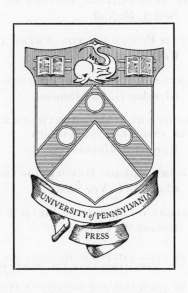

UNIVERSITY of PENNSYLVANIA PRESS

THE AMERICAN HISTORICAL ASSOCIATION

PREPARED AND PUBLISHED UNDER THE DIRECTION OF THE AMERICAN HISTOR-
ICAL ASSOCIATION FROM THE INCOME OF THE ALBERT J. BEVERIDGE MEMORIAL
FUND

FOR THEIR ZEAL AND BENEFICENCE IN CREATING THIS FUND THE ASSOCIATION
IS INDEBTED TO MANY CITIZENS OF INDIANA, WHO DESIRED TO HONOR IN THIS
WAY THE MEMORY OF A STATESMAN AND A HISTORIAN

HISTORY OF

MARSHALL FIELD &Co. FIELD

1852 - 1906

BY

ROBERT W. TWYMAN

ASSOCIATE PROFESSOR OF HISTORY

BOWLING GREEN STATE UNIVERSITY

1954

UNIVERSITY OF PENNSYLVANIA PRESS

Philadelphia

Designed by Guenther K. Wehrhan

Manufactured in the United States of America

BOOK CRAFTSMEN ASSOCIATES

Library of Congress Catalog Card Number: 54-7109

Published in Great Britain, India, and Pakistan
by Geoffrey Cumberlege: Oxford University Press
London, Bombay, and Karachi

Preface

The second half of the nineteenth century saw the coming of the great Civil War and the reuniting of the American nation on a new political basis; it saw also, just as important, the birth of a new economic age, sometimes called the "age of big business." It was an age that saw the growth of such giants as U. S. Steel, the Standard Oil Company, J. P. Morgan and Company, and in the mercantile field, Wanamaker's and Macy's. Such concerns exerted a real influence for good or ill upon the attitudes and habits of all Americans for generations to come.

The place that the story of businesses like these holds in the history of the country has been increasingly recognized by the steady production in recent years of numerous business histories. Certainly in terms of sheer size, wealth, and its influence upon a sizable portion of the American people, Marshall Field and Company deserves to find its history among such works. The policies which this outstanding firm laid down, the leadership which it so long held in both the retail and wholesale trade of the Northwest, and the important position which its wealthy founder played in the city of Chicago should make its position in the history of America secure. This book endeavors to describe the development of this great establishment and the part it played in a significant era of our past.

It is the intent of the author that this work will constitute the first of two volumes of a complete history of Marshall Field and Company during its first one hundred years. The second volume is now in preparation. Work on this, the first half of the history of the store, was undertaken with the consent of the firm in 1942; and the major portion of it was completed in 1950 as a doctoral dissertation for the University of Chicago. It has since been considerably revised and somewhat enlarged.

When first begun, the prospect for obtaining adequate and reliable source material was discouraging. Marshall Field and Company had no historical archives and the boxes of old letters, catalogues, and invoices contained in the firm's vaults, while imposing, seemed on examination scarcely sufficient in content for a thorough business history. Interest in the approaching one hundredth anniversary, however, stirred the firm to action. A "historical committee" of company executives was organized and realistic plans were laid for gathering together all available data. Long-forgotten records from the firm's warehouses, executive files, departmental offices, and other far-flung branches of the firm were systematically ferreted out and made available. An ar-

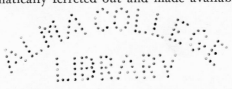

chive was created and a capable archivist was retained to catalogue and organize the vast amount of material. With this information, plus such outside collections as Marshall Field's business letters held by the Field Estate and the several collections of personal papers in the public and private libraries of Chicago, a real beginning could be made.

Despite the efforts of the firm there were naturally some disappointments. In the course of its existence Marshall Field and Company moved its offices and records many times and during each move something was lost. In addition, two disastrous fires (in 1871 and 1877) leveled the store and destroyed many valuable records preceding those dates. The final disaster came sometime after Marshall Field's death when his secretary took it upon himself to destroy many of his employer's letters in order to "keep them out of the wrong hands." As a result there are gaps in our information. Company correspondence which might have given us a clearer insight into executive policies is lacking for long stretches of time. The specialist in early labor history will regret the absence of a more complete accounting of Field's labor relations and struggle with the unions. Those interested in the marketing aspects of the firm's history will note among the statistics none on gross margins and certain expense classifications.

Most such gaps were not, however, serious and certainly are not meant to be an excuse for inadequacies on the part of the writer. The firm in all respects has given its complete coöperation without at the same time attempting to interfere. I alone must bear responsibility for the manuscript's form and content.

In the writing of this history many people have lent unstintingly of their help. It would be impossible to name all those to whom I am indebted. A special debt of gratitude, however, is owed to Dr. Bessie L. Pierce of the University of Chicago. She has given me access to her own large files of material used in the preparation of her *History of Chicago* and also the benefit of such guidance as only she could give. Others who certainly deserve to be acknowledged are the members of the Committee on the Albert J. Beveridge Memorial Fund of the American Historical Association, Dr. William T. Hutchinson of the University of Chicago, and Mr. Earl Kribben, Assistant to the President of Marshall Field's, all of whom read the text and made many excellent suggestions; Mrs. Ina Dorsey, Marshall Field and Company Archivist, for her never-ending courtesy and help; Mr. John D. Andersen, Comptroller, for his permission to use the early financial records; Mr. Marshall Field III, for the use of his grandfather's letters; the officers of Carson Pirie Scott and Company, The Fair, and Mandel Brothers in Chicago; and Mr. Lewis F. Manhart of Bowling Green State University School of Business Administration for his excellent advice on many matters. Lastly I must acknowledge my wife, my unpaid assistant, for the many years she has spent by my side thumbing patiently through dusty newspaper files, and typing notes.

Robert W. Twyman

Bowling Green, Ohio
February 1954

CONTENTS

ABOUT THE NOTES

The notes will be found on pages 179-235. In the text, referential notes are indicated by superior numbers in roman type; discussion notes by superior numbers in italics. In the note section, at the upper right-hand corner of each recto page and the upper left-hand corner of each verso page, will be found numbers indicating the pages of the text to which the notes on these two pages refer.

PLATES

Reproductions of advertisements in Chapters 9 and 11 were made possible through the courtesy of the *Chicago Tribune*.

CHARTS

TABLES

NOTE BY THE PUBLISHER

Robert W. Twyman was born in Louisville, Kentucky, on January 31, 1919. After graduating from Indiana University, he obtained the degree of Doctor of Philosophy from the University of Chicago in 1950. Since then he has taught American history at Simpson College and the University of Minnesota. He is now an associate professor of history at Bowling Green State University at Bowling Green, Ohio.

Dr. Twyman is the author of "Potter Palmer: Merchandising Innovator of the West," which appeared in Explorations in Entrepreneurial History *in December 1951.*

Marshall Field

THE EXACT BIRTH DATE OF A COMPANY IS OFTEN DIFFICULT TO DE-
termine. This has particularly been the case with Marshall Field and
Company. For over a half-century the store was dated from 1865 because it was at that time that Marshall Field first entered into the
partnership of the firm. In that year he and Levi Leiter purchased
the old P. Palmer and Company and reorganized it as Field, Palmer,
and Leiter. This event, of course, was important; for it brought into
the company its namesake, the man most responsible for creating the
international reputation of the present State Street store. Nevertheless, it has been recognized in more recent years that for those interested in the company as such, rather than in only the career of Mr.
Field, one must go further back, back thirteen more years to 1852,
when the store really first opened its doors.

In that year Potter Palmer, a husky six-footer, came to Chicago from
Lockport, New York. Though only twenty-six years old, this youth was
already a merchant of eight years' experience with five thousand dollars in gold and bank notes to his name.[1] He may have arrived on the
Michigan Southern Railroad, the only train from the East into this
raw little city of forty thousand people. If he did, he undoubtedly was
not impressed; for Chicago was only just beginning to emerge from the
ooze of the shores of Lake Michigan. The railroad station at the foot
of Lake Street into which he disembarked was an unroofed shed. The
streets over which he walked were largely unpaved and, as a result,
were always either deep in mud or sending up choking clouds of dust
as horses and wagons rumbled by. Even the largest wagons often became stuck in the bottomless slime. Placards were put up by pranksters
near the larger mud holes announcing, "This way to China," or warning that a wagon and a pair of horses had disappeared in that particular spot. On warm days garbage, dead rats, and animal excrement
fermented together beneath the wooden sidewalks and made walking
or shopping something less than a pleasure. Most houses and stores,
sitting precariously in the sticky soil, were inelegant western affairs
built of rude timbers. Even the few better business structures on Lake
Street with their yellowish limestone fronts were dreary things by
eastern standards. Since few of the stores had show windows, goods
were displayed to passers-by, and at the same time exposed to the dirt
and smoke, on dry-goods boxes out in front. Despite the town's growth
since its incorporation in 1833, the whole atmosphere when Palmer
came was still that of the frontier—rough, crude, dirty.

But, like the frontier, Chicago meant opportunity. Thousands of
Americans were streaming west, filling up the farm lands on both sides

1

of the Mississippi. Iowa had just become a state. It was the beginning of the era of large land grants to railroads; and, as a result, an economically and politically significant shift of trade was taking place. Instead of following the Mississippi River system along north-and-south lines, trade was starting to be diverted into an east-and-west movement along the new railroads a-building. Centrally located as Chicago was, the city was soon destined to outdistance even St. Louis and make the whole West its market. "The lakes, the rivers, the continually expanding railway system seem to have agreed together to make their headquarters at the foot of Lake Michigan." [2] Chicago's phenomenal growth was the talk of the nation.

The West, furthermore, was riding the back of a business boom, with Chicago in the forefront. Hundreds of small villages were popping up in the interior around Chicago, each with its general store serving the varied needs of its growing farm community. To keep the shelves of these many small merchants stocked was Chicago's job. It meant prosperity for the city's wholesale houses such as few had ever known anywhere. True, the amount of business done on a wobbly credit basis was incredible; but trade grew visibly from day to day. Everyone had faith in the future greatness of the West, and the only question, said the *Democrat,* was: "Can we keep up with the demands [for goods] made upon us?" [3]

It was into this exhilarating atmosphere of a boom town that Potter Palmer came. He went to Lake Street, the recognized retail center despite its soggy planked road, up-and-down sidewalks on teetering stilts, and homely store fronts, and, with his five thousand dollars in capital, opened up a retail dry goods store. [4] Palmer's "grand opening" of the future Marshall Field and Company consisted simply of hanging out a modest sign: "P. Palmer & Co.," and swinging wide the door. The *Daily Democratic Press* gave him a "rousing" send-off:

The dry goods store of P. Palmer will be found in No. 137. His goods are fresh from eastern markets, and appears very well. Purchasers will of course examine and purchase here or elsewhere as they think best. [5]

Palmer's store was not recognized immediately in the retail dry-goods trade as anything phenomenal. The first year's gross sales, according to one account, were seventy-three thousand dollars; [6] but a more reliable eyewitness says that four years after opening its doors, the firm was still not "over-run with business." [7] His location was a four-story frame building in which he could afford to lease only the first floor. The store front was new and described as "elegant," but no more so than the five identical store fronts ranged along side it. [8] Palmer's share of the building was heated by an airtight stove around which sat the usual loafers "with their feet on top of the stove, busily engaged in chewing tobacco." The full extent of the store's "customer services" was probably the water cooler in the corner. Andrew MacLeish, later to become famous for building Carson Pirie Scott and Company into a worthy competitor of Field's, visited P. Palmer and Company in 1856 as a young man seeking a position. He confessed later that he was actually glad at the time not to have been hired because Palmer's store appeared so "unpromising."[9]

Potter Palmer, however, did gradually introduce advanced merchandising methods that in time brought him recognition. Other stores, said Palmer, "were small and cramped, badly ventilated and on the tavern plan. You could buy codfish or calico in them. . . . I struck out for a large and distinctive dry goods store. . . ."[10] As he accumulated capital he ceased catering solely to the heavy, coarse needs of the pioneer settlers passing through. Instead he added to his stock the latest fashions to attract the wives and daughters of Chicago's financially successful. Good quality silks, velvets, and laces—things for which most other merchants apparently felt there was not a large enough market—Palmer laid out in inviting displays to tempt the feminine shoppers. Fine carpeting and upholstery goods were likewise introduced to cater to the improving tastes of a growing Chicago. It developed that not only the well-to-do succumbed to his policy of quality goods at reasonable prices, but almost all classes. Even the farm folk were lured to Chicago and to his store when some special occasion demanded the best.[11] Palmer was soon traveling to the great markets in New York in order to keep abreast of the latest fads or "novelties" as they were called then; and later, when business began to boom, he hired George W. Vail as a full-time buyer and sent him east. Vail's job was to select the better quality and more stylish of the imported and domestic dress goods, carpets, tapestries, and notions, and ship them back to Chicago by rail for Palmer's select trade.[12] P. Palmer and Company was soon recognized as the most fashionable dry-goods store in all Chicago.

Customers found that, aside from the goods, Palmer featured other innovations. Shopping, they discovered, could be pleasurable. Not so different from the modern shopper with her "charge plate," the customers of P. Palmer and Company were apparently permitted to make purchases without cash and to pay the bill by mail "on the first of the month." Palmer's charge system was quite simple. When the goods were sold, an invoice was made out and the husband's name and address, obtained from the customer, was written on the reverse side. The invoices were saved, and from them bills were later mailed out. Probably either a list of customers in good credit standing was available for the clerks to refer to, or the permission of a credit man (perhaps Palmer himself) was sought in each instance.[13] Of even more importance: with each purchase went a guarantee of satisfaction. Goods found unsatisfactory could be returned and the full purchase price would be refunded. This practice, commonplace today in most better-class stores, was not only a rarity in the America of Palmer's time, it was in Chicago unprecedented. In those days the rule of the market was still "let the buyer beware." Palmer, however, saw the shortsightedness of such a trading policy, particularly in the type of store he was trying to build. Selling in his store, he evidently felt, must be conducted in a manner befitting the quality of his goods and his customers—it must be done with scrupulous good faith. To have had it otherwise would have destroyed the store's originality and main source of attraction.

Palmer announced publicly through the newspapers that: .

Purchases made at my establishment that prove unsatisfactory either in price, quality or style, can be returned (to the Cashier's desk) for which the purchase money will be with pleasure returned.[14]

This policy, inaugurated by Palmer and over the years implemented and expanded by his successors, has become the cornerstone of the present world-wide reputation of Marshall Field and Company. The almost fantastic services performed for the modern woman shopper, the downright pampering she receives under the guise of customer services, all find their origin in this brief statement of policy first announced by the store's founder in a simple advertisement.

The fairness implied in such an advertisement was not limited to Palmer's customers. Palmer carefully cultivated also a reputation for just treatment of his employees. Nothing is known of the salaries he paid; but he did give ambitious clerks an opportunity to invest part of their earnings with him in his unvaryingly successful business ventures.[15] These included early in his career large speculations in real estate as well as merchandising. As to consideration for their comfort, employees in the mercantile trade expected little, and generally got what they expected; but in this respect Palmer was at least careful to keep up with his competitors. Clerks in those days worked regularly fourteen or more hours daily, that is, until nine or ten o'clock every evening. When the public began to complain of the incivility of these tired employees, the clerks, beginning in 1856, seized the opportunity to launch a movement for earlier closing hours. In large newspaper advertisements they appealed to the women of Chicago to make their purchases "before eight o'clock in the evening . . . to afford the young men some little time for social and moral improvement."[16] Palmer, then a young bachelor himself, lent his name as a willing supporter. By such acts he no doubt won for himself not only a spirit of loyalty among his employees but also more attentiveness on their part toward his customers, things which paid P. Palmer and Company cash dividends.

The dividends, in fact, poured in in such profusion that in October 1857 Palmer abandoned his original cramped quarters to occupy all four floors of the building next door. His newspaper coverage for the new store opening was a bit more enthusiastic than five years earlier. "No tradesman better deserves the commendations of an impartial press," said the *Times*. "He clipped the wings of extortion, by introducing moderate prices into the fashionable dry goods business, and with perhaps the most splendid stock in his line in Chicago, he adheres to the policy he has practiced so successfully for the past five years."[17] He had scarcely moved before a panic hit the country, but prosperity was to be almost a permanent fixture of early Chicago and

4

1. FOUNDING OF THE FIRM

was hard to beat down. With a trading area, as well as a population, that was doubling and tripling every ten years irrespective of events elsewhere in the country, Chicago was not to be denied. The dry-goods merchants recovered from the Panic of 1857 almost immediately, Palmer among them; and he emerged with scarcely a dent in his credit rating.[18]

Palmer was now definitely on his way. With business once more flourishing, soon even his new store felt confining to him; and in less than a year he was seeking still larger and more pretentious quarters. This time he found them a block down the street in a brand new marble-front building, a "business palace," said the newspapers. Here, adjacent to the corner of Lake and Clark, the most valuable business location in Chicago, Palmer soon led in sales, profits, and prestige over all other dry goods houses in Chicago. Although A. T. Stewart and Company of New York had long been regarded as the foremost mercantile institution of the United States, P. Palmer and Company was called the "A. T. Stewart of the West." He was "carrying with him to new quarters," according to the *Press* and *Tribune*, "a business reputation and standing in itself a fortune to any house." [19]

The new Palmer store was, for Chicago, the last word in convenience and comfort for shoppers. With more space available, goods could be better assorted and more attention given to attractive display.

The west division of the main floor is devoted to a magnificent sales room fitted up tastefully and well, and after the manner of first class stores. . . .

*   *   *   *   *

At the rear of the carpet hall [in the "east division"] a gem of an apartment which the fair shopper will readily appreciate is set apart as a shawl and mantilla room, adjacent and yet distinct from the general departments, and just the place as regards location, light, and its luxurious fixtures and attractive stock, to be visited once and again, and be widely spoken of by its fair visitors.

*   *   *   *   *

The new establishment throughout is one eminently creditable to Chicago in all its complete appointments, and is worthy of especial notice, as being a growth instead of a promise, a development of Mr. Palmer's already established success rather than a brilliant venture on future business.[20]

Such praise from the press can partly be attributed to the fact that Palmer had just lately become for them a good customer. Until 1857 he apparently made no use of newspaper advertising at all; but in that year he ran his first "ad." The typical practice in the dry-goods trade during the 1850's and '60's was to publish each season a dull, crowded little advertisement about two inches square. The same "ad" would run for several months unchanged and merely list the goods on hand, giving no prices. Occasional comments such as "lowest prices" or "just received the following by express" were the only elaboration. Palmer, on the other hand, eager to stand out from the crowd, ran his advertisements, not as two inches of crowded type, but a foot or more in length, and made use of bold type. His very first advertisement was typical in this respect—and has a distinctly modern ring:

GREAT SALE

In consequence of the
TIGHTNESS OF THE MONEY MARKET
— and other —
STARTLING CAUSES COMBINED,
and to enable me to
STAND FROM UNDER
— the —
PRESENT CRASH!
I shall offer my
ENTIRE STOCK!
— for the —
NEXT 30 DAYS!
— at a —
GREAT SACRIFICE![21]

In almost all his advertisements, too, Palmer boasted that his prices were the lowest in the city. But then, unlike the other merchants, he quoted prices for comparison. As a final touch of distinctiveness he even on occasion injected several stanzas of poetry.[22] During the Civil War, when Palmer had huge stocks of goods to dispose of, he poured money into advertising to an extent that must have amazed his competitors and surely gladdened the hearts of Chicago's newspaper publishers. It apparently paid dividends in terms of sales.

He was by this time, however, no longer advertising just retail wares. At the time of either his first or second store removal he had added a wholesale department to his business. Despite the recent panic, the West had continued to show signs of tremendous vitality and growth. Railway building since 1852 had continued at a rapid pace. Like the main strands of a huge spider web, railroads now ran into Chicago from every direction, rendering all nearby states tributary to this vigorous young city. Regular jobbing of dry goods for the country merchants had become unquestionably big business. In 1859 there were a dozen men whose wholesale trade ran into the millions. Palmer, with his capital enlarged tenfold as a result of his large retail profits,[23] was not only fully capable of launching into competition with these men but was able, after a short time, to take the lead in sales volume.

In his new location at 112, 114, and 116 Lake Street, Palmer turned over his several "airy and well-lighted" basements to the wholesale trade and filled them with fresh goods from the East. Then he ran an advertisement announcing he was in the business on a "cash only" basis.[24] That did not last long. With most other dry-goods wholesalers

6

1. FOUNDING OF THE FIRM

providing liberal credits to their little general-store merchants, Palmer found that strict adherence to a cash business often meant no business at all. Emphasis on "cash" soon disappeared from his advertisements; and like everyone else Palmer gave short-term credit to small country merchants of good standing. The prudence with which he granted credit, though, was known all over the West. All applicants were investigated; he had no taste for being caught with bad debts.[25] "We went at buyers," Palmer recounted later, "on the basis that if they could pay we could afford to be fair and if they didn't pay we did not wish their trade."[26] His advice to his salesmen according to one account was: "Get cash for your merchandise, if possible; if you can't get cash, take furs."[27]

Once a customer had proved himself reliable, however, no effort was spared to win and keep him. "I always hunted for customers," said Palmer. "If I learned of a man two hundred miles away, buried in a clearing in the forest, who might buy, I got the name of my establishment to him and invited him in. After he once got acquainted with the store, we rarely lost him."[28]

The reasons for that were many—Palmer was ahead of the field in offering advantages to his wholesale customers. One such advantage, of course, was the liberty they enjoyed, along with retail patrons, of returning goods not desired—the assurance of "money back" if not satisfied. With this went another Palmer innovation—the privilege of taking goods "on approval." The first public announcement of this was in an 1861 advertisement:

Notice to Country Customers: I will send by express patterns of different styles of Dry Goods, Silks, Shawls, Cloaks, Embroideries, or any kind of Dry Goods, from which the customer may select or not, at pleasure, the customer paying the express charges one way which will not exceed fifty cents on a package of twenty-five pounds for any distance under two hundred miles. This will give an opportunity, at a trifling expense, of seeing a choice selection from the largest stock of goods west of New York.

P. Palmer.[29]

While this taking of goods on approval was similar to money-back, it had the advantage of requiring no preliminary outlay. The buyer was able to look at the goods in his home or store without payment. He later paid only for what he wanted, sending the remainder back without the trouble of seeking a refund. This meant much to the small merchant with little capital who wanted an opportunity to see the latest fashions and novelties but found it difficult to travel frequently to market.

Palmer's biggest attraction, however, in the wholesale trade as in the retail, was his prices. Of course the only way to undersell at a profit is to buy low and cut costs. But since all Chicago wholesalers had to do most of their buying from the great wholesaling and importing center of New York, they had a middleman problem. After rendering tribute in the form of commissions to eastern importers and

7

jobbers,[30] it was difficult to compete successfully with these same persons for the trade of the western retailers. Palmer was one of the first Chicagoans to find at least a partial solution to this problem. Soon after entering the wholesale business, he eliminated the importer to a great extent by making his own buying trips abroad;[31] and for many of his "domestics," Palmer established connections directly with the New England manufacturers. On those goods which he could not avoid purchasing from New York jobbers he still won substantial discounts by buying in large quantities and, most of all, paying his bills punctually. "Even at a sacrifice we tried to make them understand that the name of 'Palmer' stood for prompt payments and that the house did not know the word 'repudiate.' "[32] With these methods he kept his credit rating high,[33] cut his costs, and thereby not only frequently undersold his Chicago rivals but more than held his own with New York. To the many small retail merchants who had been used to traveling annually or semiannually to New York and were used to shipping their small quantities of goods all the way from the coast, Palmer appealed in newspaper advertisements, reminding them of his superior purchasing facilities and that "freight from New York can be saved by buying . . . from me."[34] Many must have been convinced; for they came, and Palmer made money.

Palmer's opportunity to undersell his rivals was greatly enhanced by the coming of the Civil War. In the early days of the War, with the Union seemingly none too secure, many business men grew frightened and unloaded their stocks at ruinous prices. Palmer saw a chance to profit from other's lack of faith. Using all the capital at his command, he purchased hundreds of bales of cotton sheetings, muslin, and flannels at depressed prices and filled his warehouses. In those first weeks of war he spent all he had and borrowed more. As a result, his formerly high credit rating slumped slightly; but his exploit paid dividends. The North soon went on a wartime spending spree, and wholesale prices climbed. With large stocks of cheaply bought goods on hand, Palmer was able to supply the demand at prices a few cents lower than anyone else and at an enormous profit to himself.[35] To the amazement of his competitors, however, he did not then reduce the amount of his purchases, but instead continued to buy throughout the early and middle years of the war at what seemed ruinously high prices. Palmer's closest competitor, Francis B. Cooley, wrote to one of his junior partners in 1863:

> I took Dinner today at the same table with Mr. Shelden of Buckly, Shelden & Co. he remarked that Palmer was a strang chap. he did not know what to make of him, etc., etc., & remarked that he [Palmer] had had [sic] been buying good at high prices—etc., etc., the same thing I have noticed.

Cooley also remarked in this same letter, "I stoped [sic] buying & he [Palmer] is in no better shape than we are . . . I *may be* wrong."[36]

How wrong Cooley was quickly became evident. Prices continued to rise precipitously, only reaching their peak in 1864 and 1865. Palmer, with even the army on his list of customers, had so much business that he had to have additional salesroom; and before the end of 1863 he had added the building next door (110) to his Chicago address. His operations in New York, conducted from a new office opened on Reade Street, were even more profitable. There he bought in large amounts, held on for several months, often without so much as moving the merchandise out of the warehouses of its former owners, and then unburdened himself at peak prices. His sales ran into the millions; and Palmer, among Chicagoans, made more money than anyone else in the business.[37]

Palmer was not without a spark of practical patriotism. He invested hundreds of thousands of his dollars in government bonds and, it is said, obediently paid a large war-income tax.[38] In January of 1864, after three years of enormous earnings, he announced in the newspapers that he would devote the entire net profits of one day's retail sales to needy soldiers' families. Said his advertisement:

> While fathers, brothers, husbands, sons
> Bleed for the nation's weal,
> Shall mothers, wives and children dear
> The pangs of hunger feel?[39]

The answer, according to the "ad," was "No!" Three days later Potter Palmer calculated that his profits had been five hundred dollars in the retail department on that day. The *Tribune* reported later that he dutifully mailed a check.[40]

~~~~~~

Marshall Field: Rising Young Merchant

2

~~~~~~

PALMER AT ONLY THIRTY-EIGHT WAS NOW THE LEADING MERCHANT OF the entire West; yet already his mercantile career was about to end. Two men had arrived in Chicago who, largely by adopting his methods and improving on them, would make the momentary brilliance of the great Palmer in the dry-goods trade seem pallid indeed. These two young men, Levi Z. Leiter and Marshall Field, had both appeared on the city's dusty streets at about the time Palmer was getting a good start.[1]

The first of the two, Leiter, was not a handsome man and at times betrayed something of a bad temper, but his undoubted integrity, his boundless energy, and his ability in finance made him nonetheless indispensable in a great mercantile firm during the coming era of consolidated cost accounting. Having left a comfortable position in Springfield, Ohio, to seek greater prosperity in fast-growing Chicago, Leiter, in January 1856, found employment with Palmer's rival, Francis P. Cooley, at Cooley, Wadsworth and Company. Here it was that Leiter first met his future partner, the shortly famous Marshall Field, who was hired at about the same time.[2] Field had come to Chicago from the small Massachusetts farm community of Pittsfield, near Conway where he was born. As a clerk for four years in a country store at Pittsfield, he had been so popular with the feminine customers and had so impressed his employer with his abilities that he was offered a quarter interest in the business. Such an offer carried little charm, however, for a young man whose mind was filled with tales of the "big life" waiting in the West. So instead of accepting the offer, Field, along with thousands of others at the time, had gathered up all his worldly goods and headed for the rough but flourishing little city at the foot of Lake Michigan. Marshall Field, unlike many who went west at this time to conquer the wilderness and plow the virgin soil, was a cautious and retiring individual who felt most at ease when neatly dressed and taking refuge behind a familiar store counter. He had, in common with most of the others, ambition and determination; but Field's brand was of the cold, calculating, and dogged variety. He was, he said, "determined not to remain poor";[3] and in that resolve lies the essence of his personality and a clue to his whole future career.

Reared in the stern, cheerless atmosphere of a puritan farm family where life was frugal, Field grew up to regard money as the key that opened all doors. This attitude remained with him long after he was a millionaire many times over. Throughout his career he often judged men by what they were "worth" and appraised his own success at any particular moment by glancing at his bank balance.

When Marshall Field arrived in Chicago at twenty-one years of age,[4] he was well fortified with handsome features, valuable experience, and savings of almost a thousand dollars. His brother Joseph, who had preceded him to Chicago, went to work immediately to obtain a position for Marshall in what was then the largest wholesale dry-goods house in Chicago: Cooley, Wadsworth and Company. This firm was located in a four-storied building on South Water Street (now Wacker Drive) facing the foul-smelling Chicago River and only a little over a block from the then unpretentious P. Palmer and Company retail store on Lake Street. Joseph confidently presented Francis B. Cooley, the senior partner of the firm, with recommendations which Marshall

10

had obtained from his former employer and other residents of Pittsfield; but despite the generous praise in these letters of Field's "unusual business talent" and "strict integrity," Cooley was at first unim-
pressed and the answer was unfavorable. Only when Joseph repeatedly
returned and always on the same errand, did the old merchant, perhaps in order to rid himself of a nuisance, reluctantly promise to give
brother Marshall "a trial." [5]

Field was hired as a clerk at a salary of four hundred dollars a year.
For this sum the slim lad, besides selling goods, had to appear early
in the morning before business even began to help load the wagons,
clear the docks for the new day's work, and man the heavy rope elevator that carried goods between floors. It meant long hours of hard
work; and during the first year the weary Field did not bother even to
rent a room, but instead curled up nightly in the store. Having neither
the time nor the inclination for any sociability, his only clothing purchased during the year was a pair of overalls; and, characteristically,
he added another two hundred dollars (half his salary) to his growing
capital.[6]

In his first few months of work the new clerk was by no means immediately hailed as a mercantile genius. "As a young clerk he was not
particularly impressive," John V. Farwell, a junior partner in the firm,
recalled. "It did not take us long to find out that he had no bad habits,
that his word was always good, and that *he was with us to make money*.
Yet these were the characteristics of many other good clerks." [7] According to Cooley, "He appeared to lack confidence in himself to an
extent that would be surprising to those who have known him in
maturer years." [8] Quiet, serious, and with no interest whatsoever in
recreational or civic activities, his personality was without warmth. As
a result he made few friends and, despite his earnestness in memoriz-
ing the stock, did not arouse anyone's enthusiasm over his business
ability.

Under the unlettered but kindly Cooley's influence, however, a
warmer, friendlier side to Field's personality blossomed forth; and soon
the other members of the firm discovered that they had acquired an
extraordinary salesman. Conscientiousness in this case apparently paid
off, but the real secret was Field's sheer love of merchandising. "He
had the merchant instinct," said Farwell.[9] "He knew how to show off
a stock to its best advantage and he always knew what was in stock. . . .
The store and the stock was [*sic*] his life. . . ." [10] Field's reward was a
chance now to prove himself as a salesman "on the road."

As he gathered up his business cards and packed his two heavy
satchels, he probably told himself grimly that this was his big opportunity and he must not throw it away. He rode doggedly through
southern Iowa on horseback from one little crossroads town to the
next, washed in horse troughs, ate the frequently unappetizing fare of
the country hotels or, when the food was unpalatable, munched a
nickel's worth of cheese and crackers; but he did what he started out
to do—he came home a success. Field won new customers everywhere

he went and gained a reputation almost overnight as the most capable salesman in the Chicago area. His knowledge of the trade, his instinctive courtesy, and his unusual memory for names and faces made him irresistible. Said a contemporary: "He carried the trade of the Northwest in his pocket." [11]

While Field was growing in stature as a salesman, the firm to which he was attached was having trouble. Wadsworth, one of the two senior partners, had developed not only a disinclination to pay the firm's debts in times of financial stringency, but persisted in devoting much of his time to outside business activities that were directly or indirectly competitive with Cooley, Wadsworth and Company. Cooley, eager to improve conditions, waited only for the day when his partnership agreement with Wadsworth would end and a new company could be organized. This finally occurred early in 1857. Wadsworth was permitted to leave his money with the house but was dropped from active participation in the business in favor of the able John V. Farwell. A new firm now emerged under the name Cooley, Farwell and Company. [12]

Having no more than overcome the one problem, however, the firm drifted into a more serious one. In the midst of the prosperity of '56, the old company had, at Farwell's instigation, built larger and more elaborate quarters on Wabash Avenue. [13] This building, with its fine new steam elevators, relieved the joyous clerks of their rope-pulling exercises; but the expense of the new edifice served only to aggravate conditions when the firm plunged into the panic of 1857. Wadsworth, in order to continue to share in the profits of Cooley, Farwell and Company, had agreed to contribute 40 per cent of the capital; but in the trough of the depression, when money was needed badly, he refused to produce his full share. A large loss was taken on the stock as a result of the decline in prices; and, despite the caution which had been displayed in making purchases and in granting credits, the firm narrowly averted bankruptcy. While desperate and angry Cooley and Farwell were borrowing heavily from friends in order to make up the capital deficiency and to keep afloat, the observant Field made a mental note of a lesson learned. [14]

Luckily, good times returned quickly after the panic, and past debts and difficulties were soon liquidated and mostly forgotten in the flood of new immigration and business that came to Chicago. The city resumed its spectacular growth, and Field's career continued onward and upward; for, as the young man himself put it, "merit [his own] did not have to wait for dead men's shoes in the growing town." [15] It happened that about this time Field's old employer wrote to him from Pittsfield offering him a third interest in his store if he would return. This, Field had no intention of accepting, but the letter was a useful weapon in Chicago when displayed to the proper persons. Cooley and Farwell took the hint and in 1860, prodded by their fear lest Field accept the offer, boosted him to a junior partnership in their concern and gave him a share of the profits, even though the young man was still unable to contribute any capital.[16] Two years later, to the relief of Cooley and Farwell, Wadsworth finally withdrew from the firm entirely. Field was invited to invest fifteen thousand dollars in the reorganized company. This amount was exactly ten thousand dollars more than Field had managed to save in six years of low salaries with the firm; but despite the uncertain times, Cooley loaned Field the additional sum at 10 per cent and permitted him to pay it back gradually out of his one-sixth share of the profits.[17] Forty years later, Field, looking back, said, "Saving the first five thousand dollars I ever had. . . . That I consider the turning point." [18] Adding his five thousand to Cooley's ten made him a vested partner, and the future mercantile prince was now on his way.

The partnership papers were signed just in time for the three firm members to enjoy the same boom of wartime prosperity that was making Palmer a rich man. Under the new agreement, Cooley remained permanently in New York to do the immense amount of buying that was necessary; Farwell supervised financial affairs in Chicago; while Field hired the help, took charge of credits and of his specialty, sales.[19] The arrangement worked well; and Cooley, Farwell and Company were so rushed with army orders as well as regular business that they could afford to refuse credit in almost all cases and insist on a strictly cash business.[20] "Conditions . . . were something extraordinary," said Farwell. "Goods were up and money was down. Consequently anyone who had a stock of goods on hand was practically certain to sell them at an advance over what he had paid for them." [21] The busy clerks at Cooley, Farwell and Company had to work until ten or eleven o'clock at night. "After selling their customers all day, the salesmen would go back to the store in the evening and go with a truck from department to department gathering up the goods they sold during the day, sorting out and helping the entry clerks to enter them up." [22] From this rush of trade, the three partners of Cooley, Farwell and Company profited handsomely and Field felt so secure that in 1863 he married.[23]

In this same year, nevertheless, the firm again had to be completely reorganized. The strain of business proved to be too much for the older Cooley, and in the spring of 1863 he developed a cough so bad that it frightened him into retiring.[24] His retirement left the way clear for Field and Farwell to form a partnership, with perhaps the addition of some junior partner; but Farwell was at first disinclined to do so. His respect for the business ability of his young associate was matched by a dislike for Field personally. Field's unvarying efficiency and puritanical conscience had become, apparently, somewhat wearing on the more genial and easygoing Farwell. Farwell, furthermore, was skeptical of the future of the dry-goods business once the Civil War should end. The days of easy sales and constantly sky-rocketing prices, he felt, would not last forever. Before things go "into the old Channels [sic] again, with competition on every corner," he told Cooley, he wanted to sell out and invest his money in real estate. He therefore

13

asked his old friend to find him a buyer,[25] but Cooley either was unwilling or unable to do so.

Field, equally disinclined to join with Farwell, at the last moment in desperation approached Cyrus and William McCormick, of reaper fame, with a proposal for a partnership. The McCormicks, Field felt, could not only furnish the abundant capital that was necessary, but could lend to a new dry-goods firm their tremendous prestige throughout the Northwest. William McCormick was interested; but the proposal came so late that before the two brothers had time to discuss the proposition, Cooley, Farwell and Company had dissolved; and out of necessity a new partnership wearing the title, "Farwell, Field and Company," had been patched together.[26] In this new firm there were included, besides the principals, two new junior partners, one of whom was the bushy-whiskered and dynamic Levi Z. Leiter.

This was Leiter's first appearance as a partner, although his rise in the firm had been almost as remarkable as that of Field. Employed by the firm about the same time as Field (1856), but as an office clerk instead of a salesman, he had progressed rapidly and soon had become head bookkeeper and accountant, receiving the unusual salary for those days of $2,500 a year. Later on, Leiter's major duty came to be the "making of credits," that is, approving applications from retailers for goods on credit. The West was notorious not only for its gamblers and sharpsters who were ready to take advantage of a firm granting easy credit, but also for honorable but overoptimistic individuals who bought what they could not possibly sell and pay for. Either kind, unless carefully combed from among those to whom credit was granted, could drive the best wholesaling firm rapidly into bankruptcy. The rather austere Leiter, waiting in a little office behind a forbidding iron railing, must have seemed an insurmountable obstacle for suppliant merchants to overcome. His lack of patience, especially with persons of doubtful business character, was well known. Nevertheless, during this period, "Mr. Leiter," according to an entry clerk who worked under him, "was regarded as the foremost man of his line." [27]

During the single year of existence which the firm of Farwell, Field and Company enjoyed, prices throughout the country continued to rise spectacularly. Consequently, as in the past, by the simple expedient of announcing in their circulars and newspaper advertisements that they had goods to sell and by marking their prices a little higher each day, Field and Farwell made money. With monotonous regularity the firm was able to prognosticate truthfully for its merchant customers that the market was "very firm—tendency upward." [28] The dull business of dealing in bales of sheeting, cases of cassimeres, and assortments of notions had proved to be a veritable gold mine; and Field and Farwell, only three months after putting signatures to their partnership agreement, were already burrowing under the street and tearing out offices and stairways to provide more sales space for their huge stocks of goods.[29]

Nonetheless, all was not well with the firm. The future proved Far-

14

well and Field individually to be the two greatest merchants nine-teenth-century Chicago produced; yet their personal disagreements and their different attitudes regarding the conduct of a business were too strong to permit their working together. Marshall Field decided, there-fore, to withdraw.[30]

~~~~~~~~~~~~~~~~~~~~~~~~~~~~~~~~~~

The Man and the Opportunity   3

~~~~~~~~~~~~~~~~~~~~~~~~~~~~~~~~~~

". . . be alert and ready to seize opportunities when they present them-selves."—Advice of Marshall Field in 1896 to young men seeking success.[1]

IN HIS PLANS TO LEAVE FARWELL AND LAUNCH A NEW VENTURE IN THE dry-goods trade, Marshall Field had willing allies in Levi Leiter and several of the lesser company officials and clerks. Field now had a name for dependability and business sagacity through the Northwest that could give immediate prestige to any new business. Consequently, many of the employees in the old firm were ready to leave when he did. Field, in fact, lacked only one prerequisite to a successful under-taking; but it was a vital one—money. The War, and the tremendous growth during the previous decade of railway and lake commerce had developed Chicago commercially to such an extent that any firm with-out a capitalization running into the hundreds of thousands of dollars was sure to have considerable difficulty competing in the wholesale dry goods trade. The population of Chicago was now well over two hun-dred thousand, and millions of dollars' worth of competitive capital was being poured into the city by easterners in an attempt to share some of the large profits which could be realized by catering to the needs of such a growing metropolis. Field was not willing to enter into this competition only partially armed. Though barely turned thirty, he was no longer a young man trying to get a start and content to launch a small venture in the hope of struggling upward in the future. He was experienced, astute, and completely confident; he would be content with nothing less than to be at or near the top, and was now ready for a supreme effort to acquire undisputed leadership in the trade.

By this time Field, unassisted, had already accumulated in capital no less than two hundred thousand dollars as a result of profitable

15

partnerships and investments over the past nine years. Leiter informed Field that, if taken into the new firm, he could contribute a little over one hundred thousand dollars.[2] These amounts put together, however, were at best only half what would be needed to compete successfully with such strong firms as Carson, Pirie and Company; Bowen Brothers; Hunt, Barbour and Hale; and Potter Palmer, not to mention the store that Farwell was planning to continue at the old Farwell, Field and Company site.

Field, as early as November 1864, had turned again to the McCormicks in the hope of obtaining extra capital. To him they appeared to be the logical investors because they had, besides money, the ownership of a considerable number of good store fronts along the main business thoroughfares of Lake and South Water Streets. William McCormick did not offer Field much encouragement; but in writing to his more affluent brother, Cyrus, who was in New York at the time, William expressed the opinion that it was indeed "a rare opportunity to make a connection with such a man as Field is supposed to be in that business."[3] On December 14, he suggested that either Cyrus or his firm put two hundred thousand dollars into the proposed store.

Dear Brother

I have seen & talked with F. [Field] *here*. . .

Wm. Dogget, Bowens & other good men here speak in strong terms of Mr. F. as a close, calculating & safe business man—who devotes himself to his business [sic]. . . .

I am of opinion that either *you* or C. H. McCormick & Bros. could take half the store & carry it along.[4]

But despite the fact that William warned that Marshall Field "must know soon,"[5] Cyrus was in no hurry to make up his mind. The month slipped by while the two brothers leisurely corresponded on the matter and Field waited. When Christmas finally came and went without a decision being reached, a concise postscript to a letter written on the 1st day of the year indicated that the McCormicks had missed a great opportunity: "I suppose its [sic] too late to deal with Field. . . ."[6]

It was indeed too late, for Field had not been idle while waiting for the McCormicks to come to a decision. One day just before Christmas, Field had obtained from Potter Palmer, the richest merchant in Chicago, a proposal to sell his entire business, retail as well as wholesale. Palmer's health was bad, and he told Field his doctor had suggested a rest.[7] Such an offer, made at the peak of war prosperity might well have given the naturally cautious Field reason for hestitation. It was common knowledge in the trade that Palmer had bought in large quantities during the war; and, while he had resold most of his purchases at a tremendous profit, he undoubtedly still had his storerooms full of goods obtained at inflated prices.[8] Selling high cost war goods on a deflated market was hardly a profitable enterprise for anybody. Field had thus staved off Palmer, obviously preferring, if possible, to

16

work with the McCormicks, "buy light," and see what was going to happen to prices when the war was over.[9]

As the year 1864 ended, however, and with it the Farwell and Company partnership, Marshall Field felt he had to act quickly. If much more time were spent waiting upon the procrastinating McCormicks and they were eventually to turn him down, it might then be too late for Field to act upon the Palmer offer. Anway, to two ambitious young men like Field and Leiter, the opportunity to accomplish such a startling coup as acquiring the richest dry-goods firm in the city probably looked more attractive with each passing day, no matter what the risks. Thus when Palmer again offered his entire stock on what Farwell called "very handsome terms,"[10] Field and his friend Leiter decided to cast their lot with the Lake Street millionaire.[11]

Under the terms of some rather amazing contracts signed on January 4, 1865, the new firm of Field, Palmer and Leiter was born; and it was capitalized at the substantial sum of $750,000. This amount of money was, of course, more than double what Field and Leiter were able to contribute; so Palmer agreed to remain as a "special partner" and to leave $330,000 with the business until such time as they could afford to buy him out. Potter Palmer's brother Milton, who had been associated with him in the old firm, likewise retained a fifty-thousand-dollar interest in the company and was made a general partner, with his name (not Potter Palmer's) being carried in the title of the firm.[12] This left Field to furnish $250,000 and Leiter $120,000. Since the stock of goods purchased from Palmer by the new firm inventoried at much more than $750,000, the firm of Field, Palmer and Leiter as a whole still owed a sizeable debt to Potter Palmer personally, which it had to pay as best it could from future earnings. At the expiration of the first year, furthermore, the firm was required to return to Palmer one hundred thousand dollars of his special capital. Field and Leiter apparently had full expectations of clearing enough to pay all debts, return one hundred thousand dollars to Palmer, and more; for a clause was included in one of the contracts retaining for the two young men the privilege of purchasing the interest of Milton J. Palmer and renaming the firm "Field and Leiter" after the expiration of one year.[13]

Though both were still young, Field and Leiter were the senior partners of the greatest dry-goods firm in the West.[14] They had acquired a store known already for its distinctiveness, and now were to have an unhindered opportunity to make it even more so. They might inaugurate business policies which had long been in the back of their minds but which never before had they been entirely free to apply. The beginnings made by Potter Palmer in courtesy to customers, integrity of business character, and in reliability of merchandise were to be amplified and expanded by his successors into the now well-publicized "Marshall Field and Company Idea," or, as the man-on-the-street traditionally has credited Marshall Field with saying, the policy that "the customer is always right."

The building in which the two partners launched their new firm was, of course, the old Palmer store, and it bore slight resemblance to the modern "Field's." As compared to the present-day granite colossus with its thirty-five acres of floor space devoted to retail activities alone, Field, Palmer and Leiter occupied a brick building about one hundred and fifty feet square[15] in which the retail divisions occupied only one of the four floors.[16] The three upper floors were needed for wholesale; while in the basement the furnace, general storage, and a few retail counters that could not find room on the first floor were all rivals for the available space.[17] Instead of almost sixty smart electric elevators and escalators running between thirteen floors, there was one freight elevator of the rope-pulling variety similar to the one that Field had labored with in his first days with Cooley, Wadsworth and Company.[18] For the customers throughout the building who were trying to see what they were buying, it is likely that more light came from the sky-lights in the roof than from the inadequate artificial lighting of that day; and neither was really satisfactory.[19]

Nevertheless, it was still one of the finest establishments in the city. The outer approaches to the store had improved considerably in recent years, for Chicago was beginning to climb out of the mud. New street grades had been established allowing most of the buildings on Lake Street to be jacked up to higher elevations above the level of the river. This permitted some of the abundant rainfall to flow into the river instead of lingering in stagnant pools in the street to plague pedestrian customers. Furthermore, the city had just finished paving the street with wooden blocks; and soon delighted women shoppers found the thoroughfare running in front of Field, Palmer and Leiter being regularly swept and cleaned.[20]

Inside, so many fresh lines were added by the new proprietors to the fashionable stocks on display that it was beginning to be difficult to recognize the dry-goods store of old. For one thing, Field, Palmer and Leiter came to be unsurpassed for its variety of "notions"—the first real addition to the traditional dry-goods store which, in its purest form, had handled only the more prosaic "piece goods." It was determined that this department of the store should be made the most attractive in the West.[21] As a result, when the merchant customers climbed the stairs to the wholesale departments or the ladies squeezed their hoop skirts between the narrow aisles of the retail floor, they now found such new and interesting items as colorful sun umbrellas, ready-made Bon Ton Hova skirts, and cloaks in the latest Parisian styles, as well as the more usual buttons, combs, and thread.

A new "first class notions man," hired to make a specialty of the field, probably soon had aroused interest even in the men by placing a variety of suspenders, neckties, and shirt fronts in both wholesale and retail departments, all of which had been unknown to the dry-goods shelves of a few years back.[22] Continuing Palmer's popular policy of trying to make retail shopping less of an ordeal, it was arranged so that when the women stopped to purchase lingerie and ready-to-wear items, they were no longer forced to undergo the embarrassment of

18

3. THE MAN AND THE OPPORTUNITY

dealing with the usual male clerk, but found instead at these counters a pleasant young woman to wait upon them.[23] The feminine customers of Field, Palmer and Leiter found also that, if their credit was approved, they might charge their purchases.[24] When their shopping was completed there was no streamlined delivery truck to bring their purchases to their doors; but if a customer bought more than she could carry, young boys were sent along to help.[25]

For the attraction of wholesale customers Marshall Field, working out of the firm's New York office, was trying to buy and freight back to Chicago such quantities and varieties of goods as to suit every taste;[26] and, the firm claimed, at "under New York prices."[27] Their woolen department, they informed the trade, had been "greatly enlarged and improved" to accommodate the abundance of new items; and their lines of American cottons were now "complete."[28] Typical wholesale items offered were "gents" collars for 23 cents apiece, hairpins for 20 cents a pound, Waterville shawls for $1.30 apiece, American prints at 24 cents a yard, Dutch gingham at 24½ cents a yard, a gross of small pearl buttons for $2.50, a dozen linen handkerchiefs for $1.50, and a dozen duplex skirts for $23.75.[29] Such of these items as the merchant-customer chose to buy, if he were from out of the city, were either shipped by freight or tied in numerous small bundles for carrying. In the latter case, he was then off to the railroad station with his share of heavily loaded small boys or with the firm's horse and two-wheel dray trailing after him with his packages.[30]

During its first year of existence (1865) the firm's sales reached eight million dollars.[31] and by the second year they had climbed to over nine millions, almost as much as the combined totals of the firm's two largest rivals.[32] In fact, one day in July of 1866 Field received a letter heavily marked with "Confidential." In it was an interesting offer from the man who had come out only second best in the lively competition for the jobbing trade of the Northwest and who, at this moment, was ready to give up the fight.

> . . . notwithstanding I have thought that you & L [Leiter] had given me such treatment as at least I should not have expected, still I can forget the past and any injury I may have sustained & should you desire to rent my store and succeed to my business on the 1st of Jany next, I will entertain a proposition from you favorably. . . .
>
> Yours respectfully
>
> John V. Farwell"

It had become obvious that the new firm on Lake Street had quietly appropriated the leadership in the business that Potter Palmer had so long held. All indications pointed toward a continued supremacy.

The success of Field, Palmer and Leiter, as of any business, lay in its well-conceived organization and the men who ran it. So that nothing might be left to chance, the generalship of the company was stipulated from the first, in the original contracts. Marshall Field was to "have charge of buying all goods for the firm and a general supervi-

19

sion of the entire business," which in actual practice, besides taking charge of the store's Broadway purchasing office in New York City, meant attending auctions and making frequent buying trips to Europe. Levi Z. Leiter, who was to have charge of his old specialty, "finances and credits," took up bachelor's quarters at the Sherman House, supervised the business in Chicago, and watched with a keen eye all orders by merchants of dubious standing from distant points in Wisconsin and Iowa. Milton J. Palmer, partner by sufferance, was allotted a "general supervision of the retail department," a position in which he had apparently had experience when he was with Potter Palmer.[34]

Under these three men worked an enthusiastic and loyal group of employees. From Palmer's old organization were undoubtedly drawn the greatest numbers of clerks and ordinary salesmen.[35] But from the employees of the old Farwell, Field and Company, to whom Farwell should logically have succeeded when he purchased the business, came the key men. Edward Nevers, head bookkeeper and cashier, for example, was a man who carried devotion to duty to such an extreme that he was still working for the firm during World War I.[36] There were also enticed from the same source Lorenzo G. Woodhouse, expert buyer, and the able mathematician, Henry J. Willing. The latter was to develop a knack for plugging wasteful loopholes and devising time-saving systems in the wholesale division that in efficiency and smoothness of operation put it far ahead of any competition in the field. Finally, back from the Civil War battlefields came the fine salesman, spare Captain Lafayette McWilliams, and the broad-visioned credit genius Harlow N. Higinbotham, another former employee of Cooley, Farwell and Company. Higinbotham, working under Leiter, learned to detect potentially bad debts with precision. These men helped to round out a matchless organization.[37]

Efficient organization, and even leadership in the field, does not, however, necessarily mean profits. With the end of the Civil War came a precipitous drop in prices and many firms quickly failed. Within less than four months from the day it opened its doors, Field, Palmer and Leiter sustained a staggering loss of $300,000 in the value of the goods that it had purchased from Potter Palmer.[38] The $20,000 discount which Palmer had allowed on the cost price of the retail goods, and which may have been meant to cover any such price decline, proved, of course, to be entirely inadequate.[39] One story has it that Field and Leiter were so depressed that they asked Potter Palmer to buy back the business.[40] Whether this is true or not cannot be known; but it is certain that, not only were Field and Leiter forced to give up their original intention of buying out Milton Palmer's interest in the firm at the end of the first year, but Potter Palmer had to step in and buy back $25,000 worth of Field's original investment in order to enable his young friend to meet all his obligations.[41]

In an effort to revive business and recoup their losses, the partners instructed Leiter to adopt a more liberal policy in granting credit. A strict cash or short-term credit policy had been considered so vital to

20

the interests of the business that it had been specifically provided in the partnership agreement that no more than thirty days credit was to be allowed under any circumstances. Many of the firm's small merchant customers were faced with falling prices on their own goods. If unable to get credit from Field, Palmer and Leiter, they either had to begin purchasing from other jobbers or go into bankruptcy. Thus, in order to retain their customers and to help pull them over the crisis, an amendment was added granting permission to Leiter "to make credits in special cases (when he deems that the interests of the firm can be safely and profitably advanced) on time not exceeding ninety days." [42]

Customers stood loyally by and it would seem that most of those who were aided weathered the storm and were ready to buy for "cash" again when the crisis was over.[43] As a result, while thousands of other businessmen continued to fail, Field, Palmer and Leiter, because it still had a market, quickly recovered. By the end of 1865, each partner was realizing a 32 per cent dividend on his investment. Profits continued thereafter to run so large that by the end of 1866 the ambitious Field and Leiter were in a position to bring to fruition their greatest dream. They now could afford to relieve both Palmers of their share in the business and launch out entirely on their own. Thus on January 1, 1867, with the expiration of the old contract, Milton and Potter Palmer reluctantly withdrew their capital from what had been a highly rewarding partnership. To Chicago was then introduced a new firm, "Field, Leiter & Co." [44]

Field, Leiter and Company: 4
Retail and Wholesale

The Firm Moves From Lake Street

WHEN POTTER PALMER FINALLY WITHDREW FROM THE DRY-GOODS business entirely in January 1867, Marshall Field and Levi Leiter had by no means seen the last of him; and it was not only because they still owed him money. Despite the great wealth which he had accumulated, Palmer was apparently not very anxious to follow his doctor's orders and merely rest. He did take a trip to Europe; but within a short time, he was back in Chicago, again eager to add to his fortune.[1]

Palmer had hit upon an idea for a grandiose real estate speculation which, in order to succeed fully, called for completely transplanting the main retail business district of Chicago from one street to another; namely from Lake Street to State Street. State Street at that time was little better than a narrow lane running between rows of shabby wooden boardinghouses, saloons, and dreary little shops. In contrast, Lake Street had continued through the Civil War to be the leading retail and financial center of Chicago. At the close of the War the corner of Clark and Lake, close by Field, Leiter and Company, was considered the best business corner in the city and was selling at two thousand dollars a front foot.[2]

Potter Palmer, with the practiced eye of a shrewd businessman, was convinced, nevertheless, that Lake Street, hemmed in as it was by both river and railroad, had seen its best days. Noting perhaps that the major south-side lines of the new horsecars converged to meet the major west-side lines on State Street and made it one of the most convenient areas in Chicago to reach,[3] Palmer was apparently convinced that State would be the logical new center of trade. In any case, he proceeded quietly to buy the rundown properties along that street until he held title to most of the frontage for three-quarters of a mile south from Lake Street. He next moved every building he owned back far enough on its lot to allow a hundred-foot width for the street and persuaded all the other owners to do the same. He now had a potential business center astride a boulevard instead of a lane, with potentialities for greatness equal to that of the city in which it lay.

As if, then, to set a standard for future residents of the street, he tore down the row of shacks on the southwest corner of Quincy and State and started the construction of a magnificent hotel, the first great "Palmer House." At the other "end" of the street, so to speak, on the corner of State and Washington, he erected at a cost of about $350,000 a showy, six-story, marble-fronted store—a "dry-goods palace." By this time, he had spent almost two million dollars; but, as Palmer himself put it, "there was sense in doing things on a large scale if you could see a return."[4]

The "return" began to be seen even before the building had been completed, when he persuaded the recently formed Field, Leiter and Company to agree to occupy his new store for a rent of almost a thousand dollars a week.[5] It was a move that would prove to be of profound importance in the business destinies of downtown Chicago. Dismayed that the largest and most influential mercantile institution in the city was leaving them, the remaining major retail merchants likewise deserted Lake Street during the next few years and took up locations in the shadow of Field, Leiter and Company's new store. Between 1869 and 1871, to Palmer's utmost satisfaction, no less than

4. FIELD, LEITER AND CO.: RETAIL AND WHOLESALE

thirty new marble-front buildings were erected along his broad avenue;[6] and before he died he saw State Street become one of the greatest single concentrated shopping districts in the world. By the second quarter of the twentieth century there were more large stores close together offering a wider range of quality goods and doing a larger business than any other area of equal size in New York, London, Paris, or elsewhere.[7] And Field, Leiter and Company in 1868 were in one of the prime locations from which to dominate that area.

Marshall Field and Levi Leiter, with the coöperation of Potter Palmer, planned that the opening of their new building in October 1868 would be an event that Chicago would remember. Field and Leiter had made tremendous strides in the short time since their beginning; but it was obviously intended that this grand new store would be not only an indication of past growth and the need of a larger building, but, by its very magnificence, a promise of finer things to come. As the leading store of the city, considerable importance had to be placed on maintaining its prestige. To continue to lead in sales it was obliged to remain ahead in new ideas and fine accommodations.

The move, as a result, was accompanied by large-scale preparations. Considerable attention was given to fitting up the interior in an attempt to make it the most attractive store possible. The latest gas lighting fixtures were attached to the frescoed walls, big mirrors were placed in the wearing apparel sections, improved shelving and new walnut counters were brought in, and carpeting was laid down over large areas.[8] While this work was still going on, the huge task of transporting the immense retail and wholesale stocks from Lake Street by horse and wagon down the still unpaved State Street to the new building was begun.[9] Since "notions" were already a specialty and the firm was enjoying the largest sale of these articles of any store in the city, the entire fourth floor was devoted to them; and up the two new steam freight elevators was taken everything in the vast category of notions from soap and perfumes to hosiery, hoop skirts, and Balmorals. To the third floor were hoisted the more prosaic woolen goods, linens, blankets, and flannels, while on the second were placed the staple yard goods. Since these were all wholesale goods, and since the fifth and sixth floors had to be devoted to storage and packing rooms, it left the more easily reached first floor and the part of the basement not occupied by machinery for retail.[10]

To all these floors, in order to make the opening itself an outstanding event, were brought great quantities of new goods, many purchased undoubtedly just for the occasion—striped plush Bedouin opera cloaks, cloaks trimmed with sable fur, beautiful grenadine shawls, and women's dresses of satin and silk. One that promised to attract attention "was composed of a gold and black striped underskirt, trimmed with biased folds of the same material; the upper and over garment made of rich black silk and trimmed with rich silk." There were also "prestige pieces"—articles of particular beauty and costliness which, though they might perhaps never be sold, served to add to the magnificence of the store's displays—for example, shawls of Persian cashmere priced-tagged at $175, and point lace at $300.[11]

The actual movement and protection of such valuable goods previous to the opening consumed many anxious days. A half-dozen loyal employees slept all night in the still uncompleted building to guard the merchandise while the moving was in process; and even Palmer, eager for the success of his important tenants, made midnight visits to see that all was well.[12] Finally, in the middle of October, after a few disturbing delays, all was in readiness. The Lake Street store's doors were closed for the last time on Saturday, October 10; the last retail goods were rushed to the new building between six o'clock and midnight that evening; and on the following Monday the much publicized grand opening was held.[13] The opening was intended to be a big event, but its success undoubtedly surpassed the expectations of even Leiter and Field. Before the store was unlocked on the morning of opening day, a large crowd had already collected outside. From 10:00 A. M., when the doors were swung open and the people pushed inside, until nearly midnight, huge throngs poured in and out of the building. "No institution in Chicago, whatever its character," exclaimed the *Tribune,* "ever drew so large an assemblage together at its opening." All came to view what was for those days a gorgeous array of goods, "enough to turn almost any female head." [14] In the evening for the formal opening long lines of fashionable carriages "filled with the cream of the avenues," pulled up before the brilliantly illuminated store; and as they were ushered through the doors past the young boys in their smart blue uniforms with brass buttons,[15] hundreds of spectators watched from the streets and sidewalks. The *Chicago Tribune* the next day headlined the opening as "The Great Fashion Event of the Season";[16] and the *Chicago Times* proclaimed the house to be a "mighty firm"—"the acknowledged head of the dry goods trade in the Northwest." [17] It was everything that a businessman could wish for.

Early Retail Methods and Policies

The grand inauguration had been to a large extent a retail show. In terms of numbers of guests, certainly more of them appeared as prospective retail rather than as wholesale customers; and the women of the first families in Chicago who graced the evening opening and made of it such a grand affair were more interested in the attractive first-floor displays than in the quantity items heaped on tables on the upper floors. Yet at this time the retail department of Field, Leiter and Company was the lesser branch of the firm's business and was destined to remain so for many years to come.

Up until the year 1865, when Marshall Field and Levi Leiter decided to launch their own business, their experience had been limited exclusively to wholesaling of goods to other merchants; and certainly Field in his negotiations with the McCormicks made no mention of the possibility of entering the retail trade. In fact, it is quite probable that both Field and Leiter held off from buying out Palmer partly because of a reluctance to assume the burden of a retail division. When the contracts were finally drawn up, Palmer, as already noted, in order to make the sale attractive, had to mark the retail merchandise at a discount and include a provision that, if Field and Leiter insisted, he could be required to buy back these goods at the end of the first year.[18]

What, then, prompted Field and Leiter to keep the retail department throughout their careers? It would be interesting to know. They maintained this department despite a first-year panic that nearly ruined the firm, despite many years (beginning in 1872) of low profits and despite the growing distaste of Leiter in later years for this branch of the business. Perhaps its retention was due to the fact that a considerable part of the very first year's remarkable profits may have come from retail sales. Unfortunately no separate figures for retail profits are available. Perhaps foresight on the part of Field and the hope at that time on the part of both partners of making it a profitable venture in the future were factors.

Whatever the cause, it is certain that the interest of Marshall Field in retailing increased steadily with the passing years and that he developed definite ideas about the manner in which this phase of the business should be conducted. In 1868, in anticipation of the opening of the large new store, Field gave up his New York address; and, turning over the management of the small staff of the New York office to the capable hands of Lorenzo G. Woodhouse, he moved back to Chicago and to a residence on fashionable Michigan Avenue. He was henceforth to make Chicago his permanent home and was now in a better position not only generally to help supervise his own growing firm but, especially now that Milton Palmer was gone as manager of the retail department, to give expression to his own ideas in this branch of operation. Field, for one thing, apparently enjoyed immensely the merchant-customer relationships in retailing; for until he was a white-haired man, he appeared almost regularly among the counters of his retail store—appeared not merely for business reasons, but apparently for the pleasure of greeting his more distinguished customers at the door and of waiting upon them personally.[19] Now that he was becoming wealthy and even a bit famous, he undoubtedly enjoyed being admired and flattered at close range, rather than from afar. It was no doubt after but a short experience with the retail store in those first years that Marshall Field's partiality for this phase of his business took hold and fixed in him the determination that the branch should stay.

Once he had determined to have a retail store, its policy was a foregone conclusion. The watchword was to be integrity. In every price range, the store must carry only the best merchandise obtainable. The rarest and costliest articles down through the least expensive bolts of cloth had to be trustworthy goods. For the wealthier class, discover what the customer wants and go to the four corners of the earth to find it ("such little things are the life of our Retail trade," said Field);[20] for the other, keep prices as low as possible but never at a sacrifice of dependability.[21] Said Field later:

I made it a point that all goods should be exactly what they were represented to be. It was a rule of the house that an exact scrutiny of the quality of all goods purchased should be maintained, and that nothing was to induce the house to place upon the market any line of goods at a shade of variation from their real value. Every article sold must be regarded as warranted, and every purchaser must be enabled to feel secure.[22]

To that end, frequent retail advertisements from the first carried the same all-important guarantee as had Palmer's:

If, when you get your goods home, and do not find them entirely satisfactory, please return them, and your money will be refunded.[23]

Marshall Field's ideas, his plans, and his store of such fantastic reputation—none of these were born overnight. The fame of Field, Leiter and Company's retail store spread gradually over the years as Field, warming to the significance of his own policies, unfolded them slowly before appreciative Chicagoans. He was no innovator. Field seldom introduced an entirely novel idea. As he himself put it: "There were never any great ventures or risks—nothing exciting whatever." [24] His ability lay in recognizing a good idea and building upon it many times better than anyone ever had before.

This was true, for example, of the first principle of his business mentioned earlier—that of the customer's unquestioned right to exchange goods. This had been taken over from the "money-back" policy introduced into Chicago by Potter Palmer at least four years before Field and Leiter purchased the Palmer store. But Marshall Field so developed and glorified the policy that it became permanently identified with his name.[25] The liberality with which he accepted returned goods, in fact, obliged him throughout his life to weather a steady torrent of complaints from his major competitors. Marshall Field, they said, was too liberal—he overdid it.[26] But he did not change his policy. His store's reputation for "overdoing" an idea that another person had originated was making him a rich man.

Direct Foreign Buying

In essence, the secret of Field's success was that he overdid many things. Determined to furnish his store with the better merchandise no matter what part of the world produced it, he began, soon after returning to Chicago, to expand the firm's policy of importing direct from abroad. Previously the major burden of buying overseas had rested largely on Field alone. "Our foreign goods," said an early (1867) retail circular, "are selected with much care by our Mr. Field, now in Europe, with especial view to the wants of our trade." After 1868 Palmer's veteran New York buyer, George W. Vail, and later

26

4. Field, Leiter and Co.: Retail and Wholesale

George Stanton, able notion man, were also sent to Europe in an attempt to keep up with the demand and the high standards set for the store by Field.[27] Palmer, Cooley, and Wadsworth, if not others, had earlier dispatched at least occasional buyers to European sources to supplement what they were able to obtain at the New York auctions.[28] Field, again, simply took over the idea and was soon buying in quantities unimagined by his predecessors.[29]

Before very long Field determined to have a permanent buying office in Europe, and to retain in the major countries there a staff of resident buyers. Through this maneuver Field, Leiter and Company would no longer be limited to buying only when its representatives happened to be abroad. A permanent foreign office and on-the-spot buyers would permit a regular year-long purchasing program. The latest fashions could be procured and shipped as soon as designed, and staple items could be purchased at any time of the year that the market appeared most favorable.

By the end of 1869 the idea had materialized to the extent that Field, Leiter and Company were listing a Paris office on their letterhead, but this was only a trade connection and not an independent office.[30] In 1871, however, Field sent his brother Joseph abroad with instructions to open a small office in Manchester in the heart of the British mill district, a "good central location for our kind of business." [31] Joseph rented an unheated assortment of rooms on a second floor[32], and keeping in touch with the new resident buyers located in France and Germany,[33] inaugurated what eventually became a complex, world-wide buying organization. A half-dozen buyers representing various departments, such as notions, laces, etc., still traveled abroad semiannually; but, year-round, Joseph's tiny Manchester outpost with its few shivering clerks and bookkeepers functioned smoothly and efficiently—locating merchandise, advising Chicago what was available, relaying orders to buyers, paying all the bills, packing goods purchased throughout Europe, and shipping them by fast liner.[34] Field, Leiter and Company was growing up.

There were other problems as well; for more trouble was often experienced in getting goods from New York or Boston to Chicago than in shipping them from Europe to an American port. Warehousing expenses in New York and costly delays while awaiting customs appraisal of goods added greatly to the expense of doing business. New York firms had a definite advantage, for they might withdraw goods from government warehouses as fast as they were appraised, while Chicagoans must keep their customers waiting until sufficient quantities had been released to warrant shipping or else tie up much of their working capital by posting heavy bonds for the whole.[35]

Repeated protests by Chicago jobbers endeavoring to compete with New York brought action from Congress almost simultaneously with the establishment by Field, Leiter and Company of its foreign offices. A law was enacted in 1870 making Chicago a port of entry, with its own government warehouses, customs house and appraisers, and allowing direct shipment to Chicago from Europe without delays in New York.[36] In September 1871, when the first two bonded carloads of Field, Leiter and Company direct imports rumbled into Chicago over the Michigan Central Railroad, members of the firm, Customs House officials, the Appraiser of the Port of Chicago, members of the state Legislature, and other prominent citizens came down to the depot to hold a celebration.

In honor of this first direct importation, a dozen of champagne were opened and drank [sic] by the gentlemen present. Toasts were given and responded to, and, altogether, the "opening," not alone of the wine, but of the cars, was a very pleasant one.[37]

Thus a western firm, far from any Atlantic port, was now importing directly from European factories and fashion centers; and its foreign buyers were giving such famous firms as A. T. Stewart and Company and Claflin's of New York lively competition abroad for the more exclusive foreign products.[38] As for the city of Chicago, Field's remained for many years easily the largest of all importers.

TABLE I

VALUE OF DRY GOODS IMPORTED BY MARSHALL FIELD & CO. AND BY TOTAL OF ALL FIRMS IN CITY OF CHICAGO FOR 1873-80

Year	M. F. & Co.[a]	All Chicago[b]	Year	M. F. & Co.[a]	All Chicago[b]
1873	$1,212,439	$1,811,982	1877	$1,058,815	$1,681,939
1874	1,297,711	1,780,915	1878	1,081,549	1,410,285
1875	1,523,035	2,074,906	1879	1,208,568	2,033,863
1876	1,099,471	1,834,778	1880	2,036,228	2,935,412

[a]Accounting ledgers, 1873-80, Comptroller's safe, Marshall Field & Co. General Offices.
[b]Andreas, *History of Chicago*, III, 717.

With a steady parade of exquisite gowns and "chic" bonnets, many in their original Paris boxes, flowing from Field, Leiter and Company warehouses onto their retail shelves, the firm was soon setting the style leadership for Chicago.[39] The store almost burst with pride as it employed in its advertisements a new cosmopolitan vocabulary.

Have just received, per last steamer, a line of very fine laces . . . consisting of handsome point gaze, point duchesse, and applique collars, in the Imperial, Esmeralda, Von Moltke, and other new shapes, Point Applique Capes and Flounces, Black Thread Capes and Parasol Covers, Llama Lace Covers, very fine and very low prices. Also, an elegant assortment of Black Thread Laces, Barbes, and Coiffeurs; and a further supply of Novelties in Valenciennes Collars, Sets, Ties and Bows, the Handsomest and cheapest goods they have thus far imported.[40]

4. Field, Leiter and Co.: Retail and Wholesale

And the people who came to trade! The numbers of gracious and lovely women of society who stepped down from their carriages and swept through the doors of Field, Leiter and Company to see the latest in foreign finery kept the employees fascinated. "Ah, those were the days when women knew how to dress," said one old-time clerk.

Women didn't aim to look chic then . . . ; they were satisfied to look lovely. There was Mrs. Fairbanks and Mrs. Palmer and Mrs. McCormick—queenly, beautiful women, all of them. They were a delight to the eye.

"When the beautifully regal Mrs. Potter Palmer came into the store, all eyes followed her every move," said another. "She was the loveliest woman I have ever seen, and a perfect gentlewoman." [41] The pleasant-spoken widow, Mrs. Abraham Lincoln, appeared frequently on shopping excursions to buy for her son, Robert T. Lincoln. And one day the deceased president's daughter-in-law, Mrs. Robert T. Lincoln, pleased at the gracious treatment she received, impulsively removed a rose from her gown and fastened it an an embarrassed salesman's lapel. "I raised it in my garden," she told him, "and I want you to have it." [42] Marshall Field had obtained the kind of customers he wanted. As he greeted them at the door, he must have been happy.

Early Wholesale Methods and Policies

Had Marshall Field indulged his fondness for retailing to the exclusion or neglect of the remainder of his business, he would not have died so wealthy a man. Retail sales climbed steadily; but the spectacular totals for the whole firm chalked up in each of those early years were not so much to be credited to the retail customers as to the steadily increasing numbers of western dry-goods merchants who found it good business to buy their requirements from the wholesale division of Field, Leiter and Company. For example, the firm's sales beginning with 1867 looked like this:

1867

Retail Sales	$1,450,000
Wholesale Sales	7,621,000
Total Sales	$9,071,000 [43]

Wholesale was thus responsible for over four-fifths of the total net sales. Thanks largely to Field's expert generalship, the retail figures within five years had more than doubled—but this was also almost equally true of wholesale:

1872

Retail Sales	$ 3,109,000
Wholesale Sales	14,099,000
Total Sales	$17,208,000

Even more impressive is a breakdown of the profits. Unfortunately, for 1867 there are available only the total profits, which were $328,-000. But in 1872, when total profits stood at an imposing $869,500, as much as $828,400 of this sum came from wholesale business. The first floor's profits accounted for less than one-twentieth of the total. Field's retail store, proud of its growth, was no doubt an asset in creating prestige for the firm, but was (and would remain for many years to come) a spoiled darling in the profit ledger. If it should some day prove to be the tail that wagged the dog, it was not apparent in the 1870's.

It was, therefore, for a good reason that Field did not devote his whole interest, or even most of it, to the retail floor. Not only did the huge buying, credit, and selling organization that had to be set up for a business the size of Field, Leiter and Company's wholesale division take much more time and planning than the smaller retail store, but the latter by its very nature had to be in many respects subordinated to and dependent upon the wholesale. For example, the vast majority of goods sold over the retail counters were purchased from the firm's own wholesale department.[44] This, in fact, was one of the factors giving Field, Leiter and Company's retail a great advantage over other retail stores. Most of its goods did not have to be purchased far in advance; and it was not necessary to lease or buy large warehousing for extra stock. Both of these necessities were eliminated by the fact that its retail department had access to and first call on all goods in the firm's own wholesale stocks.[45] It could buy them as needed and usually without so much as even the expense and trouble of hauling except that involved in moving goods from one floor to another.

Fortunately, too, for the retail's policies of exclusiveness, customer satisfaction, and dependability in merchandise, the firm's wholesale branch was a source of supply that maintained these same principles of doing business. While J. V. Farwell and Company, for example, was stamping across its merchant customers' bills in red ink "POSITIVELY NO GOODS WILL BE TAKEN BACK UNLESS DAMAGED WHEN DELIVERED," [46] Field, Leiter and Company were announcing of their goods that "if not entirely approved, return at our expense," and "satisfaction guaranteed." [47] Field, Leiter and Company's reputation for integrity in its jobbing business was as widespread among the thousands of small merchants scattered over the West as was the reputation of the retail department among the women of Chicago.[48]

The store's success in dictating fashions, its ability to organize a vast importing organization, and its achievement in selling high-quality products at reasonable prices in both branches were largely due to the great buying power of the wholesale departments.[49] When Mrs. Average Chicagoan was able to buy on the first floor the latest embroidered French chemise imported over four thousand miles from Paris for only seventy-five cents,[50] it was due to the fact that alert Field, Leiter and

4. FIELD, LEITER AND CO.: RETAIL AND WHOLESALE

Company resident buyers "were the first in the French Market" and had purchased in quantity for the wholesale as well as retail.[51]

It was, in fact, the low prices maintained by both the retail and wholesale departments of the firm that made it especially difficult for their rivals to compete against them. Cincinnati and St. Louis, once formidable rivals for the wholesale trade of the West because of their favorable locations on navigable rivers, were, with the growth of the railroad, reduced to the status of serving only rather localized areas. Chicago jobbers as a whole now treated those cities with scorn. On June 8, 1867, the *Chicago Tribune* commented:

> Hereafter the pre-eminence of Chicago as the Metropolitan city of the Northwest will be a matter of record. Figures sometimes lie, but the truth of these must be so indubitable that we suspect we shall hear no more from either of the rival wood stations on the Ohio and Mississippi about their aspirations to be reckoned as rivals of Chicago.

The figures showed that in 1866 in Chicago there were fifty-nine firms whose sales exceeded one million dollars, whereas Cincinnati and St. Louis had only fifteen each.[52]

Eastern firms, however, in particular those in New York, with the obvious natural advantages that they possessed, remained formidable competitors even in the Northwest;[53] and it was mainly with them that a running battle had to be fought—a battle for the trade of the small retailers to be waged with the ammunition of price appeal. Field, Leiter and Company of all Chicago jobbers from the very first was best equipped and most successful in gaining substantial victories over all opposition. The firm never tired of informing the trade that "our intentions are to sell goods at the lowest possible living prices";[54] or "We guarantee to offer you a *superior stock* and at as low prices as can be had in any *Eastern market* for the same *class of goods,* thereby *saving freight and other expenses to the purchaser."* [55]

New York importers and jobbers countered with advertisements arguing that the western wholesaler, located a thousand miles from the nearest ocean port, could not possibly sell as advantageously as the easterner. Claims to the contrary, they said, were a snare and a delusion. One circular asserted that Chicago and St. Louis jobbers, in their desperate efforts to compete, regularly took a loss on domestics by listing them at New York prices and then made it up by seeking extravagant profits on their foreign goods. "Merchants are therefore advised to buy their Foreign and Fancy Goods from New York." Across the bottom of one of these circulars which fell into the hands of an irate Field, Leiter and Company salesman there is scrawled:

> Why not be honest about it and say that it will pay you best to buy all your goods of western merchants?[56]

Such claims and counterclaims led to strenuous price-slashing and eventually flaring tempers.[57] But no matter how low the price set by eastern firms, Field, Leiter and Company were prepared to reduce theirs further, even at the risk of taking a loss from time to time.[58] Reports were received continuously from salesmen on the road or from competitors' advertisements on prices being offered by other dealers. The big Chicago firm promptly adjusted their own, no matter what the consequences.[59] Field until the end of his career continuously admonished his lieutenants:

I fear Heads of Depts. will try to hold prices *too high* in order to save loss. That they must not do. Sell on bottom market . . . as we must hold best trade only.[60]

and:

I advocate low prices let results be what will.[61]

Prices changed so rapidly that a country storekeeper did not know from one day to the next what his goods might cost; and it became necessary to assure the customers who ordered by mail from the firm's catalogues and circulars that Field, Leiter and Company would protect their interest.

Should there be any change, we guarantee to make you the very lowest prices upon every article. Our constant aim will be to make it to the interest of all merchants in the northwest to make Chicago their market for dry goods.[62]

During the difficult period of the middle and late 1870's following the great panic of 1873, the competition and price war were particularly keen; and the manufacturers, finding their own prices being forced down by pressure from the competing wholesalers, frequently came forth with angry protests. One morning in March 1876, for instance, the following telegram from a firm of manufacturers' agents was laid on the desk of Marshall Field:

YOUR QUOTATION ON ANDROSCOGGIN L IS AN OUTRAGE UNWORTHY OF YOU AND CALCULATED TO DISTURB THE RELATIONS HITHERTO EXISTING BETWEEN OUR FIRMS.[63]

To which the usually mild-mannered Marshall Field replied:

WE HAD GOOD REASONS FOR THE QUOTATIONS. YOUR TELEGRAM VERY UNJUST. GIVE YOU TWENTY-FOUR HOURS TO RECALL IT.[64]

A covering letter from Field explained:

We will say that we much regret the necessity of making prices at any time that are injurious to your firm or the manufacture [sic] but you have no idea of outside prices that we have to contend with; from Boston travelling men, also prices given in your City. . . . We . . . will make prices to meet such competition and hold our trade.

4. Field, Leiter and Co.: Retail and Wholesale

> We will admit that our quotation (8¾¢) was rather low for Androscoggin L. . . .

Then, unable to resist getting in a last gibe:

> We must however add, that had same price been made by some of your largest New York customers, it would have been "all lovely."[65]

Companies do not, of course, stay in business by losing money. If Field, Leiter and Company were to quote lower prices than its competitors as a regular policy and yet still make a profit, it obviously had to possess facilities which other firms did not. What those facilities were has been well established. Again, none were new or unique—they were simply applied with greater persuasion. One of these—and it was to make Levi Leiter fairly famous in his own day—was the firm's credit policy.

There has been considerable misinformation in the numerous accounts of Marshall Field and Company about the store's credit policy. Marshall Field, it is often said, insisted from the begining on selling (and buying) strictly for "cash," much against the wishes of Levi Leiter, who believed in loose credits. Field's insistence, it is also claimed, won the day and was the secret of the store's great success. In point of fact, the best evidence presents quite a different story. First of all, though Field was truly a believer in close credits, it would seem that the real "bear" on the matter was Leiter. Leiter for the first sixteen formative years, during a period when long credits were the rule in the trade and pressure from customers for extended credit was consequently great, managed the firm's credit office and determinedly laid down the strict policies for which the house became so well known.[66] It was only after Leiter departed in 1881, and during a time when the firm's strategy was determined exclusively by Field, that the store's credit policy was allowed to evidence some liberality.[67]

It should be made clear, furthermore, that the strictly "cash" policy followed by both Field and Leiter never did mean at any time that every customer had to lay his money on the counter as soon as the purchase was made, or even by "the first of the month." As early as 1865—not to mention the days of P. Palmer and Company—Field, Palmer and Leiter were during the emergency of that year extending terms "in special cases" for as long as ninety days. Even under normal business relationships after 1865, terms were rarely strictly "30 days net," as they had been when the firm first started,[68] but rather varied according to the type of goods purchased. Bills for merchandise such as spool cotton, domestics, and oil cloths on which the mark-up was small usually were discounted at 2 per cent if paid within ten days and 1 per cent if paid within thirty days. Carpets and upholstery sometimes also came in that class. But for "all other goods including Department [sic] stocks usually sold on time by Eastern Jobbers," the terms were "10 days less 6 per cent. 30 days less 5 per cent. 60 days less 4 per cent."[69] Before the century was out, Field was financing hundreds of small retailers of ability over the country whom he had investigated and felt had good prospects for success.[70]

The truth about the firm's credit policy thus seems to lie not in its operating on either a literal "cash" basis or on one of "easy credits." Rather it was true that both partners were able to recognize that what was a good and safe policy toward one customer was not necessarily good and safe toward another—and before dealing with either man, looked him up in Dun and Bradstreet.[71] H. N. Higinbotham, for thirty years a dispenser of credits for the firm, confessed:

> It is hard to lay down iron-clad rules governing credit. No two cases that present themselves to us are treated in exactly the same manner. The difference in the circumstances and environments of the merchants should govern them in deciding whether they are to conduct their business on a cash or credit basis, just as it governs us in deciding upon how much credit to which they are entitled. . . .
>
> Credit and confidence go hand in hand and are a bulwark of commerce. It is as necessary for some retailers to extend credit to their patrons as it is for a wholesale firm. . . .
>
> To refuse time to some [customers] is to refuse their trade.[72]

Nevertheless, for those days when many jobbers were extending credit to their customers of four months or more, the policy of Field, Leiter and Company was naturally considered one of "close terms." [73] Leiter as head of the credit department was accepted by some as "the father of the short time, prompt-paying wholesale business of Chicago." [74] Probably both his and Field's impulse toward short-term credits came as a result of their mutual experience in the panic of 1857. Field once remarked in an interview that:

> The panic of 1857 swept almost everything away except the house I worked for [Cooley, Farwell and Company], and I learned that the reason they survived was because they understood the nature of the new country, and did a cash business. That is, they bought for cash, and sold on thirty and sixty days, instead of giving the customers, whose financial condition you could hardly tell anything about, all the time they wanted. . . . I learned what I consider my best lesson, and that was to do a cash business.[75]

Field had only scorn for his competitors who postdated bills (dated them weeks or months ahead in order to give the customer more time in which to pay) and granted absurdly long credit terms to any and all merchants. Advancing goods on time was a heavy expense to jobbers that, however disguised, had to be borne eventually by the customer in one way or another (usually in higher prices). To pretend otherwise was a species of dishonesty. Many of our competitors "seem to think they are selling time instead of dry goods," [76] he would say; and the two partners stubbornly refused, even under the stress of powerful competition, to lower their standards. Except for Marshall Field's financing of individual retailers who were trying to get started, terms remained at thirty and sixty days; and every customer, no matter

34

how strong financially, was obliged to pay promptly if he wished to retain his credit with the firm. "From a long experience we are satisfied that the only true policy for the conduct of a successful business is on a strictly cash basis." [77]

"Our policy secures the sharp, prompt paying, best merchants of the country." [78] As usual, Field was right. Only the better merchants could afford to deal on Field, Leiter and Company terms; and this variety came, without much urging, attracted by sound goods, fair prices, and liberal discounts for cash. [79] Other merchants, financially unable to pay promptly or unable to satisfy the credit office as to their responsibility, often angrily took their trade elsewhere. [80] These, many of them, were permanently lost to the firm; but as one employee laconically put it, "There were enough merchants in the Middle West discounting their bills to give Field's Wholesale all the business it could do." [81] And when the usual number of defaulting retailers fled to Canada, or a panic hit, leaving a trail of dejected jobbers face to face with bad debts and bankruptcy, among such jobbers Marshall Field and Levi Leiter were not to be found. [82]

The task of deciding in which retail merchants to place confidence, and how much, fell largely to the hard-working Leiter in the early days. [83] For sixteen years he ruled almost like a high potentate in his capacity of manager of Wholesale and chief of the credit department. In those days, with commercial rating agencies still in their infancy, most wholesale houses had to improvise their own facilities for gathering information; and Leiter's was one of the best. Again from Higinbotham, who worked under Leiter:

So thorough and searching are the means employed . . . to obtain an accurate knowledge of the standing and affairs of . . . debtors that it is practically hopeless for the latter to attempt any concealment of unfavorable conditions. [84]

Bits of information picked up on the road were telegraphed to Chicago by salesmen. Confidential estimates were regularly being sent in by friendly bankers, lawyers, and station agents. Reports on population growth and crop conditions in every farming community wherein lived a merchant-customer were carefully scrutinized. [85] These and dozens of other incidental sources, as well as the very early commercial credit ratings listed by such firms as The Bradstreet Company, Dun, Barlow and Company, and Hurst, Garlock and Company all served like a vast spy system to keep the coldly efficient Leiter informed. [86]

On every merchant seeking credit, there was a record entered in a large confidential ledger which was undoubtedly kept handy to Leiter's tall, stand-up desk. [87] If the gentleman's record did not measure up to the credit manager's specifications, the merchant was probably in for a very distasteful experience; for Leiter's refusals were not subtly proffered. As one customer approached the credit office he was likely to hear the last applicant being ushered out with angry shouts audible throughout the second floor. Thoroughly honest and painfully straightforward himself, Leiter could not tolerate a lack of those char-

35

MARSHALL FIELD & CO.

acteristics in others. "You promised it and you did not do it," he sometimes shouted, "so get out or I will have the porter throw you out!" [88]

Every article ordered, before being sent out, had to have its shipping
ticket signed and approved by the credit man. If word of any last-
minute change in the affairs of the merchant was received after his
credit had been approved, Leiter's office withheld permission to ship
the ordered goods. The scrutiny of hundreds of these shipping tags
each day was an exacting and monotonous task,[89] but it was in Leiter's
office that a reputation was built and it cut the firm's cost of doing
business. When the commercial accrediting agencies reported year
after year that the store's "losses by bad debts [are] remarkably small,"
no one was surprised.[90]

An interesting letter, illustrative of the facts that Leiter's policies
were still practiced long after he left the firm and that even a cash
business sometimes had its problems, reads as follows:

Friend Dan

*We are up a stump in a little deal in your town. Have been shipping stuff
off and on to Smith Bros. C. O. D. Drawing on them through the bank before
letting them have the goods from the freight House.*

*Shipped them a bill last week, before it reached them they were out of
business or busted I don't know which.*

*Wonder if you can't use the stuff. Enclose you duplicate Invoices showing
contents. . . . [follows the terms Field's will make "Dan" if he takes the goods]
Will appreciate the favor if you can help us out and trust do as much for you
sometime. . . .*

Yours truly,
W. F. HYPES
Marshall Field & Co.[91]

If Field and Leiter's stubborn insistence on selling only on short
terms or for cash, however, enabled them to cut costs and maintain
attractive prices, even more so did their corollary practice of *buying*
only for cash. In fact, the first policy made the other possible. With
their carefully selected customers discounting their bills as regularly as
a group of faithful employees punching a time clock, the two partners
had little capital tied up in delinquent accounts, knew with reasonable certainty how much money was coming in each month, and were
subsequently able to maintain an unsurpassed reputation themselves
for prompt payment. This reputation was so important to the firm,
said Higinbotham, "that the mail schedules, both foreign and domestic, are carefully scrutinized and constantly revised, so that it may be
instantly known how long a time will be required for a letter to reach
any city of America, Europe or other foreign lands." All that, just so
that each remittance "will be certain to reach its destination a trifle
before the date on which will occur the most advantageous moment
for the payment of the bill which the draft is to cover."[92] Field, in
this connection, is often credited with never borrowing and never giving a note.[93] This was true, but only in the later years of his career,
after he had become a wealthy man and there was no necessity for

36

borrowing. To Field, there was nothing harmful in owing a legitimate and properly negotiated debt. Honor and integrity were lost only by not paying such debts promptly. Both Field and Leiter in their first years with the firm much preferred to—and did—borrow money even at heavy interest rather than let a bill go unpaid or undiscounted and sacrifice a carefully built reputation.[94]

Prompt payment, however, was not entirely a matter of ethics. As with most of their policies it was again a matter of good business. It paid. In the first place, the growing Chicago firm's renown before long became literally world-wide and proved to be a business asset of inestimable value.[95] One of the many anecdotes regarding Marshall Field and Company is about an agent from Claflin's of New York seeking out a Calcutta manufacturer in the early 1880's to purchase goods, only to find to his surprise that he had been forestalled by a buyer from the rising young firm in Chicago. "Why," he exclaimed to the manufacturer, "they sell where the Indian and buffalo still roam. I've killed prairie wolves in front of their store. They have no business here." "We know nothing about that, sir," replied the Indian politely, "but they discount their bills promptly." [96] Such a reputation for reliability made a Field, Leiter and Company card something of an international passport inscribed in a language all its own.

In the second place, for a concern whose purchases were running into the millions of dollars, even a 1 per cent discount for prompt remittance was well worth saving; and a 2 per cent discount could mean the difference between underselling its competitor by taking a loss or being able to do the same thing at a profit. "A material part of its gains," reported Hurst and Garlock of Field, Leiter and Company, "were . . . from discounts." [97]

The biggest saving, however, lay in the firm's ability with ready money to buy in large lots at lowest market prices. Every manufacturer in America and abroad knew that a sale to Field, Leiter and Company meant a quantity purchase and cash in hand. To get that type of business it was worth while to bid low.[98] If lower prices were not willingly proffered by the seller, Marshall Field, in charge of purchasing, was not above demanding them.[99] He complained to his buyers that "we do not get the benefit in way of prices we should have by reason of making our purchases strictly for cash." [100] But the fact that he was still complaining after the turn of the century—and still paying cash—would argue to the contrary.[101] Experienced and confident Field, Leiter and Company buyers, moving quietly among the great auctions and visiting regularly the large and small manufacturers of the world, were always on the alert and ever ready to offer a small fortune in cash, if necessary, in order to buy in the best possible market and to keep a steady flow of low-priced, up-to-date merchandise traveling toward Chicago and the "Big Store." [102]

Years of Trial 5

D URING THE FIRST HALF-DOZEN YEARS OF ITS EXISTENCE, THE FIRM of Field, Leiter and Company, along with its successes, had a reasonable share of troubles: debts to pay Potter Palmer,[1] the effects of a sizable panic to stave off in 1865, and a serious warehouse fire in 1870 to cut into profits.[2] Yet 1871 was to usher in eight years of a variety of troubles for the firm that must have made the partners' past problems seem trivial indeed.

The Great Fire

On Sunday evening of October 8, 1871, a fire broke out on the southwest side of the city, quickly got out of control, and, aided by a high wind, began racing north and east from one block to another toward the business district, consuming everything in its path. The greatest disaster in Chicago's history had begun.

When John Devlin brought the news to the members of the firm that this was no ordinary fire, Henry Willing and Levi Leiter decided to load as much as possible of the more expensive goods on wagons and take them to Mr. Leiter's home on Calumet Avenue near Twenty-third Street, which was well out of the path of the flames.[3] Quick-thinking Mr. Higinbotham, meantime, had already rushed to the company barns and had ordered out all the drivers with their wagons and teams.[4] Private hack and wagon drivers were offered fantastic prices for their services by storekeepers everywhere, eager to save some of their valuable records and merchandise. Once having hired themselves out, the unscrupulous drivers were not above throwing out their first employer's goods somewhere along the route in order to accept a higher bid from someone else.[5] Field, Leiter and Company were not at the mercy of such profiteers, but instead could count on loyal, dependable service from their own crews. H. B. Parker, one of the salesmen, ran to the basement, broke up boxes, and built a fire in the boiler in order to get the steam elevators running. This helped greatly to expedite the removal of the laces, silks, shawls, and other expensive merchandise from the upper floors.[6] Under the direction of Leiter and Willing, the drivers worked feverishly, first loading the wagons to their utmost capacity and then racing them through the crowded streets back and forth between the store and the car barns at Twentieth and State streets.[7] When the gas tank exploded, putting out the store's lights, the men worked by candlelight and the gleam of the approaching flames.[8]

At this stage, despite all the effort being directed toward removing

38

the goods, hope of saving the store was still high, for the fire had temporarily by-passed the area in which the store lay[9] and numerous large fireproof buildings such as the First National Bank and the Tribune building were intact and standing between Field, Leiter and Company and the fire.[10] As the flames approached more closely, the firm's powerful pumping engines in the basement[11] were started; and at Field's request, John Devlin, with seven other volunteers, stood on the roof flooding it and the sides of the big building with steady streams of water from the fire hoses.[12] Another crew worked soaking blankets and hanging them in the windows.[13] Early Monday morning, however, the waterworks succumbed to the fire and the water suddenly stopped, making it useless to hope any longer to save the building.[14] When the block of buildings on the east side of State Street north of Field, Leiter and Company caught fire, the blaze was carried rapidly to the doors of Field, Leiter and Company.[15] The last man had scarcely left the building when flames burst from every window; and in a matter of minutes, over two million dollars' worth of goods were destroyed.[16] The next day not a wall was standing; the destruction was complete. The only testimony to the store's former existence was a rough board sign which, within the week, was placed amidst the ruins to announce that

Cash Boys & Work

Girls will be Paid

what is due them

Monday 9 A.M. Oct 16th

at 60 Calumet Ave.

Field, Leiter & Co."

Not much time was wasted on lamentation. The first day after the fire, literally before the embers had cooled, preparations were being made to start anew. Higinbotham came to Levi Leiter's home and proposed a plan that called for Marshall Field to be made responsible for finding a new location in which to do business, Leiter to inventory the rescued goods, Henry Willing to stop all goods coming from the East and warehouse them in Valparaiso, Indiana, and Higinbotham himself to adjust the insurance claims in accordance with Leiter's inventories and with the books of account that had been rescued. The plan evidently met with everyone's basic approval, for it was the one which was followed.[18]

Higinbotham, taking all the ledgers and the bookkeepers, went to his mother's home in Joliet, Illinois, where the offices of Field, Leiter and Company were temporarily located until a suitable place could be found in Chicago. After intensive work, the accounting department was able to ascertain the extent of the firm's losses and to compute the amount of coverage by insurance. The total loss in merchandise, it was found, had been approximately $2,500,000,[19] and the numerous insurance policies covering these goods were worth at par about $2,200,000.[20] Since it was suspected that numerous insurance companies were about to go into bankruptcy as a result of the Chicago disaster, Higinbotham proceeded then to call upon the insurance companies personally, traveling to Cincinnati, St. Louis, and San Francisco in order to adjust the firm's claims. After two and a half months he could show for his labors only $1,275,000 collected; but another $170,000 seemed certain to come in, and he estimated for Leiter that almost one-half of the remaining $760,000 could be safely relied upon.[21] The firm thus withstood a net loss of almost three-quarters of a million dollars, which, great as it was, was proportionately much less than that of the average 1871 fire sufferer.[22]

While Higinbotham was carrying out his share of the work toward restoration of the company, Field was searching for a suitable building in which to reopen the store. With the central business district one of the most completely burned-out areas, this was no small task. One of the few buildings available which was sufficiently out of the razed area to be at all accessible to the public was a two-story, brick, horse-car barn belonging to the Chicago City Railway Company and located at State and Twentieth streets. This Field immediately leased as a temporary place of business, despite the many disadvantages inherent in this location, chief of which was the fact that here they would be cut off from all sections of the city except the south by the barrier of debris, dirt, and dust created by the fire.[23]

The work of converting the former barns and stables into a suitable retail and wholesale establishment was begun right away. The first merchants who could reëstablish themselves were not only in a position, of course, to make the most money and recoup their losses, but in view of the city's distress, to be of positive service to people in need of everyday necessities. The hay, oats, harness, and other horsecar equipment were hurriedly cleaned out; the floors were varnished; the interior was whitewashed and painted; and the former stalls were replaced with the necessary counters and shelves.[24]

Of necessity the interior and its fixtures left much to be desired: but since Field, Leiter and Company were the only merchants who were supplementing their stocks with eastern importations, the firm's merchant-customers were only too glad to see the wholesale department re-open so soon (October 28) under any conditions.[25] When the retail department was opened on November 6,[26] the women of Chicago also overlooked the disadvantages of the location and hurried in to replace the myriads of their possessions that had ben destroyed.[27] William A. Croffut, managing editor of the *Chicago Evening Post* has left this description of the store:

Down State Street to Twentieth, and here is the largest dry-goods store in the city or the West—Field, Leiter & Company. Here are hundreds of clerks and thousands of patrons a day busy along the spacious aisles and the vast vistas of ribbons and laces and cloaks and dress-goods. This tells no story of a fire. Ladies jostle each other as impatiently as of old and the boys run merrily to the incessant cry of "cash." Yet, Madam, this immense bazaar was, six weeks ago, the horse barn of the South Side Railroad! . . . Here where ready-made dresses hang, then hung sets of double harness; yonder where a richly robed lady leans languidly across the counter and fingers point laces, a manger stood and offered hospitality to a disconsolate horse. A strange metamorphosis—yet it is but an extreme illustration of the sudden changes the city has undergone.[28]

At a meeting of merchants that had been called on the day after the fire to decide on a uniform policy in regard to the debts owed by each of the burned-out firms, John V. Farwell had suggested: "Let us first ascertain how each one stands, and then ask such an extension as corresponds with the condition of each. . . . Such a program will gain the confidence and support of creditors to any needed extent"; and his suggestion had been unanimously accepted.[29] Marshall Field and Levi Leiter, however, in order to inform everyone where they stood shortly thereafter declared that they would pay one hundred cents on the dollar and pay it immediately or at maturity.[30] In reply to an offer of aid, they were able to write:

Dear Sir:
We have your kind note of this date and can assure you that we shall continue our business in the same manner as before the fire, making our purchases in the future the same as in the past.
We have suffered some loss by the fire as you are aware, but our capital is ample to continue our business in the same magnitude for the future as during the past. We had kept our affairs very snug, making our entire purchases for cash, never in a single instance having given a note for merchandise. We are therefore today in good shape.
Before we received any money from insurance, we met our obligations promptly. This was done exclusively from our daily receipts from collections.
Thanking you for your kind note, we are
Yours very truly,
FIELD, LEITER & CO.[31]

The condition and debt-paying policy of Field, Leiter and Company soon became widely known; and the firm's reputation for integrity and stability was, as a result, not only not weakened by the calamity, but was, as the new year of 1872 dawned, undoubtedly greater than ever before.[32]

The new year of 1872 thus found Field, Leiter and Company, one of the largest victims of the calamity, in their usual sound condition. Harlow Higinbotham's plan for recovery had reached maturation: the store at the new location was flourishing; the insurance settlements had been arranged; the firm's indebtedness had been paid; and the accounts had been reorganized so that business could be conducted as usual.

On December 28, 1871, Levi Leiter confidently sent to Joseph Field in England a statement "made up from a balance sheet taken from our books immediately after the fire." It showed approximate assets of:

Merchandise (mostly saved from fire or in transit to Chicago at time of fire)	$1,000,000
Money owed to firm	1,600,000
Cash	20,000
Real Estate	30,000
Bonds	120,000
Horses, wagons & harness	16,000
Collectible insurance	1,780,000
Total assets	$4,565,000

With only $1,940,000 in liabilities, this left a comfortable balance of $2,625,000 to the credit of the firm. By adding the net profit of "at least" $125,000 which the firm had earned since the fire, a total surplus of $2,750,000 was shown to exist, an amount which, as Leiter noted, "left a very handsome capital to continue our business." [33]

Wholesale: Madison and Market

Meantime, Field, Leiter and Company was letting it be known that their present humble location in a former car barn was by no means a permanent one.[34] Less than ten days after the fire, Marshall Field arranged for the construction of a brand-new $140,000 brick building on the West Side, at the corner of Market and Madison streets, to house the wholesale division.[35] Many of the smaller jobbers in Chicago had been waiting to see what J. V. Farwell and Company and Field, Leiter and Company planned to do; for the location of the two leading firms would do much to determine the permanent future center of the wholesale trade.[36] When both firms chose West-Side sites, the location of the new wholesale district was practically assured. As shocked as many merchants were at seeing both Lake and State streets now deserted in favor of an area that was formerly one of the poorest sections of Chicago, they nevertheless followed the judgment of the larger houses and eventually found it to be good.[37] Of prime importance in making this move an advisable one at this time was the fact that the area about Madison and Market was in a position to serve conveniently customers from the northern and western sections of the city without requiring them to traverse the burned area. Land values in this district were also considerably cheaper than on State Street, the prevailing price being only five to seven dollars per square foot;[38] whereas in December Potter Palmer had sold the old site of Field, Leiter and Company at State and Washington for $350,000 or at over $2100 per front foot. Finally, as Leiter confirmed in his letter to Joseph Field, for the year to come the piles of debris clogging the area at and around the old site would make entry into the store so difficult it would certainly discourage customers. Added to that, the dust arising from the rough surroundings would damage and destroy stock.[39] Considering everything, then, Madison and Market was a logical choice;

42

and Field, Leiter and Company, while temporarily filling orders and supplying the more urgent needs of their wholesale customers in the car barns, carried in their advertisements the promise of the new, soon-to-be-opened wholesale building on the West Side.[40]

The move was finally made on March 4, 1872;[41] and for the first time in the history of the store the two divisions—retail and whole-sale—were separated and housed in different buildings. This repre-sented a permanent change in policy which was an outgrowth of the fire; for since that holocaust it had become very difficult for the firm to obtain insurance with both branches under the same roof.[42]

The removal of the wholesale departments to their own huge build-ing gave them considerable room to expand; and at the same time their departure from the car barns left aisle after aisle of space into which the retail effects could now flow. It was a fine chance to make some long overdue additions to both the wholesale and retail stocks which the store carried, and the opportunity was well taken advantage of by bringing in some completely new lines and enlarging on others.[43]

Not for at least another decade could the firm be thought of as a "department" store, and it was a full generation from the era when everything from books and toys to furniture and dishes were displayed in the one store. Field, Leiter and Company for some time were simply an expanding dry-goods store: and Marshall Field, despite the ample capital for expansion which he had at his disposal, resisted every effort to include merchandise that was not within that category.[44]

The trend, however, even in the 1860's and 1870's was toward in-creasing variety in merchandise in the larger stores; and, as seen by his expansion of the notions department in 1865, even the conservative Field responded somewhat to the needs of the times. He recognized that diversification had an advantage in that it drew more customers into the store than any single line could do, added to the total sales volume, and in turn, correspondingly cut overhead costs.[45] Thus over the years, albeit almost grudgingly, Field, Leiter and Company en-larged upon the number of lines which were carried. Each addition of "dry goods" to the firm's stocks simply required a more liberal defini-tion of that term and was, whether desired or not, a step toward the inevitable all-inclusiveness of the modern department store.

At the time of the formal opening of the State-and-Twentieth-streets store, the firm announced the addition to its display of the "largest and best-selected stocks of Carpets and Upholstery Goods to be found in the country."[46] Upholstery items and even a few rugs had previously been included among the merchandise of the house;[47] but when Field and Leiter bought Potter Palmer's stock of dry goods in 1865, they did not include his large carpet department in the purchase[48] and nothing in this line had ever been carried since. When in 1872 carpet-ing was added to the store's stock, it was an innovation of such pro-portions that Marshall Field for the next thirty years carried his retail carpets, rugs, and upholstery goods in separate departments from "re-tail dry goods."[49]

Most of the business in carpets was in the cheaper domestic ingrains which retailed in 1874 from 50¢ to $1.50 a yard. Lowell ingrains at $1.15 and Hartfords at $1.12½ were the "big sellers"; but body Brussels carpets which had solid "backs" of strong linen thread and thus stayed clean longer gradually increased in favor despite the prices of $1.25 to $2.50 per yard which they commanded.[50] The firm also carried at this early date imported French Moquette, English Axminsters, Smyrna tapestry, and Brussels and Wilton velvets at prices that ranged up to $15.00 per square yard;[51] but for sometime to come business in foreign carpets remained small.[52] The carpet department as a whole, in fact, was for many years not a large profit maker in either the wholesale or retail branch. The retail carpet and upholstery department in 1872 and 1873, for example, showed gross sales of $355,000 and $472,000, respectively; but its expenses were so large and total turnover so small[53] that the department ended these same two years with losses of $10,000 and $7,000, and in subsequent years, its outcome was the same. The comparable wholesale department finished the first two years without going into the "red" but the profits were small and remained so for some time.[54]

A short time later (October 15, 1872) in the same year that carpets and upholstery were introduced, another important addition was made: "Fine, Medium, and Low-Priced Furs." For a new line, the variety offered was impressive. Cloaks, hats, muffs, and scarves were advertised in Hudson and Russian sable, seal skin, astrachan, Alaskan mink, ermine, squirrel, rose marte, fitch, white lamb, Persian lamb, and silver and white coney. It was "by far the most select assortment to be found in the city," said their newspaper advertisement of the fur opening.[55] Within a few years would be added buffalo robes, which wholesaled at only $8.12½ to $11.50 apiece and could be purchased "by the bale" if desired — a mute testimony to the efficiency of the famous "skin hunters" of the western plains who, during this period, were destroying the remaining buffalo by the hundreds of thousands.[56]

By 1872, "gentlemen's furnishings" had also become a thriving new line.[57] A few men's-clothing items had been included in the notions department of 1865; but a separate men's-clothing department carrying a more or less complete supply of goods made its first appearance at the time of the State and Washington opening in 1868,[58] and over the years the stock was gradually expanded in both quantity and variety of articles offered. By the early 1870's, in handkerchiefs, men (or their wives for them) could buy linen cambric, Scotch lawn, silk, and Turkey red cotton.[59] A little later (1877) they could obtain stiff turn-down paper collars that came in a novel wooden bucket, in a small tin pail, or in a Zoetrope box that showed a series of comic revolving pictures.[60] Pajamas were not as yet on the market and summer underwear was something of a luxury. E. R. Dowd of the wholesale underwear department, judging by his sales, was of the opinion that the average man did not use underwear at all during the summer. Nightshirts were used by some; and Field, Leiter and Company carried a large assortment of

44

5. Years of Trial

the popular heavy red flannels for winter. In 1871, however, much of the men's winter underwear was obviously still made in the home.[61]

Other advertised items were the latest styles in linen collars (for example, "The Derby" or "The New Style Shakespeare"), silk, lisle, and cotton hosiery, "Prince Teck's" neckties, Italian silk neck handkerchiefs, "Quaker City" shirts, and "Emerson's" genuine razor strops. A man could have a choice, among others, between "Pratt's Patent Combined Shoulder Braces" and imported English web suspenders; between Silk Patent or dog skin gloves; and between "Combination Lock" and Scotch gingham umbrellas. In the store he could also obtain pipes, tobacco boxes, "CAN'T BREAK 'EM" shoe laces, and even "Jockey Club" for his hair.[62]

Women found the most significant changes in the store since the birth of the firm in the new items carried as a result of the changing styles following the Civil War and in the increasingly greater number and variety of "manufactured goods" (ready-made articles of clothing) that were now offered.[63] Whereas cloaks, hose, and shawls[64] had originally been practically the only ready-made garments carried previous to 1865, the styles of the 1870's required for some a forty-bone "Widow Machree" corset with kid covered "Everlasting" clasps. Other women purchased the "Gold Elsie," "My Mary Ann," or the "Good Enough." The newest and most popular thing in hoop skirts was the "Tape Front Hoop Skirt with Pompadour Bustle combined." To help complete her ensemble milady could buy solid color or striped lisle, silk, or balbriggan hose, "Norman two-button" or Alexandre kid gloves (or silk and taffeta gloves "in plain and eccentric colors"), collars, cuffs, Valenciennes lace handkerchiefs, an imitation hair switch, a wide variety of cloaks, or even an important llama lace jacket.[65] For her home, in addition to the usual white goods, linens, and novelties like thread and buttons, she could now obtain leather railroad traveling bags, mirrors, drapes, window shades, curtain fixtures and, in small items most everything from ostrich-feather dusters and "Receme's" silver-plated napkin holders to sewing-machine oil and "Jesse Oakley's rose geranium toilet soap." [66]

With its stocks thus generously enlarged—much of it of types unknown before the fire—the retail store at State and Twentieth, following the removal of the wholesale department, threw wide its doors for an "opening exhibition." For the entire day and evening of April 4, 1872, the retail stocks were on display for the inspection of the public.[67] Having evidently realized the futility of trying to extract beauty from the architectural lines of a building originally designed for stables, Field and Leiter put their emphasis upon the beauty and magnificence of their wares. In every instance, their aim was to call attention to the merchandise but at the same time to camouflage its background. "The very pillars were clothed in graceful folds of drapery," and "rich carpets . . . hung from the sides of the walls." In few instances in the newspaper accounts of the exposition is there any mention of the physical aspects of the building itself, except in such details as the lighting, which was from the skylights and circular gas-jet pendants suspended from the roof, and the grand staircase leading from the first floor to the only other floor above. Indeed, the entire emphasis was upon the "arrangements . . . groupings, and combinations, contrasts and assimilations, in endless succession of ever increasing beauty and novelty." True to their promise, the newly supplemented carpet and upholstery department, under the charge of the buyer, W. H. Judson, was an impressive exhibit, from the Axminster carpet with "crimson ground and white border" to the rich display of upholstery items such as the "elegantly-designed lambrequin in blue satin," the brocatelles and the brocaded terries.[68]

The wholesale departments, meanwhile, were being distributed throughout most of the commodious five floors and basement of their brand new building at the corner of Madison and Market streets. This division of the store's business was now much better located and housed than it had been even on State Street. There was more space to give attention to the displaying of goods; and from the point of view of light and convenience, the new building was better adapted to the needs of a jobbing business than was the old.[69] Temporarily, however, the structure was not completely devoted to wholesaling. In order to attract the ladies of Chicago, of the West and North sides in particular, by offering better service and to eliminate the necessity of crossing the considerable barrier of the fire belt to arrive at the doors of a Field, Leiter and Company retail establishment, part of the space in the new wholesale building was for a time devoted to a branch of the firm's retail department. During the year and a half that this branch was retained, it was referred to as "Retail No. 2." [70]

The twenty-five to thirty thousand people who turned out for an inspection of the new wholesale building and Retail No. 2 on April 25, 1872, saw a neat brick structure of five floors and a basement covering almost forty thousand square feet of ground. Such items as "Paris muslin embroidered by hand, imported expressly for the occasion, marked $150; an apricot silk, en train, $300; a sage green silk street costume, $250; a grenadine moire, $225"; and shawls and mantles as high as $2,500 were added to the more ordinary offerings of the small retail branch so that the latter received considerable notice in the press. The retail display by no means, however, measured up to—nor was it meant to—one of Field, Leiter and Company's extravagant retail "grand openings." Retail No. 2 was a transient venture and occupied only the first floor of less than half the building. Most of the other floors were devoted exclusively to the wholesale division: and if it seemed less glamorous to the press and the majority of the guests, it was undoubtedly recognized by almost everyone present as by far the more important feature of the occasion.[71]

On the wholesale floors the arrangement of goods was similar to that which it had been at State and Washington except for the addition of the new lines and the enlargement of older stock already mentioned. The new large lines of carpets, oil cloths, and upholstery goods took

5. YEARS OF TRIAL

up most of the basement and even space under the sidewalk;[72] while the new furs, which were to be added shortly, were destined to be placed on the second floor with the shawls, skirts, and blankets. There were by this time in wholesale almost five hundred employees, devoting themselves to the task of buying, displaying, selling, and delivering over fourteen million dollars' worth of goods annually. To speed their work and increase their efficiency in the new building, there were five steam elevators linking together every floor and one hundred horses and fifty wagons now at their disposal for bringing in goods and shipping them out.[73] The wholesale division had facilities sufficient not only to handle its current volume of business but, as the firm grew, even to expand and take on more.[74] It was destined thus to make this new building its home for the next fifteen years.[75]

The dry-goods field was, of course, by no means monopolized by Field, Leiter and Company. There were, for instance, Charles Gossage and Company at 235-37 West Madison; Carson Pirie and Company at 329 West Madison; J. B. Shay at 239-45 West Madison; and Hamlin Hale and Company with a wholesale house located at 31-33 South Canal Street—and all were apparently thriving.[76] Not two blocks away from Field and Leiter's new wholesale building, J. V. Farwell and Company had also built, on the northwest Corner of Franklin and Monroe, a fine new five-story structure for wholesaling purposes; and, not content with competing in merely the jobbing field, added in 1872 a complete retail division. The large floor temporarily devoted to the latter was not elaborately fitted up and decorated; but, as if once and for all to match Field, Leiter and Company in elegance of stock, Farwell brought in shawls priced at $1500, dresses costing $1000, and point lace at $250, in addition to great varieties of silks, dress goods, and imported novelties. Especial emphasis seemed to have been placed on creating an elaborate upholstery section; and, as a final touch, George Livermore was enticed from the employ of Field and Leiter and brought in as its superintendent.[77]

Both the wholesale and the new retail branch were opened with a grand flourish on March 30, 1872, at which time it was claimed that the twenty-one separate retail departments "cannot be surpassed in the country." As if, however, to forecast their eventual fate, a bad storm raged over Chicago that evening and the opening was poorly attended.[78] The retail division competed vigorously with Field and Leiter for several months;[79] but even though Farwell announced his determination to keep it well stocked,[80] that portion of his business did not thrive, and the experiment was abandoned the following year.[81]

Retail Returns to State Street

What had become obvious to Marshall Field, Levi Leiter, and to John Farwell as well, was that the West Side was not (nor the South Side either) a desirable permanent location for a large retail store. Field and Leiter's two retail branches had not done well during their few months of existence;[82] and furthermore, trade conditions were beginning to change rapidly. By the middle of 1873 the physical aspect of the old burned-out business district had altered considerably. New buildings of stone and iron were being erected rapidly along the once-busy streets of the area, and the retail trade of Chicago appeared destined to be centered again along State Street.[83] Originally, Potter Palmer had planned to build another dry-goods store at the State and Washington corner where the firm had formerly been located, but he later changed his mind and sold the property to the Singer Company.[84] The new purchaser undertook the construction of a substantial marble building on the same corner; and by the early autumn of 1873, it was nearing completion.[85] To Field and Leiter, seeking a permanent location for their retail branch, here was the logical next move.

Arrangements were made to rent the Singer building for the exclusive use of its retail departments;[86] and on the second anniversary of the Great Fire, October 9, 1873, the new retail store at State and Washington streets was opened.[87] A full cycle in the history of the firm was completed. The building was a limestone structure[88] of five stories and basement with a large frontage on both State and Washington. In the center of the building was installed a feature that was to become a familiar characteristic of Field's subsequent stores. The deep light wells which today add so much beauty to the firm's modern retail structure and occasion so much comment were first seen at Field's in this 1873 store. In the center of the building, commented the *Tribune* reporter, "the strong uniform light more than compensates for the loss of space" occasioned by the glass dome atop the wide well which opened down through all five floors. This abundant source of daylight on each floor was supplemented by elaborate gas chandeliers throughout the store.[89]

The light wells were not entirely esthetic in their purpose. It was thought that the wealth of light cast upon each floor from the glass dome would make instant detection of a blaze inevitable. To further insure the building against any future disaster, the fire-conscious builders installed stationary tubes inside the walls with a hose outlet on each floor[90] as well as heavy iron shutters at the windows.[91]

The new building was about one-third larger than the pre-fire building used formerly for both wholesale and retail.[92] That Field, Leiter and Company's retail departments alone required a structure of this size was adequate testimony to the extent to which this portion of the firm had grown. The third floor, for example, was now turned over exclusively to carpetings and the fourth to upholstery and housefurnishings. The cloaks, shawls, woolens, and similar articles took up the entire second floor; while the fifth story was devoted to general retail work rooms. This left the whole of the main floor for the fast-moving items such as dress goods, silks, gloves, notions, etc.[93] In order adequately to staff so large a store there were now five hundred retail employees[94] as compared to only two hundred, five years earlier.[95]

Years of Trial (Continued) 6

The Long Depression

BEFORE FIELD, LEITER AND COMPANY HAD EVEN SETTLED IN THEIR State and Washington home, a new set of serious problems confronted the firm. On September 18, 1873, the banking house of Jay Cooke and Company, long regarded as one of the strongest financial institutions in the United States, suddenly closed its doors. This startling development marked the beginning of a ruinous decline in values on the New York Stock Exchange, thousands of firms went into bankruptcy, and business in many parts of the country came to a virtual standstill as a result of suspended currency payments by the banks.

Nevertheless, when Mr. Leiter, in answer to a *Tribune* reporter's questions the day after the retail store opening, expressed confidence in the future and noted that "collections continue very good," [1] he was not simply assuming a bravado he did not feel. For one thing, as had been the case in the past, this international panic, serious as it was in the West, failed to obtain quite the strangle hold on this new region that it did on the older areas; and it was borne more easily by fast-growing Chicago than by the eastern cities. [2] Field and Leiter again weathered this financial emergency as they had the previous ones largely because they owed no one; and those who owed them could afford to pay. [3] Within a week after the failure of Jay Cooke and Company and the partial suspension of payments by the Chicago banks, Field and Leiter were mailing instructions to their wholesale customers on how to make their remittances; [4] but unlike their larger New York competitors, the two Chicago partners showed no signs of alarm. [5] To a reporter's query as to how his firm would be able to face the prospect of rapidly declining prices on his stocks of goods, Field replied impishly: ". . . we like to sell cheap. It pleases our customers." [6]

House sales throughout the subsequent six years of depression did not continue to increase at the rate they had in the past; but they nonetheless remained high. Because of the fact that prices declined steadily during the whole of the period, the actual amount of goods sold by Field, Leiter and Company was much greater than the dollar volume of sales would indicate. In other words, the quantities of goods sold were undoubtedly greater in 1878, a low point in the depression, than they were in 1872 and 1873 even though sales as indicated in terms of money showed a slight drop. Prices between 1873 and 1878 fell more than 30 per cent; but the firm's sales at no time declined more than 9 per cent and during most of the period were considerably higher than in 1873. [7]

Even more difficult than maintaining sales, however, is making profits on a falling market. As already indicated, buying goods at one price and then selling them at a profit at a later date, when in the meantime the price has fallen, is a difficult operation. Yet between 1873 and 1878 inclusive (six years) the firm earned $5,609,300, or a yearly average of $935,000, on an investment which at the start of the period was less than three times that amount. Putting it another way, the capital employed in 1874 was $2,500,000. Since the profit for the year was $1,210,400, this amounted to a 48 per cent return on the partners' investment! By 1878, capital and surplus ("net worth") had increased to $4,500,000, reducing somewhat the percentage return.[8] This was accomplished in hard times against some of the bitterest competition that the firm was ever to experience and despite a second fire almost as disastrous as that which it had so recently undergone.

An essential to maintaining sales and profits is the retention of one's customers, and in this direction Field and Leiter's integrity and farsightedness stood them in good stead. Recognizing that the country merchant had to prosper in order for the major branch of their own business, wholesale, to prosper, the two men concentrated for the six years of depression on keeping the small western dry-goods retailers in business. The better merchants were encouraged to hang on through the lean times,[9] and every effort was made to inculcate in their customers the methods of merchandising which Field and Leiter had found so successful in their own business.

One of these, buying for cash, as previously noted, had already long been urged, if not forced, upon their customers. During the 1870's Marshall Field became increasingly impressed with the necessity of another principle: buying light and often and keeping one's stocks "turning" rapidly.[10] In years of lean consumption when sales were slow, it was a necessity, he told his departmental buyers, to avoid carrying huge supplies. Money was scarce; merchandise was easy to get and storage space expensive. Keep stocks fresh, clean, and new, carry the latest, and be ready with cleared warehouses always to buy on a bottom market. This principle, brought home to Field in depression years, he continued to urge on his own firm throughout his life.[11]

The same business practice, drummed into his Madison and Market Street subordinates, was in turn urged on the firm's merchant-customers as equally good advice for retailers. Buy from Field, Leiter and Company, Wholesale, only in reasonable quantities for a quick turnover at small profit, they were warned. Figure your order close, move your goods out quickly, and buy soon again. Carry always fresh, well-assorted merchandise in the latest styles. Women will trade where they can get something new and different each time they call.[12] Field warned his own salesmen, thus, not to oversell their customers—a farsighted admonition. It was better business to have a customer making small, regular purchases than to ruin him with an overstock of unsalable merchandise and to lose him to the house forever.[13]

To wholesale customers, in order to keep them content and in business, were extended every courtesy and service for which Field's was to become so famous in the retail trade. A typical notice to heads of departments:

During our busy season every effort must be toward the . . . extention of every courtesy and attention to the trade in the house, so that each customer may feel that his account (however small) is an important one. Salesmen in every department should try to make customers feel so much at home in this house that they will be glad to make their headquarters with us when in Chicago.[14]

A salesman's first job was to keep his customer satisfied and treated fairly.[15] Resourcefulness was a house "must." Everything from finding missing relatives in foreign nations where company buyers were located to advising customers on purchases of horses and land came within the province of the firm's salesmen and were apparently satisfactorily handled.[16] When certain goods could not be supplied by Field, Leiter and Company, the needed items were purchased elsewhere in the city, even from competitors, in order to supply the customer with everything that he wanted.[17] Each salesman was required to keep close to his customers, work with them, and, along with the credit department, help to solve their problems. When a store got into real trouble, the firm frequently sent a manager—usually one of the house salesmen—to help the merchant and to attempt to put the store back on its feet.[18]

If, despite all advice and all help, a retailer was nevertheless unable to remain solvent, it was then a different story. With a merchant who ended up in bankruptcy and attempted to compromise on his obligations, Marshall Field had no sympathy. To pay one's debts was to Field a man's first duty, and any attempt to pay at less than their face value was a species of dishonesty. A man who was permitted to discharge his debts to the jobber at fifty cents on the dollar or some other such fraction and then start in business again with a clean slate was not only defrauding his creditor but engaging in unfair competition with other retailers who habitually paid their debts in full. Rather than agree to this, Field, Leiter and Company almost mercilessly drove such men out of business[19] and at the same time fought vigorously against bankruptcy laws which seemed to protect this type of merchant.[20]

This policy of Field's eventually raised protests even in the halls of Congress;[21] but like most other principles of the firm, it unquestionably helped to heighten the standards of business morality among its customers throughout the Northwest, and the store stood to prosper proportionately.[22] Field, Leiter and Company maintained the highest possible credit rating throughout the depression[23] and retained its lead in the western field over an ever increasing number of competing wholesale houses.[24]

Invader from the East

Competition in a certain sense never particularly bothered Marshall Field during most of his career. In wholesaling, his major competitors

51

were in the East and his own firm's location in the West gave it an advantage of availability to its western customers that was difficult for eastern firms to overcome. As for his Chicago competitors, both wholesale and retail, he not only failed to resent their presence nearby but even welcomed them as aids in making Chicago and State Street great trading centers.[25]

At one time in his life, however, he was faced by a competitor whom he not only feared but actively resented. In 1876 the great A. T. Stewart and Company, the foremost dry-goods house in America, opened a large branch jobbing house in Chicago at Field, Leiter and Company's very doorstep.[26] Here, suddenly, was a dangerous invader; and for many months Marshall Field's business correspondence was filled with ill-humored and worried references to this rival's vigorous competition.[27]

Stewart's had long had a Chicago office and had sold at wholesale in the western market to a considerable extent.[28] This, seemingly, never posed a serious threat to the business of Field, Leiter and Company. A complete on-the-spot wholesale establishment, however, was another matter. More than any competition that he had ever faced or would face, Field obviously felt that A. T. Stewart and Company was in a better position to overshadow his own firm and deprive it of its western leadership.[29] Stewart's could boast of tremendous prestige, huge capital resources, its own mills, and a foreign buying organization that was unsurpassed.[30]

On September 23, 1876, A. T. Stewart and Company opened for business amid pretentious surroundings in three large adjoining buildings on the southeast corner of Washington and Wabash, well out of the main wholesale district but just one block away from Field, Leiter and Company's retail store.[31] The new addition to the trade was publicized as the "most convenient, handsome, and commodious" wholesale dry-goods house in Chicago. Calling attention to the fact that "we get our supply direct from our factories and mills" they promised to offer their goods in Chicago "as low as we can offer them in New York." Rumors reached the press that if the branch succeeded, other New York stores would set up similar branches and even that Stewart's might shift their entire business to Chicago. It was indeed a serious threat.[32]

Not everything, of course, was in the intruder's favor. As a new firm in Chicago, A. T. Stewart was in the position of having to obtain, not only most of their customers, but even most of their salesmen by taking them away from firms well established in the field. Newspaper advertisements[33] apparently failed to entice the better class of salesmen that the new firm needed; so direct offers were made to the leading salesmen in the employ of Field, Leiter and Company.[34] Higinbotham, for example, was reportedly made an offer that would in effect have doubled his salary if he had gone into the employ of A. T. Stewart.[35] Such offers were without great consequence, however, for

6. Years of Trial (Continued)

Field, Leiter and Company salesmen and officials on the whole remained loyal.[36]

In their efforts to obtain customers quickly, the situation required that A. T. Stewart and Company offer inducements so spectacular that the retailers could ill afford not to take advantage of them. Field, Leiter and Company and every wholesale house in Chicago thus became painfully aware of the existence of the newcomers when the latter immediately began cutting prices to ruinously low levels.[37] Since prices were already much depressed by poor farm crops and a consequent sluggishness in trade,[38] the price-cutting war which Stewart's touched off meant selling at below cost on many items for all the jobbers.[39]

Field, Leiter and Company, determined not to be undersold, and yet equally desirous of making a profit, held conferences with representatives of the new firm in an attempt to reach a working agreement on prices for certain staple items. At first a few such agreements were reached, but as Field himself noted: "The fact will be ascertained by them after a while that at same prices, trade will give us the business . . . and then is when trouble will come."[40]

It was a good prediction, for before long Stewart's refused to make further extensive agreements[41] and often broke those that they had already made.[42] Prices were dropped continuously lower in a desperate effort to win customers.[43]

With each price reduction by Stewart's, Field, Leiter and Company lowered its prices also;[44] and other wholesale houses throughout the city were forced to do much the same.[45] Prices on some leaders fell so low that Field and Leiter found that their losses were less when they bought certain items from their competitors, Carson Pirie and Company and A. T. Stewart and Company, who were themselves selling at a loss, than when they attempted to supply their customers through their usual sources. An attempt was apparently made even to buy up part of Stewart's stocks on some items merely to force up the price by creating a temporary scarcity. This kept up until Stewart's refused to sell to Field, Leiter and Company any longer.[46]

"It is getting to be pretty mean competition," remarked Field after Stewart's had been in town about a month.[47] "They [Stewart's] are no doubt getting good orders by mail from list of 13th [advertising low prices]. It injures us there more than any other way."[48] Nevertheless, within a very short time a suggestion of optimism began to appear in Field's letters. "They got quite liberal orders from people that did not believe we would meet such prices but I think they [illegible] customers have learned a lesson that will last a short time at least."[49] In December, Field observed that his rivals seemed to be receiving very few goods.[50] And by April 6, 1877, there was triumph in a letter to Woodhouse in New York:

Stewarts people do not know what they want. in [sic] short they want some business but have no idea more than a child unborn how to get it . . . meantime we have no idea of learning them how to get it. . . . if [sic] they are *mad* we can't help them. it [sic] will do them good to know how it is. As you say we have nothing to guide us. we [sic] never know what foolish thing they will do next & you have no idea how ¼ or ½ ct on few Staples [sic] will turn some of these Granger merchants and many times amount [?] take his whole bills. I am fully satisfied that outside of Prints [sic] and possibly staples they have a bad name among good merchant markets . . . [illegible] but that respect they stand no possible show with us but have a *great name,* a large lot of hungry general salesmen who thus far have had but little to do but stand at door & fill up Hotels [sic] & now is cheapest time we shall ever have to let them know who is master of the situation. I feel that we have an elegant stock all over House [sic] and have more than held our own over all competition in this market.[51]

Thus, sooner than any of the Chicago wholesalers could possibly have hoped, the crisis was over. From the spring of 1877 on, the competition of Stewart's was able to perturb Field, Leiter and Company and the other western firms but little.[52]

The cause of their rival's lack of success was, however, more deepseated than they at the time suspected. Shortly before the Chicago branch of Stewart's had been established, the founder of the firm, the great Alexander T. Stewart, had died;[53] and almost immediately a marked degeneration in efficiency was evident in his firm. Apparently the famous Stewart had made little provision for an administrative organization to carry on in the event of his own death. So seriously did the firm feel the loss of its vigorous founder that it quickly lost its sales leadership and entered upon a period of steady decline which was destined to end only with its complete liquidation in 1882.[54]

One other eastern house that was long a competitor of Field's was the H. B. Claflin Co. This house reputedly at one time (1864) had the largest mercantile business in the United States, with annual sales reaching $72,000,000.[55] Thereafter during the seventies and early eighties, while under the direction of H. B. Claflin, its founder, the firm remained strong. As a competitor it caused the Chicago house an occasional annoyance both because of its price-cutting and because of its attempt during the depression years to win away some of the numerous small western merchants who formed the backbone of Field's trade.[56] Accurate information on any of these early firms is difficult to obtain and badly scattered, but one thing seems evident: H. B. Claflin and Company over the years fought a losing battle for supremacy, first to A. T. Stewart and Company, and then to Field's. Within a short time after the death of its founder in 1885, if not before, it had already been far surpassed by Marshall Field's as a moneymaker.

54

6. Years of Trial (Continued)

TABLE II

Net Profits of Marshall Field & Co., Wholesale, and H. B. Claflin Company for 1888-98

Year	H. B. Claflin Co.	Marshall Field & Co.	Year	H. B. Claflin Co.	Marshall Field & Co.
1888	⎫	$ 958,600[e]	1894	$488,312[b]	$ 895,100
1889	⎪ $737,000[a]	916,700	1895	613,969[c]	1,299,100
1890	⎬ (average)	1,276,000	1896	261,517[c]	619,800
1891	⎭	1,284,700	1897	510,944[d]	1,178,100
1892	870,006[a]	1,666,400	1898	526,545[d]	1,223,300
1893	323,786[b]	868,100			

[a]H. B. Claflin Co. Annual Statement, "Report for the season ending December 31st, 1892," attached to accounting ledgers, Comptroller's safe, Marshall Field & Co. General Offices.
[b]Ibid., 1894.
[c]Ibid., 1896.
[d]Ibid., 1898.
[e]All figures for Marshall Field & Co. from accounting ledgers, 1888-98, Comptroller's safe, Marshall Field & Co. General Offices.

By this time John Wanamaker, already famous for his Philadelphia retail department store, had also entered the jobbing business and offered himself as another strong wholesaler. In 1887 he purchased the entire businesses of three different wholesalers, among which was that of Hood, Boubright and Company, reputed to be the third largest wholesale house in the United States. Wanamaker claimed (presumably by about 1890) to be doing a business of $20,000,000 annually.[57] By that time, however, Marshall Field and Co., Wholesale, had already passed that figure.[58]

Within Chicago, Field's greatest wholesale competitor was always J. V. Farwell and Company. Despite the difficulties which Farwell experienced in getting started and his discouragement in 1866 to the point of wanting to sell his business, he nevertheless succeeded eventually in establishing a large and profitable concern; and throughout the remainder of the nineteenth century apparently continued to run second only to Field's in terms of sales. His early sales increased regularly:

1866	. . . .$6,948,328[59]	1869	. . . .$8,600,000[60]
1867	. . . .$7,109,714[59]	1870	. . . .$9,500,000[60]

By 1883, despite years of depression, falling prices, and two heartbreaking fires,[61] Farwell was able to erect a new, eight-story building for his jobbing business and at that time reported sales of approximately $20,000,000 annually,[62] a figure not far below that of Field's at the time.[63] Farwell, however, failed to keep up his earlier pace; and by the time Marshall Field died (1906), Farwell's sales were only about one-half those of Marshall Field and Company, Wholesale. He, nevertheless, apparently still held "second place" in Chicago and offered the larger firm considerable competition.[64]

The only other house that remained a consistent wholesale competitor throughout the period covered by this volume was the well-known firm that still offers Field's a lively race in the retail field: Carson Pirie Scott and Company. In the first years following the Civil War its wholesale sales were not impressive:

1866	.........$691,634[65]	1869	.........$800,000[66]
1867	.... 733,996[65]	1870	.... 810,000[66]

Carson's sales, compared to those of Marshall Field's, remained rather modest in the wholesale field well into the twentieth century.[67] In certain areas of the nation, however, she more than held her own. In later years, for example, four O'Brien brothers, by the force of their own personalities developed a few, but very strong, accounts for Carson's on the West Coast. There, said a former Field's salesman, "they were competition for us, indeed."[68]

Fire Again

Field, Leiter and Company had not finished dealing with either the depression or with its worst competitor, A. T. Stewart & Co., when a final climax to eight years of troubles in the seventies enveloped the firm. The period was destined to end just as it had begun. On November 14, 1877, the State Street store burned to the ground and sent the retail division once more on a round of temporary sites.[69]

The person who first saw the flames shooting up from the roof of the retail building at eight o'clock that fall evening and turned in the alarm did not tarry to tell the firemen where the fire was located. As a result, when the first apparatus arrived, a hose was taken all the way up a stairway to the top of No. 19 State Street, two buildings away from Field, Leiter and Company. Finding no fire, the firemen returned to the street and only then were informed where the blaze was located. Arriving finally at the burning building, they hooked up their hoses in short order but were chagrined to discover that the water would not reach the high roof.[70]

Meantime more than twenty employees had rushed from their nearby boardinghouses and were ineffectually attempting to put out the flames with hand extinguishers. Every floor was supplied with a hose and the engines in the basement were capable of pumping water to the top of the building; but before the hose could be connected and the pumps started, the flames had spread down the elevator shafts and had driven all the employees to the lower floors.[71] Attempting to repeat the methods used so effectively in the fire of 1871, Leiter and Field called out the company's horses and wagons and gave orders to the employees to save what they could, especially of the more expensive goods. The doorways were soon choked with hundreds of struggling clerks pouring in and out of the building with armloads of merchandise. The system, however, did not work as smoothly as it had six years earlier. With such huge crowds of policemen, firemen, clerks, and sightseers all rushing about, the confusion was considerable; and many helpers no doubt did more harm than good. If a wagon were not immediately available, some clerks in their excitement simply dumped their burdens of rich silks and laces into the dirty gutter and went back for more. Until he was stopped by the police, one well-intentioned individual stood at a second story window throwing out armloads of fine shawls into the muddy waters of the street and onto the heads of the workers below.[72]

Such incidents were, of course, exceptions. Ten or twelve loads of the more expensive articles were saved and taken by Field, Leiter and Company and hired Parmelee wagons to the firm's stables on Pacific Avenue and to the wholesale building at Madison and Market streets. Other goods were temporarily stored in the jewelry store of Hamilton and Rowe across the street and in the nearby St. James Hotel.[73]

When the last of the flames was extinguished at two the next morning, the outer walls were still standing; but all the upper floors were gutted and all the unretrieved merchandise in the basement and on the first floor was either burned or thoroughly soaked with water. On the morning after the fire, the clerks turned out again to see what could be salvaged from the ruins. Considerable quantities of notions, silks, velvets, carpets, and dress goods, much of it package stock in the basement, were recovered and taken to the new Taylor building at Wabash and Washington; but it could not be sold for more than 20 per cent of its original value. In all, something over $200,000 worth of goods was saved. Because of the fact, however, that November and December were always the busiest months of the year, the retail store had had on hand approximately $1,000,000 worth of goods; this meant that almost $800,000 worth was destroyed. The insurance on the building and its contents had purposely been taken out with numerous companies scattered throughout the United States, as well as England, France, and Germany. The total insurance on the merchandise and fixtures amounted to almost one million dollars and thus adequately covered their losses.[74] When Cyrus McCormick extended an offer of aid, Marshall Field confidently replied "there is nothing he can do for us."[75]

Temporary Shopkeeping

The biggest loss, of course, came from the necessity of suspending business during the year's most favorable season for trade. The paramount need was to reopen as quickly as possible in order to share in the fall and Christmas rush. The new Taylor building only one block from their old site was apparently considered;[76] but when the firm was able to obtain temporary quarters in the Exposition Building on the lake front (at the foot of E. Adams Street) for a rental of only $750 a month, the decision was made to move there. The same day that the lease was signed, a hundred carpenters, under the direction of W. Pashley, were set to work putting the building in shape.[77] A new roof was built, the old fixtures were torn out, and the exhibition booths were replaced with counters and shelves.[78] Since the firm's huge whole-sale branch with its enormous supplies was intact, it was of course a simple matter to replenish the retail stocks at the new location; and on November 27, 1877, less than two weeks after the fire, Field, Leiter and Company, Retail, was again ready for business.[79]

On opening day the weather was wretched. It rained steadily and added greater depth to the deep pools which, as a result of previous days' downpours, already covered the ground about the building. The large quantities of fire-salvaged dry goods which the firm had stacked up outside the building for sale to wholesale dealers at auction were slowly soaked and reduced to "a fine and pulpy, but hardly recogniz-able mass."

The rain, however, did not discourage the women shoppers who were out in search of the bargains that had been advertised. The surg-ing crowds could be let into the building only in detachments. Each time a door was opened to admit a few more avid shoppers, the guards and policemen manning the entrances were deafened by the cheers of the crowd. It was another typically successful "opening day" for Field, Leiter and Company.[80]

During the following week, the fire-damaged and rain-soaked goods outside the building were "dried, refolded, and put into saleable con-dition"; and beginning on December 5, they were eventually all dis-posed of at auction.[81] By December 10, Field and Leiter were able to announce that their retail stocks were completely replenished; and business once more settled back to normal.[82]

To entice wintertime retail patrons out of the main retail district to their out-of-the-way location on the cold, wind-swept lake front, Field and Leiter provided, at considerable expense, free stages which ran every five minutes from the corner of State and Randolph streets to the Exposition Building.[83] This in itself was an admission of the inadequacies of their location, and the firm continued its search for better quarters. Finally something more suitable was obtained in a row of buildings on Wabash Avenue between Madison and Monroe (133 to 155 Wabash), closer to the heart of the retail trade. Without any particular fanfare, the firm on March 11, 1878, moved all its retail departments to this new location.[84]

Final Return to State and Washington

These quarters were probably no more meant to be permanent, how-ever, than were those in the Exposition Building. Although retail sales did not fall off any more than might be expected in this, the blackest year of the depression, yet it was obviously unwise to remain in a loca-tion still considerably removed from the center of the better retail trade and in quarters unworthy of so prominent a firm as Field, Leiter and Company. Marshall Field was in fact convinced that State and Washington was still the best location in the city, and he was only biding his time until he could return his retail store to that site. With this in mind, negotiations with the Singer Sewing Machine Company were begun for the purchase of the new building which the latter firm had erected on the foundations of the old retail store at State and Washington streets.[85] Unfortunately, the price demanded for the property was $700,000, whereas Field and Leiter announced their willingness to pay but $500,000. The two partners expected the Singer Company to come down in its price; but they were surprised to have the property suddenly leased to their growing rival, Carson Pirie Scott and Company for an annual rental of $70,000. Alarmed at the prospect of losing permanently so favorable a location, Marshall Field and Levi Leiter now produced the necessary $700,000 from their own personal fortunes and bought the building outright from the Singer Company. Since this act simply made them landlords to an unwanted tenant, the two partners were unhappily forced to pay an additional $100,000 bonus to induce their competitors to break the lease.[86] The deed to the property was acquired on February 28, 1879; and thereafter the building was owned personally by Marshall Field and Levi Leiter and rented to the retail departments of the firm on a yearly basis.[87] Two months later, Field, Leiter and Company were "back home" for the last time.[88]

In the meantime the retail store's numerous moves of the past few years resulted in some interesting consequences. When the firm moved into the Exposition Building at a rental of only $750 the members of the Chicago City Council rose in angry protest. It was unfair, they said, to allow a "rich and well advertised firm" like Field, Leiter and Company to have the building at all, let alone at such a low rental. Field and Leiter had obtained the building at one-quarter the rent other firms were having to pay when there were "plenty of good buildings in the center of the city which they could have."[89] There was unquestionably some justice in their contention, for the rent was certainly very low in comparison both to what Field's had formerly paid and to what the firm was capable of paying. As an item of expense, rent for all the store's retailing activities fell from an annual rate of over $85,000 in 1876 to less than $35,000 in 1878[90] and from almost 3 per cent to only 1.29 in relation to total net sales. This one item of rent alone thus loomed large in reducing the total expenses of the latter year[91] and no doubt helped to a considerable extent to account for the large rise in net profits.[92]

After the purchase of the Singer building by Mr. Field and Mr. Leiter in 1879, the rental expense ratio remained comparatively low for many years. The two partners charged the numerous departments a total of only $50,000 a year for both land and building and the owners paid all the taxes and insurance. In 1889 a new rental was made on the basis of 6 per cent on $700,000 for the land and 8 per cent on $300,000 for the building; or in other words, the rental on this one structure was raised to $66,000, and the firm was now required to pay taxes and insurance. There were, of course, numerous other rental charges—on other retail buildings, warehouses, barns, etc.[93]

TABLE III

RATIO OF RETAIL RENTAL EXPENSES TO NET RETAIL SALES
FOR 1874-89*

Year	%	Year	%	Year	%	Year	%
1874	2.56	1878	1.29	1882	1.30	1886	1.38
1875	2.77	1879	1.72	1883	1.31	1887	1.32
1876	2.99	1880	1.61	1884	1.43	1888	1.53
1877	2.55	1881	1.43	1885	1.35	1889	1.77

*Computed by writer from figures in accounting ledgers, 1874-89, Comptroller's safe, Marshall Field & Co. General Offices.

A general invitation was extended to another opening on April 28, 1879,[94] and the popular reaction seemed to indicate that the public was just as pleased that the store had returned to its old headquarters as were the members of the firm themselves.[95] "Home" was now a six-story and basement building[96] of French Renaissance architecture with a mansard-style roof once more, crowned with eight cupolas.[97] Inside, it was said, the scene was brilliant white throughout with plentiful light shining through the oversized windows.[98] In the center of the structure the most beautiful feature of the 1873 building was repeated on an even finer scale; an immense skylight roofing a large rotunda again permitted sunshine to flood through all the floors down to the main aisle. Each floor around this well was suported by "imposing columns of ornate design, beautiful railings, and bracketed cornices,"[99] all strikingly similar to—if not so large as—the same features in Field's present elaborate structure. It was indeed one of the most beautiful buildings that Field's would ever occupy.

The additions by way of comforts and mechanical improvements which appeared in this new structure, either when it was first built or within a very few years thereafter, were indicative of the changing times and methods of catering to retail trade. A studied effort was made in this new store to surround the feminine shopper with elegance and comfort. Though to modern eyes they might still appear cramped, sales aisles in the new store were considerably wider than they had been formerly, more effort was made at display instead of merely piling goods on counters and shelves, and soft carpeting was increasingly in evidence.[100] Encircling the rotunda at the second-floor level and "overlooking the animated and ever-varying scene below" was a new waiting room where the ladies could arrange to meet friends, make use of the desks where stationery was freely supplied for letter-writing; or they could merely rest among the ferns and potted palms and watch the other shoppers hurrying past.[101] "Large, neat and commodious" lavatories and waiting rooms in the basement for the sole use of customers were still enough of an oddity to be worthy of note, as were the cloak and lunch rooms and lavatories for the men and women employees.[102]

7. PERSONNEL

Since the firm's former buildings often became extremely stuffy when large crowds flocked inside, the new building for the first time contained ventilating apparatus to add to their patrons' comfort. The two new elevators which ran between the six floors were no greater in number than formerly, but both were unusually large and were designed to provide the ultimate of the day in rich upholstery and costly woods and glass.[103]

When the big building first opened, it was equipped with the familiar gas jets for lighting; but the firm was one of the first in Chicago to replace these with the new electric globes. In 1882, two dynamos and a seventy-five horsepower engine for generating the store's own electric power were installed in the basement; and all departments were partially supplied with electric lighting, although the first two floors, because used more, were naturally the most favored with the new lights. Additional engines were installed in 1884; and even though both gas and electricity were used together for several years, each new season saw less gas burned and increasing reliance being placed upon Edison's bulbs,[104] until gas was finally dispensed with completely in 1902.[105]

≈≈≈≈≈≈≈≈≈≈≈≈≈≈≈≈≈≈≈≈≈≈≈≈≈

Personnel 7

≈≈≈≈≈≈≈≈≈≈≈≈≈≈≈≈≈≈≈≈≈≈≈≈≈

The Working Organization

WITH THE PURCHASE AND OCCUPATION OF THE NEW BUILDING IN 1879, Field, Leiter and Company completed an epoch in its history. Despite eight years of fires, panic, and cut-throat competition, the firm had emerged triumphant, increased in size, with prestige heightened, and with sales and profits greater than ever. The testing period was over. Field, Leiter and Company's leadership in Chicago was undisputed and its prosperity guaranteed. The future had only to show how large an institution it might become, what further innovations it might make.

To have achieved such a standing in the world of commerce required more than simply the construction of ever more pretentious buildings, the display of fine wares, and the installation of novel lighting systems. Behind all the exterior manifestations of success there lay the basic reason for the store's achievements: organization, the efficient human working machine that continually throughout the years made the many decisions and did the many things which brought efficient operation and resulted in mounting profits. Even from his worst critics came testimonials to Field's ability as an organizer.[1] He knew how to cut waste, how to save money in store operations, how to make the business run smoothly;[2] but most of all he possessed the greater faculty for selecting the right persons to do those same things for him.

The fine group of men that Field and Leiter gathered about them in 1865 was still largely intact by 1879. Under a less farsighted policy these men, as they gained in experience and reputation, might well have been allowed to grow dissatisfied at remaining mere employees, and they would then have departed from the firm. The loss of their abilities to Field, Leiter and Company and the gain by a competing firm might well have brought disaster. Instead, however, as they had proved their ability in their respective lines of work, these men had been permitted to rise in position commensurate with the growth of the business. By the end of the 1870's, many of them had become partners and were sharing, along with the original partners, in the over-all profits of the firm.[3]

In 1867, with the first formation of Field, Leiter and Company (as opposed to Field, Palmer and Leiter), Henry Field, who had been with his brother Marshall ever since 1861 and the days of Cooley, Farwell and Company,[4] was rewarded with a junior partnership, as were also the able Henry J. Willing and Lorenzo G. Woodhouse. Each was given a small share[5] of the gross profits by way of salary and an additional percentage of the net profits for their share in the partnership. At this time Marshall Field was furnishing 400/725 of the capital and obtaining that fraction of the net profits, while Leiter was furnishing 295/725 and also sharing in the profits proportionately. On January 1, 1869, the partnership was further broadened to include Marshall's second brother, Joseph; and at this time a contractual agreement was drawn up that was to remain the basis of partnership for eight years. Under this arrangement the capital stock was set at $1,200,000. Of this amount Field and Leiter each furnished $400,000 and obtained one-third (four-twelfths) of the profits, while each of the four junior partners furnished $100,000 and obtained one-twelfth of the profits.[7] Higinbotham's abilities were soon recognized by granting him in 1873 a portion of the profits,[8] and a half-dozen years later he was also made a junior partner, replacing Henry Field who temporarily retired from the firm.[9]

The above arrangement, as it finally evolved by 1879, brought into the partnership each of the major personalities who had been with the store from its first days and under whose leadership it had become so immensely successful. The situation might have been expected to remain static for some years to come with the half-dozen partners quietly enjoying the riches so abundantly coming their way. This,

7. Personnel

however, the nature of the men would not permit. Forces were soon at work which brought about the most drastic readjustment in leadership that the firm had yet witnessed.

The complete truth regarding the motivating forces bringing about this change may never be known, but certainly one of the strongest factors involved was the inability of the two senior partners to get along. Aside from Leiter's quick temper, some fundamental differences of opinion as to business development were said to have arisen.[10] One, according to persistent rumors, dealt with the advisability of retaining the retail division as against devoting the firm's full energies to the wholesale field. Leiter with the comparatively poor profit-showing of the Retail over past years in mind, favored discarding that branch of the business; whereas Field, always with a hopeful eye on the future, was ever its ardent champion.[11] The near loss of the State and Washington street retail store site in 1879 some laid directly at Leiter's door. Over this issue, it was said, neither partner for a time spoke to the other.[12]

Another reputed problem dealt with the ambitions of men. Field was ambitious to run the firm entirely his own way.[13] The junior partners, according to this account, were ambitious for a larger share in the business. If these various ambitions were to be fulfilled, there obviously could no longer be room for Levi Leiter. Thus, when in 1881 the junior partners made their bid for a larger percentage of the profits, Field quickly espoused their cause. By this maneuver he successfully won the support of the junior partners for his own plans. The next stop, apparently, was for Field to tell Leiter that he did not wish to renew their existing partnership upon its expiration in January 1881. Leiter was given the option of buying out Field and assuming complete control of the firm or of selling his own interest and withdrawing. Actually, he had no choice. With all the lesser partners pledged to support Field, Leiter would have had to buy them all out; and he would then have scarcely been in any position to continue the business as it had existed before. Unable to buy, he was thus obliged to sell;[14] and on January 26, 1881, the sixteen-year-old firm of Field, Leiter and Company came to an end.[15]

Levi Leiter left the firm with the reported cash sum of about $2,700,000[16] plus many more millions invested in stocks and real estate[17] to show for his years of partnership with Marshall Field. On the occasion of his retirement he announced that, outside of caring for his various investments, he desired and intended only to rest.[18] In later years as Marshall Field and Company grew ever larger and Field became fabulously rich, people talked of Leiter's "mistake" in withdrawing. But watching the latter traveling leisurely over the world with his family, enjoying the companionship of numerous friends, while Field made his way to the store alone each day, perhaps others questioned which one had made the greater mistake.[19] Leiter's investments were so well chosen that, despite a later life of comparative ease and reckless spending by his son, he left at his death a fortune variously estimated at from $10,000,000 to $30,000,000.[20]

Following Leiter's retirement, the promise made by Field to the junior partners was fulfilled. Field now assumed a 46½ per cent interest in the firm, while Woodhouse was permitted to share to the extent of 17 per cent, Willing 14 per cent, and Higinbotham 10 per cent. Henry Field returned to buy back in to the extent of 5 per cent, while J. N. Field remained content temporarily with his usual 7½ per cent share of the profits.[21]

It has been common practice to refer to Marshall Field's partnerships as a joke. It has been pointed out that, with the exception of Leiter, "they paid no money into the firm when they came to it, [and] took none out when they left," and that all the partners were completely dominated by Marshall Field.[22] This is, in a sense, true. Certainly Field could well have supplied (and often did, at least in part) the small shares of capital which most of the junior partners contributed. The point that is overlooked, however, is that after 1869 the purpose of such partnerships was obviously not to obtain capital but to retain the services of capable men by rewarding them on a profit-sharing basis.

It has been assumed further that these partnerships ended when Marshall Field chose that they should end.[23] This was also unquestionably true. Beginning with the 1869 agreement, the partnerships were always for a limited number of years;[24] and there was the provision that "if for any good and just cause Marshall Field and Levi Z. Leiter shall become dissatisfied with either of the other partners the remaining partners may at their election take their interest in said firm by paying them its cash value."[25] The explanation is, of course, the same. When, for one reason or another, a partner ceased to be of value to the house, he was retired, sometimes against his will,[26] but never with any expression of resentment against Mr. Field[27] and none with less than a million dollars to his name to show for his association with the great merchant.[28]

Field never had a partner who had not worked his way up within the firm's own organization.[29] One of the oft-repeated anecdotes about Field has it that one day he was asked, "Mr. Field, what would you do if Mr. [one of his partners] were to leave you?" "Hire another office boy," was the reply.[30] "Hiring another office boy," not only for partnerships, but for every responsible position, became one more of those deeply ingrained traditions established by the founder of the store and seldom deviated from since. It was a rare day indeed that the immense organization that was Marshall Field and Company could not find within itself the leadership necessary for efficient operation. Almost every cashier, salesman, foreign buyer, department head, superintendent—and even every presidential successor of Marshall Field himself—came from within the firm.[31] "You should also have one or more active thoroughly young men growing up about you," Marshall informed his brother Joseph, "one that can be trusted any where [sic]

64

wish to use him and learn about merchandise."[32] As if to highlight the over-all success of this policy, failure resulted in almost every instance where the rule was deviated from and employees were brought in from outside.[33] By the time of Field's death, the personnel of both the Wholesale and Retail were working under what amounted to a civil service regime. Promotions were from within the organization and strictly on the basis of merit and seniority.[34]

With this "office boy today, partner tomorrow" philosophy pervading the atmosphere of the store's organization, Field obtained from his personnel surprising feats of accomplishment and thus freed the top executives of the necessity of excessive supervision. Every man and woman in the store's employ was informed as to his job, and, as we shall see, ofttimes given some specialized training in it; but thereafter he was a businessman on his own. Marshall Field and Company was in Chicago to make money, and each employee was expected to contribute directly or indirectly to that end. According to the degree to which he succeeded he might expect promotions. If he failed, he was either released or transferred to another position.[35] But in any case he could not expect continuous directions from above as to what moves to make. Field employees, within the limits of their responsibility, were hired to think and to act, not simply to take orders.[36]

This independence of action was especially apparent—and most conspicuously successful—at the department head or "buyer" level, the key post in the entire store. Each department in the Wholesale, for example, was run as though it were an independent business firm. The department head was a merchant, completely and independently responsible for results within his own separate department or "store."[37] His capital, to be sure, he obtained from Marshall Field and Company; but he paid 6 to 8 per cent interest for its use as with the most exacting banker. He paid rent for his share of the building, and he did his own buying. As for the vast imports of the company, the buyer used only such goods purchased by the firm's New York and European representatives as he chose. He then priced his goods as he saw fit, advertised them at his own expense, and initiated any new methods he thought of on his own responsibility. If he made a mistake, he dug his own way out. If at the end of the year, however, he had made a profit, he received more than praise; for he possessed a written contract giving him a specific percentage of the profits that his department had earned.[38]

In Retail the system was basically the same,[39] but there were certain differences. Of Retail's four departments, three (rugs, carpets, and upholstery)[40] had heads who were buyers and worked in almost every respect on the same basis as wholesale department heads.[41] The fourth and largest department, dry goods, on the other hand, because of its complexity, did not have a department head. Rather, this department was broken down into numerous divisions, and each division was headed by a buyer. Considerable confusion is apt to arise from the fact that this employee was indiscriminately referred to at different times as "buyer," "division" head, "head of stock," "section" head, and worse confounded, "department" head.[42] Also, although he was the buyer for his division, the department head of the corresponding department in Wholesale was given a general responsibility for the stocks of the retail buyer.[43] After 1902, all the "departments" in Retail were abandoned and carpets, rugs, and upholstery were called simply "sections," as were the divisions of the old "dry-goods department." The title of "section manager" then became the accepted designation, and the retail divisions rid themselves of the Wholesale's supervision.[44]

Despite the retail buyer's somewhat smaller degree of independence and the fact that he worked on a straight salary rather than on any profit-sharing scheme,[45] his duties and responsibilities were much the same as those of the wholesale department heads. The retail buyers were every bit as responsible for their purchases and sales and for the performance of the employees under them.[46] Each day they visited the firm's wholesale house and made the purchases needed to replenish their shelves. They had an advantage over other retailers since they paid only 6 per cent above actual cost; but they nevertheless discounted their bills for cash just as any merchant-customer from an outside concern, for no credit was allowed between the two divisions of the firm.[47]

Above the buyer were the wholesale or retail general managers and their assistants and Mr. Field himself.[48] In the Field philosophy, however, the president and general managers were "working for the buyer." It was a "buyer-run store." To the higher executives, the buyer owed no responsibility except good results and the observance of the general rules on standards and policies set for the store by his superiors.[49] Having come up through the ranks, all department and sections heads were thoroughly schooled in general Field policies and needed little reminding along such lines. Any reminders or new policies laid down were generally brought to their attention through "notices" sent out by the general managers or Field at odd intervals.[50] Field himself seldom called a meeting of department or section heads. He preferred instead to visit them individually on his almost daily rounds of the store. On these occasions, while he sometimes made suggestions, he almost never outlined a plan of action. He was famous for listening rather than talking. Field's contribution to such sessions consisted almost solely of sharp, penetrating questions that taxed the knowledge and experience of the best buyers and at the conclusion of the conversation left them feeling mentally drained. Field, nevertheless, displayed confidence in his men, and invariably a discussion on methods and means ended with Field saying, "Well, use your own judgment." [51]

Because of their independence, department and section heads naturally possessed considerable authority over the lesser employees; and because of their eagerness to make a profit, they sometimes exhibited a tendency to develop into petty tyrants. A one-time "women's wear" clerk has told of the personnel relationships in the retail store in a firsthand account:

He [Mr. Woodcock, assistant general manager of Retail] put me at the "Comeback Window" in "Alterations" in the women's wear department. My job was to take garments that came back, call the fitter and try to get everything satisfactory. If the fitter failed I had to take it to the buyer. The buyer was Mrs. Cox, who was a czarina, and would get mad when I'd bring these garments to her, and take it out on me. Once when she had been away for some time on a buying trip her clerks had a blanket of roses on her desk to welcome her home. I was passing with a coat on my arm, and not knowing what was going on, and seeing so many roses, stuck my head into the circle and asked, "Is she dead?"

A voice hissed in my ear, "NO, I'm not DEAD!" I jumped; it was Mrs. Cox.

Along in those years [about 1900] there were five women department [section] heads. . . . They'd dress in high styles, and sweep down the aisles with their long trains swishing. You had to step aside when they passed. They were high and mighty.[52]

The fact that buyers often of necessity left the store to travel about the country or even to go abroad made necessary assistant heads in both the Retail and Wholesale. Their job was to fill in when their chiefs were away and frequently to act as buyers and acting managers of the departments.[53]

In the Retail the last remaining minor "officials" below the buyer but above the clerks were the heads of stock or "subheads"—those having in their care a particular line of goods. Like the clerks, they waited on customers but in addition had a responsibility for all the goods sold over their group of counters and for all the salespeople working under them. They in a sense also looked after their division as though they "had a store entirely distinct from the rest."[54] A good clerk was often made eventually a head of stock; and this position in turn was the recruiting ground for new assistant buyers and buyers, the immediate goal of every ambitious employee.

In Wholesale, the "departmental salesman" occupied much the same position as the "clerk" did in Retail.[55] In fact, in the early days of the firm, wholesale salesmen often sold also at Retail.[56] But operating within the Wholesale's organization was another individual not seen in Retail—the ubiquitous "general salesman." These highly paid gentlemen,[57] were the all-important link between the country retailers and the great Chicago wholesale house. Each general salesman was allotted a prescribed territory, usually one or more states; and he kept in close touch with every customer within his area.[58] He took care of the retailer upon his arrival in the city and the store, personally escorted him from department to department, introduced him to departmental salesmen and saw that he was properly served.[59] "Between seasons" the general salesman corresponded with his customers, supervised the filling and prompt delivery of their orders, and generally kept the retailers' relations with Field's a happy one. A periodic trip through his territory kept the salesman in touch with the general business conditions, the prosperity of his customers, and served once more to improve relations between the merchant and the house.[60]

For the proper performance of such an important task, a buoyant personality, well-nigh inexhaustible energy, and intelligence of a high order were unquestionably prime necessities. Men possessed of all these capacities in the greatest degree were enticed into the firm of Marshall Field and Company rather than into competing firms only by the promise of substantial pay plus considerable independence of action. They, as with the departmental buyers, had to answer for nothing except good results.[61]

Thus this intricate mechanism called Marshall Field and Company clocked off the years smoothly, efficiently, and profitably decade after decade. By its own admission this was not so much a result of bits of knowledge handed down from the quiet genius at the head of the firm as of the combined wisdom he drew from the capable men and women who made up the store personnel. "It has been the constant aim of this house, through a long course of years," said a pronunciamento of the firm in 1902, "to build up an organization of *intelligent* men and women—an organization which shall embody the foremost elements of progress—an organization built of thinking units, sturdy stock and growing capacities." [62] For so huge and seemingly impersonal a firm, Field's, by rather general consensus of contemporary opinion, was in a fair way toward succeeding in that aim.

The Working Employee

The high standards of performance set by Fields for its personnel required for many positions a superior type of person. The preëminence of Field's in merchandising was retained in part because continuously it could acquire enough such persons and retain their loyalties. By the time the title of the firm bore only the name of Marshall Field, he was employing upwards of two thousands persons even during non-rush seasons. As of January 1882, Marshall Field and Company had approximately one thousand men and women in the wholesale department and the barn, retail dry goods kept over seven hundred and fifty more employed, retail carpets and upholstery another one hundred and fifty, while the carpenter shop added seventy-five and the New York and foreign offices thirty. This was a growth from probably less than two hundred and fifty employees in 1865; and the firm was, by 1882, by no means ceasing to expand. It continued to increase in numbers rapidly and steadily until long after the period of which this volume treats. In 1906, when Marshall Field died, he was providing a livelihood for over six thousand five hundred men and women in the retail departments, over three thousand four hundred in the Wholesale, and for several hundred others in foreign offices.

The following figures on numbers of employees in the firm, because of the fact that they were gleaned from numerous and widely scattered sources, are not always entirely comparable; but they do provide some

7. PERSONNEL

insight into the remarkable growth of Marshall Field and Company over the years. The following totals (except for 1906) also do not take into account, of course, the seasonal fluctuations. Particularly in the later years the retail figures, for example, could be increased as much as 25 to 30 per cent for the Christmas season.[63]

TABLE IV

NUMBERS OF EMPLOYEES OF MARSHALL FIELD & CO. FOR 1868-1906

Year	Retail	Wholesale	Total*
1868	200[a]	200[a]	400[a]
1872	—	—	1000[b]
1875	—	500[c]	—
1877	800[d]	—	—
1882	900[e]	1000[e]	2000[e]
1884	1500[f]	—	—
1891	—	1700[g]	—
1894	3000[h]	1800[h]	—
1902	6800[i]	—	—
1906	6500 to 9000[j]	3400 to 3600[j]	12000[j]

[a]*Chicago Times*, October 13, 1868.
[b]*Chicago Tribune*, April 26, 1872.
[c]*Chicago Commercial*, September 18, 1875.
[d]*Chicago Tribune* and *Chicago Times*, November 15, 1877.
[e]Marshall Field personal memorandum, "Number of Employees Jany 1882," Marshall Field & Co. Archives.
[f]*Chicago's First Half Century, 1833-1883*, p. 87; and Barbour (ed.), *Sketchbook of the Inter-State Exposition, Chicago, 1883*.
[g]*Mercer*, I (June 1891), 15.
[h]William T. Stead, *If Christ Came [sic] to Chicago!* (London: "Review of Reviews," 125 Fleet Street, 1894), p. 61. See also, *Inter-Ocean*, October 30, 1893; *Chicago Times*, October 30, 1893; and *Chicago Tribune*, October 30, 1893.
[i]"A Modern Institution," *Northwestern Christian Advocate*, November 12, 1902, p. 18. See also, *Dry Goods Reporter*, XXXII (October 11, 1902), 17; *Inter-Ocean*, September 30, 1902; and *Chicago Evening Journal*, September 26, 1903.
[j]*Chicago Tribune*, January 17, 1906. See also, *Chicago Record-Herald*, November 29, 1905.
*The "Total" does not necessarily equal the sum of the retail and wholesale figures since the total also includes the foreign offices, etc.

The number of women employed by Fields, beginning with the first two or three in ready-to-wear and lingerie, increased almost imperceptibly over the years. As the store grew and added new sections, more and more of those hired were women; and some even rose to be department heads with salaries and bonuses comparable to those of the men.[64] By the middle eighties there were approximately six hundred but over half of these were "sewing girls" rather than clerks.[65] The working girl by no means dominated the store even by 1900,[66] although Field's found them easier to obtain than other firms because it was known to be so "respectable" to work at Field's.[67]

Mr. Field succeeded in retaining a surprising degree of loyalty from his large staff. Although personnel records were not kept in as much detail as in later days, Field's turnover in labor appears to have been small.[68] Long service was usual rather than unusual. "Fifty year men," those employed by Field's for fifty years or more, by the 1920's were already no longer a novelty, and by that time even "sixty year men" were not unknown.[69]

Many factors account for the store's success along this line, some of which were the result of a purposive company policy and others of which were not. The encouragement offered to work up in the firm, along with the fact that the ever expanding nature of the store provided more opportunity in this direction than could be provided in other firms, unquestionably had much to do with this loyalty. Allied with this was the great prestige which went with the name of Marshall Field and Company. Men and women took pride in their employment at Field's and enjoyed the opportunity to bask in the reflected glory of their store's wealthy founder. "When a boy got a job at Field's," said one employee, "he was a point out in the neighborhood and started to shine his shoes." [70] Thus, many worked, often at menial positions, for the better portion of their lives and died proud of their association.[71]

If Marshall Field and Company's size and success seemed to offer opportunity and if the firm's prestige was high, its wages and salaries did not always measure up to this standard. Like most employers of his day, Field paid only that amount which was necessary to retain the services of the type of employee he wanted. Wages to the unskilled, lower ranks of his employees were small,[72] by common agreement smaller even than those of his competitors.[73] If these people left, they could easily be replaced; though as it was, enough remained with the firm because of other compensating factors. Where skills and experience were demanded, and not so easily replaced if the employee were to quit, Field, on the other hand, was ready to pay well. When Field was asked how he could afford to pay his merchandise manager, John G. Shedd, such an extremely high salary, his reply was supposed to have been, "I cannot afford to pay him less." [74] Field lost top salesmen and a few executives, but it was the exception rather than the rule.[75]

Field did not pay low wages to some of his people through any particular heartlessness, but he felt, apparently, that it "ruined" a man to have too much too quickly. He himself had started at the same low wages he was paying many of his employees. If they were hard working and worthy, they had the same opportunity to achieve success as he had had. A person should get ahead by saving and by making the most of opportunities as they came. He advised the young men of America that "the five, ten or fifteen cents a day that is squandered, while a mere trifle apparently, if saved would in a few years amount to thousands of dollars." [76] In the meantime he had a business to run and it was necessary to operate it as cheaply as possible.

To a modern generation becoming accustomed to "time and a half for overtime" Marshall Field and Company's attitude on this question is interesting. It was the custom then to pay nothing extra and to provide only "supper money" on such occasions. To the store executives, however, even this seemed unnecessary. They admonished their department heads to "avoid supper money wherever possible. Almost every man," they said, "can do a little more work and move a little faster during the times when overtime work would be necessary. By securing this additional quick action all through the stock you may oftentimes save supper money." [77]

One of the lowliest positions at the "Big Store" was that of the "cash boys" who in 1882, for example, made up as much as a full third of the entire complement of the retail dry-goods section.[78] Starting at a wage of two dollars per week[79] these eleven-, twelve-, and thirteen-year-old lads[80] had to be on duty from eight to ten hours daily, five and one-half to six days a week.[81] As each clerk completed a sale and called lustily, "Cash!"[82] it was the duty of these youngsters to rush from their bench (where they had been sitting stiffly in their tight-fitting uniforms with their arms folded), take the money, merchandise, and sales slip on the fly from the clerk to the inspector for wrapping and checking, then to the departmental cashier to make change and finally to return the package and change on the double to the sales-clerk.[83] Their gradual disappearance after 1900 meant a virtual revolution in sales procedure and brought to an end one of the most distinctive features of the nineteenth-century department stores.[84]

Also in the two-, three-, and four-dollar-a-week category were the errand boys and girls, door boys, office boys, and boy apprentices in general.[85] Though overworked, underaged, and victims of a poverty that forced many of them to walk miles to and from their work in order to save the five cents carfare, these young people added a variety of human interest to the story of the store that only extreme youth can. Typical of their maneuvers was one described by a former delivery boy:

> They'd [i.e., the firm] give us streetcar tickets for use while delivering packages, and if a boy was wise enough he could save $2.00 a week on this. I'd ask for a transfer and get the conductor to punch it a half hour ahead, get off and deliver packages in that region and then get back to the cross line in half an hour and use this transfer. We'd do this on all the lines we used and save on tickets. Then we'd sell the tickets back to a conductor who wanted to get rid of his pennies.[86]

The "Delivery Boy Book," a terse "personnel" record kept by the boys' superintendent attests to the evils resulting from low wages and the employment of children. According to this record, one of the boys, for example, was discharged because he "got away with McButyan's lunch"; another "skipped for parts unknown, left 21 suckers [creditors] to mourn his loss"; a third was "discharged for losing 10 dollars, Mother drunker pretends she stold [sic] it"; and one poor fellow "left mysteriously, with cop."[87] Among the thousands of these boys who were recorded as having passed through Field's employ between 1865 and 1900, these comments were all too typical. Behind many of these brief remarks could undoubtedly be read a description of slum living, inadequate schooling, and an invitation to delinquency. The improvement in the child-labor legislation which came about in 1903 and 1904 helped bring a gradual end to this type of employment in Field's, as well as in other wholesale and retail establishments, and was unquestionably a considerable boon to society.[88]

Higher in their wage scale and comprising the largest total number of employees were the great mass of sales clerks, stock boys, watchmen, stenographers, and other office help who fell in what might be called the middle salary bracket. Beginning salesmen "got down early, stayed late, did the 'last man' chores [sweeping, dusting, and arranging blinds], but still had time to sell," [89] and made eight dollars a week on up.[90] As a rule, men found it easier to obtain the higher salaries. Some women earned as much as $12.00, but the average was about $9.00 for women and $12.00 for men.[91] Increases for sales clerks, about the turn of the century, were supposedly on a "scale"—$1.00 a week raise for each $1,000 increase in sales per year. To grant more than a $2.00 raise at any one time, however, was apt to "spoil the help." [92]

Male stenographers averaged around $1,000 a year. Mrs. Ella Chambers, hired by Field as his personal stenographer in 1884, came in at $8.00 per week. Her salary rose to $16.00 in four years and other female stenographers received as much as $25.00, which, announced the firm, was the "limit." [93] Most porters received $10.00 to $12.00 a week;[94] but one more fortunate man's contract ran:

Conrad Brown
New Retail when we open—to have charge of shutters and do any other Porter's work we want—to repair shutters evenings or in night & no extra pay—but if works after 10 o'clock in the evening to have equal amount rest next day.

$18.00 wk.[95]

Other typical weekly salaries were receiving-department labor $12.00 to $16.00; elevator operators (male), $4.00 to $10.00; watchmen, $15.00; ushers, from $6.00; and some "city buyers," who purchased for the firm in Chicago only and were not department heads, as little as $7.00.[96]

In the lower and middle brackets, wages and salaries remained relatively constant throughout most of the period following the Civil War. A rising scale within Marshall Field and Company did not become apparent until after 1900.[97]

Charges of unfair and unkind treatment were lodged against Field's, as against many other business enterprises. Writing to Henry D. Lloyd one Chicagoan declared:

Miss Maggie Graham of 2128 Indiana Avenue has been in the employ of Field, Leiter Co. 12 years. She has left them to give her influence against their oppression of sewing girls. I am surprised at the facts she is willing to attest to. I do not doubt her word. . . . "Too bad she said, for the poor and alone girls. Do you know they cry all day some of them as they work, and its hunger too. There is lots of them that do not make thirty cents a day. When they engage a chair is given them which they are to occupy whether there is work for them or not. Sometimes for days they have no work then a nickle [*sic*] only is given daily to such [?] unemployed for a lunch. When work comes they are paid by the piece. Some experts have made as high as fifteen dollars a week but the greater number do not receive more than six or seven dollars. While a large class do not make anything like that sum." Miss Graham tells me that it is next to impossible for outsiders to get at the facts by going to the establishment. The employees allowed to converse with persons coming in are under instruction. . . . Miss G made up her mind that she could get a living outside Field & Co. and left determined to use her own language to tell how things was.[98]

Such accusations, however, considering the low salaries paid, were surprisingly rare.

For the higher-ranking personnel Marshall Field showed not only a greater inclination to pay increasingly higher salaries as the firm enlarged and required more talent, but also considerable ingenuity in obtaining more for his money. In the early days of the firm, no general policy for determining salaries seems to have prevailed. Rather, each salesman, department head, and superintendent was obliged to bargain individually with Mr. Field to obtain the best contract possible. The terms of the agreement were written briefly, sometimes in code, in one of Field's little personal record books, apparently the only record of the transaction. Salaries varied considerably for the same positions depending on the man's ability, experience, length of service, importance of the department with which he was connected, and somewhat on his bargaining ability.

Marshall Field obviously believed thoroughly in the incentive system, for almost every contract called for a bonus for work well done. Mr. Lafayette McWilliams, for example, was employed in June 1869 as a salesman in Wholesale on the following basis:

> one yr July 1/69 at $2250# & if does
> well & we can afford it $250 more left
> entirely with us.[99]

A Mr. J. J. Fishburne was employed in 1872 as a salesman in Wholesale on a contract calling for:

> Jany 30/72 one year $1400.00 if sells
> less than $300,000—if 300,000 & less
> than 350,000 $1500.00—if over 350,000
> $1600.00.[100]

Mr. Fishburne did well; so the following year his contract read:

> For year 1873 $2000 & 200.00 more
> at end of year if bus. of House war-
> rants.[101]

Under such a system in these early days of the firm's existence to outline any salary scale for comparative purposes is not easy. Salesmen's compensation in Wholesale, for example, ranged all the way from $10.00 weekly to $6,000 yearly. Even $4,000, however, was rare as a top salary; and $2,000 plus a $250 bonus was much more common for leading general salesmen. While salaries for retail department heads ranged as high as $4,000 plus $1,000 "if manages well and business of firm warrants," here again more typical was a salary of $2,250 plus $250 bonus.[102]

As years passed and business expanded Field continued to bargain individually with most of his many employees and only gradually, in the late seventies and early eighties, began turning this function over to junior executives. Wishing to keep a hand in, he did not give up completely the task of engaging top executives until shortly before he died.[103]

When higher salaries became necessary, $6,000 was fixed upon as the maximum to be paid anywhere in the firm. Actually, however, this figure meant little; for it came to be the accepted practice to pay department heads and general managers, in addition to their salaries, either a stipulated bonus or a percentage of the profits of their department or division,[104] and salesmen, liberal bonuses or a percentage of their total sales, usually 1 or 2 per cent.[105] These provisions generally boosted the salaries considerably over the $6,000 figure. The latter, in fact, soon was more often serving not as a maximum, but as a minimum guarantee, with no ceiling existing above that amount. In 1876, Field, Leiter and Company, by formal contract, agreed to pay Dixon Bean, head of the wholesale and retail carpet departments, 10 per cent of the net profits over and above $35,000. If profits did not amount to more than $35,000, he was to receive a flat salary, in this case, of $5,000.[106] By 1880 he was contracting to receive 10 per cent of all profits plus a flat salary of $6,000. On the back of this particular contract was the notation:

> Chicago, Oc. 13, 1882
> Received of Marshall Field & Co.,
> $12,000 in full of all claims against
> them under the foregoing contract.
> D. Bean
> Guaranteed salary and share of esti-
> mated profits $12,000[107]

A Mr. Frank Ames, in charge of the carpet, rug, and oilcloth departments from 1887 until 1894, drew the following amounts on the basis of a $6,000 guaranteed salary and 10 per cent (from 1888 on, 12½ per cent) of the profits:

1887	$10,624.49
1888	9,501.60
1889	11,619.65
1890	16,056.60
1891	16,205.64

7. PERSONNEL

1892	22,337.83
1893	12,845.72
1894	11,297.75[108]

The fact that the superintendent or general manager of retail in 1889 and 1890 *contracted* to receive a guarantee of $6,000 plus a $14,000 bonus (!) illustrates the extremes to which Field went to avoid departing from his $6,000 "maximum salary." [109] The extent to which some men benefited by working on a percentage of the profits basis is illustrated by a department head in 1906 who made over $100,000 in addition to his "salary" of $6,000.

Following are the total profits shared by department heads alone between 1898 and 1906:[110]

Year	No. of Dept. Heads Sharing	Total Amount
1898	9	$ 88,501.56
1899	9	130,697.00
1900	16	235,129.61
1901	16	224,543.00
1902	12	215,895.41
1903	11	190,681.00
1904	10	168,552.86
1905	10	235,721.00
1906	10	281,762.00

An interesting bias of Marshall Field's was a certain scorn which he had for office employees. Perhaps because he had acquired his own original success in the role of salesman, it was the latter employee whom he considered the key man of the firm. His cost-accounting ledgers, much to the dismay of some of his more alert personnel, distinguished between "productive" and "non-productive" employees;[111] and those in the latter category, apparently considered as near-parasites, with few exceptions worked for smaller bonuses and much lower salaries.[112]

By way of added compensation for all employees, whether high salaried or low, was the privilege which they enjoyed of buying goods from the house at a discount. Employees at the Wholesale, from the beginning, were permitted on one day a week, usually Saturday, to purchase any articles they desired for their own personal use at wholesale prices.[113] They, along with the retail employees, also were privileged to buy from the retail stocks at a modest 6 per cent discount.[114] In order to keep employees from spending too many of their working hours in shopping and to keep them from reselling goods to outsiders, use of the discount was hedged with considerable restrictions. Nevertheless, judging from the prevalence of store correspondence on the matter, employees took full advantage of the privilege.[115]

Salaries cannot be judged solely by the amount of money paid because there are often additional compensating factors. The number of hours the employee was expected to work each day, for example, obviously affected his choice of employer. From the days in 1856 when P. Palmer and Company closed at seven in the winter and at eight during the summer,[116] a good many years passed before a regular six P. M. closing was adopted for both the Wholesale and Retail by Field, Leiter and Company in the early seventies (probably 1873).[117] At this time "everyone" was "expected to report by 7:30 in the morning, take one hour for dinner; and remain at the store until 6 o'clock P. M." [118] The employees were checked in with the timekeeper when they came in the morning and when going to and from dinner.[119]

In adopting a six o'clock closing hour, Marshall Field anticipated most of the other dry-goods firms by at least five years; for the majority of them did not fall into line in this respect until 1878.[120] "I have never believed in overworking," commented Field, "either as applied to myself or others. It is always paid for with a short life, and I do not believe in it." [121] In line with this philosophy and the ever-changing times, he reduced the store hours again in 1881, requiring only that his employees arrived by 8:00 A. M. and remain until 5:30 P. M.[122] These same hours were kept as long as Field lived.[123]

In the Wholesale, however, until about 1900,[124] there were a few weeks during the period of heavy trading in the spring and fall when the 6:30 to 6:00 limits were allowed to prevail in order to provide time to accommodate the flood of buyers. These "rush periods," when retail merchants did their spring and fall buying usually lasted from the end of February until the first part of May and from the latter part of August to the middle of October.[125] A few of the young lads also had "early weeks" every so often when they were required to get to the store before the others in order to polish glass, dust the furniture, and sweep the floors; but they were allowed an hour's rest between 8:00 A. M. and 9:00 A. M. by way of compensation.[126] An interesting rule introduced near the turn of the century and indicative of the changing times provided that while the men were to continue to report for duty at 8:00 A. M. and leave at 5:30 P. M., the women employed were not to report until 8:30 A. M. and were to leave at 5:20 P. M. "We endeavor," explained Field, "to throw about our young women an atmosphere of protections [sic]." [127]

John G. Shedd, rather than Marshall Field, is credited with inaugurating the half-holiday on summer Saturdays. When a movement for such a half-holiday began to spread in the middle eighties among the smaller wholesalers, Shedd, head of the lace department in Wholesale, decided on his own authority to order it for half his force each week. Though at first it created something of a furor among the executive partners, the story goes that Shedd had his way and the idea was soon made to apply to other departments also.[128] In 1887, an agreement was reached among all the major wholesalers to adopt the practice during the months of July and August; and it was continued every year thereafter by Marshall Field and Company in both its retail and wholesale branches.[129]

Except in the case of watchmen, Sunday work was not permitted by Marshall Field. This was not so much a matter of allowing a holiday and a needed day of rest as it was a religious requirement inherited from his New England Calvinistic background. In 1902, when every employee was busily preparing for the opening of the new retail store, this notice was sent throughout the house.

Notice to Section Managers:—
We find that there is a little inclination to overlook the expressed wishes of the house in reference to Sunday work for the approaching opening. We do not wish the present to be any exception to the general rule, and the rule is, of course, that no Sunday work take place in this establishment. Any section manager who is planning to bring his people down on Sunday will immediately change his plans and complete the work to-night, staying as late as is necessary or beginning very early Monday morning. *The decorations which cannot be placed to-night will be placed after twelve o'clock midnight, Monday morning,* and for this important event in the history of the house we wish to preserve the same dignified attitude regarding Sunday work as heretofore.[130]

Another factor which made working at Marshall Field and Company attractive to its employees was a comparatively liberal, if paternalistic, policy in regard to sick leave, vacations, and holidays. There is no evidence to indicate that Marshall Field, in the very early years of the firm, was willing to commit himself to any definite store policy as regards employee vacations, any more than he was in regard to any other employee benefit. Of the strict, individualistic school, he held the opinion that that which he gave he had the right to take away. Field did, nevertheless, from the outset allow vacations to his employees, and with full pay. By 1869 he was already beginning to write two-week paid vacation provisions into individual salary contracts of even some of the ordinary salesmen, stipulating only that they be taken during the "dull season." [131] By the middle eighties there was still no fixed policy; but by this time custom had decreed that July and August, the least active months in both Wholesale and Retail, were the general vacation months and most of the employees were obtaining a vacation every year.[132] When Field's finally announced in 1897 a definite store-wide policy to the effect that "a vacation of two weeks will be allowed . . . to those who have been here for twelve consecutive months, and one week to those who have been here for six consecutive months," it was simply confirming an already well-established practice.[133]

In this enlightened policy Field's was well ahead of the times. In 1899, over thirty years after Field, Leiter and Company had started granting vacations, the *American Artisan* commented:

The commendable practice of taking vacations has taken a wider hold this year than ever before. . . . There was a time not so many years ago, that such things as vacations were not dreamt of, and no merchant would think of leaving his business for a week's fishing trip or would allow any of his employees to do so.[134]

In addition to their standard vacations, the employees enjoyed a limited holiday schedule which usually included Thanksgiving, Christmas, New Year's Day, Independence Day, and at least a half-day on Decoration Day,[135] plus an occasional additional recess for such civic events as patriotic celebrations and election days.[136] After 1882 employees regularly obtained the right either to report late for work or to leave early in order to vote—even in primaries.[137] Infrequently on election day the store closed early.[138] Those working at the polls were excused for the entire day.[139]

When an employee did not appear at the store for reasons other than vacations and holidays, it was the job of the department head to find out why; and records were kept of such absences.[140] In cases of illness, there was in the earlier years again no formal policy, no standard sick benefits. The matter was to be cared for in each individual instance as seemed to fit the case, but in practice this almost invariably meant that full salary was paid by the house, no matter what the length of absence or how insignificant the position was.[141] Sometimes, in instances of acute distress, Mr. Field personally cared for the family of the ailing worker, sent baskets of food, paid doctor bills or supplied needed cash.[142] After 1903, the company, however, finally announced a definite platform to which it was willing to stand committed: half-pay when ill.[143] Unfortunately it proved to be less generous than the practice prevailing since the beginning of the firm.

The problem of old age was handled, as might be expected, in a similar manner. The house promised nothing; there were no pensions, no program of tenure. Older persons were, however, purposely kept on in the employ of the firm long beyond their period of usefulness; and those who found themselves in financial difficulties following their eventual retirement "privately and unofficially" received checks from the firm. Thus, without the aid of a modern retirement system, the men and women of Field's were able nevertheless to attest to a strong feeling of security.[144] This compares favorably with A. T. Stewart and Company where apparently no thought was given to the desire of employees for security and people were simply hired "from month to month" and discharged at will.[145]

Field's in this period of its history was modern enough in its labor relations to deliberately attempt to make life more pleasant on the job itself. The store established something of a reputation for accommodations which it provided not alone for cash customers, but for its own people. In the State and Washington streets building constructed in 1879, for example, each employee was provided with an individual locker for his clothing; and there were separate toilet, cloak, and lunch rooms for men and women, all kept neat and clean by special

7. PERSONNEL

attendants.[146] When the buildings begun in 1902 provided the necessary space, these facilities were expanded to include more elaborate rest rooms complete with shower baths, as well as an employees' restaurant, library, men's gymnasium, girls' recreation rooms, and even a company hospital.[147] The store's employee-recreation program was made to include such things as occasional picnics, and interdepartmental baseball competitions.[148] The health and spirits of the working girl were further maintained with a free cup of hot bouillon served daily;[149] while the young cash boys were indulged with an opportunity for free schooling in regular academic subjects four hours out of each week. The latter innovation, though not compulsory, was taken advantage of by most of the boys and helped to overcome, at least partially, any deficiencies they experienced because of having left school too early in life.[150] At least one lucky lad, with higher ambitions, found one of the firm's partners willing to give partial financial aid to provide the youth during his spare hours a more advanced education in one of Chicago's art colleges.[151]

Such marked interest by Field's in its employees also had its other side, of course. Mr. Field was determined that his gentlemen employees be gentlemen and his lady employees be ladies; and he was not unwilling that his supervision of his people's activities extend to their behavior and deportment outside as well as inside the store. A clerk, cash boy, or salesman, on and off the job, was a representative of the store; and consequently his conduct, good or bad, reflected upon the store. Field personnel, whether it was their natural inclination or not, had to live up to that same model of decorum to which the firm as a whole aspired.[152]

The educational features of Field's employee policy mentioned above were admittedly but one step in an effort to achieve these high standards of behavior by the members of the firm. It was the duty of the teacher employed in the cash boys' school not only to increase, by education, the efficiency and behavior of the boys but to keep a record of the abilities and personal traits of her pupils, in order to mark the more capable and personable for promotion, and to weed out the stupid and obstreperous from the employ of the firm.[153] This academic preparation was then further supplemented by a regular training in store procedure conducted by the older hands in the firm. Every department head and his assistants were made responsible for seeing that each new employee understood the rules and regulations and that he was thoroughly indoctrinated with the "Field Idea" of courtesy and service.[154] This task was not taken lightly and Field's became famous for the thoroughness of its training as reflected in the excellence of its clerks.[155]

As the store developed into a vast and complicated merchandising institution, however, and the problem of coördination of sales methods became acute, it was seen that, if Field's were to remain famous for its personnel, further methods were necessary. The retail section managers were called together in 1902 by the aggressive retail manager, Harry G. Selfridge; and the whole problem was thoroughly discussed.

From the meeting emerged a plan for individual departmental education preceded by a short period of uniform training in general methods to be conducted by a centralized training school.[156] As set up, this became a three-day period of training—with pay—for all new employees. Conducted at the start by a woman educational director and by three teaching assistants, this "school" undertook to teach the store rules, how to make out sales checks, display goods, approach customers, and to help, incidentally, in the necessary process of eliminating undesirables before they reached the customers.[157] This did not relieve the department head of his responsibility for conducting further specialized training in a knowledge of his department's wares when the new people actually arrived on the job.[158] If the department were men's neckwear, for example, he had to be sure his new clerk understood how ties are manufactured, understood something of the qualities of material, of tasteful colors, and of real values. The new man must know that ties come in different lengths and different widths, and that only certain ties are suitable for particular occasions. Field clerks were expected to know.[159]

Even when once set to work, the supervision and indoctrination of the new man had only just begun. His behavior at all times was carefully observed and regulated by his superiors; and even his fellow employees were required to report any infractions of the rules on his part. If he arrived late, he was fined; and if he made any mistakes in filling out a sales slip or shipping order, he paid the cost of the error from his own pocket. He was forbidden to waste any time or to leave his department (on pain of dismissal) except when serving a customer. During business hours and while on duty he could not read the newspaper, drink, eat, smoke, chew tobacco or gum, clean his fingernails, engage in loud conversation, use profane language, or make any other unnecessary noise.[160]

The male clerk was not too closely regulated as to the clothing which he wore to work; but the women employees, in order not to offend the customers, were asked to avoid any "excess" in attire.[161] Dresses were to be modest—"conspicuous for their neatness and tidiness and inconspicuous for the color and pattern of material."[162] A prescribed dress consisting of a black skirt and a simple black or white blouse was decided upon in later years for all saleswomen. Low necklines and even short sleeves were forbidden. Until long after Marshall Field died "artificial complexions" as well as exaggerated hair fashions and the excessive use of jewelry were likewise banned.[163]

After the Field employee left the store in the evening, he still was answerable for the good name of the house. He was warned against frequenting pool halls, dance halls, gambling houses, or any place of amusement where intoxicating drinks were served.[164] If his pay was small, he might even be brought in before a superior and cautioned against marrying, should he seem so inclined.[165] He was positively forbidden to engage in outside mercantile or manufacturing operations,[166] to borrow money from other employees,[167] or to contract loans elsewhere "at exorbitant rates of interest per month." [168]

On the positive side, he was urged constantly to imitate the founder's path to success by saving. A message on the outside of each pay envelope and frequent bulletins reminded him that the Illinois Trust and Savings Bank was a safe depository and was paying 6 per cent interest. Field even made special arrangements with the president of this institution to handle the small accounts of his employees.[169]

The most important training which the members of the staff obtained, of course, related directly to the treatment of customers and the treatment of other employees in the presence of customers. While there were certain rules to be followed in this case, it was more an attitude—almost a philosophy—rather than an observance of a set discipline that was necessary. The employees must at all times by their conduct enhance that atmosphere of quiet gentility and of comfortable respectability that was Marshall Field and Company.[170]

Field fought hard against the age-old fawning habits of merchants and their clerks. He insisted that it was possible for his people to assume a position of dignity and equality at the same time that they acted in a thoroughly friendly and courteous manner toward customers. Employees were instructed to refer to each other in the firm as "Mr. ———" or Miss ———," not simply by their given names; and never was the attention of a clerk or salesman to be obtained by shouting "forward!" On this same note, women shoppers were to be addressed as "madam," and not "my dear" or "lady." Male attire at Marshall Field and Company after 1880 was "men's goods," not "gent's goods." [171] In the earlier days of the firm, clerks had been taught to open the conversation with a customer by saying, "Have you been waited upon?" Since, however, this seemed to put the clerk in too subservient a position, the introduction was changed to a polite "May I help you?" [172] And, incidentally, the clerk found it a great deal easier to maintain the desired poise when he knew, as he did, that the house frowned upon the undue urging of customers to buy and that monthly sales totals were not the sole measure of pay and advancement.[173] The general public, it followed, as well as the employees themselves, learned to appreciate and enjoy the difference.

By way of contrast the experience of a young woman while clerking in two of the other Chicago department stores about this same time are of interest:

Our business was first to dust and condense the stock, and then to stand ready for customers. We all served in the double capacity of floorwalkers and clerks, and our business was to see that no one escaped without making a purchase. The confusion can be readily imagined. As soon as the elevators emptied themselves on the floor, there was one mad rush of clerks with a quickly spoken, "What would you like, madam?" or, "Something in toys, sir?" and the responses to these questions were indicative of the characters of the people making them. The majority were rude, some amused, and a few alarmed at the urgency of the clerks. One young boy, on being assailed by half a dozen at once, threw up his hands in horror, and said: "For God's sake, let me out of here!" and fled down the stairs, not even waiting for the elevator. The cause of such watchful activity on the part of so many employees was the 5 per cent commission which was to eke out the two or three dollars a week salary.[174]

All in all, the result of the Field policy toward its employees was one of considerable success. Despite what might seem to have been excessive interference by the firm with personal liberties,[175] morale was high and labor efficiency at a peak. Many employees were underpaid, overworked, and hampered by numerous restrictions; yet these conditions were prevalent to an equal or greater degree in all other drygoods firms, and Field's unquestionably had many things to offer by way of compensation which most other firms did not. Marshall Field and Company, as the most successful firm in the West, meant prestige of employment, job security, and rapid promotion for the able. The wealth of the firm and its founder meant at least sporadic generosity and some security during illness and old age. Its progressiveness in merchandising methods usually meant pride in one's work.[176]

Only by first understanding these things is it possible to appreciate the Field employee—why he was filled with such unusual loyalty to the store, why he seemingly struggled as hard as the partners to maintain the firm's reputation for progress and dependability, and why he was manifestly so content in his job. Despite the feeling of awe which he held for his superiors in the firm (and dislike for a few), the average employee still felt that in general these men had his interests at heart and that his own particular job was considered to be of importance to the store.[177] Over and over employees attest to the fact that in order to keep up with their work, they voluntarily went without meals, worked extra hours and extra days without pay, and still came up praising their employer. "We did this," they said, "because we were interested." [178]

A Mr. J. J. Reilly, after several years of keeping shipping records was transferred into traffic work in the Adjustment Bureau:

> Right off, I saw there was work here I didn't understand. I always wanted to be able to give an answer to the other fellow. So at nights I went down to the Illinois Central depot and got a job loading cars to learn how freight was handled, how they kept their bills and tallies of freight cars. I was there about a month. Then I got a job with American Express at Federal Street and with Wells Fargo on South Wells Street and learned how they operated. Then I pitched mail at the Post Office for several months. While I was with Wells Fargo I'd work Saturdays and go as far west as Fort Dodge on express cars handling express.
>
> All this fortified me for my job at Field's.[179]

A Mr. F. O. Stevens started in as a cash boy in the retail store in 1893:

82

I went to North Division High School at night, taking a course in business to fit myself for advancement. I decided on this extra study soon after arriving for I promptly got the idea at Field's that its policy of merchandising was the best in the world. I heard about Mr. Field's principles and regarded them as ideal.[180]

There was also a feeling of camaraderie certainly unusual in so large an institution. Field's was known as a friendly place to work. The staff, by reputation, was "one big family" where every employee felt his presence was valued. The writer of a 1902 article in the magazine the *Interior* was an eyewitness to an incident that illustrates the point:

The head of a certain section, summoned from the city by sad news, was just leaving as we entered. He excused himself from an interview very politely and went out. As he passed the desks of subordinates, hands were outstretched to give a grip of sympathy; even a little cash boy coming in on an errand, stopped to say "good bye," and get a hand clasp. It seems a little thing to notice, or to mention; it merely shows how the feeling of fellowship and coöperation penetrates the whole fabric.[181]

That this spirit was to a great extent spontaneous, rather than inspired by a deliberate company effort so familiar today, makes it the more remarkable.

New Hands at the Helm 8

Marshall Field Finds Interests Outside the Firm

ON JANUARY 3, 1881, WHEN THE NEWSPAPERS HEADLINED THE STORY that Marshall Field had bought out Levi Leiter and was for all practical purposes the sole owner of Chicago's greatest dry-goods firm, it served to emphasize what most people had long suspected—that Field had become a very wealthy man. Field publicly admitted at the time that his wholesale and retail firm was doing a $25,000,000-a-year business. Since he had just paid Leiter over $2,000,000 for his share in that business, it was not difficult to deduce that his dry-goods activities alone had made this merchant several times a millionaire. The news accounts, however, also gave publicity to the fact that by no means all of Field's wealth was being acquired in the dry-goods trade.[1] In order to prevent just such information from leaking out, the news of the dissolution of the firm was released by Field and Leiter in a carefully guarded interview in which they refused to divulge anything of real interest concerning their affairs.[2] But they underestimated the press. An enterprising *Times* night reporter was ready that same evening with a complete inventory of the real estate properties which Field had been accumulating over the years.[3] Much to the latter's surprise and discomfiture, this list, with an estimated valuation of each piece of property, was printed next day in the *Times* as prominently as his uninformative interview was in the *Tribune*. The value of his properties alone added up, the *Times* told the public, to a total of $2,180,000.[4]

The truth is, Field had been quietly buying Chicago real estate as an investment for his surplus wealth almost from the day that he freed himself from debt to Potter Palmer. In March 1867, only the third month after the creation of Field, Leiter and Company, Marshall Field's "outside property" was estimated at $50,000 to $60,000.[5] He continued thereafter to invest,[6] buying sometimes with a view to the future needs of his firm, but usually for the purpose of collecting rentals and of profiting from the almost fantastic increase in real estate values taking place in Chicago.[7] "As to the future of Real Estate here," he wrote in 1875 to a London banking friend,

I think if selected with judgment, that it will pay at once fair income on investment & chances are will appreciate in value. I have made some investments since returned [from England] & shall more during next few months if anything comes up that suits me. Money is a drug here allmost [*sic*] and out of the question to loan it at the present time.[8]

By the early eighties Field possessed corner lots and high income producing buildings and store fronts scattered all over the business district of the city.[9] Continuing to buy heavily during the remainder of his life,[10] he was declared by many at the time of his death to be the largest single property holder in Chicago.[11] Estimates of the value of his seventy-four different pieces of real estate in 1906[12] placed the figure at about $40,000,000.[13]

The significance of this for the firm becomes clear when one discovers that Field had acquired possession, not only of all the land and buildings occupied by his own retail and wholesale houses, but also of the land where two of his largest department store rivals stood (Mandel Brothers and Schlesinger and Mayer—and later Carson Pirie Scott and Company).[14] Field and Leiter, at the time of their separation as partners (1881), owned jointly the Singer building, property occupied by the Retail. In 1886 Field acquired Leiter's half-interest by directing the firm to pay Leiter a $50,000 bonus in addition to his own purchase payment of $500,000. Field then collected from his own firm a tidy rental of $50,000 per annum, later increased to $113,000.[15] When the Retail in subsequent years began to expand and spread over the entire block bounded by State, Washington, Wabash, and Randolph, Field bought up the land ahead of time in anticipation of each move.[16] The firm, as his tenant, eventually occupied land and buildings conservatively valued at over $12,500,000[17] and bringing an annual rental of over $1,000,000.[18]

Levi Leiter, as it happened, was a reluctant accessory in aiding Field to acquire the valuable State and Madison site on which Carson's stands today. Leiter had purchased the property sometime previous to 1881,[19] reported as costing only $212,000;[20] and he apparently had no intentions of ever letting it go. When, however, his son Joe, in a gigantic effort in 1898 to corner the wheat market, "overstayed" and lost an estimated $9,750,000 of his father's money, Levi Leiter was forced to sell this corner, along with other choice properties. Turning to his old partner mostly because he was one of the few men who could produce the necessary cash, Leiter sold the corner for $2,100,-000.[21] Field found the land encumbered with a 106-year lease signed by Leiter and Schlesinger and Mayer only two months earlier, but it called for a payment of $112,000 per annum; so Field apparently minded not at all.[22]

While Marshall Field was an exacting landlord and took care to obtain in rentals all that his land would yield,[23] he did not use his large holdings in "Loop" property to keep rivals away, but rather to encourage his competitors to settle close by. When Mandel Brothers, for example, desired to expand, Field did not seek to hamper their growth but leased to them the land for the building which they so earnestly desired. Earlier when Carson Pirie Scott and Company lost their lease and there was danger of the firm moving some distance away, Field encouraged them to settle at their present location only one block from his own store.[24] "If we do anything to thwart their growth in this neighborhood," Field is supposed to have said, "they will go elsewhere—and draw crowds of customers after them. Better to keep them near us. Let them draw people here. If the crowds come here and we are not able to get our share of their business, it will be because we do not deserve to have it." [25]

Adventures in Chicago real estate were not the only means by which Marshall Field made his millions produce more millions. Field early in his career had invested in stocks and bonds and even personal notes.[26] In January 1874, in a confidential memorandum he listed his assets in this particular category as:

    Note made by J. N. Scammon [?] and by J. M. Tyler ... 5000
    100 Shares 1st nat. BK ....value 14000
     50 Shares German Bk ....value 4000
     50 Shares Bank Commerce ....value 4000
     40 Shares Manfg Nat Bk 2000
    100 Shares Ill Loan & Trust Co. 10000
     50 Shares Dry Goods Bk New York 4000

```
100 Shares American Express Stock ................... 5000
100 Shares Chicago City RR Stock ...................12500
       L. H. Fields Note ....................... 5000²⁷
```

This comparatively modest amount was but a starter, however. "It has been my intention," he stated in his will, "to keep at least half of my property in real estate and the rest in personal property." [28] And with this in mind, apparently, he invested heavily in such securities—so heavily, in fact, that eventually his private secretary could no longer handle the task alone but was forced to hire a confidential book-keeper for the sole purpose of keeping a record of his investments. [29] By 1906, Field held stock in eighty-two different companies; and it was worth over $34,000,000. In bonds of thirty-nine companies he had at least $7,400,000. [30]

Field was generally considered by his contemporaries to have been one of the shrewdest investors in the United States. [31] And well he might have been, for he seemd to have the magic touch. Little that he ever purchased failed to produce ample dividends and increase in value after he purchased it. [32]

Though he by no means limited himself to any particular types of investments, his preferences seemed to be for steel companies, banks, and railroads. [33] These purchases, just as with his real estate holdings, had a double purpose. They not only produced profits but were complementary to his dry-goods business. The railroads made Chicago a great trading center and distributor of goods, and Field was a major distributor. Steel companies created wealth and attracted labor. Field intended to provide supplies to the people. To conduct all such businesses the banks were, of course, a necessity.

In 1887 Field joined a syndicate that included John D. Rockefeller and other prominent financiers and purchased 20,000 acres of the Vermilion iron range in Minnesota. [34] This tie-up, along with his large holdings in the Federal Steel Company, won him a seat on the board of directors of the United States Steel Corporation when the former company was incorporated into this huge trust. Field's influence and threats of resigning, according to Schwab, had much to do with the location of the future United States Steel mills in and around Chicago rather than in the older Pittsburgh area. [35]

In the Chicago banking world Field was even more influential. His original small holdings in banks of the city were soon enlarged, and he eventually sat as a director on the boards of several different financial institutions. [36] The Merchants' Loan and Trust Company, however, was "his" bank; and through his virtual control of its board, upon which he sat for almost thirty years, he was a power to be reckoned with in the banking world. [37] In times of banking crises, the Clearing House Committee of bankers sometimes found itself obliged to seek the advice and assistance of Marshall Field as a man of greater financial power than any one of them possessed. This was illustrated in 1905 in the failure of the John R. Walsh banks, which included the

Chicago National Bank, the Home Savings Bank, and Equitable Trust Company.[38]

One of Field's earliest investments in railroads was in the stock of the Chicago City Railroad;[39] and because he eventually owned a considerable share of the company, not many moves were made without his consent.[40] Field perforce became associated with Charles T. Yerkes, who had the reputation of negotiating some of the unsavory deals involving Chicago street railways.[41] The great merchant, as a result of such connections and of his bitter opposition to public ownership of the lines,[42] injured his own reputation.[43] Field was accused of helping to manage this company largely in the interest of State Street and especially of his own retail store. The most important car lines were all made to run to the very doors of his retail establishment, and between 1899 and 1903 there were even "Marshall Field Specials" which ran from Harlem to Randolph and Wabash.[44]

The Field establishment occupies most of the block between Randolph Street, Wabash Avenue, Washington and State Streets. There is an entrance on the second floor of the store directly from the "Loop," where passengers from the Northwestern, Oak Park, Metropolitan and South Side elevated lines may disembark and do their shopping without going into the street. The four elevated railroads using the "Loop" tap the most populous residence districts of the city and suburbs.

In addition to the elevated roads, the surface lines also feed steady streams of passengers into the neighborhood of the Field store. For example, the Cottage Grove avenue, Indiana avenue and several crosstown lines from the South Side have their northern terminus at Randolph Street and Wabash avenue. The State street, Archer avenue and other crosstown cars run to Randolph and State, looping around on Wabash avenue.

The North State and North Side lines touch the corner of State and Randolph. The Northwestern surface lines, such as Milwaukee avenue, Grand avenue, and the several east and west lines that run into the heart of the city on those diagonal thoroughfares—Chicago avenue, Division Street, Elston Ave., etc.—run to State street and turn a corner at the Marshall Field store, either State and Randolph or State and Washington. The same is true of the main West Side surface lines, such as Lake street and Madison street, with their tributaries. Dearborn street, just one block west of the Field store, is traversed by several other well patronized surface lines. Two blocks east on the Lake front, the Illinois Central suburban service has its northern terminal at the foot of Randolph street.

The fact—too significant to be accidental—is that the people who constitute the most desirable class of buyers in the city of Chicago and its suburbs are deposited at the doors of Marshall Field & Co., or within sight and easy walking distance of the big store.[45]

Supposedly in part to assure adequate and cheaper shipping for his business, Mr. Field early acquired large stock holdings and directorships in such western railroads as the Chicago, Milwaukee, and St. Paul, the Rock Island, and the Chicago and North Western.[46] Since, even after these purchases, he lacked control of any one road between Chicago and the Atlantic coast, he joined with P. D. Armour, another large Chicago shipper, and James J. Hill and others in taking over the shaky Baltimore and Ohio and personally invested at least $10,000,000 of his own money to help restore it to an efficiently operating system.[47]

In addition, Field was for many years the largest single owner of stock in the Pullman Sleeping Car Company and exercised considerable control of its operations.[48] Marshall Field and Company profited handsomely from enormous orders of pillows, sheets, carpets, etc., which the Pullman Company bought at the dry-goods house.[49] The business of the sleeping car company, however, occupied a great deal of Field's time; and when, after Pullman's death in 1897, Field installed his friend Robert Lincoln in the presidency, it still did not relieve the aging merchant from stopping at the Pullman offices as regularly as his own in the Marshall Field and Company Wholesale building.[50]

Youth Takes Over

The greatest importance of Marshall Field's increasing absorption in his expanding outside investments was the fact that he was able to spend less and less time performing the duties of commander-in-chief of his equally expanding dry-goods firm. During the last twenty years of Field's life, Marshall Field and Company almost tripled its sales volume[51] and greatly enlarged its scope of operations. To administer adequately so large an institution required more time and energy than the aging Field could give to the task. Thus, in tune with his philosophy of providing room at the top for merit from within his own firm, Field began to turn over many of his responsibilities to younger men. While Field retained until his death the post of president and maintained an energetic hand on the helm, two carefully chosen lieutenants, the general manager of Retail and general manager of Wholesale, assumed a virtually independent command of their respective branches.

The two men who rose to these posts in the last years of Field's career and achieved prominence in the mercantile world were worthy successors to him. John G. Shedd, general manager of Wholesale and Harry G. Selfridge, general manager of Retail, were destined to rise to such success in the trade as few men dream of. The more patient of the two, Shedd, followed Field as President of Marshall Field and Company and in 1926 died worth $15,000,000.[52] Selfridge, who lived until 1947, eventually created a business in London worth $50,000,000 and died with a reputation in his adopted city of London equal to that of Shedd's in Chicago.[53] Both, during their stay as Field's underlings, made contributions to the firm's greatness that were incalculable.

John Graves Shedd and the Wholesale

John G. Shedd first appeared at Marshall Field and Company about a year after the Great Fire (August 1872).[54] He was then just twenty-two years old[55] and looking for a job. Though physically unimpressive, this young lad was not lacking in self-confidence. According to Shedd's own account, Field asked him, "Are you a salesman?" "Yes, sir," answered Shedd. "What can you sell?" "Anything," was the reply.[56]

Field jotted down the following terms in his personal salary book and Shedd thus began his career as a salesman and stockboy in Department D[57] (linens, laces, hosiery, gloves and underwear),[58] headed by Henry J. Willing[59] in Marshall Field and Company, Wholesale:

> J. G. Shedd
> Aug. 7 to Jany 1/73   Per wk. $10.00
> and if suits $12.00 from that date to July 1/73.
> To let him go at any time does not suit.[60]

Shedd was fortunate to have been placed under the care of as capable a man as Willing. Though not prone to share credit unnecessarily with others for his own deeds, Shedd admitted later in life that Willing taught him much about the art of merchandising and salesmanship.[61] Under Willing's guidance and by dint of hard work, young Shedd, despite his extra duties as stockboy, sold over $10,000 worth of goods in his first five months on the job.[62] Field was so pleased that he crossed out his original entry that was to determine Shedd's salary for the coming year

> J. G. Shedd   D
> Jany 1/73 to July 1/73 $12.00
> to let him go any time does not
> suit—

and substituted in its place

> J. G. Shedd   D
> From Jany 1/73   one year 14.00 wk

But before another six months were up, Field had changed his mind again; and he boosted Shedd's salary for the third time in a year:

> J. G. Shedd   D
> July 1/73   one year $900.00[63]

Within only four more years (by July 1876), Shedd had become an established house salesman, earning a guarantee of $1200 plus a $200 annual bonus.[64]

Shedd's secret as a salesman was the same as that of the man who hired him: he was a hard worker; he had an earnest, persuasive personality; and, most of all, he truly loved merchandise. He made it a point, as he grew in experience, to find out what the American consumer wanted to buy. Thus when he urged certain items upon his merchant customers, his arguments carried conviction. His popularity with customers was so great that long after he had ceased selling, in order to be general manager of the house, many retailers continued to ask for him and insist that he wait upon them.[65]

Shedd's first opportunity to move up the ladder came in 1883. In that year Willing retired from the firm,[66] and Field recognized the abilities of his able young salesman by subdividing Willing's old department into two and asking Shedd to head a new department, number 21, dealing exclusively in laces and ladies' underwear.[67] His salary was at the same time increased to a $5000 guarantee plus a $1000 annual bonus if he succeeded. As it happened, Shedd had the misfortune to take over the department just at the beginning of a mild recession in business that occurred in the middle eighties. Sales and profits of the wholesale departments generally ceased their steady rise and during several years even declined.[68] To make any showing under such circumstances was difficult for a new department head; but Shedd was up to the occasion—the sales and profits of his department held up well.[69]

In fact, he was doing so well and was so full of confidence as to his abilities that he seriously considered going into busines for himself.[70] Field, however, was eager to retain him. In 1884 he offered him an attractive two-year contract putting him in charge of an additional department, number 22—embroideries, frillings, rufflings, ladies' muslin underwear, infants' robes and tidies.[71] At the same time Shedd was guaranteed a $6000 salary plus $2,000 additional in bonuses *every six months*.[72] No more talk of leaving the firm was heard.

When Shedd was for the first time placed on a profit-sharing basis in 1887, he received, in addition to his guarantee, $7\frac{1}{2}$ per cent of the net profits of the two wholesale departments he headed and of the retail departments selling the same goods and thus "controlled" by him. At the end of six months, lace curtains were added to Shedd's stock, apparently because they were currently losing money[73] and Field hoped Shedd could do something with them.[74] Shedd must have fulfilled all of Field's hopes and expectations; for the lace curtains department account jumped from a $5,000 loss in 1887 to a $2,600 profit in 1888, a $17,100 profit in 1889, and continuously larger profits thereafter.[75] Shedd's personal gain from his first year's efforts was a neat return of $9,200 over and above his $6,000 guarantee, an amount well above that of any of the other four new department heads who were all given their first opportunities in that same year.[76] For 1889 and 1890 his percentage of the net profits was increased to $12\frac{1}{2}$ per cent;[77] and by 1891, after the linen department was also placed under his control, he was the highest paid department head in Wholesale. His earnings were averaging close to $40,000 a year through profit-sharing alone.[78]

Other reasons than his remarkable sales ability, of course, accounted for Shedd's rapid rise in Field's esteem. One was the effect of his personality on those with whom he worked. Possessing great self-confidence,[79] Shedd was a keen judge of men and on friendly terms with them all. Not so secretive and shy as Field, he found it easier to be on

90

intimate terms with his employees to whom he gave advice and encouragement. He could joke and enter into a friendly wager with his salesmen. In short, Shedd knew the value of personnel morale and thus took a genuine interest in the men who worked under him.[80] One of Shedd's favorite maxims was: "If we'd burn down, we could pick up somewhere tomorrow, and the customers would come, but if we'd lose our staff the customers wouldn't come back"; and the people working for Shedd felt that he meant it.[81] In the meantime Shedd's own unflagging energy, conscientiousness, and unquestioned intelligence aroused their admiration; and the example he purposely set was not lost upon them.[82]

Shedd's early training at the hands of Willing, a man with a passion for discovering time-saving methods and demonstrating through cold statistics more efficient ways of doing business, obviously motivated Shedd to think along similar channels. He, like Willing, acquired a fascination for finding new ways of doing things; and in turn, he inspired those under him to develop the same urge. When employees spoke of the future president of the firm, they used terms like "dynamic," "energetic," "sharp," and "bustling." "The employees recognized Shedd as the one with the progressive ideas," said one man. "Shedd took the initiative. . . . [He] had the vision and the courage to make innovations—the things that our rivals weren't doing. We all felt that if new things came it would be via Shedd."[83]

Shedd's first new contribution of significance was made in the 1870's while he was still a salesman working under Willing and endeavoring to make a reputation for himself in the house. Eager never to lose a customer unnecessarily, it irritated Shedd to find that even under the close buying methods of Willing,[84] that most popular items and sizes of goods were frequently out of stock. Extremely large and extremely small sizes seemed to pile up in ever greater abundance, while the best sellers were often "fresh out." This not only led to accumulation of unsalable merchandise, but, at the same time, it required that the popular items be purchased in haste regardless of market conditions. Shedd, upon investigation, discovered that the fault lay with the somewhat antiquated purchasing methods that had been used almost since the beginning of the firm's history. Purchases for each coming season, he found, were based to a considerable extent on a tabulation of the purchases of previous seasons plus guesswork. The result was that mistakes of previous years tended to be repeated, rather than corrected; and dead stock continued to clog the shelves.

Approaching Willing on the question, Shedd was encouraged to work out a purchasing plan for his own department and to present it for approval. This he did, basing his buying schedule on a statistical analysis of previous seasonal *sales* and stocks on hand, rather than purchases. The plan catered to the actual demands of the consumer as to color, pattern, and size, and not to the whims or ignorance of buyers. "When a buyer stops selling he ought to stop buying," he said;[85] so his plan called for the keeping of regular sales records and want lists by department heads as a constantly up-to-date source of information. Stocks were to be kept as low as possible and at all times well assorted. The scheme was adopted and its basic essentials was continued over the years as a highly successful policy.[86]

For the benefit of any department heads who were inclined to forget, there were constant reminders from Field and Shedd: "What we want is best assorted stock in America in every department";[87] . . . keep your stocks thoroughly well assorted";[88] and "surplus stocks must go."[89] Field's, it came to be said, were for all practical purposes "always sold out." "Any surplus in Field's is not stock, it is cash."[90]

Shedd was logically in line for promotion as a result of the success of his new buying plan, his proven skill at handling men, and his marked ability at making money. Thus, in the latter part of 1892 he was called in to Marshall Field's office and presented with a junior partnership in the firm. His share was the smallest in the firm, only two and a half eighty-eighths of the capital and profits; but he had his foot in the door and with a man of Shedd's drive that was about all that was necessary.[91] To go with this new recognition there was very shortly afterward conferred upon him what appeared to be the duties of a merchandise manager.[92] In 1901, he was made vice-president.[93] Though this was in practice merely giving a title to duties which for the most part he had held for some little time as close adviser to Field,[94] he now had the clear-cut authority to make his wishes felt more directly in the firm. Important changes were bound to come.

The Traveling Salesman

Many of these important changes in Wholesale had been impending for some time and only the rather natural conservatism of the aging Field had held them in abeyance. The influence of younger men, including Higinbotham and Shedd, which began to make itself felt in the 1880's came none too soon. One such change made in this period had to do with the method of contracting and selling to the outlying country merchants. For years Field had insisted that the only satisfactory way to do business was to have his merchant customers come to Chicago at regular intervals to place their orders directly and in person at the great wholesale building. In contrast to ordering from a mail-order house or from a traveling salesman showing a limited number of samples, Field's customers, he argued, could see and select in person from the store's huge stocks that offered a complete range of styles, sizes, colors, and prices.[95] Under this method, ordering was more accurate, shipping and billing were simplified, and the customer in every way was certain to return home a better satisfied man.

Shortly after the Civil War, however, traveling men from eastern wholesale houses began to appear throughout the Middle West; and the competition from this source became greater every year.[96] Many a small country merchant liked the idea. It saved him a long, expensive trip to Chicago; and with the salesmen coming directly to his store, he had the help and advice of his own clerks in selecting from the bewildering varieties of goods offered.

During the early seventies Field yielded to the extent of mailing unsolicited samples and goods on trial[97] and vigorously sought additional mail-order trade by sending out circulars and postcard advertisements.[98] But for some time still he refused to dispatch salesmen to compete on the road on equal terms with the wholesalers who did not carry a fraction of the wide varieties of goods that Field stocked for his customers in his Chicago house.[99]

An eventual surrender on the point, however, was of course inevitable. Marshall Field and Company was no longer a small jobbing house catering to the immediately surrounding area. Its customers were being drawn from an ever-expanding area that eventually stretched from the Appalachians to the Pacific Coast and from border to border. All the merchants in such a wide territory could hardly be expected to continue to journey twice a year to Chicago.[100] As a result, under pressure of constant complaints from his salesmen that the smaller merchants were not coming in and that when they did, they had already purchased part of their supplies from road salesmen of competing houses, Field capitulated. In 1877-78 he reluctantly agreed to permit Dixon Bean, head of the carpet department, to try out three of his men on short trips. When the three returned to Chicago in a short time with thousands of dollars' worth of orders, there was no more denying their argument.[101]

Field's continued to urge its customers to visit the house in person, but the traveling man was on the way to becoming a permanent feature of carpets—and of the other departments at Marshall Field and Company, Wholesale.[102] House expenditures for "country traveling" was increased[103] by two-thirds in 1879 over the previous year and, as the following figures indicate, they mounted steadily thereafter. During the next ten years (after 1879) the amount spent on "country traveling" increased more than tenfold; and by the time Mr. Field died the firm considered this feature of its business so necessary that it was spending over one-half million dollars in travel expenses.

TABLE V
"Country Traveling" Expenses of Salesmen of Marshall Field & Co., Wholesale, for 1873-1906*

Year	Amount	Year	Amount	Year	Amount	Year	Amount
1873	$ 2,276	1881	$ 27,330	1889	$133,200	1898	$231,166
1874	3,230	1882	40,410	1890	132,000	1899	259,265
1875	3,821	1883	53,390	1891	141,434	1900	309,693
1876	2,751	1884	48,830	1892	149,780	1901	375,643
1877	6,431	1885	54,600	1893	142,940	1902	430,473
1878	6,091	1886	71,600	1894	142,900	1903	498,912
1879	10,212	1887	88,600	1895	168,628	1904	518,251
1880	13,219	1888	120,800	1896	167,358	1905	518,345
				1897	183,422	1906	597,693

*Accounting ledgers, 1873-1906, Comptroller's safe, Marshall Field & Co., General Offices.

The introduction of this type of salesman not only revolutionized Field's selling methods, but it added a new element of interest and color to the story of wholesaling. Setting out with his grips, a couple of trunks-full of samples or "swatches" of goods, and his vest bedecked with lodge emblems, the Field traveling man journeyed patiently and laboriously from one town to the next within his allotted territory. Arriving in town, he engaged a room at the local hotel and obtained permission to display his samples either in the lobby or in one of the other hotel rooms. Having several days earlier sent an advance card to each of the merchants in town notifying them that he would be there, he was now ready for business.[104]

In the earlier days, selling by this method was comparatively easy. "Merchants would drop customers and stop to meet the traveling representative. They felt honored at being called upon by a representative from such a house as Field, Leiter and Company."[105] Over the long pull after the novelty had worn off, however, the traveling men were sometimes forced to resort to less subtle measures to win out over competition. For example, W. F. Hypes, one of the most successful salesmen,[106] and a good singer, gave concerts to please his customers whenever they arranged it and invited him. Some of the smaller towns in the isolated areas of the Dakotas looked forward to his coming and generously rewarded him for his performances with large orders.[107] Other salesmen operating out of Denver toward the ranch and mountain regions were forced during the winter to make trips in bobsleds over open country in order to reach the stores in the smaller towns off the railroads.[108]

The farther the sales area expanded and the greater the variety of wares the firm carried as the years passed, the more difficult the problem of coverage became. With many goods to display, the salesman found it impossible to carry over the vast distances in the West sufficient samples to do justice to every line carried in stock. As a result there evolved, of necessity, really two kinds of traveling men. The "specialty salesman" usually represented only one of the more important departments and one line of goods. He sold only linens, gloves, or perhaps lace goods. Such a salesman had a wide area to cover and was away from the firm sometimes most of the year. A single merchant in a western town might be contacted within any one month by a dozen different Field's specialty salesmen, each selling a different line.[109]

The "general lineman" on the other hand, was really the old general salesman with new responsibilities. He was allotted a comparatively small area but was required to cover it approximately every fortnight or every month. His major interest was in the smaller merchants neglected by the specialty men and he carried within his trunks samples of everything from yard goods and carpeting to toys and jewelry.[110]

Of course the most important thing that both types of salesmen had to sell in this period was the same thing that Field's had been selling since 1865, namely an unsurpassed reputation. First there were the known standards it had set for itself: Field's was honest, its good were dependable; in short, it was one of the outstanding wholesale houses of the nation.[111] Secondly, there was the name it had for looking out for the customer: Field salesmen guaranteed to satisfy him; they stayed close to his business; and they worked with him. In other words, they labored to keep the customer in business as well as their own firm.[112]

A Revised Credit Policy

In its struggle to maintain customers and acquire new ones in the ever-expanding area of operations, Field's made another basic change in its policy in this period: a pronounced liberalization of the store's credit terms. After Leiter left in 1881, Higinbotham took over the task of dispensing credit.[113] He had been trained under Leiter and was by no means reckless; nevertheless, under the effect of Marshall Field's more expansive policy and backed by a vastly larger capitalization than was the case in the beginning days of the firm, the credit department under Higinbotham was able to launch (1881) a policy of helping to extend wholesale sales by liberalizing the firm's credit policy toward new retailers. Between 1870 and 1880 the population of the West had increased over 78 per cent and during every *single year* of the eighties it jumped an average of 7 per cent more; while the Middle West was averaging a 3 per cent increase every year. Such tremendous growth in population meant new towns, new stores, and potentially new customers for Field's Wholesale.[114] Often by extending a line of goods on credit, by liberally "dating" invoices far in advance (especially in areas where the merchants depended on the seasonal farm trade), and sometimes by having the firm "grub-stake" new merchants outright, Marshall Field and Company's customer outlets were extended ever westward to the Pacific.[115] The idea was to find men who knew merchandise and then back them; that was the way to create customers. Young prospective merchants often wrote or came to see Field and Higinbotham and described their opportunities. The situation was investigated, and if the prospects were good, the young man would be told to go ahead—open up a store and Field's would finance him in part or give him long-term credit. A typical arrangement was that, if the merchant was to have a $20,000 stock, Field gave him perhaps $5,000 to $10,000 credit. Even this seemingly small help usually meant that nearly everything that the merchant handled thereafter would be purchased from Marshall Field and Company, Wholesale.[116]

This close tie between credit and sales was maintained for the remainder of Field's lifetime. Field and Shedd were much interested in opening up the West. In addition to the business advantages, both enjoyed participating and aiding in the growth of this vast new area. The road men were a continuous source of information as to the financial condition of distant merchants and helped keep the credit department informed. Field acted as banker. When the firm wished to extend credit, it did not have to borrow the money from a bank and obligate itself with a thirty- or sixty-day note; instead, the necessary millions of dollars were borrowed from Marshall Field, also at interest, but with the privilege of paying the money back as fast as it came in from the retailers. Since this might be within a matter of only a few days, considerable interest money was saved to the firm during the years.[117]

Wholesale Departmental Expansion

Another move in Marshall Field and Company's search for trade in the period subsequent to Leiter's departure was the further development of new departments in Wholesale and the expansion into new lines. Unobtrusively, almost surreptitiously, new products had a way of showing up in old departments, and then growing in sales to such an extent that they soon required a separate department to handle their sales. This growth in stocks, referred to incidentally in other connections, deserves some special attention of its own. For one thing, the ultimate culmination of this continuous expansion was the necessity of erecting a new wholesale building in 1887.[118] This building provided the necessary room both for new lines already introduced before this date and also for further extension into still other fields that the firm had long wished to enter.

Marshall Field, as far back as 1881, had, by purchasing a piece here and a piece there, acquired in the wholesale district title to an entire block bounded by Adams, Quincy, Wells (then called "Fifth") and Franklin Streets.[119] There, between 1885 and 1887, he constructed a massive seven-story building, covering this entire area. The building, though designed by the famous architect, Henry Hobson Richardson, of Boston,[120] had little of beauty to recommend it to the modern eye. A gloomy structure of rough-hewn granite and brownstone, the building had only its appearance of strength and the absence of excessive nineteenth-century ornamentation to recommend it. The structure was strictly utilitarian; it was, in a sense, simply eleven and a half acres of perfectly rectangular floors held aloft by straight walls of stone and iron, methodically perforated with rows of windows.[121] But, of course, size and space, rather than beauty, were the urgent requirements of Wholesale.

With almost none of the publicity usually associated with its retail openings, Marshall Field had the doors of the old building on Madison and Market closed at one o'clock, Saturday afternoon, June 18, 1887; and the doors of his new building opened on the following Monday, June 20. Thus the firm evidenced very little disturbance to the conduct of its business.[122] The goods now displayed on its half million square feet of floor space,[123] however, indicated that Field's had grown in the process and was planning to continue to grow. The variety of articles—and the contrast with those displayed at the opening in 1872 —was startling. Practically all of the same items mentioned in the earlier year were there fifteen years later in much greater quantities and choices of style and pattern; but the really impressive feature was the number of completely new items. One room alone on the seventh floor carried enough articles unknown to the 1872 store to refute any claim that Field's was still solely in the "dry-goods" business. There were in this room, for example, such new and unrelated item as carpet sweepers, baby buggies, dining-room tables, tricycles, art squares, and copper rivets. Elsewhere in the house could have been seen other interesting evidences of the changing times: rubber diapers, clocks, opera glasses, atomizers, baseballs and bats, fish hooks, glue, sandpaper, harmonicas, machine oil, music rolls, wire mattresses, thermometers, teething rings, and toothpicks. It was a different Marshall Field and Company.[124]

Private Branding

The expansion of sales territory, improvements in credit facilities, plus the continuous introduction of new lines, all unquestionably helped to build trade; and low prices, consistent with quality, remained a most important factor in holding customers. But as the firm's competitors gradually adopted many of the same methods for buying economically and cutting costs which had long been used by Field's,[125] the great Chicago wholesale house was continually forced to find newer devices for staying ahead.

The smaller jobbing houses at this time did a great amount of selective price-cutting. Prices were set at ridiculously low figures on a few leader items in order to win customers. The loss was, of course, made up on other goods sold to the customer at the same time. Under this practice, prices were frequently even cut for one customer and not another. In fact, the salesmen of Field, Leiter and Company had never been entirely freed from the necessity, in the heat of competition, of indulging in the practice themselves. This was particularly the case with regard to so-called "staples," such as sheeting, cotton dress goods, and curtains. A local jobber might make Ellison flannels a leader and cut the price to a very low figure. The Field salesman trying to sell in that area was forced to shave his price on that particular type of goods and try to make it up on something else. This, of course, not only cut into the store's profits; it meant an abandonment of Field's traditional "one-price" policy and led to the showing of preference for one customer over another. The whole idea was abhorrent to Field and inconsistent with his business principles. He was not long in seeking a way to make such price competition unnecessary.[126]

At least a partial solution was found in the adoption for the house of certain exclusive designs and brands. When Field's was the only house selling a particular brand-name product or design, it gave to the firm many of the advantages of a monopoly in that item. It could set its price at a profit-making level and charge the same to everyone. And once a Field's salesman had succeeded in placing his line with a retailer, the latter was obliged to go to that salesman for any reorders.

The acquisition of a popular design or brand that was unobtainable to any other firm thus eliminated direct competition and gave Field's an almost certain money-maker. The house, furthermore, was put in the more estimable position of treating its customers all alike.

The effort to acquire exclusive designs was naturally begun first in staples where the competition was greatest and then gradually extended to other lines as Field's grew larger.[127] This was accomplished by negotiating with supplying firms a contract calling for Field's to have for a particular product the sole agency in the West or the entire United States, or by buying in such large lots as to control the entire output of certain manufacturers. As early as 1870, Field, Leiter and Company had already obtained the exclusive sale of the products of certain mills manufacturing woolens, flannels, and blankets.[128] Within two more years they also had the entire production of the "American Hosiery Company" and were sole agents for either the West or the whole United States of such basic items as the Quaker City products (shirts, pajamas, etc.), Imperial Rugs, Pontoosuc Shirts, and Clark's O. N. T. thread.[129]

So successful was this method of attracting and holding trade that the practice was extended rapidly to other departments. During the late seventies, and the remainder of the century Wholesale's buyers, making full use of the firm's vast purchasing power and the weight of its prestige, won exclusive selling rights to a long list of standard goods. A carpet advertising circular of 1877, for example, notified retailers:

We are now prepared to offer for the Fall trade a full line of carpets, mattings, oil cloths, etc. Having the control, and taking the production of several Mills, enables us to offer an extensive variety of private designs, especially adapted for a fine retail trade. In addition, we have in stock all the Standard Makes, many of which we have the exclusive sale for the west: Body Brussels; Roxbury Tapestries; Higgins' Tapestries; Sanford's Tapestries, etc.[130]

In other lines by the end of the century Field's Wholesale was the sole western agent, or agent for the entire United States for such varied merchandise as, for example, Morris and Company Art Goods,[131] Excelsior Sole Leather trunks, women's Ferris Good Sense corset waists,[132] Mary E. Cobb's Manicure articles, Wm. Rieger's "Celebrated" Soaps, Perfumeries, and Toilet Articles,[133] "U.S." and "National" playing cards, Henrichs' Patent Sectional Cases.[134] At least as early as 1893 Mr. Field was even subsidizing some companies with cash loans in order to keep afloat (and retain control of) factories producing the types of goods he wanted.[135]

One of Field's most successful ventures in the direction of product differentiation was made in 1880. In that year Marshall Field left Leiter in sole charge of affairs in Chicago and traveled to Paris where he approached Fortin Fils and Deschamps, manufacturer of the famous "Alexandre" brand of kid gloves.[136] For years this latter company had dealt solely with the house of A. T. Stewart, and had permitted no one else to distribute its product in America.[137] Field's had retailed and wholesaled the gloves before;[138] but its only source of supply, ironically enough, had been one of its greatest rivals. There was no clearer recognition of the decline of the once-great firm of A. T. Stewart and Company and of the rise in world esteem of Field's than the fact that Fortin Fils and Deschamps was now ready to negotiate with the Chicago firm a contract identical in purport to that formerly negotiated only with the New York house. It read in part:

All gloves manufactured by Fortin Fils et Deschamps for the United States shall be consigned to Field, Leiter & Co. on joint account and all of which consignments as to quantity, quality, colors and so forth shall be subject to the direction and control of Field, Leiter & Co.[139]

Kid gloves were a very large item in dry goods in those days.[140] Fabric gloves were less expensive and considered less desirable than leather, except for certain specific occasions;[141] while kid gloves, the productions of the French from the hides of their own domestic goats raised in southern France, were held unequaled.[142] Field was so delighted with his new acquisition that he proudly advertised these gloves on frequent occasions thereafter[143] and ordered that a label bearing the trade name of the new product, "Alexandre," be affixed to every letter written thereafter by the general salesmen.[144] Fortin Fils & Deschamps must have found their association with Field's profitable, for the contract was periodically renewed even after the death of Marshall Field.[145]. With Marshall Field and Company's own retail store alone as early as 1887 providing an outlet for a full third of all the gloves imported, Wholesale never found any difficulty in disposing of all that the French firm manufactured.[146]

With this experiment in foreign wares an immediate and outstanding success, Field's began to enlarge upon its comparatively meager facilities for importing foreign manufactures. To the store's Manchester office, established by Joseph Field in 1871, there had already been added one in Paris by 1872;[147] and during the seventies, an average of $1,200,000 worth of goods had been imported annually. For a young western firm, this was a worthy enough feat; but to give Field's the quantities of exclusive new designs it needed in order to meet competition, even these figures had to be enlarged. As a result, through the eighties and nineties the firm's imports were permitted to climb steadily. By the late eighties the firm was sending abroad twice as many buyers as it had in the seventies and was importing over $2,600,000 worth of goods, more than double that of the previous decade. By 1900 this figure had reached $4,300,000 and by 1906 almost $6,000,000.[148] As of the latter date, Marshall Field and Company was paying three-fifths of all customs duties at the Port of Chicago and was the largest importer in the United States.[149]

As the quantity of imports grew, an elaborate organization evolved in Chicago to handle the trade. A "foreign office" was set up in Wholesale to expedite the handling of goods, records were kept of the prevailing exchange rates and export rates of gold, and for communicating with the European offices, cable codes were established.[150] Constant checks were made seeking the least expensive and most efficient routes for the shipment of goods both from New York and abroad, and buyers were kept closely informed.[151] Since adjustments in the American tariff so vitally affected the prices at which foreign goods could be sold, Marshall Field and Company, acting as spokesmen for most of the Chicago dry goods, became something of a counterforce to most other types of business; for it did everything it could to put pressure on Congress to keep the tariffs within reason and to refrain from constantly changing them.[152]

In the meantime, between 1880 and 1906, Field's also expanded its two foreign offices into a network of agencies that covered all of western Europe. The Manchester office in England, which formerly had handled everything that was shipped to the United States,[153] now specialized in English cottons and linens; and a new office in Nottingham carried English lace curtains and one in Bradford, woolens. The Paris office continued general French merchandise, and now in addition one in Lyons was devoted to silks and one in Calais to French lace. Need for a more direct source of German hosiery, gloves, and toys led to the establishment of an office at Chemnitz, and one at St. Gall for Swiss embroideries and handkerchiefs.[154]

Buyers from Chicago usually docked first at Liverpool and then entrained for Manchester close by. Four or more men in the Manchester office were delegated to escort the buyers to the English mills, introduce them, and help in any way they could. Everything purchased was sent to that office to be shipped. The buyers then traveled to as many of the other offices in England and on the Continent as they felt necessary, and they were assisted there in much the same manner.[155]

The location of these foreign offices in no sense represented the limits of the buying field, for as early as 1875 Field himself made buying trips to Italy.[156] In later years, some department heads even traveled as far as Turkey, India, and Japan in their search for the unusual or in an effort to buy directly at the source those staples formerly purchased at higher cost from importing firms.[157] The buyers' activities were not confined, either, to the large cities and the great factories. Much of the finer materials were hand made, and sometimes they were purchased directly from the Oriental, Swiss, or Turkish weavers in their own homes.[158]

For competing firms to duplicate these goods which Field put on display was difficult. Patterns, all that a manufacturer could produce, were purchased in their entirety to prevent any other firm from acquiring the same designs. Simply buying in enormous quantities and engrossing all of the design did not necessarily guarantee sale in Chicago, of course; for European and even American manufacturers were not always the best judges of American taste. This fact necessitated the taking of the next logical step. Field's Chicago department heads, who had immediate contact with the buying tastes of the public, began to develop ideas, sketches, designs, and patterns of their own. These were submitted to the American and foreign manufacturers to produce for Marshall Field and Company only.

In linens we used to put in six to eight new designs a year, have the designs drawn here and then sent to Europe to our manufacturing centers to be made up, guaranteeing certain amounts. The minute we sent off these designs we'd begin to drop an equal number of designs in stock, and instruct the sales people to push these doomed designs. They'd push all they could without any mark-down, then, if there were some left we'd keep on slicing prices till they were moved out entirely by the time the new materials arrived from Europe.[159]

In the field of exclusive designing for foreign manufacture, however, it was the carpet department that obtained the most satisfactory results and certainly the greatest publicity. As has been seen in an earlier connection, the carpet and rug department, after it was first opened in 1872, floundered badly for some time. With such poor sales the department frequently failed to show a profit of any sort.[160] In the early seventies Oriental rugs were little more than objects of curiosity,[161] and foreign carpets in general failed to move sufficiently to warrant even an annual buying trip to Europe.[162] According to the trade journal, *Interior Furnishing:*

The period which marked the revolution or sharp advancement in the furnishing of homes in the United States commenced soon after the World's Exposition at Philadelphia in 1876. Chicago, at that time and since, probably more than any other American city, has been peculiarly situated, owing to the large area of homes destroyed by fire, and to its very rapid growth, to adopt modern ideas in architecture and modern furnishing [sic].

Marshall Field & Co. . . . have been influential by their progressive methods in cultivating the general public to a better appreciation of thoroughly correct designs and colors as applied to carpets, rugs and upholstery.[163]

Beginning, therefore, about 1878, the market for foreign carpets began to pick up,[164] and the difference was reflected noticeably in the wholesale carpet departments' totals. Wholesale sales in 1879 were $1,136,300 as compared with only $836,709 for 1878. Thereafter representative sales figures by ten-year intervals were:

1886	$1,769,700
1896	2,048,100
1906	5,683,300

Wholesale profits in 1879 were $64,100 as compared to a $1900 loss in 1875 and by the year 1906 profits had reached $189,000.[165] Field's buyers increasingly made regular journeys abroad, particularly into all parts of the Near East, constantly seeking fine "Orientals" in designs not available to any other American firms.[166] While bemoaning the lack of a "school of textile industry" in America which might have served as a prolific and continuous source for new designs, Field's went to great expense to bring back to Chicago worn and even ragged, but beautiful, rugs some centuries old. These were for the purpose of serving as guides in creating other designs acceptable to the American taste.[167] These in turn were sent to Kashmir, India, where by 1903 Marshall Field and Company had over one hundred seventy looms manufacturing rugs exclusively for them and according to their designs.[168]

The logical final step to cutting costs and guaranteeing an exclusive source of supply is, of course, to make the goods in factories and workshops owned by the seller. The "manufacturing division" of Field's or "Fieldcrest Mills," as it came to be called, with its huge cotton mills and other factories located mainly in the South, is almost entirely a product of Shedd's presidency beginning in 1906 and, consequently, will not be discussed in this volume. The firm, however, had begun to manufacture on a smaller scale long before 1906. Within only three years of the store's founding in 1867, Field and Leiter advertised, on the occasion of the opening of their new cloak department, "a great variety of New and Beautiful Designs of their own manufacture. . . ."[169] From this beginning grew numerous "workshops" serving both Wholesale and Retail with a wide variety of goods and employing hundreds of people.[170] Within the next decade after opening the first workrooms, sewing girls were also making fur garments, lace in Department H of the manufacturing room, and suits and dresses as well as cloaks, in Department E.[171] Elsewhere they turned out bundle shirts, overalls, jackets, linens, flannel and jean drawers,[172] and spring beds, "one of the best in use."[173] Later were added the manufacture of neckwear, suspenders and other types of underwear,[174] plus literally scores of made-to-order articles for the firm's own retail trade.[175] The quantities of men's, women's, and children's wearing apparel, towels, napkins, umbrellas and other articles turned out eventually necessitated the opening of an "Eastern salesroom" in New York City (apparently in 1902 or 1903).[176] In 1900, an average year, the Lace Factory alone made $9,000 in profits; the Underwear Factory, $14,600; the Neckwear Factory, $4,500; and the Suspender Factory, $5,400.[177] Even John Wanamaker of Philadelphia was impressed.[178]

Probably the most interesting single factory was the one for making fur garments. By the time Wanamaker made his visit in 1903, Field's claimed to have the largest factory of this kind in the world.[179] Almost from the time (1872) when furs were first introduced into the firm's wholesale and retail stocks,[180] Field's had made all its own furs in its own factory. This included by 1876 not only women's fur coats, but also muffs, ladies' and children's hats, and men's fur caps and fur gloves.[181] In the early 1880's, with the return of prosperity, the wholesale market for furs began to develop rapidly;[182] and in 1886 a new department (30) in Wholesale was created largely for the purpose of handling furs alone.[183] Sales continued to climb in both Wholesale and Retail[184] until by 1900, it was claimed, Field's was disposing of, on the average, one article of fur apparel every seven minutes and keeping three hundred workers in the fur factories busy the year around producing more fur garments than any other firm on the globe.[185] Field's announced to the wholesale trade that:

> Orders already on our factory's books, call for 100,000 of one kind of skins alone. We maintain a stock of over 200 different kinds. Last year we absorbed 15⅛ per cent of the world's output of Alaska Sealskins.[186]

For preserving the furs, Field's had its own cold-storage rooms[187] and, in fact, built in 1902 a huge fireproof vault, four stories high, that was supposed to be the best equipped and the largest constructed to that time. It contained room for twenty thousand garments at once, and the half-million dollars' worth of sable, silver fox, and Persian lamb, down through coon, calf, goat, and dog-skin coats sold by the wholesale division alone made it a most profitable investment.[188]

The best gross-sales years in wholesale furs about this time were:

1899	$565,000
1900	582,800
1901	575,900
1902	590,600

The best profit years during this same period were:

1903	$23,600
1904	48,800
1905	64,600
1906	70,600[189]

All large companies which control their source of supply or otherwise gain exclusive control of certain merchandise develop as a matter of course their own trademarks for the purpose of identifying their goods. Among other advantages, this enables a firm to win a reputation for a brand bearing its trademark and to own 100 per cent of the good will attaching to the article. Anyone familiar with modern Field's is well aware of the hundreds of such trade names which the store controls and under which its numerous manufactured items are sold. Not much is known, though, about Field's early efforts in this area.

The firm's first trademark was an emblem very similar to the modern shield found on all "Fieldcrest" goods, namely a simple adaptation of the Marshall Field family coat of arms:

This was a "blanket" trademark first introduced in 1871 with the announcement that it "will be upon all goods of our own importation."[190] This simple use of the new trademark was apparently continued through most of the seventies.[191]

A blanket trademark, however, has obvious limitations, particularly when applied to goods not uniform in either style, value, or quality. Field's thus eventually adopted the technique of applying distinct trade names to many individual articles of merchandise which is controlled. A miniature Field shield was printed in the center of many of these trademarks. Just when the first such trade name was devised is difficult to ascertain. One, "Cachemire Italian," a variety of imported silk cloth was mentioned in 1876 as the firm's "OWN BRAND," but there were surely earlier ones.[192]

The failure of any wholesale catalogues which may have been printed during the eighties to endure makes it difficult even to determine exactly when other trademarks were added. That there were many, however, is apparent from the fact that the several existing catalogues of the nineties list many Field's trademarks which had obviously been familiar to the trade for at least several years. An 1890-91 edition, for example, offered "Seamless" dress shields with the familiar Field shield shown in the center of the trademark and listed as patented in November 1886. In the same catalogue other examples of trademarks bearing the Field crest were "Feather Weight" dress shields and "Reversible" ribbons. Some goods, interestingly, simply bore the name of the firm, such as "Marshall Field and Company's Knitting Silk."[193] In 1895 there appeared "The Field Sewing Machine—A first-class high arm Machine with all the Latest Improvements," as well as such Field crested items as "Tartar" and "Santa Maria" ribbons and twenty-one different styles—individually named —of men's linen collars made in Field's workrooms.[194] In 1898 Field's "Perfecto Aristotype Paper," as well as "Marshall Field and Company Dark Room Lamps" were available for photographers. Men's and women's watch movements could be had in Field trade names which reminded the retailer of the exact address of the firm's wholesale house, namely "Adams Street," "Quincy Street," "Franklin Street," and "Fifth Avenue."[195] We do know that as Field's entered the twentieth century its prestige had been well boosted by a long list of trademarks registered in Washington, and the salesmen of all departments were urged to take full advantage of the situation. "Sell more goods put up under our own private brands!"[196]

These innovations, the use of road salesmen, the stepping up of the importation program, and the increased efforts to control manufacturing outlets, all had their effect on the prosperity of the wholesale division in general. Total wholesale sales, after keeping to a long plateau during the years of steadily declining prices in the eighties and early nineties, eventually gathered momentum following the panic of 1893. Beginning with 1897, aided by rising prices and returning prosperity, the sales and profits totals climbed amazingly. Within the last ten years of Mr. Field's life (1897-1906) sales nearly doubled and profits almost tripled.[197] Wholesale had never before been so prosperous. By no means all of the success of the wholesale division was due to Shedd, yet the major innovations and the greatest rise in sales and profits came during his years of influence in this branch. He had good reason to be proud. Marshall Field apparently thought so; he described Shedd as "the best merchant in the United States." [198]

New Hands at the Helm (Continued) 9

Harry Gordon Selfridge and the Retail

To compare John Shedd of the Wholesale with his counterpart in Retail, Harry Selfridge, is to compare a fine team horse with a Kentucky colt. While Shedd, as we have seen, was intelligent, hardworking, and deliberate, Selfridge was brilliant, dramatic, and very much in a hurry. A handsome, dashing, young man, complete with long, carefully trimmed sideburns and a gracious smile, he fascinated people by his presence. His superabundance of energy enabled him to participate actively in civic affairs and the highest society and at the same time foment small revolutions at the store.[1] Unfortunately for Selfridge's soaring ambitions for himself and his branch of the firm, he found that Wholesale came first and that his efficient but less scintillating rival at the head of that division sometimes used his position to thwart Retail's plans. Said Selfridge, impatiently, on one such occasion, "Shedd wears too small a collar." [2]

Selfridge joined Field's in the year 1879, as a young man of twenty-one.[3] Like Shedd, seven years earlier, he started as a stockboy and salesman in Wholesale. Showing considerable ability and determination in this position, he was later raised to the rank of general salesman and allotted Indiana as his territory. His winning personality and electric energy made him a natural person to meet the public; so again he did well. Field, however, in September 1883, asked him to transfer to Retail.[4] In those days, if a salesman was in any position to do so, he resisted any such move; for Retail was considered as distinctly secondary to Wholesale in esteem and lacking in opportunity for the ambitious.[5] Selfridge, however, probably went to Retail with the understanding that he would soon be made an assistant superintendent (under Superintendent J. M. Fleming), if indeed he was not given this title immediately. His performance must have pleased Field, for his salary was increased from $2,000 for his first full year (1884) in Retail to $2,400 for the next.[6] In 1886 he obtained a $1,600 bonus;[7] and by 1887 he had not only taken over Fleming's job, but also had the new title of "General Manager" which carried considerably wider powers than the old "Superintendent." [8]

In Retail, Selfridge proved to be a man bursting with ideas and something of a genius at organization. His "radicalism," disliked in Wholesale, was badly needed in Retail to stir it from the lethargy into which it had temporarily fallen. The former superintendent, though capable enough and a thoughtful appraiser of merchandise, had not been a hustler. Rather than build up the business through advertising and constant improvement, he had been largely content to coast on the firm's reputation and let his department remain under the dominance of Wholesale. When Selfridge came, he hit Retail like a whirlwind. Always dressed in the latest style, he wore a frock coat and "the tails of it," everyone agreed, "would whisk, stand out behind as he'd fly through the store!" [9] Whether it was a plan for tearing out old counters and shelving, rearranging the display of goods, putting in a new system for marking sales slips, remodeling the main entrance to the store, developing a different kind of newspaper "ad," putting in telephones and pneumatic tubes, or building an entire new building, Selfridge was in favor of it if it was new, sounded practical, and stimulated sales.[10] When he had exhausted his own ideas, he obtained permission from Field to visit Boston, Philadelphia, and New York so that he could study the leading department stores of the East and acquire still other ideas with which to experiment. "I can say quite precisely," he later commented, "that I never let well enough alone. . . . No part of an intricate machine such as the retail trade can ever be so 'well' that it cannot be better." [11]

During his managership (1884-1904) a considerable improvement was wrought in the morale of Retail. Everyone sensed that here was a man who was trying to do important things for their branch of the firm; and they were proud to be part of his regime.

Selfridge was that way; he'd inspire you; make you feel you knew how to do things; and he'd do it by talking it out with you, treating you with respect. There was no big front to Selfridge with the help. He was dashing, impressive, and cut quite a figure in the town; but he'd let young men, especially, in the firm argue with him.

* * * * *

He would drop in at your desk sometimes all of a sudden, sit there and talk ten minutes, ask about this and that, debate a thing with you, never talk down to you—and the result was you'd be thrilled for a week. I would literally walk on air for two weeks after he'd done this at my desk. I never met a man capable of putting such inspiration into his employees.[12]

It was the same with the customers. Undoubtedly the hold which Selfridge acquired on Marshall Field's confidence was partly due to the fact that he was so successful in carrying out Field's long-standing determination to make Retail unique as a service institution. Selfridge succeeded in convincing customers that he was looking out for them and that he was personally at their service. When they wished to speak with the head of the retail store, he was available, for every clerk had instructions to telephone Selfridge whenever such a request was made.[13] He seemed to anticipate what customers wanted, particularly the increasingly fashion-conscious women; and Selfridge made every effort to keep Field's the style center of Chicago.[14] Beginning as early as 1900, for instance, he offered the younger set the newest thing in "automobile coats" and "automobile hats" to wear in the new explosive buggies of that era.[15] To fulfill the needs of the coming age of greater recreation, Field's began also to carry a more complete line of sports clothing and equipment, eventually (1906) even manufacturing their own golf balls.[16]

As in Wholesale, keeping up with public demand for more and more goods and services often necessitated creating a brand new department or vastly enlarging an old one. Selfridge became famous for doing both. For example, in order to attract the more select trade, fine pictures and artware were secured for sale and exhibit in the retail store.[17] This included the exclusive control and sale for the West of art goods designed by the much-talked-of William Morris of England. In fact, a complete "Morris Department" was installed for a time in the Singer Building.[18] To broaden the store's appeal generally, Selfridge created Field's famous tearoom, the bargain basement, and the important shoe, furniture, toy, jewelry, and boys' and children's clothing sections.[19] The latter was located in the new 1902 store opposite the women's rest rooms for the convenience of mothers.[20] More for the benefit of patrons than for profit, additional retail workrooms were set up where customers could have their photographs taken or developed, their gloves cleaned, jewelry and shoes repaired, or eyeglasses ground, in addition to the service provided by the older garment and upholstery factories.[21] By 1904 Selfridge had either created or greatly enlarged and improved practically every section in the store.[22] In 1883, there were less than fifty "departments"; when he left, there were one hundred and fifty.[23]

It is a tribute to the greatness of Marshall Field that he did not allow his own natural conservatism to block most of Selfridge's projects. Often Field objected to ideas and occasionally he refused permission to go ahead with them, as when Selfridge proposed what he himself referred to later as a "visionary scheme for establishing Marshall Field stores in the capitals of Britain, France, Germany, Russia, and Spain."[24] For the most part, however, Field wisely let his energetic young manager go ahead and try out his ideas. When they were not

107

entirely successful, he did not reprove. But, as Selfridge himself complained, neither did Field, when an idea was successful, issue many compliments.

Often I prevailed upon him to do things, take chances, much against his will, and when they came off, he seldom was inclined to unbend and confess that, perhaps, he had been wrong. I fancy he always regarded me as a young man in a great hurry.[25]

Although by 1889 Selfridge had risen in only ten years from an ordinary stock boy to the head of a multi-million-dollar retail store and was earning $20,000 a year,[26] it did not occur to him to rest upon his laurels. He knew that December 31, 1889, marked the end of another two-year agreement between Field and his other partners,[27] so Selfridge, with characteristic assurance, went into Mr. Field's office and asked to be taken into the new partnership to be formed for the coming year. "To say that Mr. Field was astonished and delighted," Selfridge recalled, "would be a gross misreading of that famous man's feelings. He was dumbfounded, and rather angry." [28] Nevertheless on January 1, 1890, when the new partnership was announced, Selfridge found himself included and drawing a 2/85 share.[29] The necessary $200,000 was mostly provided by Marshall Field; but Selfridge's share of the profits enabled him to pay the amount back within a short period of time.[30] In 1893, when Shedd was also permitted to come into the partnership, Selfridge was raised to a 2½/85 share. The shares of both men were then gradually increased until they reached their maximum in 1900, Selfridge owning 9 per cent of the business and Shedd 10 per cent.[31]

Retail Departmental Expansion

Selfridge's expansion of old departments and inclusion in the store of so many new lines were but the final steps in making Marshall Field and Company a "department store." In this one respect Field's had fallen considerably behind the trend set by such stores as The Fair in Chicago, Macy's in New York, and Wanamaker's in Philadelphia, which were making little pretense of being ought but universal providers, carrying everything and anything that could be sold at a profit.[32] Selfridge, with an eye to the future, undoubtedly saw that if business and profits were to grow, Field's must, like these stores, expand its appeal to the public. Each new department meant new customers for all departments. If a customer liked the store for one article, she was apt to buy others when she came—but only if they were there to buy.[33] There were, furthermore, certain economies in retailing on a large scale just as there were in any business. The cost of buying, advertising, selling, and delivering, other things remaining equal, did not seem to increase in equal proportion to the quantities of goods sold. Thus, if new goods could be introduced and sold without an equal increase in expense, it was only good business.[34]

108

9. New Hands at the Helm (Continued)

It required, nevertheless, all of Selfridge's persuasiveness to convince Field of the merit of such rapid expansion; and each new section was acceded to with considerable reluctance. Field to the very end continued to deny stoutly that the retail branch of his firm was a "department" store,[35] and more than once on those grounds had his way in keeping out new branches. When two of Selfridge's assistants, sent to gather new ideas in the large eastern stores, returned with the suggestion that Field's put in a book department such as John Wanamaker's had, Field objected: "Let Col. McClurg[36] sell the books; we're in the dry-goods business. Never forget that."[37] But call it what he might, Retail would never be the same again.

It was said that:

> . . . When each fresh department was added to Marshall Field's store it was as if a cyclone had gone forth among the smaller houses which were in the same line of business. When Marshall Field opened any new department, say of cutlery or hardware or millinery, jewelry [sic], etc., or what not, he would run it at cut rates so as to give him the command of the field, contenting himself with the profits of the other departments. Against such a power, so concentrated in turn against each detachment of the enemy, or the competitor, nothing could stand. The consumer is loath to pay a nickel more to an old tradesman for what he can get for a nickel less down town. So it has come to pass that Chicago is honeycombed from end to end with elderly men who twenty years ago had businesses of their own in retail stores by which they expected to make a living of their own and to have a comfortable competence on which to retire in their old age. They reckoned without their Marshall Field, however, and others of his class who have passed through the streets of Chicago with much the same effect upon the smaller stores as that which the angel of the Lord had upon the besieging host which surrounded Jerusalem under Sennacherib.[38]

Unfortunately, there was undoubtedly some truth to the charge.[39] But, of course, as the writer of the above admitted, that was business; and it would have been more surprising had Field resisted the opportunity to enlarge his store and his sales (which, as we have noted, he sometimes did!). Once he had consented to open a new section, it was naturally pushed with all the energy and by all the legitimate competitive devices that the law allowed. Selfridge was, more than anything else, a promoter. After he had won Field's approval of a new department, he worked hard and advertised vigorously to make it a paying success.

On March 29 and 30, 1889, Chicagoans read in their newspapers the advertisement reproduced on page 110. Emphasizing quality and wide selections in style, Selfridge gave the shoes plenty of publicity;[41] and like most of the other new sections, this one prospered mightily.[42] Only seven months after opening the section, it had to be enlarged;[43] and at the end of its first year Selfridge was able to boast that:

> Our Shoe Department can probably point to a more rapid growth in sales than can any similar department ever organized in Chicago.[44]

MARSHALL FIELD & CO.

RETAIL.

We announce for TODAY the first

OPENING

Of our newly organized department containing

Fine Shoes.

The public is cordially invited.

Within a decade, Field's held in stock "more than 50,000 pairs of women's and children's shoes," alone.[45] And in 1902 the reliable trade journal, the *Chicago Dry Goods Reporter,* announced:

> The shoe section [of Marshall Field and Company] is perhaps the largest of its kind in the world, with more space devoted to the retailing of shoes than in any other store. It is arranged in separate sections for the different classes of goods and includes everything from baby shoes to the heavy hunting boots for men.[46]

Field's, to keep so large a section staffed and to keep up with the demand, was forced to advertise for salesclerks, a rare thing for the house.[47]

The furniture section had its real beginning in 1896-98.[48] Until that time, the firm had carried some furniture but only as an incidental feature of other departments. In the fourth-floor "bedding section" in the midst of pillowcases and blankets, patrons could find mattresses and springs and the then fashionable brass beds.[49] Most other furniture items were part of the upholstery department and Manufacturing Division. All upholstered furniture was made by Field's in its own workrooms and placed on display still uncovered. The customer could then select her own fabric to be made to order.[50] The only furniture items which did not fall into this category were antiques and expen-

110

9. New Hands at the Helm (Continued)

sive imported pieces from France and England which were carefully kept within a glass-enclosed room. This room most nearly approached a real furniture section; but, as one employee appropriately remarked, the department was more "like a museum." People would come [to Field's] and look and then go to the Fair to buy." [51]

In 1896, an enlarged furniture section within the upholstery department was created;[52] and an attempt was made to build up the sales volume. In an effort to do this the mistake was made at first of purchasing many inexpensive, locally-made pieces of too poor quality to appeal to the typical Field customer. It did not sell even after several years' trial and could be disposed of only through the annual and special sales.[53] In 1898, Mr. W. H. Miller, an assistant to the buyer in the bedding section, was put in charge.[54] He, along with W. E. Clarke, head of the upholstery department, of which furniture remained one section for a time,[55] won permission to make a buying trip to Grand Rapids, where they purchased carefully the better quality merchandise, purposely to avoid further competition with the less expensive lines sold by the mail-order houses and such large houses as John M. Smyth. Field's own Wholesale handled the cheaper furniture, but Miller and Clarke hoped to attract to Retail a clientele more interested in good styling and fine quality than in price alone. The first purchases were mostly of the conventional heavy oak furniture popular in that day. Later Field's worked with several of the good manufacturing houses to develop new lines and to improve the staple items. Thus "Mission" furniture, with its plainer surfaces, "Flanders," a design worked out by Miller and the Berkey and Gay Company, and the always popular "Eighteenth Century" and Colonial patterns were added. The floor area devoted to furniture was enlarged and the new tables and chairs, "high-boys," folding beds, and box-couches were put on display right along with the antiques and the overstuffed furniture still made in Field's workrooms.[56]

Good results were not immediate, and for some time the old reliable brass beds continued to be as much a feature item as any of the other pieces in the section.[57] Total sales picked up only gradually; and the profit aspect of the venture was discouraging, to say the least.

	Sales		Profits	
1898	$123,200		$ 7,142	(loss)
1899	122,000		11,733	(loss)
1900	161,900		171	
1901	161,000		4,635	(loss)
1902	282,500		17,773	(loss)

Sales eventually took a strong hold, however; and beginning in 1903 the furniture department started to climb once and for all out of the "red" in the profit and loss ledger.[58]

The most novel addition made by Selfridge, and one always mentioned in popular accounts of his career, was the "bargain basement."

The use of the basement as a salesroom was not new when Selfridge came to Retail. At least from 1858 a part of the area below the first floor had been allotted to display and sales as well as to storage and furnace. The basement in those days was not, however, a separate entity in itself and was by no means a special "bargain" salesroom. It was simply an extension of the regular retail or wholesale departments made necessary by cramped conditions on the upstairs floors.[59] Not until 1879 did the idea of a basement salesroom to present a new, lower-priced line of retail goods disassociated from those shown on the upper floors take form. On May 1, 1879, for the first time, a Marshall Field and Company advertisement announced a newly opened, special "Department of CHEAP DRESS GOODS" in the basement, in addition to the printed cambrics, domestics, cottons, and prints already on display there.[60] This was followed in 1880 by featuring in the "Basement Salesroom" a sale of domestic cottons, such as sheetings, pillowcase muslins, shirtings, and canton flannels at "greatly reduced prices" and, more significantly, by the establishment of a "Permanent Department" for the sale of low-priced houskeeping linens.[61] The basement was obviously already on the way to becoming an established "residue" area for each of the correlated departments on the floors above.

For some reason, however, the scheme was not pushed. Although the basement departments were continued,[62] there is little mention of them in the firm's advertising from May 1880 until the first part of 1885.[63] It remained, thus, for Selfridge, who by 1885 was gradually insinuating himself into the place of Fleming, to snatch up this embryo department and make it a distinctive feature at Field's. Selfridge's original plan was to create for himself an outlet for the odds and ends of stock from upstairs that were marked down in price and for which formerly a special department was sometimes created,[64] if it were not simply placed on sale within the department.[65] A bargain basement is a solution in particular to two common problems in merchandising. First, in this way, the regular stock in the main departments can be kept in perfect order all the time. That is, when an assortment goes out of style, becomes limited in quantity and broken in size or color, or when there is an assortment of seconds, the lot can then be sent to the basement and placed on sale at an inviting price.[66] This frees the shelves in the regular sections for a new shipment of a complete line. Secondly, goods will occasionally not find a ready sale. When this happens, if they can be reduced in price to a point where they will appeal to the purse of the basement shopper, they soon find their way to the bargain counters in the downstairs store. Thus a quick turnover of the fine quality goods in the regular retail sections is assured, and stocks there are always fresh and new.[67]

Undoubtedly enjoying the prospect of promoting his idea, Selfridge enlarged the basement's lower-priced section and, early in 1885, began a persistent campaign of advertisement. On March 23, 1885:[68]

State and Washington-sts.

Announcement!

Realizing the Growing Demand for

Lower Priced Goods!

And to meet the wants of our

Rapidly Increasing Business,

*We have enlarged our Salesroom on Basement Floor,
and will open*

Today!

Several Departments, including

*Cheap Silks, Dress Goods, Embroideries, Housekeeping Linens,
White Goods, Underwear, Hosiery, Handkerchiefs,
Gloves, Ribbons, Cloaks, and Shawls,*

And These Lines Will Be Kept Full
and Complete.

Specially Attractive Bargains
Will Be Offered!

This notice was followed by a regular outpouring of basement advertisements during the remainder of the eighties and thereafter.[69]

The emphasis on the words "low priced" and "cheap" in the basement's early advertisements[70] had, however, one unfortunate effect.

113

They seemed to give credence to the suspicion that Marshall Field had seen the handwriting on the wall and was sacrificing his merchandising ideals to the pressures of the times. One writer in 1890 commented:

There used to be such a thing as an "established" business. There isn't any longer. The public isn't sentimental nowadays. . . . Even Marshall Field must meet the demand or the demand will leave him. He is too good a merchant not to see which way the wind is blowing, and, although basement bargain counters may be distasteful to him, nevertheless you can find the basement bargain counters at State and Washington Streets, with the same class of goods on them exactly as you find on the cheap counters at State and Adams streets.[71]

Even before this book was published, either Field objected or else Selfridge anticipated such comments; for a noticeable change took place in the phraseology of his advertisements. While low prices continued to be hawked, beginning as early as 1887[72] the emphasis was placed increasingly upon the idea of "Less Expensive but Reliable" grades of goods.[73] This sort of advertising and the resultant success of the basement store had unexpected results; for as its sales continued to grow over the years, Selfridge was forced more and more, not only to sell marked-down quality items, but to sanction the purchase of entirely separate lots of different-grade merchandise for this part of the store in order to supply the demand. These goods duplicated in less expensive wares what was carried upstairs and thus made the basement more than ever a store in itself.[74] And as business steadily increased,[75] he rushed into the basement line after line of merchandise not formerly carried there until by 1890 there were thirty departments[76] and by 1906 the basement was a complete store, selling, along with everything else, trunks, men's and ladies' furnishings, parasols, toilet articles, hosiery, laces, linens, shoes, carpets, bedding, and even furs.[77] In 1902 Field's announced that their "GREATER NEW BASEMENT SALESROOM" [78] (as a result of the erection of a new building)[79] was the "largest single salesroom in the world, taking up about seven-eighths of the block." [80]
Basement sales compared with those in the main sections were as follows for 1900 to 1906:

	Main	Basement
1900	$ 9,748,560	$3,064,840
1901	10,684,590	3,490,180
1902	13,507,230	4,241,950
1903	16,005,930	5,467,860
1904	16,737,210	5,886,690
1905	18,533,880	6,237,930
1906	19,441,870	6,165,760[81]

Here then was over the years a complete evolution of the basement, from a place for storage and a few overflow sections of the first floor Retail, through a section serving as an outlet for odds and ends from all the upstairs sections, to its culmination in a store by itself.

114

PLATE I

MARSHALL FIELD

24-year-old stellar salesman for Cooley, Farwell & Co.

PLATE II

LAKE STREET EAST FROM CLARK ABOUT 1867

The large building in the center with flag was occupied by Potter Palmer 1857-1865. Picture was taken when Field, Leiter & Co. occupied the premises after adding fifth story.

PLATE III

FIELD, LEITER & CO., STATE AND WASHINGTON STREETS BEFORE THE GREAT FIRE

Rise of Retail

Selfridge's ingenuity in developing new lines, in expanding the numbers of departments, and in displaying and advertising goods was reflected in the sales columns. During the period of his general managership (1887 to 1904) sales for the retail branch as a whole climbed from $4,932,000 to the startling total of $22,295,000, an increase of which any merchant might well be proud.[82]

Fortunately Marshall Field's retail chief proved that he could not only get rid of goods but also sell at a profit.[83] The purchasing under Selfridge was done with efficiency and dispatch; and although there were not the numbers of opportunities for introducing sensational new methods into buying that there were in selling, Selfridge instituted some new ideas even into this aspect of merchandising.

One of the major factors preventing any very radical departure in purchasing methods was the long-standing subservience of the retail branch of Marshall Field and Company to the wholesale. In the early days of the firm the close ties between the two branches had given the Retail a distinct advantage over its competitors. Marshall Field and Company's Retail could buy its products for less at the Wholesale; it had first choice of the new goods; and the delivery of goods to its shelves was almost instantaneous. The entire accounting, administrative, and buying organization had been devised on the assumption that Retail would continue, by its very nature, to remain dependent on Wholesale.

The system was of such long standing by the time Selfridge arrived that any attempt to compel Wholesale to weaken its hold on retail functions was bound to be a difficult undertaking, despite the fact that the two branches were obviously headed in different directions. Marshall Field and Company, Retail, was in these latter years of the nineteenth century catering increasingly to a more and more sophisticated customer.[84] No longer was Chicago a rough-hewn, muddy-laned, frontier metropolis as when Field and Leiter first opened their doors. By 1890, when Selfridge was beginning his career, Chicago was already an industrial and transportation center of well over one million people eagerly conscious of fashions and finicky in their tastes. Particularly did this seem to be true of the class of women who made it a habit to trade at Field's; they knew what was the best, were used to having it, and wanted it.[85] Wholesale, which continued to cater, as always before, to the less exacting, small rural and western merchant, had difficulty in appreciating the needs of its own Retail and was, as the years passed, less and less able to supply its wants.[86] Yet the rules remained: "All orders . . . placed by Retail, must be done through Wholesale."[87] "All goods bought in Retail . . . must be confirmed by Heads of Dep'ts. at Wholesale. This order must be strictly enforced."[88]

The severing of this tie was not complete even by the time of Field's death. It was a gradual process, accomplished by the recurring necessities of the moment, and it came hard. The older heads in the firm were reluctant to interfere with the traditional section head's independence; but as the retail buyers tended more and more to seek their goods elsewhere than the firm's own Wholesale, the latter were constantly reminded by the executives of the advantages of the old system. Among the topics referred to at a meeting in November 1902, for example, were:

The great advantage to the Retail, in being able to supply its needs through the Wholesale, and the great importance of the Wholesale and Retail acting conjointly in purchasing.

In the same meeting:

Regarding the extraordinary buying power of this house. Great businesses are combined, so that large orders can be placed, and consequent concessions in prices obtained. We are already in this strong position as the Wholesale and Retail together are enormous users of goods.[89]

As time went by, retail buyers, nevertheless, continued increasingly to strike out on their own. The volume of sales of Retail alone was so tremendous that it found itself able to take advantage of some of the cost-saving tactics that were practiced by Wholesale, without at the same time having to buy the type of goods that the Wholesale used. Retail purchased ready-made clothing, jewelry, furs, and upholstery directly from the firm's own manufacturing division, which gave it exclusive styles at no greater cost than Wholesale acquired them.[90] In addition, Retail bought directly from other manufacturers and succeeded in obtaining exclusive agencies in Chicago of numerous other famous and fashionable articles. It acquired, for example, the exclusive handling of such items as Tiffany glass, Grueby pottery,[91] Morris art goods and wallpaper,[92] and Brokaw's men's clothing.[93] Furthermore, the Retail buyers, like Wholesale, bought extensively in foreign markets; they created their own designs; and they had goods made to their specifications by numerous American and European manufacturers.[94] The number of retail dry-goods buyers sent abroad increased from two in 1875 to twenty-one in 1906.[95]

More and more Marshall Field and Company, Retail, thus not only purchased elsewhere than its own Wholesale; but it sought to eliminate *all* jobbers and middlemen. Direct buying from the manufacturer meant quicker delivery from the original source of supply and thus immediate response to changes in fashion and price. Contrary to the popular conception, eliminating the middleman does not always cut costs; for the retailer must then perform for himself all the freighting, warehousing, financing, and selecting formerly done by the middleman. But for a huge institution like Field's, already equipped for such tasks,[96] it did mean important savings. Like Wholesale, Retail was able to pay cash, buy in huge quantities, and take advantage of instances where manufacturers unloaded their excess goods at low prices;[97] and the results were good.[98]

Two important indices of the efficiency of a firm's management are the annual gross margin and stock-turn. Unfortunately no accurate

9. New Hands at the Helm (Continued)

annual gross margin figures have ever been computed for Field's for the years before 1906 or apparently ever can be. Early accounting methods make it impossible to determine whether or not discounts were included by the firm in its costs and even whether certain discounts that are mentioned refer to the vendor or the buyer.

As seen in Table VI, however, accurate stock-turn figures from 1878 are available and are of considerable help even by themselves. For the Retail as a whole they seem to indicate a continuously high rate of performance throughout those years. The store's rate of turnover in relation, first of all, to that of most modern department stores shows up very favorably. A typical large department store today has a stock-turn of between four and five. As seen below, Field's retail turnover never fell below four and for almost half the years was five or over. These figures, secondly, are interesting to compare with Macy's, a great New York retailer of those days as well as of the present time. Professor Ralph Hower in his history of this store has been able to find few figures for the seventies and eighties, but these few indicate a higher annual stock-turn than Marshall Field and Company. Yet, while Macy's rate dropped rapidly during the nineties, Field's rate remained relatively constant until by the late nineties the two stores were experiencing an almost equal turnover of their wares. Professor Hower attributes the early high rate to a management policy of that time which called for limiting stocks only to fast-selling merchandise, and frequent and drastic price cutting in order to clear less popular items from the shelves. This was done even in the face of lowered profits and loss of customer good-will which resulted from the lack of selection and the inability of customers to depend on Macy's to satisfy their particular needs. Later under different management more attention was given to keeping large assortments of goods and maintaining higher margins. As a result by 1897 Macy's turnover declined to an average of a little less than five.[99]

This comparison with Macy's serves to point up some significant facts about Marshall Field and Company, Retail. In the first place Field's in contrast to Macy's, benefited from the guidance of a single management during all those years. Even while such individualists as Selfridge and Shedd directed the separate destinies of the Retail and Wholesale there remained always the strong, overall guiding hand of Marshall Field to insist on certain basic principles of merchandising. One such policy in both Wholesale and Retail was that "stocks must be kept *low, clean and well assorted.*"[100] As noted in Chapter VI[101] Mr. Field frequently admonishd his subordinates from Shedd and Selfridge on down to "Keep Stocks Turning"[102] by not overbuying any particular items; but at the same time a warning was always added: "Assortments of goods should be complete all the year!"[103] Field's management worked hard to keep prices low, but, conscious of the importance of complete customer satisfaction and of the institutional aspect of the store, put the major emphasis on quality rather than price. "Volume of business doesn't make any real difference," he told his employees. He wanted no artificial or forced growth of sales volume by unusual advertising or other selling pressure but the "steady, cumulative patronage of satisfied customers." [104]

In comparing Retail with the company's own Wholesale it is interesting to note that there is a similarity in the two divisions both in the average rate of turnover for the entire period and in the rates of particular years. In those years in which Retail had an especially low turnover, Wholesale tended to experience the same phenomenon; and the like was true in times of high rates. As might be expected, these deviations from the norm usually coincided with stages in the business cycle. One notable difference between the two divisions, however, was the fact that while Retail figures after the turn of the century showed no marked difference from those in the seventies, a glance at the Wholesale column reveals a noticeable trend over the years toward a lower turnover. It is obvious from the official bulletins issued by those in charge of management that this change was the result of no alteration in policy.[105] Rather it was evidence of the growing difficulty of jobbing efficiently such a huge variety of merchandise. As noted in the preceding chapter, Wholesale was required by the changing times continually to add new merchandise to its stocks—this in the face of greater specialization by many retailers and direct buying on their part from manufacturers. The fact that the Wholesale's turnover failed to rise as did Retail's in the prosperous years after the turn of the century is not in itself conclusive evidence this early of any inherent sickness in this division of the business, but there were those in the firm at that time who seriously wondered.[106]

Stock-turn rates in both retailing and wholesaling vary considerably by type of merchandise. In modern retailing, for example, food stores and butcher shops must sell their produce quickly or it will spoil; and since food customers buy almost every day the turnover is very great. Furniture and jewelry stores, on the other hand, maintain large assortments, can keep their stock for long periods without deterioration, and thus have a lower turnover. Unfortunately not much is known about the breakdown of Field's individual retail sections except as indicated in the table below. Obviously dry-goods items in most years sold more rapidly than the house-furnishings items listed. For the wholesale departments we have a more detailed information and it bears some interesting contrasts to the statistics on Retail. Among wholesale departments, rugs and carpets, for example, enjoyed a turnover as great as or greater than any other department. Other high-ranking items (stock-turns of six to ten) were printed yard goods, blankets, notions and cabinet hardware. Merchandise with the lowest turnovers (one to three) were gloves, underwear, hosiery, and ready-made clothing in general,[107] items which in modern retailing are usually the faster-moving goods. The reason for this variation between the merchandise of the two divisions no doubt lies in the fact that Wholesale purchased its ready-made articles in huge lots from the manufacturers once or twice a year. The retailer is inclined to buy

118

clothing in small lots only as he needs it. Furthermore, Marshall Field's Wholesale obviously experienced some difficulty selling the newer, ready-made articles where the style factor was strong in comparison with such staples as yard goods and carpets.[108] Most retailers, perhaps with considerable justification, felt that their chances of satisfying the demand for the very latest style in clothing were much better

TABLE VI

AVERAGE STOCK-TURN OF MARSHALL FIELD AND COMPANY BY RETAIL AND WHOLESALE FOR 1878-1906[a]

| Year | Retail | | | | Total | |
	Dry Goods	Rugs & Carpets[b]		Uphol-stery	Retail Average	Wholesale Average
1878	5.5	4.0		3.5	5.3	5.9
1879	5.3	3.2		3.3	5.3	5.4
1880	5.0	2.4		3.5	4.4	4.4
1881	5.2	3.3		4.0	5.1	5.2
1882	5.6	3.0		4.1	5.2	5.1
1883	5.7	3.3		3.6	5.1	5.0
1884	5.8	2.6		3.1	4.7	4.7
1885	5.9	2.6		3.4	4.6	4.5
1886	5.2	1.8	2.4	3.2	4.1	4.1
1887	5.8	2.0	2.7	3.2	4.5	4.5
1888	6.4	2.2	3.6	2.9	4.7	4.4
1889	6.3	2.1	3.1	2.9	4.8	4.6
1890	6.3	2.4	4.2	3.3	5.1	4.9
1891	5.7	3.2	2.0	4.3	4.8	4.8
1892	5.9	3.7	2.0	3.7	5.4	5.4
1893	5.6	3.9	1.7	3.7	4.4	4.3
1894	5.2	4.8	1.8	3.4	5.3	5.5
1895	5.8	3.7	2.2	3.7	4.9	4.8
1896	6.0	2.6	1.9	4.8	4.3	4.0
1897	6.2	3.2	1.8	4.6	4.8	4.1
1898	5.8	3.8	1.6	4.1	4.6	4.4
1899	5.5	5.2	1.9	4.4	4.8	4.5
1900	5.3	3.9	2.1	4.1	4.1	3.7
1901	5.7	4.8	2.3	4.5	4.8	4.6
1902	6.4	3.6	2.3	5.0	5.1	4.8
1903	7.2	4.1	2.6	5.4	5.0	4.4
1904	8.2	3.8	2.7	6.5	5.3	4.5
1905	7.5	4.5	2.8	6.9	5.4	4.8
1906	6.9	3.4	2.5	7.4	5.0	4.5

[a]Accounting ledgers, 1878-1906, Comptroller's safe, Marshall Field & Co. General Offices.
[b]After 1885 "Rugs" and "Carpets" were organized as separate departments.

when they were dealing directly with the manufacturer themselves than with any sort of middleman.

Anti-Department-Store Agitation

Not everyone was happy to congratulate Field's on the success of its expansion into new lines and on its cost-cutting methods. Hundreds of small retailers whose fields were invaded found themselves undersold and outsold as Mandel's, The Fair, Carson's, Schlesinger and Mayers, and Field's endlessly expanded.[109] When the departmentalizing of the great State Street houses and similar firms all over the United States reached its climax in the middle nineties, it suddenly brought down upon itself an outpouring of pent-up wrath from smaller merchants and from a fearful public that was becoming all too aware of the dangers of monopoly in "big business." It began during the panic years of 1893 and 1894 when the pressure on the independent man was particularly great. The large department stores, by running "bargain" advertisements, convinced the economy-minded shopper that they were the places to buy.[110] Thousands of smaller merchants, with little capital to tide them over the depression, failed in 1893 and the years following.[111] By 1898 so much of the business was flowing into the hands of the department stores, it was gloomily predicted that if they were allowed to continue to grow and expand, the small, independent dealers would be ruined.[112]

The denials of Marshall Field that his store was a department store[113] did not spare his firm any of the verbal bombardment received by the others. Rumors even developed that Wanamaker had combined with Field's and Jordan Marsh and Company of Boston to make a colossal mercantile combination that would be able to sweep away all opposition.[114]

Fears of this sort brought on a wave of anti-department-store agitation and attempts to legislate the largest stores out of business. Retail associations of smaller businessmen were formed to bring a combined pressure on the state assembly for the necessary laws;[115] and despite the lack of newspaper support, considerable publicity was given to the dangers involved in the situation.[116] In some instances, in other parts of the country, minor successes were obtained. In Denver, for example, this took the form of a graduated tax so devised that it made a store of more than four departments almost impossible to operate.[117] But on the whole, the wealth and influence of the department stores, and above all, the insatiable desire of the women for the bargains and superior services provided by the larger stores, won the day for the big institutions.[118] Numerous bills were introduced but were always eventually side-tracked.[119] By the time the agitation died down, Field's and the other department stores had grown larger than ever.[120]

Customer Services

10

The Field Customer

I T HAS BEEN CORRECTLY SAID THAT

In the larger cities there are well-defined gradations in department stores. One attracts to itself the better class trade, and handles the more expensive lines of goods. To another goes the medium-class trade, while the management of a third seeks to cater to the cheaper and lower class trade.[1]

Most contemporaries would undoubtedly have agreed that Field's in the late nineteenth century was the store for society people. Many a little Chicago girl of the nineties skipped rope to the tune of "tar-ra-ra-boom-de-ay" and sang the words:

> All the girls who wear high heels
> They trade down at Marshall Field's
> All the girls who scrub the floor,
> They trade at the Boston store.[2]

Attracted by the elaborate lace robes,[3] the latest Paris millinery,[4] and the diamond and pearl brooches,[5] and the general absence of "clap-trap and sensationalism,"[6] the carriage trade drove up in style in their expensive equipages, boasting a retinue of coachman, butler, and maid.[7]

In harmony with the quality of such customers, the store endeavored to provide these women with every possible convenience. The aim was to make trading as easy and comfortable as possible.[8] To this end the stock was arranged with care. In order that madam, in the new 1902 store, might not be made uneasy or nervous by the hurry and bustle of crowds on this first floor, piece goods, which required some time to select, were purposely relegated to the second floor, where her decision could be made in an atmosphere of restfulness and quiet.[9] In order that the shopper might have a certain privacy and also not be obliged to take more steps than necessary, the stocks were divided and arranged as they belonged together—men's furnishings were grouped together in seclusion in the north end of the first and second floors where a gentleman could "do his shopping without passing through the sections so largely patronized by women"; and by the same token, in the lingerie section the feminine shopper could find complete privacy to select a trousseau or a layette; while notions, novelties, and the "many little things a woman wants each day in the year" were displayed together on the first floor.[10] In the ladies' garment section, to retain an unhurried air, only a few costly gowns were displayed in cases; and little stock boys were employed to carry away all the gowns shown the

121

customer while she was making up her mind.[11] To aid her in coming to a decision and at the same time to prevent her from becoming fatigued, models were employed to display the gowns.[12]

If the expensive and the exclusive attracted the "Gold Coast" to Field's, the advertisement of prices that were "during every business day in the year . . . unquestionably the lowest in Chicago," [13] also drew a very liberal representation from all the other classes in Chicago.[14] The services and comforts of the Field's way of trading too were theirs to enjoy. From the first Field's carried a variety of goods designed to appeal to almost all classes of trade.[15] In later years it was apparent, however, that Field's felt it had acquired too much of a reputation for catering to the rich, and it made thus a particular effort to broaden its appeal. The opening of the basement bargain center was only one indication of this trend in the firm's merchandising policy. By the end of the old century and the beginning of the new, while it was still soliciting the patronage of the more wealthy,[16] much of its advertising was especially aimed at the popular trade—the economical buyers.[17] *"We have built this great institution for the people,"* Field's ads claimed, "to be their store, their down-town home. . . ." [18] That this policy was in effect was brought out even in the arrangement of stock. On one side of the millinery aisle, for example, were the "parlor millinery," cases sheltering fabulously expensive matched sets of trimmed hats and neckwears, while on the other side long tables were "crowded with popular priced 'ready-to-wear' hats." [19] "We wish to wipe out completely," the Retail manager told his employees, "any thought that merely because this store includes in its great stocks some of the finest merchandise made that it is necessarily a high-priced store." [20]

Field Courtesy and Service

If Field's had extended its courtesies and services only to the heavy purchasers, and subtly denied them to the bargain hunters, the store certainly would not have become famous. Field's fame for its treatment of customers has come from its unique ability to give masses of people the feeling that they have been served individually—and whether they bought anything or not. In the firm's youth when his customers numbered in the hundreds[21] Marshall Field was able to convey an air of gentility, leisure, and respectability to the store. When in later years he succeeded in providing the same atmosphere for hundreds of thousands,[22] he made Marshall Field and Company one of the most talked-about stores in the world.[23]

The fact that it *pays* to follow a generous policy in the matter of customer treatment[24] can be considered the cornerstone of the entire structure of the idea. From the small beginnings of personal greetings which Mr. Field extended each morning to the visitors who entered his store[25] came the inspiration for the actual stationing of an official host or "greeter" inside the Washington Street entrance. Had this individual been a mere tip-collecting doorman, he would have been a most ordinary fixture to be sure. But Field's greeter was a well-paid[26] man of considerable importance to the store. He welcomed all patrons with a flourish, calling many of them by name, and made them feel genuinely at home.

I'd get a name, write it down, and at night at home I'd go over the names fixing them with faces in my memory. If I wasn't sure who they were, I'd check them up . . . and see if the right spelling was what I had in my book. I could only write down the names the way I heard them. If a lady would come two or three times I'd remember her. They'd be surprised when I'd call them by name, and pleased. Sometimes a lady would say, "Why, I'm from out of town. I haven't been here in four years." I had names of hundreds of people from out of town. I'd get their names when they arrived by listening. I'd get the blue books from out of town and look up the names there, too. . . . After autos came it was much easier for I'd get their licenses and check up that way.

Country people in the old days were more shy than city people, and didn't come so much to Field's, but later on they started to come. . . .

I always made it a point to watch out for out-of-towners. I can tell them right off. In my business if you've got half sense you learn to tell things like that right off. I made it a point in old days to take an out-of-towner as he came up to the door and show him right in to the ushers and present them. . . .

My job has been to be the same to everybody, to make them feel Marshall Field's has been polite.[27]

The door man and ushers (floormen), identifiable by the traditional carnation in their buttonholes, were called upon to reply to queries concerning not only the store proper but the surrounding environs of the city.[28] From this grew by 1902 the full-fledged information bureau, "in charge of courteous attendants," with its myriad subsidiary services such as a cab and messenger call, a local theater ticket office, sub post office, a telegraph office, a railroad, steamer, city, and store guide, local and long-distance telephone exchange, free stenographic service, dictionaries and directories, not to mention the universal clock showing the exact time of day at a given moment in almost any city in the world.[29] By way of special services, schoolteachers, who could not cash their pay checks in the nearest saloon like other folk, were, beginning in 1895, permitted to bring them to Field's for payment. Sometimes as much as $20,000 worth were cashed in one day.[30] For the benefit of the foreign visitors during the 1893 World's Fair, the store stationed interpreters at the doors, "guides ready to take any nationals through the store, talking to them in their native tongues if it be French, German, Spanish, all the major modern tongues." There was also a booth set up in the store to offer assistance in language either in buying or sightseeing.[31]

Again from the small beginning, where doorboys opened doors and in bad weather brushed snow from the coats and furs of customers and checked their umbrellas, came eventually the parcel checkroom. In 1902 this was located adjacent to the reading and writing rooms.[32] These reading and writing and waiting rooms had their origin in 1879 (or shortly thereafter) on the second floor of the Singer Building in a small area surrounding the open well[33] and in the businesslike rest rooms in the basement for the sole use of patrons.[34] In 1893 when the annex was opened to the people of Chicago, the covered bridge over Holden court was utilized as a haven of rest for the weary,[35] in addition to its own newly appointed and complete waiting and rest rooms and lavatories.[36]

In 1902 these facilities were still further expanded and considerably enhanced. Wood-paneled library and writing rooms fitted with deep, luxurious Oriental rugs and comfortable mahogany and green leather furniture provided the latest thing in comfort. Tired patrons found an unlimited supply of popular magazines and daily newspapers to while away the time; or the maid in constant attendance would, on request, pass out literature and poetry from the large catalogued library. Desks were supplied with an abundance of stationery for writing notes to one's friends.[37] Beyond the library and writing rooms was the new "rest room" proper, "large, airy and inviting" with its green willow rockers, armchairs, and settees, and Madras window hangings filtering the light from the windows.[38] As in the writing rooms, a maid was in constant attendance here, also.[39] In the inner recesses of this room were three maids who were in charge of the lavatory, one of thirty-nine identical such rooms located throughout the building. These maids supplied free of charge to the guests of the store, "soap, face and talcum powder, individual flannel cloths for powdering, hair pins, safety pins, needles, thread, tape shoe laces, shoe buttons, pearl buttons, button hooks, scissors, sewing silk and hooks and eyes." [40] The floors were of white marble, the fittings of porcelain, the walls lined with mirrors; and the furniture and dressing tables were of white enamel. Each dressing table was provided with an electric curling iron, brushes and combs.[41] Also to be found here were scales and "measuring machines"—another convenience for the feminine shopper. As a final touch, the surroundings were sometimes enhanced by bouquets of fresh flowers.[42]

In addition to these rooms, the store in 1902 and 1903 boasted a "silence room," for "quiet rest for women and children," [43] and in 1907 waiting rooms exclusively for men.[44] Starting in 1902 in conjunction with these various types of rest rooms, there was a medical room with all the appliances of a regular hospital and staffed with a trained nurse.[45]

Associated with the rest rooms was the children's nursery. At first the library and writing rooms contained small rockers and desks with tot-sized wastebaskets and chairs for the particular benefit of the youngsters of tired mothers.[46] Not long afterwards, in response to many inquiries and requests, a baby nursery was provided, in charge of a competent nurse, where mothers could leave their children while on shopping errands in the store. The room was furnished with the necessary cribs, cradles, rocking chairs, and a stock of toys. Unfortunately, however, experience soon showed it to be unwise to make the quarters too attractive lest unscrupulous mothers take advantage of the privi-

10. Customer Services

leges of free nursemaid care and leave their offspring almost all day of every day. In general, infants under six months had to be refused in the nursery because of the ever-present danger of the management having little foundlings left in their permanent care.[47]

The Tearoom

The tearoom was another innovation in department-store management which was said to have been first introduced by Field's and Mr. Selfridge.[48] Macy's of New York, however, had a ladies' lunchroom as early as 1878,[49] Wanamaker's, about 1882;[50] and in Chicago, the Fair store for one, by 1885, had a "café" on its second floor.[51] Thus Field's had examples to guide it in the promotion of this type of inducement to trade.

In the week of April 14, 1890, the firm opened as a convenience to its customers—there was a noticeable asbence of fanfare[52]—a small tearoom tucked away in a corner of the fur section on the third floor of the State and Washington Streets building (Singer). This original room boasted fifteen tables which could seat approximately sixty people. Evidently the tables were all filled to capacity once and then the first day was considered ended. This "capacity crowd" was served by four women in the tiny pantry and eight maids moved carefully among the tables laid with linen and silver. The orange punch served in an orange shell garnished with smilax, and Field's rose punch (ice cream with dressing, served with a rose on the plate)—these things had a glamorous but brief existence. On the very first menus, however, appeared many of the dishes which remained to become traditions, such as corned beef hash, chicken pie, and chicken salad.[53] The tearoom proved immediately popular. By June of the following year its facilities had already been expanded, and it was serving twelve hundred to fifteen hundred people daily.[54] At the end of its first full year it showed a profit of $14,800 and continued to operate "in the black" even in the depths of the 1893-94 depression.

1892	$12,168
1893	10,200
1894	340
1895	4,400
1896	7,017[55]

The atmosphere of the new tearoom was one of quiet elegance, enhanced by appointments of dainty china, fine table linen, and high-backed leather chairs, as well as by the neat caps and gowns of "perfectly trained attendants." It was a woman's restaurant designed to suit a lady's taste.[56] In 1893 at the time of the opening of the annex, the tearoom was moved, this time to make use of the entire fourth floor of the Wabash Street building,[57] or an area measuring 150 by 180 feet. The palm-decorated room contained some one hundred tables which seated probably three hundred or more people at one time.[58] In 1902 the whole establishment was moved finally to the State Street side of the store to occupy the entire seventh floor, running from the old Singer building at Washington Street to the newly opened State Street building at Randolph. Thus, the restaurant became a block long and a half block wide, or 400 by 150 feet.[59] At this time a new room, the grillroom, later called "English Room," [60] for men, was an added feature. In contrast to the tearoom where the appointments were more feminine in nature, the men's grill was decorated in heavy, dark, weathered oak, sanded ceilings and walls, and carpet and draperies of a rich dark red. Here the tables were devoid of cloths, "after the old English chop house style," and the only relief to this comparative severity was the bud vase on each table. The grillroom specialized in good hot chocolate and coffee and in meats broiled to order in "plain view of the customer." [61]

By 1902 the tearoom alone was serving 2,000 persons,[62] and in another year this number had increased to over 3,000 daily.[63] There were six ushers to seat guests, and more than 350 people by this time were employed in the kitchens and for serving the patrons.[64] In 1906, the Crystal Buffet was added to the accommodations, thus making it possible to seat 2,000 people at once and to serve about 5,000 each day.[65] In 1907, the Walnut Room and the new South Grill followed the Crystal Buffet, increasing the seating capacity to 2,800 and the total area to over 80,000 square feet.[66]

"Whether You Buy or Not . . ."

More and more during the last years of Marshall Field's life the task of carrying on the store's tradition of hospitality was necessarily taken from the hands of the busy executives and left to the responsibility of the salesmen and clerks. That the sales force by its own friendliness could adequately substitute for the days when department managers and even the partners personally met the customers on the floor was a tribute to Field's gradually perfected system of training employees.

Marshall Field and Company from the very first had been noted for its "polite and attentive clerks";[67] but in later years its graciousness and courtesy became almost legendary.

No effort is made in this place to induce any visitor to make purchases. If moved thereto, he will find able and courteous assistance; but the casual sightseer is as welcome as the purchaser, and in some indescribable way is made to feel so as soon as he steps inside the great entrance.[68]

Or as a woman customer put it:

They have a way of making me feel that the whole store is there for my convenience, whether I come to buy, or to return goods I don't want, or just to look around.[69]

That this was literally true was no accident, of course, but the result of a deliberate company policy. No other single subject was a basis for more discussion and emphasis in the house rules than this matter of courtesy and service.[70] Field's had acquired a reputation; they knew it and were determined not to lose it:[71]

The greatest courtesy is required from employees in all matters relating to the business of the house, whether customers wish to purchase; to exchange merchandise or return it for credit; to inform themselves regarding an article on sale; or merely to visit the different departments. Under no circumstances allow the customer to leave the house dissatisfied.[72]

More specifically this meant that while the customer was to be given immediate and polite attention, there was to be no undue urging to buy. Sales people were instructed to have patience in serving customers, "showing goods willingly and pleasantly, without asking too many questions as to price, width, size, or color wanted."[73] And "don't neglect a customer who happens to be poorly dressed," clerks were warned.[74]

The Return Privilege

The one store courtesy that was probably of most significance to the average customer was Field's willingness to refund the full purchase price of any article sold and—most important—to do it without the slightest question. This money-back guarantee, one of the oldest policies of the house,[75] continued to be the cornerstone of the firm's reputation for pleasing the general public. According to the employee rules:

All merchandise which has failed to give satisfaction is exchanged or redeemed, at choice of purchaser. This privilege, however, is subject to the following exceptions:
1st. When article has been worn.
2nd. When sufficient time has elapsed between purchase and return to make article unsalable.
3rd. When goods are marked "down," and sold with the understanding that they shall not be returned.
We wish to make important the point of receiving merchandise which has been returned, without going through any unnecessary or unpleasant questions or remarks, which remarks make the customer ill at ease and really accomplish no good. We would much prefer to be occasionally imposed upon than to feel that we have made any errors in the other direction. The employe is not the loser by the returning of goods, except in a very slight way. The house is the loser, and if we prefer to stand the loss cheerfully, please let us have corresponding cheerfulness from employes.[76]

Not only did it mean more pleasurable shopping for the customer, when she knew she had the privilege of later changing her mind, but it implied complete confidence by the firm in the quality and value of its merchandise. Employees were instructed never to "misrepresent an article for the sake of making a sale."[77] This admonition was, of course, almost superfluous. Anything other than quality of product and honesty in sales procedure and statement of price was pointless when the customer could return the merchandise as soon as the deficiency or falsehood was discovered. "Money-back" underwrote the entire business and everything it sold.

Whether Marshall Field ever expected that his pampered customers would take advantage of the return privilege to the extent they did is doubtful. Almost all stores which sell better quality—and thus higher priced—merchandise, of course, suffer a greater rate of returns; for the clientele which such a store attracts is one more demanding of complete satisfaction. Large department specialty stores experience a greater rate than smaller stores. Field's returns, however, were especially high and the cupidity of some customers sometimes caused even Mr. Field himself to wonder at humanity.[78]

Yet despite the annoyance and great expense involved, the firm never deviated from its original position and, if anything, became more liberal as time went by. In 1873, the earliest year for which figures are available, Field, Leiter and Company, Retail, had a "returns" ratio of 4.67 per cent; or to put it another way, the store had to buy back $4.67 worth of its own goods for every $100 in final sales. The rate remained about the same for several years but after 1877, as is evident in Table VIII on page 130, the ratio increased steadily until 1890. It leveled off during the "panic" years—a typical phenomenon during most depressions—but then began to shoot up during the late nineties. By 1906 it had reached a surprising figure of almost 17 per cent, four times what it had been a little over a quarter of a century before.

There are several factors which probably account for this rapid increase in the rate at which Chicagoans took advantage of Field's liberal return policy. Studies made in recent years indicate that one of the biggest reasons for returns is "unsatisfactory fit." [79] When Field and Leiter first reopened their doors following the Great Fire ready-to-wear clothing was still relatively new. Many, if not most, women still purchased "piece goods" and made their own clothing. The percentage of returns on such merchandise for obvious reasons is always small.[80] As the years passed and it became fashionable to buy ready-made clothing the chances of a customer obtaining a poor fit or—with all the variety of sizes, colors, styles to choose from—of her simply "changing her mind" when she got home were increased tremendously. As Field's sales of ready-to-wear increased, so did its returns. This same truth, of course, applies to other types of goods. Many of the numerous new items of merchandise which Field's during the eighties and nineties added to its original list of "dry goods" were goods with high return rates—such things as hardware and house furnishings. As these more complex—and some were even mechanical—goods were added to the stock more returns were no doubt made because of "defective merchandise," a cause high on modern lists but relatively infrequent in the era of simple dry goods. Other reasons for the increase in the percentages over the years were in all probability the increasing size and complexity of store operation and greater use of mail and phone orders, all of which provided more opportunities for mistakes. Finally,

10. CUSTOMER SERVICES

Marshall Field and Company unquestionably has long been a victim of a certain amount of lazy salesmanship. Knowing the firm's liberal policy on returns, clerks tend to encourage their customers to defer a decision until they get home and then return the goods they decide not to buy.

Retail Credit

Part of the answer to the growing rate of returns lay with another service provided by the store, namely charge accounts. As Table VII illustrates, despite Leiter's close credit policy, sales to charge customers closely approximated cash sales even in the earlier years and remained thereafter as an essential feature of the business.

TABLE VII
NET RETAIL CASH AND CREDIT SALES FOR 1877-1906[a]

Year	Cash Sales	Credit Sales[b]	Year	Cash Sales	Credit Sales[b]
1877	1,562,630	1,309,894	1892	2,843,057	4,564,406
1878	1,390,064	1,286,299	1893	3,509,914	4,617,712
1879	1,520,712	1,456,889	1894	2,909,773	3,952,947
1880	1,781,954	1,894,287	1895	3,379,136	4,243,262
1881	1,760,397	2,089,883	1896	3,645,239	4,140,023
1882	1,906,586	2,253,687	1897	3,994,018	4,343,160
1883	1,945,790	2,463,546	1898	4,609,576	5,005,431
1884	1,890,338	2,344,951	1899	5,317,765	5,870,669
1885	2,012,701	2,540,130	1900	6,126,171	6,414,584
1886	1,992,100	2,618,620	1901	6,565,473	7,286,827
1887	2,112,609	2,819,641	1902	8,508,801	8,791,072
1888	2,183,199	3,171,402	1903	10,779,850	10,256,692
1889	2,423,296	3,625,174	1904	11,474,622	10,820,279
1890	2,644,332	3,974,312	1905	12,403,197	12,074,347
1891	2,678,992	4,135,213	1906	12,573,966	12,738,650

[a]Accounting ledgers, 1873-1906, Comptroller's safe, Marshall Field & Co. General Offices.
[b]"Credit Sales" refers only to charge accounts, not installment buying.

Like its other services, this accommodation to customers resulted in a large amount of work and expense for the firm. Though actual losses from bad debts were small, charge accounts did necessitate a special retail credit office and much accounting work and correspondence.[81] But, of course, the fact that charge customers undoubtedly did the bulk of their buying where they had their account made the undertaking of such expenses not only wise but necessary. From the customer's point of view, a charge account was another important aid to easy shopping. The danger of loss or theft in carrying large amounts of money was avoided. Even the simple inconvenience of having to wait for one's change was made unnecessary.[82]

129

It was particularly agreeable to have an account at Field's. When a woman patron, for instance, wished to think over her selection, she had several dresses "sent out";[83] that is, she charged them, and had them all delivered free of charge to her home. After making the final selection at home, the other dresses were picked up by the store[84] and her account credited.[85] Nowhere in the operation was it necessary to pay out any cash, receive back any change or refund, or carry the merchandise to or from the store.[86] A cash customer had the same privilege of delivery to her home and of refund of the purchase price; but besides the necessity of paying out so much money to make the original purchase, she necessarily had to bring back the unwanted merchandise herself in order to obtain her money back. As might be expected, therefore, the return ratio for charge customers was considerably higher than for cash customers. Field's high proportion of charge sales —which at times made up three-fifths of total sales[87]—thus helps to account for its extremely high average return ratio.

TABLE VIII

PERCENTAGE RATIO OF RETAIL RETURNS BY CASH AND CREDIT CUSTOMERS TO NET RETAIL SALES FOR 1877-1906*

Year	Cash Returns	Credit Returns	Total Returns	Year	Cash Returns	Credit Returns	Total Returns
1877	1.37	8.67	4.70	1892	3.70	16.00	11.28
1878	1.42	8.65	4.89	1893	3.35	16.14	10.62
1879	2.22	9.16	5.62	1894	3.69	17.79	11.81
1880	3.23	9.14	6.27	1895	3.75	16.67	10.94
1881	3.30	9.31	6.56	1896	3.97	18.29	11.58
1882	3.10	11.04	7.40	1897	4.67	19.34	12.31
1883	3.10	11.67	7.89	1898	4.96	21.14	13.38
1884	2.99	11.52	7.71	1899	5.17	21.49	13.73
1885	2.89	12.43	8.21	1900	4.69	21.20	13.14
1886	2.95	13.08	8.70	1901	4.90	23.57	14.72
1887	3.16	15.45	10.19	1902	5.51	24.08	14.95
1888	3.08	15.58	10.48	1903	5.77	27.10	16.17
1889	3.64	17.17	11.75	1904	4.98	24.21	14.31
1890	3.75	17.81	12.20	1905	5.40	24.93	15.04
1891	3.66	16.39	11.39	1906	6.15	27.03	16.66

*Computed by writer from statistics in accounting ledgers, 1877-1906, Comptroller's safe, Marshall Field & Co. General Offices.

Even without taking into account charge customers, of course, Field's returns figures still were unusual. Unfortunately few statistics are available for other large firms of that time but Professor Ralph Hower has published some comparable figures of Macy's for 1891 to 1906. These reveal that this large retail firm—which had no charge customers—experienced a rate of returns during those years that ranged consistently from less than one-third to one-half the ratio which Field's accepted from its cash customers alone.[88] In the particular case of Macy's this difference is at least in part attributable to Macy's pricing policies. While many customer conveniences were provided, the major emphasis in that firm was on price, rather than service. Most department stores during the twentieth century have gradually liberalized their policy on returned merchandise; yet few today have even such a high ratio as Field's Retail experienced during the lifetime of its founder.[89]

The Wholesale for obvious reasons did not fare so badly. The percentage of returned goods to net sales ranged around only 3 per cent and the increase over the years was very small. How this compared with other Chicago wholesale houses is unknown but Mr. Field's rather frequent notices to his salesmen regarding what he considered an alarmingly high rate of returns would indicate that Field's rate was higher than those of its competitors and added considerably to the firm's expenses.

TABLE IX

RATIO OF WHOLESALE RETURNS TO NET WHOLESALE SALES FOR
MARSHALL FIELD & CO. FOR 1878-1906*

Year	%	Year	%	Year	%	Year	%	Year	%
1878	2.99	1884	3.27	1890	2.85	1896	3.06	1902	3.34
1879	2.57	1885	2.88	1891	3.06	1897	2.76	1903	3.58
1880	2.74	1886	3.20	1892	2.80	1898	2.92	1904	3.48
1881	2.56	1887	2.93	1893	3.19	1899	2.86	1905	3.23
1882	2.84	1888	2.80	1894	2.69	1900	3.24	1906	3.33
1883	3.07	1889	2.75	1895	2.81	1901	3.22		

*Accounting ledgers 1878-1906, Comptroller's safe, Marshall Field & Co. General Offices. The amount of goods returned to Wholesale, like Retail, varied considerably by departments. The departments which suffered most throughout the years were furs, and cloaks and suits. Ready-made apparel of all types had a high rate of return, while the simplest yard goods boasted the lowest. (Ibid.)

Delivery

From the days when its delivery facilities consisted only of Field, Palmer, and Leiter's single two-wheel dray and one horse,[90] the firm's delivery service made rapid progress. From this original cart, which was for delivery of wholesale goods alone, eventually evolved two separate delivery systems, one for Retail and one for Wholesale each of which came to serve hundreds of square miles of territory daily.

The wholesale delivery system, to be sure, was no special customer "service." It was more in the nature of a necessary and inseparable part of the business; for the merchant-customer could hardly be expected to carry home with him his extensive purchases. In the first State and Washington Street building, which housed both the wholesale and retail branches, the entire sixth floor was devoted to packing and crating. Said the *Times:*

> Scores or more of men are busily engaged in hammering together boxes of merchandise, fastening bales of silks and shawls, marking them plainly with brush and ink, and shipping them off to all parts of the country.[91]

After being packed, the crates and boxes were carried by the elevator to the ground floor, loaded in the wagons, trucks, and drays—even by 1868 the house had several—and carried to steamboat landings and railroad offices.[92]

Though the firm's facilities for wholesale delivery were increased and improved commensurate with the growth of its business, it prided itself, even in these early days, on filling and shipping all orders the same day as received.[93] When in 1872 the delivery service of all Chicago houses was threatened with dissolution because of an epidemic of horse distemper, the resourceful young Field, Leiter and Company announced calmly to its customers that "there will be no delay in Shipping Goods. . . . All Orders will be filled promptly. . . ." To pull its wagons through the streets of Chicago, the company used oxen.[94]

By 1875 the Wholesale on Madison and Market boasted of fifty wagons and one hundred horses as necessary for conducting its business.[95] Field built extensive barns located on Pacific Avenue[96] for the accommodation of his horses and took particular interest in their care and treatment. He and the Wholesale general manager gave personal attention to the buying of finely bred animals and ordered that none were to be whipped, none to be used more than half of each day, and all were to be kept clean, well fed, and healthy.

> We'd see Mr. Field sometimes put on his silk hat and go down on the street to examine horses that Phil Niebergall [head of the barns], was buying. Phil would have the horses brought up to the street outside Wholesale and then would go up into Mr. Field's office and ask him to come down and look at the horses. Mr. Field obviously liked this very much.[97]

So outstanding were his wagons and horses that they were entered in the shows against the horses and wagons of other merchants, packers, and manufacturers at the World's Fair of 1893 and won awards in all classes.[98]

By 1906 Marshall Field and Company maintained not only regular daily wholesale delivery schedules to all parts of the city and to railroad and lake shipping points, but even had an extensive special delivery service, called "green ticket deliveries," for the benefit of "Loop" retail stores.[99] By this same year, Wholesale spent over $320,-000 for special delivery alone as compared to only $36,000 in 1873.[100]

Such an expense by Wholesale, however, was unavoidable. It is when the store first turned its attention to the problem of carrying home the purchases, large or small, of its retail customers, that the delivery service can be looked upon in the light of strictly an accommo-

10. CUSTOMER SERVICES

dation for the customer. At first, the "basket trade" did just what the appellation implied — brought along baskets in which to cart away their purchases. At the same time, the "carriage trade" experienced no great problem in this respect since their maids or butlers usually relieved them of the menial task of carrying their purchases out to the waiting carriages. The first step of the management in the direction of trying to aid a woman with her parcels was the stationing inside the door of several "bundle boys" whose duty it was to relieve the shopper of her bundles and deposit them in her carriage.[101] This practice was continued right down until 1906.[102]

As a result of this small beginning the need for a delivery service, evidently, became more apparent; for in addition to the bundle boys a service of "delivery boys" gradually developed on a small scale in the last years of the sixties and finally to a greater extent in the early seventies, particularly after the Great Fire[103] when a regular retail delivery department was established.[104] It became a common sight then and for many years thereafter to see young boys, carrying a full khaki bag in one hand as well as numerous bundles tied together with string in the other hand, on their regular round of deliveries. The boys delivered on foot where that method was feasible and rode the horse and cable cars where it was not, and in this manner they covered their territory in one morning and one afternoon trip.[105]

At the same time that the delivery-boy system was establishing itself as a regular department of service in the store, a wagon delivery service was also begun. Taking up where the youngsters left off, the wagons delivered in the more outlying areas. During the depression era of the seventies, the firm spent in the neighborhood of only $25,000 to $30,000 per year on delivery to its retail customers;[106] and even by 1881, the retail delivery expenses for the boys as well as for the horses and wagons had risen only to about $40,000. As business revived, however, the cost of deliveries quickly rose to an annual bill of approximately $50,000 in 1885 and continued to mount thereafter as sales increased and the city expanded in size.[107]

By 1883 the packing and delivery room had become an old and seasoned department of nearly sixty employees. Under the supervision of R. M. Hitchcock,[108] the steady stream of bundles brought in by the floor boys were efficiently wrapped (or boxed), tied, addressed, and passed outside to the delivery agent. They were then assigned to one of the six "neat, stylish turnouts" then used in the delivery of more than a thousand packages each day.[109] One boy accompanied each wagon and driver—two-horse wagons for the outskirts of the city and one-horse for closer in. It was the boy's job to jump off, run in with the package, and if it was cash-on-delivery, "keep your hand on the package until you got the money." [110] Still another service "arranged for the convenience of the shopping public" was the crew of messenger boys kept always within call for use as a special delivery staff to send "hurry" packages.[111]

Otherwise, a regular delivery schedule was adhered to. By 1904 this meant two or three deliveries daily.[112] The delivery service had grown to such proportions that frequently as many as thirty horse-drawn wagons could be seen at one time pulled up to the loading platform at the rear of the store.[113] Over one hundred wagons, requiring nearly two hundred drivers to operate them, traveled an average of 1320 miles per day and delivered an average of 14,545 packages, most of them on the same day they were purchased.[114]

Competition was, in fact, so keen that free delivery was extended even into the suburbs; and by 1902 Field's had established separate suburban barns to care for its far-flung trade.[115] These were located at strategic points along the outskirts of Chicago. Packages to be delivered were loaded into trunks and sent by Adams or American Express to these points where the firm's wagons waited. The drivers sorted out the packages, checked them, and then delivered them to the individual homes. By this method, daily delivery was made to such distant points as Evanston, Oak Park, La Grange, Riverside, Rogers Park, and Austin, as well as to all parts of Chicago.[116]

The first "motor wagons" for delivery purposes were purchased shortly after the turn of the century. By 1902 three were in regular use and two years later at least twenty.[117] But in spite of the automobile's behavior, which the company felt was "praiseworthy in the extreme," it was still considered definitely in the experimental stage as a factor in the delivery system. At that, the firm used only electric machines, as "the odor of gasoline . . . injures the goods to quite an extent."[118] For this reason Field's continued to add to their complement of horse-drawn wagons until by 1907 the store utilized over three hundred wagons and seven hundred horses, in addition to their motor vehicles, to cover the 350 square miles of their delivery area.[119] The annual bill to the company for this one type of convenience to customers was over $686,000.[120]

As an item of business expense, delivery loomed large and had a way of continuing to get larger. As seen in Table X retail delivery expenses in relation to sales increased more or less steadily after the depression years of the seventies. Almost without exception each year's delivery costs not only reached a larger dollar sum than the year before but increased proportionately as an expense factor. Comparable figures for other retail firms again are largely lacking, but Macy's delivery expenses published by Professor Hower are of value.[121] They show, for example, an interesting similarity to Field's statistics during the nineties and early years of the twentieth century not only in the ratio of delivery costs to net sales and in the gradual rate of increase over the years, but also in particular years where increases were unusually small or particularly great.[122] Apparently such factors as the general business cycle with its consequent effect on sales, the gradual extension of the metropolitan delivery areas for both stores, and the introduction of motor transport at about the same time were factors which operated somewhat uniformly on both stores. The fluctuations in percentage ratios during the seventies can be attributed more to

134

10. CUSTOMER SERVICES

disturbances in the sales picture than to any startling changes in delivery department efficiency.

TABLE X

RATIO OF RETAIL DELIVERY EXPENSES TO NET RETAIL SALES FOR MARSHALL FIELD & CO. FOR 1874-1906*

Year	%	Year	%	Year	%	Year	%
1874	.84	1883	1.01	1891	1.30	1899	2.11
1875	1.05	1884	1.04	1892	1.49	1900	2.30
1876	1.08	1885	1.08	1893	1.49	1901	2.34
1877	1.00	1886	1.10	1894	1.72	1902	2.30
1878	.97	1887	1.17	1895	1.71	1903	2.33
1879	.98	1888	1.29	1896	1.85	1904	2.28
1880	.84	1889	1.25	1897	1.85	1905	2.28
1881	1.02	1890	1.24	1898	1.97	1906	2.71
1882	.98						

*Computed by the author from delivery and total sales figures in accounting ledgers, 1874-1906, Comptroller's safe, Marshall Field & Co. General Offices.

Even with Field's offering such services and hospitality, it was not without its share of customer complaints. As a matter of fact, like any well-run business firm, it solicited them as a matter of policy.[123] Despite everything the store did, there were complaints of discourtesy in attention and of short-changing on the part of clerks;[124] there were complaints relating to injuries received in the store;[125] there were complaints regarding payment of bills[126]—and there were some complaints that must have perplexed even Marshall Field:

Dear Sir
I have been a customer of your house over 20 years and have been well tended always only in one particular of which I wish to complain. The elevators at the south end of your store are too low in the door to admit a man of full stature. I have broken and spoiled two good silk hats there and am tired of the sacrifice. I am 6 feet 1 in. in shoes.
Very Truly[127]

On the whole, however, it can be safely said that Mr. Field succeeded in firmly establishing his firm's reputation for courtesy and service and in making it, as he wanted to do, the people's "downtown home."[128] Women became accustomed to use Field's as a rendezvous with their friends.[129] Once in the store, they were not likely to do much of their shopping elsewhere.

Newspaper Advertising, 1865-80

I̲N THE REALM OF ADVERTISING THERE WAS, AT THE OUTSET, LITTLE TO distinguish Field's from its competitors. Like those of most dry-goods firms, Field, Palmer and Leiter and Field, Leiter and Company's advertisements in the newspaper were infrequent and repetitious and uninteresting in phraseology and form. Except for a few houses, such as Ross and Gossage[1] and Ross, Foster and Company[2] which ran frequent and sometimes comparatively large advertisements, the prevailing practice in the sixties among Chicago merchants was to insert an advertisement at the start of each trading season, let it run unchanged for a week or more, and then not to advertise again until the following season except to announce an infrequent sale or other special event.

All these advertisements were small, one-column wide, and seldom over three or four inches long, and were printed together on the first or second page of the paper. Similar to modern classified advertising, all dry-goods advertisements were placed consecutively in long columns.[3] Most of the advertisements were similar in format, and Field's were no exception to the others. Almost like "legal notices," simply for the purpose of notifying the public that they were in business, each firm listed what it had to sell and quoted few or no prices. The only effort made by a merchant to entice buyers to his firm in particular was through some such comment as "lowest possible prices" or "cannot fail to please."[4]

The first Field, Palmer, and Leiter advertisement to appear was an announcement in January 1865 of the new firm; and thus it was more "newsy" and varied than might ordinarily be expected:

GREAT REDUCTION
Field, Palmer & Leiter
110, 112, 114 & 116
LAKE STREET

11. ADVERTISING

Having bought P. Palmer's entire stock of Dry Goods at a large discount, have marked down their Retail Stock of

Dress Goods,
Silks,
Cloaks,
Shawls,
Cloths,
Flannels,
Embroideries, &c.,

FULL

20 per cent

BELOW FORMER PRICES

Alexandre's Kid Gloves
at $2.25 to $2.50

CALL AND SEE FOR YOURSELVES

WHOLESALE

Our Jobbing Stock is large and we are offering it under New York prices. Shall be pleased to see all our old friends when in the market, or in the meantime receive their orders, which we will give prompt and careful attention.

FIELD, PALMER & LEITER

Marshall Field, formerly of Cooley, Farwell & Co.,
and Farwell, Field & Co.,
L. E. Leiter, formerly of Farwell, Field & Co.,
M. J. Palmer., formerly with P. Palmer.[5]

After the above advertisement had appeared on January 17 and 20, nothing was printed concerning Field, Palmer and Leiter for ten days. Then on January 31 through February 4 appeared a typical advertisement:

137

LOW PRICES

FOR

MERINOS,

DRESS GOODS,

CLOAKS,

SILKS,

SHAWLS,

CLOTHS,

EMBROIDERIES,

&c &c &c

Wishing to make room for Spring Goods, we are offering our entire stock at largely reduced prices.

Field, Palmer & Leiter

110, 112, 114 & 116

LAKE STREET[6]

On March 25 and 29, the firm notified the trade that they were selling their stock at "PANIC PRICES,"[7] and a strictly wholesale advertisement appeared in May;[8] but following this there were no more until November.[9] The store's final advertisement for the year appeared on December 20, 1865.[10] These advertisements were so general it was not always clear whether they were announcing wholesale or retail goods or both.

As early as 1866, Field, Palmer and Leiter advertisements already showed considerable change in format and phraseology. They were longer; they gave evidence of more attention being paid to spacing in

11. ADVERTISING

order to lend emphasis to certain words; and, most important, a few were quite specific and dealt with the goods of only one department at a time rather than the whole firm.[11] By 1867, after the firm had become Field, Leiter and Company, its advertisements continued along these lines and also became somewhat livelier and made greater use of large and heavy type (see below). Not long after this appeared, Field and Leiter ran two advertisements similar to the one below at the same time, printing them in parallel part-columns by way of extra emphasis.[12] While this was by no means the first time it had ever been done in Chicago,[13] it was nevertheless a distinct innovation for Field's and was not frequently repeated.[14]

Silks!   Silks!

We will offer on TUESDAY, September 17th, a choice and full assortment of SILKS, selected in Europe expressly for the RETAIL TRADE comprising all the best grades and consisting in part of

Plain Taffetas,
    Gros Grains,
        Velours, Brocades,
            Chenes, Stripes,
                Moire Antiques,
                    Satin Cachemires,
                        Scotch Plaids.

Drap de France,
    Faities,
        Cachemere de Soles,
            Bonnets,
                Taffetas, &c.

FIELD, LEITER & CO.
110, 112, 114 & 116 LAKE ST.[15]

The claim was made by the house in its advertising at this time that:

We guarantee to make Lower Prices than any House in Chicago, and as LOW as any in New York.[16]

This is as strong a statement as Field's had ever made in the public press. From then on the firm's advertising became even more conservative. An air of we-do-not-need-to-stoop-to-the-level-of-others was assumed and was eventually developed, in fact, into a basic policy of the firm. Marshall Field's natural conservatism, his desire to maintain a reputation for complete honesty and integrity, were unquestionably the motivating forces behind this attitude. Compare this typical Field's advertisement:

FIELD,
LEITER
& CO.

Are now opening a full assortment of Broadcloths, Tricot, Pique, Crepe and Granite Coatings, in all colors; 3-4 Cassimeres, suitable for Pants and Suits, in every variety, $1 to $2 per yard; 6-4 do. from $2 to $3 50; 3-4, all wool, for Boys' wear, 65c. and upward. A full line of fine Linen Ducks and Duck Coatings for Gents' wear, and Fancy Linen for Boys' wear, 25c. and upward.

Merchant Tailors, and purchasers generally are invited to examine our stock, as many BARGAINS will be offered the ensuing week, worthy of attention.

STATE & WASHINGTON STS.

with this double-column advertisement run by a competitor on the same date:

141

Despite Field's conservatism, however, marked improvements were evident during the seventies in the company's advertising as compared to its first attempts. Advertisements were no longer confined to just the first or second page, and they appeared much more often than before (more frequent instances of two and even three advertisements on the same day),[19] and the copy was changed at shorter intervals.[20] Advertisements listing specific goods with their prices were more frequently in evidence; sometimes departments were listed one by one and attention called to the wares and prices in each.[21] Some of the advertisements were larger;[22] and there were more feature items such as "holiday gifts" or "close outs," "openings," "special bargains," and "sales," often on particular items or in certain departments rather than simply "panic prices" throughout the store as formerly.[23]

Sunday Advertising

Until very recently the Field firm never advertised on Sunday according to popular belief.[24] No less important a figure in the company's development than John G. Shedd helped to perpetuate this conception by a statement in the latter part of 1919:

Answering your inquiry of the twenty-fourth ultimo. we will say that during fifty odd years of business, Marshall Field & Company never have advertised in Sunday newspapers. They have followed the rule that six days of labor and the seventh for rest was best for employer and employe.

We regard Sunday advertising as an unnecessary infraction of this very wholesome, many-century old, religious dictum, and we are glad to follow it. . . .[25]

The fact is that from the time that Field and Leiter took over the store through 1872, they advertised frequently in the Sunday papers.[26]

It was not until the spring of 1876 that the firm of Field, Leiter and Company, along with six other dry-goods merchants, pledged itself to abstain from retail advertising in the Sunday issue of any newspapers published in Chicago.[27] This agreement was adhered to strictly except under what Field's must have considered mitigating circumstances; for a year later, in 1877, following the destruction of its retail building at State and Washington in November, Field's ran advertisements again on Sunday to announce its new location in the Exposition Building and the auctioning of damaged stock.[28] After this emergency, the firm reverted to its still-new policy and discontinued Sunday advertising.[29]

That it did this is the more singular in light of the fact that each of its competitors after a time ceased to observe his pledge.[30] The Sunday paper, after all, was becoming too popular in America by the last quarter of the nineteenth century for businessmen to ignore it as an advertising medium. Monday was "bargain day" in department stores throughout the United States and the Sunday advertisements were the stores' main device for bringing in the customers.[31] That Marshall Field and Company could ignore this trade-pulling stratagem for so many years and make its own "bargain days"[32] was as much a tribute

142

11. ADVERTISING

to its commercial standing in the community as it was to Marshall Field's religious devotion.

Field's advertised most frequently on Monday. This was especially true during the seventies and eighties when daily advertisements were not yet the rule. The firm for months on end advertised almost every Monday and only infrequently on other days. The first day of the week was chosen undoubtedly because few other firms advertised then, and therefore Field's advertisements stood out prominently.[33]

Wholesale Advertising to 1906

During the seventies most of the Field, Leiter and Company newspaper advertising was by the retail departments. The wholesale branch of the firm ceased almost entirely to advertise in the dailies except to announce changes of address, the opening of a new building, or similar uncommon occurrences.[34] Public quotations of prices in the wholesale trade would not have been good practice, especially for a firm like Field, Leiter and Company which was also engaged in the retail end of the business. Thus it could not make use of newspaper advertisements for this purpose; and its reputation by this time was already such that the old-fashioned appeals to the trade phrased in general terms were unnecessary.[35] Furthermore, since the clientele of Wholesale was not limited to Chicago, as was that of Retail, it could better reach its customers directly by mail than through an advertising medium limited largely to the Chicago metropolitan area. For these reasons, Wholesale, beginning in the seventies, began listing its offerings in catalogues, circulars, letters, or postcards, using whichever best suited the needs of the moment.

The wholesale catalogue of Marshall Field and Company seems to have been first published in the spring of 1870 as an annual, for it was promptly followed by another in 1871. These two catalogues were little pocket-sized books resembling modern souvenir notebooks given away by firms to create good will, rather than a true mail-order catalogue. The entire stock of goods carried by Field's was listed by departments; but there were no prices quoted, and many pages were left blank so that the recipient would be more tempted to keep it handy as a useful memorandum book. Its service as a catalogue was limited to informing the retailer in general terms as to what goods the house carried and what its policies and terms were, and to giving directions on how to order.[36]

Prices were not listed in the catalogues for the simple reason that they changed too rapidly under existing competitive conditions to be quoted in a publication printed only annually. For that matter, even the firm's policies and wares were liable to change greatly in the space of a year and render the catalogue out of date.[37] To remedy this deficiency, circulars, form letters, and postcards, containing announcements and lists of prices good for a brief time (sometimes only a single day), were mailed or handed out from time to time.[38] These tended more and more as the complexity of the firm's stock increased, beginning in the late seventies and early eighties, to be only announcements covering the goods of a very few departments or just a few specials from several departments; for it became an impossible matter to lay out a format for a short, mailable circular that could encompass the myriad offerings of the entire house.[39] The postcard announcements, in fact, usually carried news of but a few particular items within one department.[40]

Doubtless this same problem of the expense and difficulty of listing so many different goods and the interruption of the Great Fire caused the firm to discontinue the publication of the general catalogue after only two years. In any event, no third issue covering the wares of the entire house appeared in 1872. When another catalogue was attempted in 1877, it was for the notions department alone.[41] This was published irregularly as late as the nineties, and some other departments individually or together followed suit.[42] As the trading area of the firm spread all over the United States and mail orders increased, these catalogues became a necessity to many customers. As a result the catalogues were gradually improved and printed in more detail as the years passed. Those issued in the nineties were similar in appearance to a modern Sears, Roebuck and Company or Montgomery Ward mail-order catalogue. They were profusely illustrated and carried specific prices to be used in ordering.[43] Once again in 1900 a general catalogue was printed. Its success must have been considerable, for in 1902 it was decided to make it a permanent feature to be published in both a spring and fall edition.[44]

Retail Newspaper Advertising, 1880-1904

The Retail's conception of what constituted a good advertising layout changed little during the early eighties. Although it ran an occasional full two-column-wide display and used a little more variety in type than in the seventies,[45] its advertisements were for the most part still single column in width and uninspired in content.[46]

The main feature distinguishing Marshall Field and Company advertisements from those of other firms continued to be simply their marked conservatism.[47] While other advertisers ran copy filling several columns (even full-page spreads)[48] and introduced their advertisements with such copy as this:[49]

LOOK, SEE, AND BEHOLD!
THE GREATEST STORE
ON EARTH
The Fair The Fair The Fair The Fair

the following typical Field advertisement makes clear that Field's
could never be accused of sensationalism:[50]

European Modes.

State & Washington-sts.,

Are in receipt of

"PARISIAN STYLES"

IN

"Costumes,"

"Mantles,"

AND

"Cloaks,"

And will continue to add daily the
latest NOVELTIES as they appear in FOREIGN MARKETS.

The Fashions in these Garments
are unusually attractive this season.

Ladies', Misses',

AND

Children's

Dresses and Cloaks

Are a special feature with us.

EXAMINATION INVITED.

145

The turning point in the history of advertising at Marshall Field and Company, Retail, was 1885; and, as with many of the changes taking place about this time, the man held responsible was the energetic new assistant-superintendent, Selfridge. Fleming had not believed in advertising; Selfridge was enough of a modernist to appreciate its power when properly directed. Every change or improvement in the retail store he felt should be the occasion for a burst of advertising. He was permitted to have his way.[51] Back in 1872 and 1873, as early as figures are available, the Retail had spent $9,600 and $7,200 a year on advertising.[52] Ten years later, with a store of much greater sales volume,[53] Fleming was spending little more than before. For the years 1880 through 1884, Retail advertising expenses were only $8,600, $9,400, $15,000, $13,300, and $13,500. In 1885, however, after Selfridge's arrival, this item jumped suddenly to $28,100 and continued to increase almost every year thereafter.[54]

Selfridge encouraged the writing of more, larger, and better advertisements.[55] This at first meant the two-to-four-column variety,[56] neater and more distinctive-looking advertisements with a greater amount of white space, and more often several separate spreads in the same issue of the same paper.[57] After 1892 he held forth with many advertisements that covered three-fourths or a full page; and they were undeniably well-written.[58] Selfridge often wrote "messages" at the top of these notices—chatty, optimistic, and sometimes patriotic pieces—that his admiring employees called "H. G.'s Declarations of Independence."[59] These little editorials gave information about store policies, services, and the degree of business success as items of news in which the general public would be interested. For example:

Our Linen Sale of '92 has proven phenomenally successful. In amount of sales, in amount of stock displayed (all of which was new and fresh), and in beauty and extreme variety of patterns, qualities and weaves offered, this sale has, beyond all question, surpassed by a very large percent, any similar effort ever made in America, or, as far as we can discover, in Europe. Every day in January has shown a handsome increase in business over the large sales of 1891.[60]

This type of copy is illustrative of what is usually called the "institutional" approach to advertising. It is advertising designed not necessarily to produce immediate sales but to create a favorable attitude toward the store.[61] The use of this type of copy, mixed in with the conventional sort (goods and prices), gradually became important in Marshall Field and Company's advertising from 1890 on; but it became particularly important following the construction of the 1893 Annex and in connection thereafter with the remainder of the building program. Deliberately the grandeur of the store and its place as a unique community service institution were emphasized rather than the profit-seeking aspect of the business. Field's, due to the physical beauty of its store and the reputation of its house, was able to make

Courtesy of Chicago Historical Society   PLATE IV

FIELD, LEITER & CO. RUINS FOLLOWING GREAT FIRE OF 1871

Courtesy of Chicago Historical Society   PLATE V

MARSHALL FIELD & CO. ABOUT 1896

Singer building in center—1893 annex at right—the two buildings at left of Singer also used by firm. Central Music Hall is building at left of block with clock tower.

MARSHALL FIELD & CO. IN 1907

PLATE VI

use of this type of advertising with an artistry and perfection un-matched by competitors.[62]

Marshall Field and Company, despite Selfridge's aggressive in-fluence, was one of the last department stores to make use of illustra-tions in its newspaper advertising. Neither Field's nor many other firms in the early post-Civil War days made much use of the assort-ment of unimaginative woodcuts kept on file by the newspaper offices,[63] but as the technique of photoengraving was perfected and made com-paratively inexpensive during the early nineties, many firms took ad-vantage of the opportunity to enhance the visual appeal of their advertisements by inserting numerous pictures of their stores or their products.[64] Apparently the traditional conservatism of Field's and the desire to hold costs to a minimum, however, caused the city's largest store to be one of the very last to make use of this device. Except for very occasional small "cuts," [65] Field's did not use illustrations until almost the turn of the century.[66]

To keep its advertising consistent with the general store policies of honesty and integrity (and perhaps also as a subtle way of advertising in itself) Marshall Field and Company made it a standing and well-publicized rule that all its advertisements were to be truthful and un-exaggerated. As a result of the keen competition for customers, many Chicago merchants had carried sensationalism and exaggeration in their newspaper advertisements to such a degree as to cause consider-able unfavorable comment from the general public.[67] Field's wisely turned this situation to its own advantage by making of moderation and honesty in its own advertising almost a fetish. If remnants were marked at "half-price," for example, this must be literally true;[68] and if goods were to be sold at a reduced price because they were "sec-onds," this fact must be so stated in the advertising.[69] The policy was fully exploited by keeping the public informed of it. Their advertise-ments proclaimed:

> We allow no misstatement—no exaggeration in even the slightest degree to enter into our announcemnts. Every statement in our advertisements can be absolutely depended upon.[70]

But at the same time, the firm made it an actual thing by informing its employees through its book of rules that:

> It is our intention that every advertisement which we publish shall be *abso-lutely true and correct in every particular*. It is further our desire that em-ployees become familiar with the advertisements as rapidly as they appear. In order to draw many critical eyes to our advertisements, and, furthermore, to give double interest to the reading of the same, we hereby offer one dollar to the employee who first calls the attention of the Manager's Office to an error (other than typographical) in any of our advertisements. Errors will be considered such:
> When there is in any way an exaggeration.
> When the price is wrong.
> When a word is misspelled.

When the advertisement is grammatically incorrect.
Or when a false statement occurs.[71]

Field's care to avoid any exaggeration led them to make such statements as this in their advertisements: "Cut Glass Tumblers at less, *in one instance,* than wholesale prices. . . ."[72] Such a policy, as it became known to the public, made every Marshall Field and Company advertisement worthy of attention. Thus the firm's very conservatism in its advertisements, which at first made them seem unimaginative and unprogressive, in the end, with the proper promotion, proved to be the most enlightened and modern approach of them all.

Special Events Advertising

Marshall Field and Company's aversion to the sensational did not prevent it from having well-advertised price-cutting sales, just as did the other merchants, in order to clear its stocks for the coming season and to entice new customers into the store. Ordinarily Field's sales did not include the entire store but rather covered the goods of only one or a group of departments.[73] Beginning in the eighties, there developed the custom of annual sales held at a particular set time every year by each separate department. The annual linen sale, for example, was held every January;[74] and the home-furnishings sale came in April.[75] These were dignified sales—or as dignified as any sale can be—and the advertising copy announcing them was as generally free of sensationalism as that in the firm's other announcements.[76]

Apparently the first such annual sale was held by the linen section in 1883.[77] Though not referred to in the beginning as an "annual" affair, its initial success prompted the department to hold another the following year, and by that time it was officially labeled "annual."[78] One was held each year thereafter.[79] Other sections followed this example, and soon most of the more important ones had established set dates for the holding of their particular event. The first annual muslin underwear sale was in January of 1887;[80] the first for home furnishings (furniture and china) in 1904;[81] and the first for ladies' corsets in 1903.[82]

Another type of well-publicized special event at Field's, particularly after 1900, were the annual "Children's Days," "special exhibits," "expositions," and seasonal openings.[83] One such event in 1905 drew a quarter of a million people in one day.[84] "Children's Day" in 1904 was attended by even more, a record 400,000.[85] To attract such crowds, Field's put on displays that probably few other stores at the time could have afforded to undertake. On one such "Children's Day" there was, for instance, among other exhibits, a complete printing shop set up in the art room to show old and new methods of setting type. A linotype operator was there with his machine to form each visiting child's name on a sample lead slug and present it to him as a souvenir. A potter entertained with his wheel, making vases as gifts for the children. Elsewhere glass was blown, flax was spun, jewelry and beads made, even

148

underwear and hosiery knit by machinery; and there were many more souvenirs for the youngsters.[86] On such occasions Field's decorative schemes were also becoming known as out of the ordinary. In 1905:

> From the Washington Street entrance, the main aisle presents a forest scene, with trees and shrubs tinged with autumn sunset hues; from the Randolph Street entrance, a woodland under a harvest moon is presented, the foliage being silvered and shadowy under the paler light. On other floors also, the autumn colors predominate, with the entire color scheme following that of the main floors.[87]

The good will and prestige created by such events, when so well attended and so roundly praised in the press, were substantial.[88]

Newspaper Advertising After 1904

Selfridge's strong belief in large and frequent advertisements resulted in a continuous rise in the cost of Retail's newspaper advertising until, in his last year with the firm (1904), this expense had reached $231,900.[89] But when Selfridge left in May of 1904,[90] a slight "reaction" set in for a short time. It was apparently felt by James E. Holden, his successor,[91] that Selfridge had overdone the quantity feature of advertising and neglected the quality. As a result, the amount of money spent for newspaper advertisements in particular was drastically reduced (to $167,300 in 1905);[92] and a new tempo was set by departmental notices issued from the new manager's office.

> It has been clear to us for some time that certain radical changes in our advertising customs might be made with ultimate if not with immediate advantage. . . . We are now ready to take this step. . . .
> It is our purpose to do much less advertising than heretofore; to require a higher standard of importance before any announcement is issued; to lean more on the dignity and power of the store, so that a word from us may come to mean more than a paragraph from another house, or a single column more than a whole page; to hold this store entirely out of comparison with other stores,—in short, *to do more and say less about it*.[93]

Though, as noted, the amount of advertising was reduced under this policy during 1905, the experiment was apparently unsuccessful; for in 1906 the Retail once again began to advertise profusely, spending more than Selfridge ever had.[94] In fact, judging from the complaint of the *Daily News,* a certain amount of indecision and confusion seemed to be characteristic of Field's advertising department during these last years.[95]

Newspapers as Advertising Media

Before placing their advertisements, big stores with large advertising budgets like Marshall Field and Company needed to make careful studies of the character and the circulation of each newspaper. They had to know how many people bought the newspaper so that they

149

could insist on paying less for advertisements that were to be seen by fewer readers. Equally important, they needed to know what class of people tended to buy a particular daily or weekly. Some were favorites of the lower-income groups; others had a wider circulation in the better residential areas. And finally taken into account was the fact that morning newspapers were apt to be read more quickly and evening papers more slowly.

Unfortunately no Marshall Field and Company records of very early date relating to these matters had been preserved, but excellent figures for 1905 show that at least by that date Field's was amply aware of the significance of these various factors. It was taken into account, for example, that advertising rates in the *Daily News* were higher than in the *Tribune,* the *American,* the *Record-Herald,* or any of the other newspapers;[96] nevertheless, the large circulation of the *Daily News*[97] and the fact that it was an afternoon paper warranted giving it a considerable share of the store's advertising. It was apparently decided further that more people in the upper-income brackets read the *Chicago Tribune,* for within its pages Field's more often placed the advertisements of higher-priced goods and less often the "bargains." Though Field's more than made up the difference by running more of the other types of advertising in the *Daily News,*[98] the latter newspaper gave evidence that it was not particularly flattered that "high toned houses like Marshall Field's used the *Daily News* only for their cheap basement business and not for the 'fine silk' business upstairs." [99] On the matter of expense, it has often been insinuated that the real motive for Field's not advertising on Sunday was that Monday advertising rates were cheaper. It is true that the rate per line was a full 20 per cent less during the week than on Sunday. The *Tribune* rates for 1906, for example, were 22½ cents a line for the daily and 27½ cents on Sunday (Monday was no cheaper than other weekdays).[100]

Other Retail Advertising

Marshall Field and Company did not put its complete faith in newspaper advertising either at the outset or in later times. For one thing, circulars and souvenir pamphlets were used by the Retail much the same as they were used by the Wholesale. Even the earliest ones, while not illustrated, were attractively printed in gold or in a variety of colors. For the most part they were used to announce openings of new departments. Doubtless many were wrapped with parcels and mailed out with the monthly bills to customers; but some bear a specific date and are set up as form letters. This suggests that the firm kept a general mailing list even in its first years of business.)[101]

By the eighties the straight circular was becoming less important, but little booklet "announcements" and souvenir pamphlets, both types giving early evidence of the institutional approach to advertising, increased in number and elaborateness. Typical were foreign lithographed cards bearing sentimental colored pictures or Christmas

150

11. ADVERTISING

greetings on the front and a modest statement of the firm's name and place of business on the back.[102]. On the occasion of the 1884 Republican and Democratic conventions in Chicago, the store published a sixteen-page booklet containing a record of previous conventions and space for tallying the votes in the current balloting, as well as a polite invitation to visit Marshall Field and Company.[103] During the nineties and later, as the value of this medium of institutional advertising became apparent, expenditures for these items were increased roughly proportional to that for newspaper advertising. There were eventually included under this category everything from the ordinary circulars and booklets to posters, folders, store guides, painted signs, "drumming" letters, and horse-show programs.[104]

In normal years Selfridge allotted only from $10,000 to $15,000 for such purposes;[105] but there were numerous "special occasions" which he apparently felt called for something out-of-the-ordinary from a store such as Field's. In 1893, at the time of the opening of the new Annex, a special booklet of engraved colored pictures of the retail store was distributed to Field's customers as a souvenir.[106] The National G. A. R. Encampment of 1900 in Chicago called forth from Field's an even larger pamphlet filled with excellent views of the retail store, fine photographs such as are not often seen in free literature even today;[107] and the "pamphlet and circular" expenses for the year 1899 when these letters were printed jumped to $25,200.[108] If the expenses dropped again thereafter (and they did for a year or two), they hit an all-time high in 1902, doubtless mostly in connection with the huge opening of that year. Field's spent $58,500 on this type of advertising alone for 1902, an amount almost three times that of the previous year.[109] Expenses of this sort never fully returned to former low levels during the few remaining years before Selfridge left because he immediately launched into an extensive direct mail advertising campaign that kept costs high.[110] Not until after Selfridge left and Holden's new "do more and say less" policy took hold in 1905 did expenses again materially dropped.[111]

As a cost item in the total retail expense picture Field's advertising never loomed very large. The store's expenditures in the earliest years were pathetically small. Even after Selfridge began to make greater use of this type of sales stimulant Field's advertising-expense ratio was very low in comparison to modern advertising budgets. More to the point, of course, was its relationship to other similar firms of that day. Here a rough survey of lineage in both the Chicago and New York newspapers seems to indicate that Field's used this medium to a smaller extent than its rivals in either city, especially in the earlier years. Comparing Field's advertising-expense ratio against those published by Professor Ralph Hower for Macy's confirms this. Field's ratio never exceeded that of Macy's and usually remained between one-half and two-thirds the annual rate of the New York firm.[112]

Other than those already accounted for, the few sudden increases in Field's advertising expense, such as in the years 1878, 1893, and 1902 can probably best be explained by the purchase of elaborate newspaper coverage announcing the transfer of the store to a new location in the first instance and the erection of new buildings on the latter two dates. The percentage decline in 1903 was actually not so much due to a drop in dollar expenditures as to a sudden spurt in retail sales following the opening of a beautiful new building the year before.

TABLE XI

RATIO OF RETAIL ADVERTISING EXPENSE TO NET RETAIL SALES FOR
MARSHALL FIELD & CO. FOR 1872-1906

Year	%	Year	%	Year	%	Year	%	Year	%
1872	.31[a]	1879	.25	1886	.57	1893	.99	1900	1.22
1873	.23[a]	1880	.23	1887	.50	1894	.85	1901	1.24
1874	.48[b]	1881	.24	1888	.55	1895	.82	1902	1.39
1875	.48	1882	.36	1889	.48	1896	.98	1903	.89
1876	.45	1883	.30	1890	.56	1897	1.14	1904	1.04
1877	.34	1884	.32	1891	.68	1898	1.34	1905	.68
1878	.58	1885	.62	1892	.81	1899	1.32	1906	.93

[a]Computed by writer from figures in Expense Record, 1872-73, A. B. Jones folder, Marshall Field & Co. Archives.
[b]Computed by writer from figures in accounting ledgers, 1872-1906, Comptroller's safe, Marshall Field & Co. General Offices. Hereinafter all figures in this table are from this source.

Window Displays

The sixty-five big show windows facing the streets on all four sides of the retail building and the excellent displays regularly featured in them have long been a source of particular pride to Marshall Field and Company. The larger twelve-feet-deep windows have, according to the firm, "won renown the world over for the beauty and uniqueness of their decorations. They are planned carefully in advance and changed frequently." [113] But all this is a far cry from the meagre beginnings of the "deeply recessed" (two-feet) windows of the first State and Washington Streets store. These windows of 1868 were of plate glass and measured 6 feet in width by 14 feet, 9 inches, in height, quite large for that day; but their sole purpose was to let in light and generally to add to the attractiveness of the store.[114] No displays were attempted in this or any of the succeedings stores of the firm until 1883.[115] In that year and in 1884[116] two windows, small and shallow by modern standards, were built, one to the south and one to the north of the main State Street entrance. These served as the only show windows of Marshall Field and Company until 1890, when finally a number of good-sized display windows were added along State and Washington Streets.[117]

Shortly thereafter in 1893 when the "Annex" was erected to the east of the Singer building, show windows were built in from the start. The windows of this building were much smaller and definitely less spectacular than most of Field's present ones; but with their new concealed electric lighting,[118] they nevertheless made a considerable im-

11. ADVERTISING

pression in Chicago and seemed amply large when first displayed to the public. "Each one," claimed the *Evening Journal*, "is large enough to hold the goods in an ordinary retail store. The window dresser of the firm will certainly have no cause to complain of any lack of room for the carrying out of any of his plans for showing goods." [119]

This was an accurate enough statement, as it proved, for these same windows still serve the store at the Wabash and Washington corner; however, in 1893, Field's major concern was with the window trimmers, rather than with the windows to be trimmed. The art of window display, being new, was not thoroughly developed; and it was believed that little skill was required simply to show goods in a window. As a result, the work was handled at Field's by trimmers, "who were considered just a notch above the store porters." [120] When Mandel's began to make a name for itself because of its excellent window displays created by a Mr. Ambrose, Field's then began to seek greater talent for its own windows. A succession of men and expedients were tried. Mr. Ambrose was even enticed away from Mandel's for a few months, but for some reason he grew dissatisfied and left. Finally, when Field's first window trimmer was asked to take the job again, he recommended instead one Arthur Fraser as a person of considerable talent. Fraser was hired for a trial in 1895 and held the job for forty-nine years.[121]

Fraser was not only clever with design and color but had a marked flair for showmanship. Since the curtains of the window displays were always lowered during Sunday anyway as a gesture of religious reverence,[122] Fraser would start changing his windows on Saturday night. The curtains on several windows would then sometimes remain closed for several days. Finally, like the opening of a new show, the unveiling would suddenly take place to receive the admiration of the crowds of people passing by.[123] Fraser's displays were usually tied together with some central theme. In 1897, for example, six of his largest and most conspicuous windows were all devoted to the display of only one color (red) because it was to be the fashionable color that season.[124] On another occasion a whole series of display windows was given over to the portrayal of an exact reproduction of the interior of a large hall or gallery in a seventeenth-century English mansion in order to suggest the high standards of the interior-decorating section of the store.[125] When the Retail expanded in 1902, and a long array of big windows was added, thirty to forty full-time trimmers were placed under his direction and Fraser was able to give free play to his talents.[126] At Christmas time and during the numerous "grand openings," his windows never failed to draw almost as much attention as the attractions on the inside.[127]

153

The New and the Old

Retail Building Program

T HE RESULT OF MARSHALL FIELD AND COMPANY'S SUCCESS IN THE IN-troduction of new lines and in the development of older ones was a desperate need for more retail sales area.[1] A program of building expansion was, consequently, a marked feature of Selfridge's seventeen years as Retail head. During this period were erected most of the sections of the buildings which still house the present huge retail store. Selfridge's persuasiveness has been credited in large part with bringing this great achievement about.[2] Mr. Field, however, was apparently not very difficult to persuade on the matter; and the man who actually footed the bill each step of the way certainly deserves much of the credit for the final accomplishment.[3]

The first step taken in the search for more space was to acquire the two five-story buildings on State Street immediately north of the Singer building. These buildings, acquired in 1888, gave the Retail an additional one hundred feet of valuable store frontage along State Street. The Central Music Hall on the State and Randolph corner was the only remaining building along the State Street side of the block which did not belong to Field's.[4]

Aware that even this large addition of sales space would be insufficient for future needs, Field acquired, between February 1888 and December 1891, the property on the northwest corner of Washington Street and Wabash Avenue (east of the Singer building).[5] This required the purchase of six different deeds at a cost of over $800,000, but a building erected on this corner would give his firm the entire frontage along Washington Street and considerable space along Wabash Avenue.[6] Field promptly leased the land to the firm at 6 per cent per annum and later charged an additional 8 per cent on $800,000 of the cost of the new building,[7] which was rushed to completion by late summer of 1893.[8]

This building, of Italian renaissance architecture,[9] was a nine-story structure of granite[10] and terra cotta.[11] Minus a few layers of Chicago soot, it would be recognized even today as a rather beautiful building. The five[12] top floors, served by elevators, were arranged as elaborate office suites done in fine cabinet woods and marble.[13] The four lower floors[14] devoted to sales area were designed to make them the finest in the city. There was a large handsome entrance decorated with gold-plated ironwork and marble at the corner of Wabash and Washington; and the interior featured expensive plate-glass and solid mahogany showcases, combination gas and electric chandeliers, and

154

12. The New and the Old

double-doored, hydraulic elevators. Perhaps most significantly, it was the first store with modern show windows to be erected by the firm.[15]

The opening on Monday, August 7, 1893,[16] was a typical Marshall Field and Company affair. The store was transformed into a veritable conservatory by a lavish use of blooming plants and cut flowers. The section heads put on display their finest wares; thousands of people came to visit and shop; and the newspapers were very generous in their praise. Everything was "handsome," "magnificent," or "greatest." The success of the event was complete.[17] Selfridge had a new door cut into the southeast corner of the Singer building so that customers could go straight across the alley (called "Holden Court") from one building to the other. With a characteristic Selfridge flourish, he laid down a long jute matting, euphemistically described as a "carpet," between the two exits to eliminate any risk of patrons slipping or soiling their clothes.[18] In addition, the new annex was connected with the main store by tunnels at the basement level and by a covered bridge over Holden Court at the second-floor level.[19] The two buildings thus made conveniently accessible to each other gave the Retail a total of nine acres of floor space and provided the much-needed room for such customer conveniences as the tearoom, parcel room, and additional rest rooms, as well as for the firm's new jewelry section.[20]

The serious Panic of 1893 closed in upon the firm just as the new building was being erected and was full-blown at the time of the formal opening. Before another year had passed, hundreds of banks and mortgage companies and over 15,000 businesses had failed throughout the country. Unemployment was general, and the want and distress of the poorer folk in Chicago led to labor strikes and riots.[21] Retail sales of Marshall Field and Company declined, instead of increasing, for the first time in a decade, despite the glamour of the brand new building.[22] It would appear that any plans for further expansion were dead.

Yet, if few predicted the depression of 1893-94, fewer still foresaw the period of prosperity that was to follow.[23] Retail and Wholesale both quickly recovered and entered upon an era of good times such as they had never before known.[24] By 1897, Selfridge was his old jubilant self. He publicly announced:

At the present time our sales are larger and we are getting more money than ever before. This certainly looks as though the good times had arrived.[25]

The next year (1898) the home of the Retail began again to grow. The cupolas were removed from the old Singer building at State and Washington Streets and in their place was constructed a "remodeled" sixth floor plus two additional stories topped by a flat roof, making the old Singer building eight stories in all.[26]

The last and most significant phase in the building program, however, began in 1900. Its result was the occupation by Field's Retail of the entire city block bounded by State, Washington, Wabash, and Randolph streets, and the erection of a series of buildings which, when completed, appeared to be (except for the Washington and Wabash Annex) but one continuous rectangular structure. Despite plans which dated at least from 1891,[27] this program was not completed until 1914, eight years after Marshall Field's death.[28]

Field gave the structure its start, nevertheless, in 1900, when he obtained from the Chicago Commissioner of Buildings a permit for the erection of a twelve-story building on State Street north of the Singer building and extending to Randolph Street.[29] In the same year he effected the purchase of the Central Music Hall.[30] This gave him complete ownership of the frontage on State between Washington and Randolph Streets and enabled him to raze all three of the buildings (Spear, Hale, and Music Hall) north of the Singer building[31] in order to replace them with his projected new store.

The building which Marshall Field erected for his firm in 1902 and which still stands as part of the retail store is an imposing, dignified structure of white granite and steel. There is nothing of particular beauty in its exterior (except its large show windows) to cause one to stop to comment. But the simplicity of its lines has given it a less "dated" appearance than any of its Marshall Field and Company predecessors so that it appears today almost as modern as when it was built. At the time that it was erected, while the exterior was still a gleaming white and skyscrapers were more of a novelty, it appeared to Chicagoans as a beautiful addition to the city and worthy of the fine store it housed.[32]

This first building filled only about three-fifths of the block along State Street, since the remodeled Singer building was left standing. The huge "main entrance" on State Street, flanked by massive stone columns, was placed at the south end of the new building so that it was in the middle of the whole block and is today in the center of the entire finished building. It was apparently expected that this entryway would be the most used of the entire building (or perhaps used by the carriage trade); for behind its doors was placed a sumptuous vestibule with mahogany-paneled walls, red marble floors, and specially designed chandeliers weighing over twelve hundred pounds apiece. It was as large in itself as many a store.[33] The middle of a busy Street Street block, however, proved to be anything but a convenient vehicle loading point. The vestibule has, as a result, long since been sacrificed to the need for more sales space, even though the huge monoliths still loom impressively before this little-used entrance.[34]

To a new visitor, after viewing the plain, straight lines of the outer walls, the interior of the store must have been a pleasant surprise. Entering the building at Randolph near State Street, there stretched before him for the entire length of the building a spacious central arcade formed by parallel rows of classic white Grecian columns. At the same time, symbolic of a new age, was the total absence for the first time of unattractive gas jets and the substitution of completely electric Tiffany chandeliers. These reflected a much more brilliant light than heretofore on the wares encased in polished mahogany and French

12. The New and the Old

glass counters. Aisles were comfortably wide, and all floors above the first were covered with thick pile carpeting or Oriental rugs. Most striking then, as today, in this building was the atmosphere of spaciousness and grandeur given by the great open light well reaching through twelve floors to the huge skylight in the roof, and on which the intervening floors opened like galleries. This space-wasting feature has through the years caused so much favorable comment that it has successfully resisted all suggestions to eliminate it and add the space as much-needed sales area to each floor.[35] "The premises," boasted the firm in 1902, "are the best that can be erected . . . the fixtures are the most carefully thought out and built . . . and the opening decorations are attractive in the extreme. . . ."[36]

Conscious by this time of its own dignity and importance in the public mind, Marshall Field and Company conducted the erection and opening of its building in 1902 as it might a civic celebration. While the building was under construction, regular reports were issued to the public through newspaper advertisements on the progress of the building and on the wonders which would be revealed when it was completed. In June 1901:

> The great interest shown by the public in the massive foundations now being sunk for our new granite building causes us to print this architect's sketch—which is drawn to scale and is correct—together with the following brief explanation: This building, which is to be *217 feet high* and of great weight, is to be built on 84 enormous *pillars or "caissons" of concrete,* each of which extends downward almost 100 feet through soft clay, hard clay, loam and various kinds of soil until we reach *"hard-pan"*—so hard that no pick will pierce it—and within a few feet of solid rock.
>
> These "caissons" are from 6 to 9 feet in diameter; and at the lower end are belled out to about three times this size. They are being dug by hand, all material is hoisted and lowered by machinery, and every precaution is taken to prevent accident. All day and all night this work is going on—and as a whole these caisson foundations are *vastly greater than have ever before been undertaken for any building.* Thus far the contractors are far *"ahead of the schedule time."* The first ground was broken May 8th, the first caisson touched "hard-pan" May 12th, and at this writing (Saturday noon), of the total number, 38 *are completed* and ready for the steel superstructure, and 24 more are nearly complete. The weight of each caisson is nearly 200 tons—its cubic contents are 2,400 cubic feet, and each *caisson will carry "one million two hundred and twenty thousand pounds."*[37]

In February 1902:

> Our new 12-story steel and granite addition, which together with our present area, will give us over a million square feet of floor space (the largest area in the world devoted to retail merchandising), is being rapidly pushed to completion.[38]

In April 1902:

Every night except Sundays, for the past few weeks an army of people has been employed throughout the store, accomplishing tasks of really great magnitude. Between the closing hour in the evening and the opening hour in the morning (8:00), it has become a common thing to remove an entire section to another part of the building, tear up the old fixtures and floors which have done so excellent service for many years, put down new floors, install the new fixtures, rearrange the goods and be ready for business when the first customer arrives in the morning.[39]

For the grand three-day opening, two hundred thousand formal invitations were mailed to prominent Chicagoans and other interested people in all parts of the world; and full-page newspaper advertisements issued similar invitations to the general public.[40] An estimated 150,000 or more persons came the first day, so filling the store that business was almost suspended. The $10,000 worth of silver spoons, gold bowls, silver pin trays, and postal cards given away as souvenirs was quickly exhausted.[41] When the crowds continued to jam the aisles on the second and third day, the opening had to be extended an additional three days.[42]

The building had cost Mr. Field $1,750,000;[43] but in 1903, the first full year after the completion of the building, the firm made over 70 per cent greater profit than the year before;[44] so Field was ready to invest again and the expansion continued. Arrangements went quietly ahead to acquire more property in this same square block bounded by State, Randolph, Washington, and Wabash streets. Some time previously (1891) Marshall Field had for $100,000 purchased the Whittemore property, with a frontage of 25 feet on Wabash Avenue and a depth of 150.8 feet back to Holden place. That left two lots (the Botsford and Hettie Green properties) separating this acquisition from his Annex building.[45] Field had allowed negotiations previous to 1892 to break down;[46] but in later years the need was too urgent, regardless of the price. The last lot, the Botsford property, was eventually leased (not purchased) as of June 22, 1904.[47] Field then proceeded to tear down the old buildings on the land and to erect in their place, immediately adjacent to the 1893 Annex, another twelve-story granite edifice. This building was consistent in design and appearance with the new State Street store, though not so long, for Field still lacked possession of the Randolph and Wabash corner.[48]

This "middle Wabash" building was not even completed before plans were launched to raze the old Singer building and to erect another section of new building similar to the first two. This was a step that Field was obviously reluctant to take. His sentimental attachment to the old Singer building was strong.[49] But, more important, each new building increased the firm's overhead in rent and taxes and unless sales continued to increase commensurate with the firm's physical growth, the destruction of a building valued at $464,500[50] and the erection of another at a cost of $1,500,000[51] was hardly worth while.[52] Furthermore, the labor unrest in Chicago, the constant talk of city ownership of the street railways, and similar conditions bothered him. "Now you must remember," he wrote Shedd, ". . . how reluctant I am

158

to invest any more money in Chicago with such a government as we have had for fifteen years, *now have* & likely (I am sorry to say) to have. . . ."[53] "If I could see any chance for improvement in City Government, I should feel quite different. . . . Here (in Switzerland) the Gov own most of the RR & you can travel 25 miles an hour & it costs including Baggage full double what it does with us. All fair minded Swisses, are againtst [sic] Gov ownership even when Polotics [sic] is hardley [sic] know [sic] in the management."[54] Nevertheless, on July 4, 1905, he had told Shedd: ". . . if I am willing to go ahead & build I will cable the word 'Singer,' inside 30 days meantime if you have any thing more to say in favor of Building than have said please give it to me on the other hand if I cable the word Singer & you have any reason for not building you will *not* go ahead."[55]

Field took more than thirty days to make up his mind; but finally on August 6, a cable arrived from Burgenstock, Switzerland, for Shedd. It bore only one word: "Singer."[56] Plans were promptly pushed and, on January 2, 1906, the public announcement was made that the old Singer building was to come down and a new building would be erected in its place.[57] Before the old building was razed, it was planned that the basement salesroom should be removed and 57 caissons be sunk 110 feet to solid rock to form the foundation. Also previous to demolition, it was arranged that the Wabash store be finished and be made ready to receive the merchandise from the Singer building so that there would be no disturbance to business.[58]

When the "New Completed Retail Store" was formally opened to the public during the week of September 30 to October 5, 1907,[59] Marshall Field and Company occupied a retail store covering an entire city block, with the sole exception of the Randolph and Wabash corner.[60] According to the firm's own estimate at this time, it was "the world's greatest store at its best."[61] The illuminated Mosaic vault of Tiffany favrile glass gracing the top of the rotunda in the south State Street building (corner of State and Washington) between the fifth and seventh floors was said to be "the largest single piece of glass mosaic in the world, and the first dome ever built of iridescent glass."[62] Requiring almost two years to produce and erect and containing over one million pieces of glass, this many-arched vault was, undeniably, a real work of art.[63] All told, the combined buildings in 1907 provided Marshall Field and Company with almost thirty-five acres of floor space.[64] A conservative evaluation (for tax purposes) placed the worth of the land and buildings which the Retail occupied at a little over $8,000,000.[65]

One result of the erection of the numerous new buildings was to increase retail rents sharply. The acquisition in 1888 of the two buildings north of the Singer building was (along with an adjustment in the method of determining rent)[66] responsible for bringing about much of the rise in the rental expense ratio from 1.32 in 1887 to 1.77 in 1889. In 1893 the building of the Annex, coupled with a drop in net sales caused Retail's rent, as an expense factor, not only to rise again, but to more than double itself. It should be noted that the 1894 percentage of 3.27 was a peak figure, however, and as the sales volume rose to new heights, the ratio dropped rapidly. It was never as high again. In 1898, after two additional stories were added to the Singer building the book value of this particular structure was increased from $300,000 to $464,500.[67] The actual increase in rent, only a little over $13,000, was not, however, reflected seriously in the expense picture even though the total amount of annual rent paid was slightly higher. Finally the erection between 1901 and 1906 of the various sections of the present retail structure was largely responsible for causing the rent to double itself in dollar value,[68] but again as sales continued to mount, the annual percentage expense ratio failed to rise appreciably and it became obvious that the retail market had well warranted the entire building program. Without the increased selling area the store would have become seriously overcrowded and would no doubt have failed to experience much of the great expansion in sales and profits that it did.

TABLE XII

RATIO OF RETAIL RENT TO RETAIL NET SALES FOR MARSHALL FIELD & COMPANY FOR 1887-1906*

Year	%	Year	%	Year	%	Year	%
1887	1.32	1892	1.56	1897	2.82	1902	2.73
1888	1.53	1893	2.00	1898	2.58	1903	2.44
1889	1.77	1894	3.27	1899	2.72	1904	2.26
1890	1.66	1895	3.12	1900	2.41	1905	2.19
1891	1.64	1896	2.99	1901	2.78	1906	2.64

*Computed by writer from figures in accounting ledgers, 1887-1906, Comptroller's safe, Marshall Field & Co. General Offices.

The final summation of all Field's retail expenses in the table below (Table XIII) reveals little that is surprising. The relatively high expense ratios of the seventies (except for 1878 and 1879) reflected both rapidly falling prices[69] and sales rather than any significant dollar increase in expenses. In 1878 and 1879, however, actual costs did drop —largely due to the low rentals of those years. Field's total dollar expenses thereafter showed a steadily rising trend throughout the eighties and early nineties. As already noted, Selfridge's new buildings, his increased advertising budget, and the expanding delivery service plus other such customer services as charge accounts and the liberal acceptance of returned goods made Field's way of doing business more expensive as each year went by. After 1878, with only one exception (1894) there was never a year in which the firm did not find its retail dollar expenses greater than the year before. That this does not always reflect itself in Table XIII is, of course, due to the fluctuations in net sales. As a matter of fact, one of the best evidences of the Re-

12. The New and the Old

tail's sales success during the last years of Mr. Field's life is the fact that while its expenses between 1894 and 1906 rose from about $1,500,-000 to over $5,700,000, the ratio of these same expenses to net sales rose scarcely at all.

In any comparison with other retail firms, most of which offered far less in the way of customer services than Field's, it would be expected that Field's total expense ratio would be higher. An analysis of Macy's expenses tend to bear out this expectation, although the difference in most years was not overly great—approximately 2 to 3 per cent.[70] As already noted, Field's advertising expenses were relatively lower than Macy's and delivery was no higher. The extra services which Field's provided were reflected rather in a high percentage for rentals (customer hospital rooms, playrooms, elaborate waiting rooms, and deep light wells all take up expensive selling space) and probably in a high ratio of salary expense for the numerous non-selling employees necessary to perform such tasks as crediting accounts, checking returned goods, etc.[71]

Some further insight into the real meaning of Retail's annual expense ratio can be attained by comparing it with the firm's own wholesale division. Competition on a strictly price basis is, of course, much greater in the jobbing field than in retailing. Field's Wholesale consequently could ill afford to permit its expenses to climb to such figures as did Retail. It was, moreover, unnecessary since such things as large waiting rooms, elaborate displays, and doorstep delivery are not an expected part of wholesale service. In relation to net sales, wholesale expenses ran along at a rate usually close to one-half those of Retail.

TABLE XIII

RATIO OF TOTAL EXPENSES TO NET SALES, RETAIL AND WHOLESALE,
FOR MARSHALL FIELD & CO. FOR 1874-1906*

Year	Retail %	Who. %	Year	Retail %	Who. %	Year	Retail %	Who. %
1874	14.22	5.41	1885	13.72	7.75	1896	21.72	11.94
1875	15.01	5.93	1886	15.07	8.08	1897	21.23	11.02
1876	15.29	..	1887	14.51	..	1898	19.37	11.02
1877	16.48	7.71	1888	15.36	..	1899	20.26	10.76
1878	14.20	..	1889	15.26	9.18	1900	19.58	10.80
1879	13.05	..	1890	15.31	8.94	1901	20.02	10.20
1880	12.02	6.46	1891	15.36	9.01	1902	21.69	10.72
1881	12.07	..	1892	16.74	8.97	1903	21.17	11.15
1882	12.16	7.13	1893	19.00	10.13	1904	20.83	11.39
1883	12.59	5.71	1894	22.13	10.81	1905	22.86	11.30
1884	13.73	..	1895	21.09	10.86	1906	22.81	10.80

*Only those figures for Wholesale are included in which comparable statistics could be obtained (accounting ledgers, 1874-1906, Comptroller's safe, Marshall Field & Co. General Offices).

It is somewhat surprising, in fact, that wholesaling expenses were even that high; but delivery costs, returned goods, and increased country traveling all raised expenses. If these costs continued to increase it could only serve eventually to raise prices, hurt sales, and cut into profits. The fact that Wholesale for many years showed a rate of increase in her expense ratio comparable to that of Retail certainly boded ill for the future.

The Last Years

Unfortunately Marshall Field never saw the completed retail store as it stands today or even as it looked when the Wabash building was completely occupied.[72] Marshall Field died in January 1906.[73]

The last few years of Field's life were particularly memorable. So many newsworthy events occurred connected either with his personal life or with the firm that few months were permitted to pass without his name appearing in the newspapers. The building program and the continuous prosperity of the firm undoubtedly gave him great personal satisfaction, but not all of his other experiences were equally happy. In many respects he died a disillusioned man.

One of the first blows to Marshall Field was the loss to the firm in 1904 of Harry G. Selfridge. Other partners had retired, usually because of illness, old age, or at Field's own request. This was probably the first time that Field ever lost a partner whom he very badly wanted to keep: for Selfridge was at the peak of his career at the time he chose to leave.

As to why he left, there are more stories told than there is space here to recount them. One of the most widespread reports, still believed by many today, is that Selfridge "demanded his name over the door"; that is, he demanded that the store be renamed "Field, Selfridge and Company" and, when Marshall Field refused, Selfridge withdrew from the firm. A second story is to the effect that Field's refusal to agree to Selfridge's plan to set up a chain of Field's stores across the country brought about the rupture.[74] The entire truth may never be known; but by Selfridge's own admission, it was his ambition that brought about his break with Mr. Field. "Well as I was doing for myself as one of his junior partners," he said, "I wanted to do still better. . . ." He wanted his own store; so in June of 1904 he successfully negotiated the purchase of Schlesinger and Mayer, a State Street competitor in the retail trade. "When I . . . told Mr. Field what I had done," Selfridge recalled, "he took the news very quietly—more quietly than I liked. 'Very good, Selfridge,' was all he said. 'I hope you are successful.' But I could see that he was mortally offended."[75]

12. The New and the Old

Knowing Selfridge to be the type of man that he was, one has little difficulty in understanding his dissatisfaction with the partnership arrangement as it had existed for several years at Field's. In 1901, following the retirement of H. N. Higinbotham,[76] it had been decided to convert the firm from a partnership into a corporation.[77] Marshall Field, grown old, was eager to take a less active part in the business and at the same time prepare for the eventuality of his death. A natural pride in his accomplishment made him want to see his company continue beyond his own lifetime.[78] Yet at the same time, it had become obvious that his only son (Marshall Field II), a frail and retiring young fellow, was not the man to succeed his father and carry on the business.[79] The next best thing was by incorporating, to provide a way for the business to continue under other heads while the Field family inherited a negotiable, profit-sharing interest in the firm.[80]

At the time of incorporation (February 23, 1901), 60,000 shares of stock with a par value of $100 each were issued, giving the company a capitalization of $6,000,000.[81] These shares were then distributed among the "partners" as follows:

Marshall Field	34,000	shares
John G. Shedd	6,666⅔	"
Robert M. Fair	6,666⅔	"
Joseph R. Field	6,666⅔	"
Harry G. Selfridge	6,000	" [82]

When it came time to elect officers, Marshall Field was, of course, made president; and John G. Shedd, vice-president.[83] From Selfridge's point of view, not only did this arrangement delegate to him the smallest share of the profits, but placed his rival, Shedd, in the position of acting head of the entire firm. That Selfridge eventually left is not nearly as surprising as the fact that he stayed on for three more years.

When the announcement of Selfridge's departure was made on May 14, 1904, it created a mild sensation, for he had become a prominent figure in Chicago business and social circles. It was page-one material for almost every daily.[84] Selfridge issued this statement:

I have severed my connection with the house that I have been working for nearly twenty-five years. I have only done so because of a great desire to become the head of a business of my own—to gain the pleasure of direct personal ownership. If I were not absolutely confident of success in my new enterprise I should not have taken this step. I have purchased the entire interests of Schlesinger & Mayer and shall take over the active management of same on June 13 and from that time shall conduct the business as its sole owner, using the firm name of Harry G. Selfridge & Co. I have no associates in the firm and nobody is back of me. As a matter of course I have disposed of my shares in the corporation of Marshall Field & Co. . . .[85]

The amount that he was paid for his shares of stock he later said was "nobody's business but my own." He insisted, however, that it was a "very considerable sum of money," and unquestionably it was a great deal more than the face value of $600,000.[86]

For the stock and leasehold of Schlesinger and Mayer, Selfridge paid a reported $5,000,000 and on Monday, June 13, bravely launched his own new firm.[87] It lasted exactly sixty days. On August 12, State Street merchants were startled to read in the papers that Selfridge had suddenly sold out to Carson Pirie Scott and Company.[88] Working at the head of an army of strangers in competition against people he had known and liked for twenty-five years took all the pleasure away from owning his own store.[89] Furthermore, the excellent employee training and spirit, and the efficient business organization, which he had formerly taken for granted, were lacking. "There are a million things to do and nobody to do them," he told his old assistant at Field's soon after buying the store.[90] Convinced that he had made a mistake, Selfridge got in touch with Carson's, which had also wanted to buy out Schlesinger and Mayer. He found to his pleasure that it still was of this mind. With Shedd acting as intermediary, negotiations were successfully conducted in the deposit room of the Illinois Trust and Savings Bank.[91] Selfridge triumphantly emerged with a payment for his store equal to what it had cost him three months before, plus an additional $250,000 "bonus." Carson's thus had to pay $3,765,000, but it had what it wanted and badly needed—an excellent State Street location.[92]

Neither Selfridge, nor apparently anyone else, gave serious thought to his returning to his old post at Field's. Instead he was lost sight of to the business world for a time until suddenly in 1909 word came from England that Harry Gordon Selfridge was about to launch his most interesting experiment of all, a brand new H. G. Selfridge and Company in London. Beginning this time from the ground up, equipping and training his own organization in his own way from the start, he was a distinct success. Selfridge introduced to Londoners for the first time in his store many of the myriad shopping conveniences that Chicagoans had long taken for granted; he taught his employees what he had learned from Field's about customer treatment; and he had a fine time with his newspaper advertisements, topping them off with little philosophical and moral essays that became almost famous.[93] Selfridge's firm rose to top rank among London department stores.[94]

Another series of events that marred the last years of Marshall Field's life and, in a way, also took the edge off the usual good feelings existing among the personnel of the store were the labor disturbances involving the firm between 1902 and 1905. These were characterized by radical leadership and a great deal of violence, which resulted immediately in the animosity of Marshall Field.

Though not unreasonable in regard to the treatment of his own employees,[95] Field was outraged almost to the point of fanaticism at what he called "lawless strikers."[96] In a day when many looked upon strikes as an illegitimate method of improving labor conditions, it is not strange that Field held strikes in contempt and even hatred. He had been one of the original organizers of the secret, anticommunist and antisocialist Citizens' Association,[97] a heavy contributor to the maintenance of the national guard in Chicago,[98] and was at the fore-front in urging swift action by the police and courts in punishing any disturbance to peace and commerce.[99] At the time of the railroad strike in 1877, he had all the men at Wholesale drilled in how to handle weapons. The guns were kept ready in a rack installed in the carpet department. At the height of the emergency he reputedly posted the men behind bales of cotton at the entrance to repel any mob attacks.[100]

Anything or anybody that served to arouse disrespect for law and order or implied that the business interests had anything but the high-est of motives was sure to feel Field's wrath. When the *Daily News* in 1903, for example, published the headline:

RAILROADS DEFY FREIGHT MEN

Victor Lawson, the editor, heard from Field immediately.

Dear Mr. Lawson

Enclosed clipping is from the News of last evening. I think you will agree with me that the head line only inflames the laboring classes and does no good.

You well know that the railroads of this city are in the hands of the very best men in this country, who desire to treat everybody fairly and justly and to pay their men liberally, and I regret exceedingly to see anything that inflames the public mind.

Trusting you will see this in the same light, believe me,

Very truly yours,

MARSHALL FIELD[101]

On the other hand, a later Lawson editorial advocated that children's "trampling over private lawns . . . ringing door-bells," etc., "should be regarded as serious offenses, subject to constant police repression" in order to "prevent the forming of the habit of disregarding others' rights and of general lawlessness. . . ." This also won a response from Field:

The communication in yesterday's News signed "L" (which I trust means your good self) covers the whole ground. What you say is the cause of most of our troubles for the past fifteen years. I trust you will give us plenty of such good reading.[102]

Mr. Field was obviously interested in all aspects of the labor situa-tion in Chicago, but the disturbances of these last years that particu-larly affected Marshall Field and Company were the two teamsters' strikes of 1902 and 1905. The first of these, launched by a newly or-ganized Chicago department-store driver's union, lasted only ten days during June of 1902;[103] but Marshall Field was nevertheless deter-mined that no union was going to interfere with his business. He asked for volunteers from his own employees to man his wagons, obtained police protection for them, and sent them on their rounds.[104] The strike was settled quickly due to the timely intervention of the Illinois State Board of Arbitration.[105] Field's personal secretary, James Simpson, for several weeks thereafter, nevertheless, hired spies from the McGuire Agency to attend the union meetings of his shipping-room employees in order to provide his chief with information in case of future trouble.[106]

Trouble came when a second strike was called in 1905; and it was more serious than the first. This time the Board proved to be helpless to stop it;[107] so it dragged on from April 6 until late in July.[108] Dr. Howard B. Myers, in his study of Chicago labor disputes, called this strike "undoubtedly the least excusable and most violent labor struggle the city has ever witnessed."[109] The fact that it was merely a "sympathetic" strike—the teamsters had no direct grievance against the Chicago firms—and the fact that the corruption of its leaders was well known, made the employers the more ruthless in attempting to suppress it. Marshall Field and other prominent merchants of the Chicago Employers' Association used their combined wealth in a desperate attempt to break the union once and for all.[110] Marshall Field and Company alone spent $55,000 in subscriptions to the Association and general "strike expenses."[111] Thousands of Negroes and professional "toughs" were imported and added to the force of volunteer employee strikebreakers and deputy police in the pay of the employers. Both sides were armed and Chicago became a virtual battleground. Over twenty persons were killed and over four hundred others injured.[112]

To Marshall Field's typically nineteenth-century way of thinking, there was no question of where the right lay. "We have no quarrel with anyone," he told Lawson, "and only ask the right to use the streets for all lawful purposes entirely unmolested."[113] While the strike was still at its height, he left Shedd to deal with it and went vacationing abroad; but he kept constantly in touch with the progress of events.[114] When the strike finally began to collapse in July, he was elated.

I see by Morning papers that the drivers are beginning to want their old places . . . it took them a long while to find out Shedd. Yesterday I had a letter from my Grand Son Marshall (the one that was so ill) [Marshall Field III], he added a P.S. Grandpapa, don't let the Strikers get the better of you.[115]

By the end of the month it was all over; the union had been crushed.[116]

The last remaining months of Marshall Field's life were marked in rapid succession by events both of great felicity and of great tragedy. On September 5, in 1905, in a ceremony in London at once quiet yet elaborate, Field married a widowed socialite and long-time friend, Delia Spencer Caton.[117] The *Chicago Tribune* reporter on this occasion commented of Field that "the quiet smile that lingers beneath the white mustache was oftener in evidence than in many years gone by";[118] but his happiness was quickly cut short, for only two months later, on November 27, 1905, his only son, Marshall II, died.[119]

12. THE NEW AND THE OLD

The news of Field's marriage and of the death of his son had scarcely passed from the columns of the newspapers before Field's own death was suddenly brought to the attention of the country. Marshall Field died only four months after his marriage and less than two months after the funeral of his son. At the time of his wedding, Field's good health had been the subject of some comment;[120] but on New Year's Day of 1906 he chose to go golfing in the snow (using colored balls) with Robert T. Lincoln, and he caught cold. He still had the cold two weeks later when he took the train to New York on some business related to his railroad holdings. By the time he reached his destination he had developed pneumonia. Though met at the train by a physician and given prompt treatment, he died in New York the day after he arrived (January 16, 1906).[121]

The respect and sorrow expressed by the members of the firm's staff and by persons all over the world upon the death of Field were undoubtedly genuine. Everywhere the consensus of opinion was that here was a millionaire about whom there was no question—he had obtained his money honestly.[122] "He did more to build up the mercantile interests of Chicago than any other man," claimed Henry C. Lytton of the Hub.[123] The *Tribune* printed on January 17, 1906, a cartoon by the famous McCutcheon showing death closing Marshall Field's book of life. The last page of this book read, in part:

A man who by legitimate means built up a great fortune, in the acquirement of which he has never lost the confidence and trust of his fellow-men; whose business triumph has not been by means of financial trickery or the evasion of his Country's Laws; about whose fortune (unlike many other great American fortunes) there has never been a suspicion of taint.

It was unfortunate that such widespread praise of the man had to turn so quickly to partial disillusionment. Field's will, published in all the papers less than a week following his death, was a distinct disappointment. The paucity of his charities need not concern us in this, a history of the company; but his effort to retain almost his entire fortune within his family (and not scatter it too widely even among his few relatives) is of significance. Obviously his major concern was to perpetuate his fortune in the hands of his male descendants and to facilitate continued family control of the business. He left a million dollars each to his wife and his daughter-in-law, six million to his daughter, and scattered a few hundred thousands of dollars among his various distant relatives. A few other millions went to the Field Museum and lesser charities. To his employees Field left a relatively small sum, $100,000 to be distributed only among those with twenty-five or more years of service. To specific executives he gave $200,000.[124] The bulk of the fortune,[125] however, was carefully assigned to his two grandsons with the provision that should one or the other die, the surviving boy was to have everything. Further provisions of the will prevented either grandson from frittering away any sizable portion of his inheritance, at least until he had reached maturity. Field earnestly hoped that "they will each seasonably adopt some regular occupation in life, inasmuch as such an occupation will, in my judgment, greatly promote their usefulness and happiness. . . ."[126] The boys would in any case have a voice in the management of the firm as soon as they reached twenty-five and eventually, if they wished, complete control.[127] To those in the firm who knew Field well this will probably came as no surprise; but among some jurists and much of the public generally it was a bit disappointing. It was one thing to allow a man to accumulate vast wealth; it was quite another thing to permit him to continue to dictate its expenditure for over a quarter of a century after his death for the apparent purpose of creating a family aristocracy of wealth. It was feared that Marshall Field & Company might be destined to become a soulless corporation run by trustees of the estate whose only interest would be to increase the worth of that estate.[128] At the next session of the Illinois General Assembly a law was passed declaring null and void any provisions of future wills which attempted to delay the acquisition of an inheritance by the heir beyond the age of his majority.[129]

Conclusion

Wholesale and retail firms, through their position as distributors of the world's goods, have had the great responsibility not only of supplying many of the actual needs and wants of the world but also of helping to develop the public's tastes, of creating a demand for new products, and of transferring from the consumer to the manufacturer and worker that vital life-giving blood of business, the capital of the world. When Marshall Field died, he left behind him a firm which was apparently at one and the same time the largest single distributor in America in both the wholesale and retail fields.[130] By this time thousands of stores scattered from the Alleghenies to the Pacific coast had learned to depend upon Marshall Field and Company, Wholesale, for their seasonal stocks to the extent of rendering to the Chicago firm almost $50,000,000 in business annually. Other thousands of Chicagoans and suburbanites relied upon the Retail to dictate their fashions and to supply many of ther daily needs to the extent of another $25,000,000 annually.[131] In 1865 this firm was only a small supplier of simple dry goods and confined its $8,000,000 in wholesale and retail sales[132] to the four crowded floors of a modest brick building. The firm then grew within little more than a generation into a huge distributor of a complex variety of articles that required the space of an entire seven-story block-square building for its wholesaling alone and another thirteen-story edifice for its retail efforts, not to mention numerous warehouses, a New York branch, and foreign offices in most of the important countries of the world. That it did this while yet maintaining a deserved reputation for integrity and honesty made it indeed an institution whose history is worthy of note.

Many of the major reasons for this remarkable success of Marshall Field and Company rested in its progressive policies and carefully maintained traditions. The close coöperation insisted upon between the Wholesale and Retail served to provide Retail with an ever-available supply of all types of goods and at a cost lower than that paid by its rivals. Wholesale, in turn, benefited by having so large a customer as Retail and by the close touch which the latter provided with swiftly changing consumer demands. Field's strategy of buying in large quantities and for cash, its insistence wherever possible on buying directly from the manufacturer at home or abroad, and its short-term credit policy, all so helped to lower costs that despite the high quality of its merchandise the firm consistently undersold its competitors. At the same time in the Retail, Field's customer treatment came to be not only unique but nationally famous. The quality of its merchandise, the trustworthiness of its advertising, and, most important, the justice of its returned-goods policy gave customers an unlimited confidence in the value of their purchases. The sheer magnificence of the store and the studied courtesy of the clerks and officials made buying a pleasure; whereas the multitudinous services such as the store hospital, checkrooms, post office, lounges, rest rooms, and delivery service added such a premium of comfort and convenience to shopping at Field's that to go elsewhere seemed pointless.

On the staff side the firm enjoyed similar individuality. Marshall Field's administrative organization was unusual for its efficiency and encouragement of individual initiative. For the lesser employees the firm exhibited, in every respect except wages, a forward-looking policy. Field's grew from a store of perhaps two hundred employees to one providing jobs for twelve thousand men and women; and yet, despite this rapid increase, the firm had an amazing ability to retain throughout the years the loyalty and devotion of its employees. The paternalistic interest in their subordinates which caused the partners of the firm to provide for illness and retirement compensation, clean locker rooms, recreational facilities, and medical care was only a small part of the story. More important was the fact that at Marshall Field and Company the profession of merchandising was elevated from a fawning, menial task for the clerks to a position evidencing skill and dignity. For the increasing numbers of women hired by the store Field's provided a "respectable" place to work. Consideration was shown for their limited physical capacities, need for somewhat shorter hours of labor, and desire for clean, attractive rest rooms and dining facilities. For everyone of ability there was proffered, not just in theory but in practice, the opportunity to rise up the scale of promotion to any of the higher positions, not even excluding partnership in the firm. That the firm never had a partner who had not risen from the ranks is no small compliment to the efficiency of its staff organization.

In many instances Marshall Field alone was responsible for these advanced policies. But while recognizing his undoubted ability as a merchant, it must also be recognized that Field lived in an era that suited his talents. It was the age of big business—an era of national growth, expansion, and consequent speculation. The men who had a little capital and invested it early enough in the right places made money. Marshall Field lived in one of the fastest growing cities in America and put his money and skill into two of the most lucrative fields for investment—trade and real estate. His store profited from his wisdom in both fields. Its situation in Chicago, the "Queen City of the West," its wisely chosen locations within that city, and the good reputation which it inherited from Potter Palmer enabled it to ride the crest from the start and to set the pace for others to follow.

CHART I

RELATIVE RATES OF INCREASE:

SALES OF MARSHALL FIELD & COMPANY

IN COMPARISON WITH TOTAL MANUFACTURES

AND WHOLESALE SALES OF CITY OF CHICAGO

FOR 1867 - 1906[a]

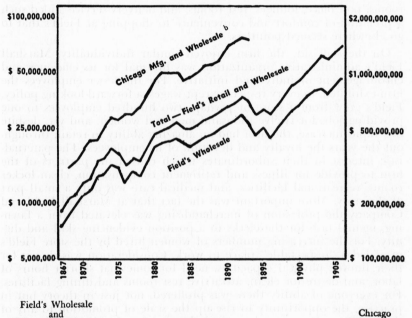

Field's Wholesale
and
Total — Field's Retail
and
Wholesale

Ratio Scale

Chicago
Manufactures
and
Wholesale

[a]*Industrial Chicago*, IV of "The Commercial Interests" (Chicago: The Goodspeed Publishing Co., 1894). See also Table XIV, p. 175.
[b]"Wholesale" sales include the produce trade.

To find any index for comparing the relative growth of Marshall Field and Company with that of other wholesalers and retailers in America at that time is very difficult. Some scattered figures are available for one type of business or another, but to discover any that cover all years of the period under study or that are uniformly accurate and comparable seems to be impossible. Mr. Harold Barger of the National Bureau of Economic Research, however, has arrived at some estimates of separate retail and wholesale dry-goods- and department-store sales in census years for the entire United States. When compared to Marshall Field and Company's retail and wholesale sales, they strongly indicate that the Chicago firm was expanding at a remarkably faster rate than were the dry-goods industry and the department stores for the nation as a whole.[133] This is as might be expected. Of more interest is how Field's fared in relation to other similar businesses in Chicago. For this purpose the best statistics available are those covering the total of the produce and wholesale trade and manufacturers of the city of Chicago for 1868-93. While not complete to 1906 and obviously not in every way comparable to the sales figures of Marshall Field and Company, when plotted on a graph as in Chart 1, they do indicate one interesting possibility, namely that Field's as a firm—or Wholesale separately—apparently did not progress in sales at a rate any faster than similar businesses as a whole in Chicago, if indeed as fast. This same fact seems to be borne out by scattered statistics on later years. For example, total sales in the Chicago wholesale dry-goods and carpet trade for 1893, 1894, and 1900-1904 are available.[134] By computing the average sales of the years 1893 and 1894 and the average sales of the years 1900-1904 we discover that this branch of the Chicago wholesale trade experienced a sales increase of 94 per cent between these two periods. Computing the same averages for Field's Wholesale shows, on the other hand, only a 51 per cent increase. While these figures are by no means conclusive, they would, nevertheless, seem to bear out strongly the belief that Field's growth was no more phenomenal than that of the city in which it was located and even that much of it was only a product of the growth of both Chicago and the West.[135]

Unquestionably Marshall Field also owed much to the fact that he was able to purchase from Potter Palmer a firm which already led the field. Like the proverbial snowball, initial success brought immediate large profits; and large profits meant increased capital which, reinvested in a growing city, brought still further profits. The original $750,000 ventured in 1865 brought a 32 per cent dividend or a return of $240,000 in the first year of business for the two Palmers, Field, and Leiter. Within two years Marshall Field, by reinvesting his portion of such large earnings, had increased his share of the capital from $250,000 to $400,000; Leiter had increased his from $120,000 to $295,-000; and they had been able to buy out the Palmer brothers. In only two more years the capital stock had risen to $1,200,000, and Field and Leiter already had sufficient funds to begin to finance deserving employees who wished to purchase junior partnerships in the firm. Thereafter the capital invested rose steadily, but the two senior partners' incomes provided them with so much more money than was needed to capitalize the firm that they were forced to use their money in enterprises outside the firm. In addition, for those times of the year when the firm's credit was heavily extended to wholesale customers, Field made his growing private fortune continuously available for short-term loans to tide the house over until the receipts came in.[136]

Marshall Field was careful never to take the strong financial position of the store for granted and to coast on its early leadership and reputation. Instead, he constantly strove to maintain and improve its position, but the original impetus given the store at the start was unquestionably of fundamental importance. When the time for testing came in 1873-79, those retailers and wholesalers who had been unable to create a strong financial backlog in the days of plenty found their shelves loaded with high-priced goods purchased on credit and no place to dispose of them at a profit. Only the large firms, such as Field's, which had promptly accumulated the capital that enabled them to buy in large quantities for cash and directly from the manufacturers at home and abroad, could sell cheaply enough to exist in a world of declining prices. Marshall Field and Company was thus early in its career freed of serious competitors to an extent that would arouse the greatest envy from a merchant of the mid-twentieth century. But for the occasional exceptions already noted (*viz.* early competition of the eastern wholesalers and their traveling salesmen and the brief competition of A. T. Stewart's Chicago branch), Marshall Field and Company was never seriously troubled with that finely drawn, day-by-day competition that so characterizes the present stabilized and legally regulated economy of a mature nation. In an age lacking large corporation taxes, excess-profit taxes, social security premium payments, and even personal income taxes, Field's found it comparatively easy, once financially in the lead, to remain there.

Both as an employer and as a buyer and seller Marshall Field and Company was in many ways a "rural" institution. In fact, the very history and success of Marshall Field and Company support the thesis of the growing importance of Chicago as the key city to a greatly expanding agricultural hinterland. Because Chicago as yet was not an extensive manufacturer of many of the things in which Field's dealt, it was necessary for the Company to be an "importer"—a buyer of eastern and foreign manufactured goods for the purpose of supplying the small country stores of a rural and agricultural West. In the early years of its existence, Field's purchased only 3½ per cent of its wholesale needs in the city of Chicago. New York, on the other hand, supplied 88 per cent and foreign imports the remaining 8½ per cent. Even by 1906 Chicago and the Middle West continued to be so preoccupied with things agricultural that Field's was still making 82 per cent of its purchases for Wholesale in New York, had increased its foreign imports to 11 per cent, and was buying only 6 per cent in Chicago.[137]

As America's attention was directed largely toward the land, so did American attitudes tend to come from the land. It was a rural philosophy that until the turn of the century sanctioned Field's employment of young boys for such long hours of work. A people with an agricultural background was slow to see any wrong in youth sharing the burden of responsibility to support the family. Hours of 7:30 A.M. to 6:00 P.M. at the store, though they interfered with school, were no worse than those that many a boy and girl worked on the thousands of American farms. On the matter of hours, furthermore, Field's was no less and usually more considerate than its competitors; but the damage done to the physical and intellectual well-being of hundreds of these youths was all too evident from the employee records of the store.

The same generalization as to rural attitudes can be made in regard to the store's wage policies. Starting rates at Field's were very low and for most categories of work wages never did rise to a very high figure. Only the highest ranking salesmen and the administrative officials obtained good incomes. All wages and salaries were individually bargained for with the heads of the firm and were realistically based, not on the needs of the individual, but on the degree of indispensability of the employee to the store. As a consequence the gap existing between the lower and higher income brackets was extreme. On the whole, wages and salaries, until the turn of the century, rose only very gradually and were slowest to rise at those levels where the need was greatest.

With all this a nineteenth-century America, however, was slow to find fault. When state child labor legislation helped put an end to the store's "cash boy" system in 1904, when labor disturbances rose up to plague it in 1902 and 1905, and when the small retailers and the general public brought forth a rash of anti-department store agitation in the late nineties, all these events were appropriately timed to warn any who cared to notice that a new era was at hand. Rural America was growing up to its new urban and industrial responsibilities.

Into the Future

Marshall Field and Company, before 1906, drew most of its income from wholesaling when large scale dry-goods wholesaling was a profitable and growing business. Today it is not;[138] and there were signs even at the time Field died that wholesaling if not already a declining business, had at least reached its zenith. During the last two decades before 1906, Marshall Field and Company's annual wholesale sales increased 117 per cent; but in that same period its retail sales increased over 450 per cent.[139] While these comparisons are impressive, even more significant is the fact that by 1906 the Retail, which dealt in single items over the counter, was selling more than half as much as the Wholesale, which theoretically supplied it.[140] Actually, as has been indicated, Wholesale no longer did supply all of Retail's needs; but obviously without its own tremendously successful retail branch as a customer, Wholesale's sales would not have increased even to the extent that they did. In 1886 Marshall Field and Company, Wholesale, had depended on its retail branch for only 16 per cent of its

173

12. The New and the Old

total sales; but by 1896 the figure stood at 24 per cent, and by 1906 it was dependent to the extent of 35 per cent.[141] The accompanying Chart 2 showing the relative rate of increase in the sales of the two divisions indicates that Retail was clearly the most rapidly growing of the two. If the trend continued, the retail tail would soon be wagging the wholesale dog.

CHART II

NET SALES OF MARSHALL FIELD & CO.

BY RETAIL AND WHOLESALE

FOR 1867-1906*

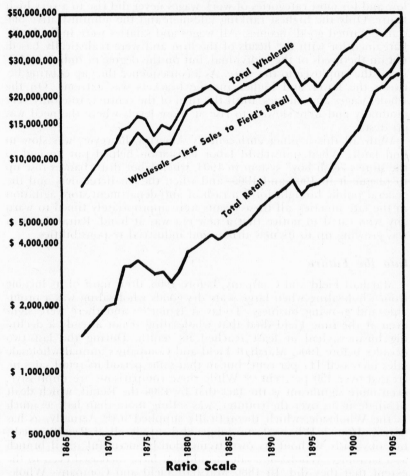

Ratio Scale

*See Table XIV, p. 175; and accounting ledgers, 1877-1906, Comptroller's safe, Marshall Field & Co. General Offices.

174

12. The New and the Old

Obviously, the same technique of buying directly from manufacturers that had been used by Marshall Field and Company's own Retail to cut costs was open for adoption by other large retailers throughout the country.[142] The spread of railroads and manufacturing into the West put sources of supply closer to the retailer and made the general wholesaler of Field's type less and less necessary. There was no mistaking the tendency, and Marshall Field, along with everyone else, saw it. "The Wholesale is a dying business," he is reported to have said; "the trend is to Retail."[143] When in later decades the wholesale divisions of, first, John V. Farwell and Company (1925),[144] then Field's (1935),[145] and finally Carson Pirie Scott and Company (1941)[146] collapsed, it seemed that the obvious signs of aging that had begun to appear even before 1906 had but pointed their natural course toward death.

TABLE XIV

Net Sales of Marshall Field & Co. by Retail and Wholesale for 1865-1906

Year	Retail	Wholesale	Total
1865	....	....	$ 8,000,000[a]
1866	....	....	9,221,000[b]
1867	$1,450,000[c]	$ 7,621,000[c]	9,071,000[c]
1868	....	....	10,419,000[d]
1869	....	....	11,000,000[e]
1870	2,000,000[e]	11,000,000[e]	13,114,000[f]
1871	2,041,000[g]	11,539,000[g]	13,581,000[g]
1872	3,109,000[h]	14,099,000[h]	17,208,000
1873	3,135,000[h]	14,478,000	17,613,000
1874	3,357,000[h]	16,216,000	19,573,000
1875	3,139,000[h]	15,438,000	18,577,000
1876	2,869,000[h]	13,310,000	16,179,000
1877	2,873,000[i]	14,732,000	17,605,000
1878	2,676,000	14,315,000	16,991,000
1879	2,978,000	16,678,000	19,656,000
1880	3,676,000	20,060,000	23,736,000
1881	3,850,000	20,852,000	24,702,000
1882	4,160,000	21,655,000	25,815,000
1883	4,409,000	22,872,000	27,281,000
1884	4,235,000	20,921,000	25,156,000
1885	4,553,000	20,454,000	25,007,000
1886	4,611,000	21,647,000	26,258,000
1887	4,932,000	23,189,000	28,121,000
1888	5,355,000	23,571,000	28,926,000
1889	6,048,000	24,958,000	31,006,000
1890	6,619,000	26,487,000	33,106,000
1891	6,814,000	27,655,000	34,469,000
1892	7,407,000	29,792,000	37,199,000
1893	8,128,000	27,319,000	35,447,000
1894	6,863,000	23,323,000	30,186,000
1895	7,622,000	24,769,000	32,391,000

TABLE XIV—Continued

NET SALES OF MARSHALL FIELD & CO. BY RETAIL AND WHOLESALE FOR 1865-1906

Year	Retail	Wholesale	Total
1896	7,785,000	22,412,000	30,197,000
1897	8,337,000	25,630,000	33,967,000
1898	9,615,000	28,507,000	38,122,000
1899	11,188,000	32,093,000	43,281,000
1900	12,541,000	33,853,000	46,394,000
1901	13,852,000	37,773,000	51,625,000
1902	17,300,000	39,959,000	57,259,000
1903	21,037,000	40,741,000	61,778,000
1904	22,295,000	38,760,000	61,055,000
1905	24,478,000	42,792,000	67,270,000
1906	25,313,000	47,321,000	72,634,000

aA. T. Andreas, *History of Chicago*, II, 695.

b*Chicago Tribune*, June 8, 1867.

cMarshall Field, personal income tax memo, 1868, Marshall Field & Co. Archives. See also *Chicago Times*, May 9, 1868, for a somewhat variant figure.

dEarly memorandum, Marshall Field's handwriting, 1869, Marshall Field & Co. Archives. See also *Chicago Tribune*, October 13, 1868.

e*Hurst, Garlock and Company's Western Reports* (Chicago: [Hurst, Garlock & Co.], 1871), p. 521.

fRetail and wholesale figures do not equal this exact total because they are round numbers (accounting sheet, Field Leiter & Co., 1870, A. B. Jones folder, Marshall Field & Co. Archives).

g*Ibid.*, 1871.

hJohn Shedd record books, 1872-1902 and 1902-6, Marshall Field & Co. Archives. Hereinafter, the wholesale figures cited are from this source. Comparable figures will also be found in accounting ledgers, 1873-1906, Comptroller's safe, Marshall Field & Co. General Offices. See also accounting sheet, Field, Leiter & Co., 1870-73; and salary record, 1872-74, Marshall Field & Co. Archives.

iAccounting ledgers, 1877-1906, Comptroller's safe, Marshall Field & Co. General Offices. Hereinafter all retail figures cited are from this source.

12. THE NEW AND THE OLD

TABLE XV

NET PROFITS OF MARSHALL FIELD & CO. BY RETAIL AND WHOLESALE
FOR 1865-1906

Year	Retail	Wholesale	Total
1865	....	....	$ 240,000[a]
1866	....	....	....
1867	....	....	328,000[b]
1868	....	....	....
1869	....	....	....
1870	....	....	....
1871	....	....	....
1872	$ 41,100[c]	$ 828,400[c]	869,500[c]
1873	18,700	731,300	750,000
1874	72,800	1,137,600	1,210,400
1875	68,000	1,023,700	1,091,700
1876	44,900	754,900	799,800
1877	63,500	810,400	873,900
1878	162,500	721,000	883,500
1879	193,400	1,312,100	1,505,500
1880	384,300	1,441,500	1,825,800
1881	400,400	1,222,500	1,622,900
1882	413,500	1,336,100	1,749,600
1883	433,900	1,298,300	1,732,200
1884	374,000	1,116,200	1,490,200
1885	397,600	1,270,500	1,668,100
1886	408,200	1,157,900	1,566,100
1887	472,400	930,500	1,402,900
1888	512,400	958,600	1,471,000
1889	570,700	916,700	1,487,400
1890	740,000	1,276,000	2,016,000
1891	750,900	1,284,700	2,035,600
1892	744,000	1,666,400	2,410,400
1893	582,100	868,100	1,450,200
1894	318,900	895,100	1,214,000
1895	448,700	1,299,100	1,747,800
1896	501,100	619,800	1,120,900
1897	563,600	1,178,100	1,741,700
1898	714,100	1,223,300	1,937,400
1899	836,600	1,745,900	2,584,500
1900	998,300	1,496,500	2,494,800
1901	989,500	1,351,700	2,341,200
1902	845,500	1,739,700	2,585,200
1903	1,445,000	2,225,600	3,670,600
1904	1,793,300	2,201,200	3,994,500
1905	1,281,700	2,865,300	4,147,000
1906	1,497,700	3,300,000	4,797,700

[a]Computed from information based on Articles of Co-partnership, Field and Leiter, January 1, 1867.
[b]Marshall Field, personal income tax memo, 1868, Marshall Field & Co. Archives.
[c]John Shedd record books, 1872-1902 and 1902-6, Marshall Field & Co. Archives. Hereinafter, the figures cited are from this source.

TABLE XVI

ANNUAL PURCHASES OF MARSHALL FIELD & CO., WHOLESALE, BY
SOURCE FOR 1873-1906[a]

Year	New York Purchases	Chicago Purchases	Foreign Purchases
1873	$12,483,365	$ 515,931	$1,212,439
1874	13,109,629	458,912	1,297,711
1875	13,335,948	553,057	1,523,035
1876	11,442,666	563,546	1,099,471
1877	12,704,181	606,672	1,058,815
1878	12,237,702	645,102	1,081,549
1879	14,808,258	804,876	1,208,568
1880	15,891,862	909,825	2,036,228
1881	16,393,491	840,594	1,549,100
1882	16,815,987	979,310	2,300,423
1883	18,052,740	941,503	2,448,455
1884	15,674,847	846,932	2,246,320
1885	17,147,947	896,585	2,025,647
1886	17,102,509	997,117	2,271,329
1887	18,220,669	1,198,484	2,199,396
1888	18,858,707	1,219,780	2,397,962
1889	20,397,600	1,346,400	2,624,500
1890	20,819,196	1,356,869	2,755,036
1891	21,412,058	1,522,504	2,486,422
1892	23,573,976	1,681,876	3,376,397
1893	20,324,927	1,445,230	3,156,300
1894	18,049,045	1,261,141	2,157,247
1895	20,740,241	1,335,491	3,604,236
1896	16,707,144	1,194,068	2,930,726
1897	20,773,287	1,366,850	3,328,669
1898	23,096,930	1,442,454	3,115,824
1899	28,269,538	1,668,204	3,513,261
1900	27,015,829	1,661,069	4,275,166
1901	30,711,048	1,976,561	3,866,636
1902	35,340,257	2,666,800	4,796,670
1903	35,151,277	2,984,521	4,969,991
1904	35,068,556	3,154,389	4,345,650
1905	40,955,765	3,533,841	5,317,864
1906	43,124,886	3,476,500	5,941,303

[a]Accounting ledgers, 1873-1906, Comptroller's safe, Marshall Field & Co. General Offices.

CHAPTER ONE

1. Palmer had already been a clerk for three years in a general store at Durham, New York, and in business for himself for five years at Oneida and Lockport of the same state (*Chicago Tribune,* October 13, 1868).
2. William O. Stoddard, *Men of Business* (New York: Charles Scribner's Sons, 1895), p. 282.
3. *Weekly Chicago Democrat,* April 29, 1854.
4. [Andrew MacLeish], *Life of Andrew MacLeish, 1838-1928* (Chicago: privately printed, 1929), pp. 27-28; and *Chicago Tribune,* October 13, 1868.
5. November 19, 1852.
6. *Chicago Tribune,* May 5, 1902.
7. MacLeish, *Life . . . MacLeish,* p. 29.
8. *Daily Democratic Press,* November 19, 1852.
9. MacLeish, *Life . . . MacLeish,* pp. 28-29.
10. Potter Palmer, "Memoirs," quoted in Harold I. Cleveland, "Fifty-Five Years in Business: The Life of Marshall Field," *System,* July 1906, p. 24.
11. Letter, Mrs. L. M. Brock to Marshall Field & Co., May 8, 1925, Marshall Field & Co. Archives; bills of sale, P. Palmer & Co., of various dates, *ibid;* and *Chicago Times,* October 6, 1857.
12. Bills of sale, P. Palmer & Co., of various dates, Marshall Field & Co. Archives; *Dry Goods Economist,* [April 15, 1896]; and MacLeish, *Life . . . MacLeish,* p. 29.
13. Bills of sale, P. Palmer & Co., May 17, 1859, Marshall Field & Co. Archives.
14. *Chicago Tribune,* November 26, 1861; and *Chicago Evening Journal,* November 27, 1861. Gibbons in his biography of John Wanamaker, the great Philadelphia merchant, gives the latter credit for originating this "money-back" policy in 1865 (Herbert A. Gibbons, *John Wanamaker* [New York: Harper, 1926], I, 92-94); but Professor Ralph M. Hower has discovered several European firms and at least two New York firms advertising a clear-cut money-back guarantee before Wanamaker had even entered business (*History of Macy's of New York, 1858-1919* [Cambridge Massachusetts: Harvard University Press, 1943], pp. 90 and 94). Palmer was also at least four years ahead of Wanamaker and, as stated above, for the city of Chicago seems to hold very first honors. The following advertisement of L. D. Olmstead and Company, it is true, appeared in the *Chicago Daily Journal* as early as 1852: "We will guarantee our prices in all cases to be as low as the same quality of Goods are sold, at the time, by any one in the city. If it should prove otherwise, in a single instance, we will make it satisfactory or refund the money" (May 1). The limitations of this privilege, however, are obvious. Only when the price was not right could the goods be returned. Palmer's advertisement was distinctly modern in that it covered all contingencies.
15. *System,* July 1906, p. 23.
16. *Daily Democratic Press,* February 13, 1855, and May 24, 1856; and *Chicago Daily Press and Tribune,* November 15, 1858.
17. Palmer's new store was located at 139 Lake Street (*Chicago Times,* October 6, 1857).
18. *Bradstreet's Book of Commercial Ratings,* I and II (1857-58), as quoted in letter of John J. Thornton of the Bradstreet Company, Chicago, to Samuel McClintock, December 5, 1922, Marshall Field & Co. Archives.
19. *Chicago Daily Press and Tribune,* September 30, 1858. Palmer moved

in September 1858 *(Ibid.,* September 21).

20. *Ibid.,* September 30, 1858.
21. *Chicago Times,* October 6, 1857.
22. See the *Chicago Tribune,* September 10 and November 26, 1861; May 19, 1862; and January 23, 1864 for typical Palmer advertisements. No claim can be made for Palmer for any particular cleverness in his advertising copy. Compared to the advertisements of Macy's in New York, for example, the phraseology of Palmer's advertisements lacked subtlety.
23. Palmer's capital at the end of 1858 was fifty thousand dollars *(Bradstreet's Book of Commercial Ratings,* IV).
24. *Chicago Daily Press and Tribune,* September 22 and 30, 1858.
25. *Chicago Tribune,* October 13, 1868; and *Bradstreet's . . . Ratings,* I, II, and IV.
26. *System,* July 1906, p. 24, quoting Palmer's "memoirs."
27. S. H. Ditchett, *Marshall Field and Company, the Life Story of a Great Concern* (1st ed.; New York: Dry Goods Economist, 1922), pp. 15-16.
28. *System,* July 1906, pp. 23-24, quoting Palmer's memoirs.
29. *Chicago Tribune,* November 9, 1861; and *Chicago Evening Journal,* November 8, 1861.
30. This is not to imply that a middleman's margin is always an imposed and unnecessary cost. Certain middlemen perform necessary marketing functions that cannot be properly or economically performed by others. Palmer, however, as a large purchaser of imports and manufactures, was able to perform these functions more economically himself than through others.
31. The *Press and Tribune* in June 8, 1859, gave Palmer credit for being the "pioneer" in eliminating the importer; but Cooley, Wadsworth & Company had at least given the idea a trial as early as 1854 *(Daily Democratic Press,* April 1, 1854). Obviously, however, it was still an unusual practice in so far as the majority of merchants were concerned.
32. *System,* July 1906, pp. 22, 24.
33. *Bradstreet's . . . Commercial Ratings,* I, II, IV.
34. *Chicago Tribune,* October 2, 1861.
35. *Chicago Evening Journal,* November 8, 1861; *Chicago Tribune,* October 13, 1863, November 9 and 26, 1861, and May 19, 1862.
36. Letter, Francis B. Cooley, New York, to Marshall Field, Chicago, April 17, 1863, Marshall Field & Co. Archives.
37. *Chicago Tribune, Annual Review for 1864,* pp. 21-22. Palmer's four-year war profits are usually given as more than $2,500,000. See, for example, *Chicago Tribune,* May 3, 1902.
38. *Inter-Ocean,* May 5, 1902; and James Burnley, *Millionaires and Kings of Enterprise* (Philadelphia: J. B. Lippincott Co., 1901). p. 417. Estimates on Palmer's bond holdings run as high as $2,200,000. See *Chicago Tribune,* May 5, 1902.
39. *Ibid.,* January 23, 1864.
40. *Ibid.,* January 26.

CHAPTER TWO

1. Leiter arrived in the fall of 1854, and Field in January 1856 *(Chicago Tribune,* October 13, 1868).
2. Leiter worked a little over a year for the firm of Downs & Van Wyck before being engaged by Cooley, Wadsworth & Company *(Chicago Tribune,* October 13, 1868; *Chicago Times,* January 27, 1881; and *Chicago Chronicle,* June 10, 1904).
3. Interview, T. Dreiser with M. Field, "Life Stories of Successful Men: Marshall Field," quoted in *Success,* December 8, 1898, p. 7.
4. Marshall Field was born September 18, 1834, according to Conway, Mass., birth records.
5. Letters of recommendation from the Pittsfield employers of Marshall Field: Henry G. Davis, Ez. R.

Colt, and Julius Rockwell, January 19 and 21, 1856, Marshall Field & Co. Archives; and Letter, F. B. Cooley to A. B. Jones, October 10, 1898.

6. T. W. Goodspeed, *University of Chicago Magazine,* VIII (1922) , 26, quoting a letter from Field's sister, Mrs. Philip W. James, to himself, Goodspeed; David W. Wood, *Chicago and Its Distinguished Citizens* (Chicago: Milton George & Co., 1881) , quoting John V. Farwell, p. 459; and Mrs. Abby Farwell Ferry, *Reminiscences of John V. Farwell by His Elder Daughter* (Chicago: Ralph Fletcher Seymour, 1928) , I, 119. See also John V. Farwell, Jr. (ed.) , *Some Recollections of John V. Farwell: A Brief Description of His Early Life and Business Reminiscences* (Chicago: R. R. Donnelley & Sons, 1911) , p. 66.

7. Italics mine (McClintock typescript) .

8. Letter, F. B. Cooley to A. B. Jones, October 10, 1898.

9. T. W. Goodspeed, *University of Chicago Magazine,* VIII (1922) , 26-27, citing a personal interview.

10. Cleveland, *System Magazine,* June 1906, p. 564.

11. E. P. Bailey, Vice-President, Chicago Trust Company and former employee, unpublished reminiscences, Marshall Field & Co. Archives. See also letter, F. B. Cooley to A. B. Jones, October 10, 1898; and McClintock typescript.

12. Circuit Court, Cook County, Illinois, *The Joint and Several Answers of Francis B. Cooley, John V. Farwell, and Marshall Field, Defendants, to the Bill of Complaint of Elisha S. Wadsworth.* [1863] Pamphlet, pp. 1-14 and 30, Chicago Historical Society. Hereafter cited as Cooley, Farwell and Field *vs.* Wadsworth.

13. Ferry, *Reminiscences of J. V. Farwell,* II, 119. The address was Nos. 42, 44, and 46. (Business card, M. Field, traveling salesman for Cooley, Farwell & Co. [1857].)

14. Cooley, Farwell and Field *vs.* Wadsworth, pp. 14 and 21-22.

15. Interview, T. Dreiser with M. Field, quoted in *Success,* December 8, 1898, p. 7.

16. Field's share in the profits was a flat $3,000 yearly (Articles of Agreement, Cooley, Farwell & Co.. with Marshall Field, February 1. 1860, Marshall Field & Co. Archives) .

17. Note made to Francis B. Cooley by Marshall Field, February 1, 1862, Marshall Field & Co. Archives; and Articles of Co-partnership, Cooley, Farwell & Co., and Marshall Field, January 29, 1862, Marshall Field & Co. Archives.

18. Interview, T. Dreiser with M. Field, quoted in *Success,* December 8, 1898, p. 7.

19. Co-partnership, Cooley, Farwell & Co., and M. Field, January 29, 1862; and Bailey, Reminiscences.

20. *Chicago Tribune,* June 9, and September 10, 1861, and Invoice, Cooley, Farwell and Company, May 8, 1863.

21. McClintock typescript.

22. E. P. Bailey, reminiscences, Marshall Field & Co. Archives.

23. *Chicago Chronicle,* January 16, 1906.

24. Letter, F. B. Cooley to M. Field, April 17, 1863.

25. Farwell, *Recollections,* photostat facing p. 72.

26. *Chicago Tribune,* February 3, 1864; and letter, William S. McCormick to Cyrus H. McCormick, January 31, 1864, McCormick Historical Association, Chicago.

27. Bailey, reminiscences and *Chicago Record-Herald,* June 10, 1904. See also *Chicago Chronicle,* June 10, 1904, quoting Harlow N. Higinbotham, a partner in the firm of Field, Leiter & Co.

28. For example, see circular, Farwell, Field & Co., to wholesale customers, 1864, Marshall Field & Co. Archives.

29. *Chicago Tribune,* March 16, 1864.

30. Letter, J. V. Farwell to M. Field, July 5, 1866; and McClintock typescript.

CHAPTER THREE

1. Letter, "Elements of Success," Marshall Field to the Reverend Newell Dwight Hillis, D.D., February 15, Marshall Field & Co. Archives.
2. Co-partnership, Field, Palmer & Leiter, January 4, 1865; and Contractual Agreement for transfer of stock, Field, Palmer and Leiter, January 4, 1865, Marshall Field & Co. Archives.
3. Letters, William S. McCormick to Cyrus H. McCormick, November 29, and December 14, 1864, McCormick Historical Association, Chicago.
4. *Ibid.*
5. *Ibid.*, December 19.
6. *Ibid.*, December 31.
7. Letter, W. S. McCormick to C. H. McCormick, December 26 and 31, 1864; and *Chicago Tribune*, January 17, 1906.
8. Letter, F. B. Cooley to M. Field, April 17, 1863. See also *Chicago Tribune*, October 13, 1868.
9. Letter, W. S. McCormick to C. H. McCormick, December 26, 1864.
10. T. W. Goodspeed, *University of Chicago Magazine*, VIII (1922), 28.
11. Copy of contractual agreement for purchase of the interests of Marshall Field and Levi Z. Leiter in the firm of Field, Farwell & Co., by John V. Farwell and S. M. Kellogg, December 31, 1864, Marshall Field & Co. Archives.
12. Letter, William S. McCormick to Cyrus H. McCormick, December 31, 1864; and Co-partnership, Field, Palmer and Leiter, January 4, 1865.
13. *Ibid.;* and Agreement . . . stock, Field, Palmer & Leiter, January 4, 1865.
14. Though no comparative figures are available for 1865, the *Chicago Tribune* of June 8, 1867, shows the sales in 1866 of Field, Palmer & Leiter's nearest St. Louis competitor to be $3,127,223, and their nearest Cincinnati competitor to be $2,700,000, whereas Field, Palmer & Leiter, as the largest Chicago firm, had sales of $9,220,967. See also *ibid.*, January 23, 1868.
15. Palmer's original location at 112-116 Lake Street consisted of "two floors [store fronts], each fifty-six feet in width by one hundred and fifty feet in depth" *(Chicago Daily Press and Tribune*, September 30, 1858). Later 110 Lake Street was added *(Chicago Tribune*, December 22, 1863), which should have given a total of approximately one hundred and fifty feet of frontage.
16. *Chicago Daily News*, August 25, 1926, quoting John Devlin, fifty-year employee. Two years later (1867) an additional story was added (see Plate II).
17. Letter, Levi Z. Leiter to Marshall Field, March 13, 1867, Marshall Field & Co. Archives; and McClintock typescript.
18. Walter Scott Clark, presentation address, as quoted in pamphlet commemorating banquet tendered R. M. Hitchcock, fifty-year employee, July 1, 1915, Marshall Field & Co. Archives.
19. *Chicago Tribune*, October 13, 1868; and *Chicago Evening Post*, August 25, 1926, quoting John Devlin, fifty-year employee.
20. Bessie Louise Pierce, *A History of Chicago from Town to City, 1848-1871* (New York: Alfred A. Knopf, 1940), II, 317-19; and *Chicago Daily News*, August 25, 1926.
21. *Chicago Tribune*, May 4, 1866; and *Chicago Times*, May 8, 1866.
22. The term "notions" was used in a broader sense than it is today. In 1865 a notions department included everything except the simplest dry goods. *(Chicago Times*, May 8 and June 2, 1866; and miscellaneous invoices, Field, Palmer & Leiter, Marshall Field & Co. Archives).
23. McClintock typescript, citing a personal interview with Willard R. Wiley, employed in 1865. The use of women clerks dates back as early as 1852 in Chicago *(Daily Democratic Press*, October 20, 1852); but it was still a matter of controversy in 1855 *(Daily Democratic Press*, February 13, 1855) and did not begin to become common, in the sense of large numbers, until late in the nineteenth century.

24. Miscellaneous invoices, Field, Palmer & Leiter, Marshall Field & Co. Archives.
25. *Herald-Examiner,* August 25, 1926.
26. Co-partnership, Field, Palmer & Leiter, January 4, 1865; letter, R. M. Hitchcock to James Simpson, May 10, 1922; and letter, L. Leiter to M. Field, March 13, 1867.
27. *Chicago Tribune,* January 17, 1865.
28. Form letter to wholesale customers, Field, Palmer & Leiter, August 10, 1865.
29. Invoices, Field, Palmer & Leiter, June 15, October 13, December 28 and 30, 1865; and May 28 and October 15, 1866, Marshall Field & Co. Archives.
30. *Chicago Daily News,* August 25, 1926; and *Journal of Commerce,* March 28, 1938, citing early delivery department employee.
31. See Table XIV, p. 175.
32. The exact amount of sales for 1866 for Field, Palmer & Leiter was $9,-220,967 *(Chicago Tribune,* June 8, 1867). J. V. Farwell & Co. sales reached $6,948,328; and Bowen, Whitman & Winslow, $3,458,876. With one exception, the sales of all other dry-goods firms fell below one million (John S. Wright, *Chicago: Past, Present, Future* [Chicago, 1868], p. 148). The above figure for Field, Palmer & Leiter includes both wholesale and retail, while the other firms named were solely jobbers. Judging from 1867 figures, however, Field, Palmer & Leiter's sales exceeded those of the above firms even in wholesale alone *(ibid.).*
33. July 5. The offer was repeated on November 26, of the same year (Marshall Field & Co. Archives).
34. Co-partnership, Field, Palmer & Leiter, January 4, 1865.

35. See, for example, letter, C. P. Griffing to Marshall Field, December 26, 1897, Field Estate, Chicago. See also salary record book, 1872-74 (pages not numbered), Marshall Field & Co. Archives (hereafter cited as "Salary Record, 1872-74").
36. Salary record book, 1871-87 [pages not numbered], Marshall Field & Co. Archives (hereafter cited as "salary record, 1871-87") ; and "Edward Nevers," *Dry Goods Economist,* August 28, 1920, p. 52.
37. Salary record, 1871-87.
38. *Chicago Tribune,* October 13, 1868.
39. Co-partnership, Field, Palmer & Leiter, January 4, 1865.
40. Statement, F. W. Boyden, employee, quoting Mr. Merritt of Conway, Mass., executor of estate of John Field (Marshall's father), Marshall Field & Co. General Offices.
41. Co-partnership, Field, Palmer & Leiter, January 4, 1865. See addendum to contract.
42. *Ibid.*
43. As evidenced by sales figures for 1865 and 1866 (see Table XIV) and small loss from debts *(Bradstreet's . . . Commercial Ratings,* Vols. XVI and XVIII, quoted in letter of John J. Thornton to Samuel McClintock, December 5, 1922; and *Dun, Barlow & Co.'s Book of Commercial Ratings [1859-1881],* 1865, as quoted in letter of A. E. Sullivan, Dun & Bradstreet, Inc., N. Y., to Robert W. Twyman, February 12, 1948) .
44. Contractual agreement for purchase of stock from Field, Palmer & Leiter by Field, Leiter & Co., January 1, 1867, Marshall Field & Co. Archives.

CHAPTER FOUR

1. *Chicago Tribune,* May 3, 1902 and October 13, 1868; and *Inter-Ocean,* May 5, 1902.
2. Homer, Hoyt, *One Hundred Years of Land Values in Chicago: 1830-1933* (Chicago: University of Chicago Press, 1933) , p. 89.

3. *Ibid.;* and *Inter-Ocean,* May 5, 1902.
4. Cleveland, *System Magazine,* July 1906, quoting Palmer's "memoirs"; *Chicago Tribune,* January 27, 1881, and October 13, 1868; "Chicago," *Scribner's Monthly,* X

(1875), 544; Hoyt, . . . *Land Values in Chicago*, p. 90; and *Chicago Times*, October 13, 1868.

5. *Chicago Times*, October 13, 1868.

6. Hoyt, . . . *Land Values in Chicago*, p. 90.

7. James Simpson, "Simplifying Buying for the Merchant," *Nation's Business*, July, 1929, pp. 41-42; *Chicago Herald-American*, May 4, 1949.

8. *Chicago Tribune*, October 13, 1868.

9. *Chicago Daily News*, August 25, 1926.

10. *Chicago Times*, October 13, 1868; and *Chicago Tribune*, October 13, 1868.

11. *Ibid.*

12. *Chicago Daily News*, August 25, 1926; and *Chicago Evening Post*, August 25, 1926.

13. *Chicago Times*, October 4, 5, 6, 7, 8, 11, and 12, 1868; *Chicago Tribune*, October 12 and 13, 1868; and *Evening Post*, October 10, 1868.

14. *Chicago Tribune*, October 13, 1868.

15. McClintock typescript, quoting Ferdinand A. Bischoff, fifty-year employee.

16. October 13, 1868.

17. October 13, 1868.

18. Co-partnership, Field, Palmer & Leiter, January 4, 1865.

19. Personal interview, Dr. J. L. Munson, head, Marshall Field & Co. health department, July 1947; and interview, J. G. Hall with Fred Bonk, greeter, October 18, 1939, courtesy History of Chicago Project.

20. Letter, Marshall Field to L. G. Woodhouse, November 25, 1875, Field Estate.

21. Letter, William L. Hipsley, Table Grove, Illinois, to W. F. Hypes, general salesman, December 28, 1922, Marshall Field & Co. Archives; and statement, John McKinlay, Marshall Field & Co., General Offices.

22. Interview, T. Dreiser with M. Field, quoted in *success*, December 8, 1898, p. 7.

23. For example, see circular, Field, Leiter & Co. [1867], Marshall Field & Co. Archives; and *Chicago Tribune*, April 17, 1866.

24. Interview, T. Dreiser with M. Field, quoted in *Success*, December 8, 1898, p. 7.

25. See, for example, *Chicago Herald and Examiner*, May 26, 1918; and William P. Green, "Marshall Field Store Reflects Business Building Policies," *Associated Advertising*, XII (December 1921), 5.

26. Stanley, nephew of Marshall Field, and the latter's representative on the State Street Managers' Association, had to hear most of these complaints (statement, Stanley Field, Marshall Field & Co. General Offices). Marshall Field has also erroneously been given credit for being one of the first to introduce the "one-price" policy (Lloyd Wendt, "Marshall Field's," *Holiday*, May 1947, p. 42; and "The Meaning of Field Leadership," Marshall Field & Co. Archives. Typescript). Actually, not only in New York, Philadelphia, and the larger foreign cities but also in Chicago there were several stores advertising "one-price" long before Field and Leiter opened their doors — some at least as early as 1849 *(Chicago Tribune*, April 23). See also *Chicago Daily Journal*, December 8, 1852; and *Daily Democratic Press*, April 1, 1854.

27. Marshall Field and Company, "Beginnings of Foreign Importations" (unpublished typescript, Marshall Field & Co. Archives), citing interviews with Edward F. Ernst and other employees. Also, undated "Memorial Sheet" from *Dry Goods Economist*, Marshall Field & Co. Archives.

28. *Press and Tribune*, June 8, 1859; and *Daily Democratic Press*, April 1, 1854.

29. Accounting ledgers, 1873-1906, Comptroller's safe, Marshall Field & Co. General Offices.

30. Marshall Field and Company, "Beginnings of Foreign Importations," typescript. Earliest letterhead still available and listing Paris office is of March 1, 1872 (form letter, Field, Leiter & Co., to wholesale customers, Marshall Field & Co. Archives).

31. Letter of instruction, Marshall Field to Joseph N. Field, May, 1871, Marshall Field & Co. Archives.

32. Hilton Thorpe, "Joseph Nash Field—As I Knew Him" (Unpublished typescript, Marshall Field & Co. Archives, November 1945), pp. 1-2.

33. *Chicago Tribune,* April 26, 1872; and *Spring Catalogue,* Field, Leiter & Co., Wholesale, 1871, Marshall Field & Co. Archives.

34. Thorpe, "Joseph Nash Field—As I Knew Him," p. 2; Letter of instruction, M. Field to J. N. Field, May, 1871; statements, Hilton Thorpe and Stanley Field, Marshall Field & Co. General Offices; letters, Marshall Field to Joseph N. Field, June 30, 1875; and to Field, Leiter & Co., New York, December 5, 1875, Field Estate.

35. *Chicago Tribune,* October 5, 1871.

36. *Ibid.,* October 1, 1870.

37. *Ibid.,* October 3, 1871.

38. Statement, Hilton Thorpe, Marshall Field & Co., General Offices.

39. "The Dry Goods Market," *Economist and Dry Goods Reporter,* March 20 and April 3, 1872, J. D. Stone Scrapbook, p. 17, Marshall Field & Co. Archives; statement, Hilton Thorpe, Marshall Field & Co. General Offices. Also see Field advertisements in *Chicago Evening Journal, Chicago Times,* and *Chicago Tribune* for these years.

40. *Ibid.,* April 28, 1872.

41. *Chicago Herald and Examiner,* October 23, 1924. See also, *Chicago Evening American,* October 22, 1924.

42. *Chicago Herald and Examiner,* October 23, 1924; and *Chicago Daily News,* October 22, 1924.

43. For sources of these and all subsequent sales and profits figures see Tables XIV and XV.

44. Accounting ledgers, 1873-1906, Comptroller's safe, Marshall Field & Co. General Offices.

45. Contractual agreements, Alfred Ray with Field, Leiter & Co., January 24, 1873; and Marshall Field & Co., with John E. Jenkins, superintendent of retail and wholesale dress goods department, January 1,

1882, A. B. Jones folder, Marshall Field & Co. Archives.

46. Invoice, J. V. Farwell & Co., February 18, 1868.

47. *Spring Catalogue,* Field, Leiter & Co., Wholesale, 1870, pp. 15 and 74; and advertising circulars, Field, Leiter & Co., [late 1870's]. Also see wholesale invoices, Field, Palmer & Leiter, June 15, 1865 and July 26, 1866, Marshall Field & Co. Archives.

48. Dun, *Barlow's . . . Ratings (1859-1881),* as quoted in letter, A. M. Sullivan, Dun & Bradstreet, Inc., to R. W. Twyman, February 12, 1948; *Chicago Tribune,* October 13, 1868; and letter, Marshall Field to Field, Leiter & Co., N. Y., August 20, 1875, Field Estate.

49. Accounting ledgers, 1873-1906, Comptroller's safe, Marshall Field & Co. General Offices.

50 Advertising circular, Field, Leiter and Company [late 1870's], Marshall Field & Co. Archives.

51. Advertising circular, Field, Leiter and Company, Wholesale, autumn, 1877, Marshall Field & Co. Archives.

52. See also *Chicago Tribune,* May 4, 1872.

53. Letters, Marshall Field to Field, Leiter & Co., N. Y., August 20, 1875 and December 2, 1877; and to L. G. Woodhouse, April 6, 1876; and letter, Field, Leiter & Co. to Field, Leiter & Co., N. Y.; February 11, 1876, Field Estate. See also J. Moses and J. Kirkland, *History of Chicago, Illinois* (Chicago: Munsell & Co., 1895), I, 288.

54. *Spring Catalogue,* Field, Leiter & Co., Wholesale, 1870, p. 72.

55. *Ibid.,* p. 5. See also advertising circular, Field, Leiter & Co., Wholesale, February 28, 1876, Marshall Field & Co. Archives.

56. Marshall Field & Co., "Beginnings of Foreign Importations."

57. Letters, Marshall Field to Field, Leiter & Co., N. Y., March 30, 1877; and to L. G. Woodhouse, April 6, 1877, Field Estate.

58. Letters, Marshall Field to Field, Leiter & Co., N. Y., November 18, 1876 and to L. G. Woodhouse, April 16, 1877, Field Estate.

59. Field, Leiter & Co., Chicago, to Wright, Bliss and Fabyan, New York, Field Estate; March 29, 1878; and M. Field to Field, Leiter & Co., New York, August 20, 1875.

60. Wholesale record, Marshall Field & Co., August 7, 1896, p. 213.

61. Letter, Marshall Field, Switzerland, to John G. Shedd, August 7, 1905, Marshall Field & Co. Archives.

62. Advertising circular, Field, Palmer & Leiter, December 3, 1866, Marshall Field & Co. Archives.

63. Letter, Field, Leiter & Co., to Wright, Bliss & Fabyan, New York, March 29, 1876.

64. *Ibid.*

65. *Ibid.*

66. *Chicago Tribune* and *Chicago Chronicle,* June 10, 1904. See also, "Marshall Field & Co.'s [sic], Chicago," *Mercer,* I (June 1891), 19.

67. This later credit policy is discussed in Chapter VIII, pp. 95 ff.

68. Co-partnership, Field, Palmer and Leiter, January 4, 1865.

69. Advertising circular, Field, Leiter & Company, Wholesale, March 1, 1872, Marshall Field & Co. General Offices.

70. The earliest instance of anything of this sort of which there is any record is found in a letter, Field, Leiter & Co. to T. C. Powers, Ft. Benton, May 21, 1875, Field Estate. See also letter, S. G. Gould, Salem, Oregon, to Marshall Field, May 15, 1890, Field Estate; and Marshall Field personal record book, real estate and salaries [1866-1901], Marshall Field & Co. Archives.

71. Wholesale record, Marshall Field & Co., p. 208. Also, statement, E. F. J. Kuliecki, Marshall Field & Co. General Offices; and inter-office communication, Marshall Field & Co., Counting Room, Credit Division, to C. A. Day, October 5, 1906, Marshall Field & Co. Archives.

72. "Mr. Higinbotham's Views of the Cash and Credit Systems," *Chicago Dry Goods Reporter,* XXVII (February 20, 1897), 11.

73. *Chicago Tribune,* June 10, 1904; and *Mercer,* I (June 1891), 19; and *Hurst, Garlock and Company's Western Reports,* 1871, p. 522.

74. *Chicago Tribune,* June 10, 1904.

75. Interview, T. Dreiser with M. Field, quoted in *Success,* December 8, 1898, p. 7.

76. *Inter-Ocean,* January 28, 1890.

77. *Spring Catalogue,* Field, Leiter & Co., Wholesale, 1870, p. 5.

78. *Inter-Ocean,* January 28, 1890. See also letter, M. Field to Field, Leiter & Co., New York, August 20, 1875.

79. *Ibid.*

80. Harlow N. Higinbotham, *The Making of a Merchant* (Chicago: The Curtis Publishing Co., 1902), pp. 145-46.

81. Statement, Philip James, Marshall Field & Co. General Offices.

82. *Hurst, Garlock and Company's Western Reports,* 1871, p. 521, Marshall Field & Co. Archives; and *Dun, Barlow's . . . Ratings, 1865-1881,* as quoted in letter, A. M. Sullivan, Dun & Bradstreet, Inc., N. Y., to Robert W. Twyman, February 12, 1948.

83. *Chicago Tribune,* June 10, 1904.

84. Higinbotham, *The Making of a Merchant,* p. 41.

85. *Ibid.,* p. 143; statement, Joseph Yates, wholesale, Marshall Field & Co. General Offices; letters, M. Field to L. G. Woodhouse, August 11, 1875; and Field, Leiter and Company to Field, Leiter and Company, Manchester, July 24, 1875, Field Estate.

86. See early copies of such reports in Marshall Field & Co. Archives.

87. Field, Leiter and Company book of confidential wholesale credit ratings, 1873-79, Marshall Field & Co. Archives.

88. McClintock typescript.

89. Wholesale record, Marshall Field & Co. [circa 1873], p. 3. See also Higinbotham, *The Making of a Merchant,* pp. 168-69.

90. *Hurst, Garlock and Company's Western Reports,* 1871, p. 521.

91. Letter, W. F. Hypes, salesman, wholesale, Marshall Field and Company, to D. R. Nicholson, Madison, Nebraska, April 24, 1905, R. H. Bettcher record book, Marshall Field & Co. Archives.

92. Higinbotham, *The Making of a Merchant*, pp. 179-80. See also letter, "Elements of Success," M. Field to the Rev. N. D. Hillis, D.D., February 15, 1896.

93. For example *Chicago Tribune*, January 17, 1906; and Ditchett, *Marshall Field and Company*, pp. 56-57.

94. For example letter, L. Leiter to M. Field, March 13, 1867.

95. Thorpe, "Joseph Nash Field—As I Knew Him," pp. 3-4; and *Chicago Dry Goods Reporter and Wholesale Price List*, July 7, 1894, pp. 6-7.

96. Cleveland, *System Magazine*, November 1906, p. 464.

97. *Hurst, Garlock and Company's Western Reports*, 1871, p. 521.

98. Contractual agreement, John and James Dobson, Philadelphia, with Marshall Field & Co. (for plush for fall season of 1891), July 1 and December 31, 1891, Marshall Field & Co. Archives; "Topics Referred to at the Meeting [of section managers] of November 4th, 1902" (unidentified scrapbook), Marshall Field & Co. Archives. Typed.

99. Letters, Marshall Field to Lorenzo G. Woodhouse, New York, June 26, 1875; and Marshall Field to Field, Leiter & Co., New York, June 24, 1875, Field Estate.

100. Wholesale record, Marshall Field & Co., June 27, 1896, p. 211.

101. *Ibid.*, January 5, 1904, p. 401.

102. *Inter-Ocean*, January 28, 1890; statement, Porter Case, wholesale salesman, Marshall Field & Co. General Offices; and *Chicago Tribune*, December 29, 1867.

CHAPTER FIVE

1. Letter, L. Leiter to M. Field, March 13, 1867; and Contractual agreement . . . stock, Field, Leiter & Co., January 1, 1867.

2. *Chicago Tribune*, January 27, 1881.

3. *Chicago Daily News*, August 25, 1925; and *Chicago Tribune*, August 25, 1926.

4. Harriet Monroe (ed.), *Harlow Niles Higinbotham: A Memoir with Brief Autobiography* (Chicago: Privately Printed, 1920), p. 15.

5. Dorsha B. Hayes, *Chicago, Crossroads of American Enterprise* (New York: Julian Messner, Inc., 1944), p. 157, citing *Paper*, prepared in 1939 by Mrs. Cornelius Wacker McLaury who was about 23 years of age at the time of the fire; and MacLeish, *Life of MacLeish*, pp. 52-53.

6. McClintock, citing account of fire rendered by Mr. Parker, salesman of firm at the time.

7. Monroe, *Harlow Niles Higinbotham*, pp. 15-16. Almost $600,000 worth of goods were saved in this fashion (letter, Levi Leiter to Joseph N. Field, December 28, 1871, enclosure, financial statement of October 9, 1871, Marshall Field & Co. Archives).

8. Mabel McIlvaine, *Chicago: Her History and Her Adornment* (Chicago: C. D. Peacock, Inc., 1926), pp. 31-32.

9. Monroe, *Harlow Niles Higinbotham*, p. 15.

10. A. T. Andreas, *History of Chicago* (Chicago: A. T. Andreas, Pub., 1885), II, 734, citing Horace White editor of *Chicago Tribune* in 1871; and McIlvaine . . . *Chicago During the Great Fire*, p. 641, citing letter, Horace White to M. Halstead.

11. *Chicago Times*, October 13, 1868.

12. Letter, Frank R. Swartout, son of C. R. Swartout, former employee, to Samuel McClintock, May 5, 1924, Marshall Field & Co. Archives; and *Chicago Tribune*, August 25, 1926.

13. Monroe, *Harlow Niles Higinbotham*, p. 15.

14. *Ibid.*; letter, J. Hale, Chicago to H. Townsend, Iowa, October 8, 1871; and *Chicago Tribune*, October 11, 1871.

15. E. J. Goodspeed, D.D., *History of the Great Fires in Chicago and the West* (New York: H. S. Goodspeed

& Co., 1871), p. 266; and G. P. Upton and J. W. Sheahan, *The Great Conflagration: Chicago, Its Past, Present and Future* (Chicago: Union Pub. Co., 1871), p. 79.

16. Letter, F. Swartout to S. McClintock, May 5, 1924; and *Chicago Tribune,* August 25, 1926. *Infra,* p. 39.

17. See Plate IV.

18. Monroe, *Harlow Niles Higinbotham,* p. 16.

19. *Ibid.,* p. 17.

20. Letter, Leiter to J. N. Field, December 28, 1871, enclosure, financial statement of October 9, 1871.

21. *Ibid.*

22. *New York Evening Post,* July 22, 1872, Stone Scrapbook, Marshall Field & Co. Archives.

23. *Chicago Tribune,* November 3, 1871 and January 27, 1881; and *Chicago Times,* October 20, 1871.

24. T. W. Goodspeed, *University of Chicago Magazine,* VIII (1922), 33, quoting William A. Croffut, managing editor, *Chicago Evening Post.*

25. "New York Dry Goods Market," *New York Economist and Dry Goods Reporter,* October 27, 1871, J. D. Stone Scrapbook, p. 1, Marshall Field & Co. Archives; *Chicago Tribune,* October 28, 1871; *Chicago Evening Post,* October 24 and 28, 1871; and *Chicago Times,* October 28, and November 8, 1871.

26. *Chicago Tribune,* November 3 and 6, 1871.

27. *Chicago Times,* November 8, 1871.

28. T. W. Goodspeed, *University of Chicago Magazine,* VIII (1922), 33, quoting William A. Croffut, managing editor, *Chicago Evening Post.*

29. Farwell, *Recollections,* pp. 70-71.

30. *New York Economist and Dry Goods Reporter,* October 27, 1871, Stone Scrapbook, p. 1, Marshall Field & Co. Archives.

31. Letter, Field, Leiter and Company to H. Greenbaum, November 15, 1871.

32. *Dun, Barlow's . . . Ratings,* 1871, as quoted in letter, A. M. Sullivan, Dun & Bradstreet, Inc., to R. W. Twyman, February 12, 1948; and Paul M. Angle (ed.), *The Great Chicago Fire; Described in Seven Letters,* citing letter, Anna E. Higginson, wife of George M., real-estate broker, to Mrs. Mark Skinner in Europe, November 10, 1871. Most of the other dry-goods firms in Chicago were also able to pay in full and on time; but Field's and Leiter's greatest Chicago competitor, John V. Farwell, asked for a settlement which allowed him as long as three years to pay. As a consequence, the latter withstood considerable criticism and injury to his credit standing *(ibid.);* and *New York Economist and Dry Goods Reporter,* October 27 and November 3, 1871, J. D. Stone Scrapbook, p. 3, Marshall Field & Co. Archives.

33. Letter, Leiter to J. N. Field, December 28, 1871, and enclosure, financial statement of October 9, 1871.

34. *Chicago Times,* November 3, 1871.

35. Robert M. Fair personal record book of rents and property, "compiled June 1, 1901," Marshall Field & Co. Archives; *Chicago Tribune,* October 20, and 21, and November 3, 1871.

36. See opinion of Frederick F. Cook in *Bygone Days in Chicago: Recollections of the "Garden City" of the Sixties* (Chicago: A. C. McClurg & Co., 1910), pp. 187-88.

37. Farwell, *Recollections,* pp. 70-71.

38. *Chicago Evening Journal,* December 11, 1871.

39. Letter, December 28, 1871.

40. *Chicago Tribune,* October 20 and 21, and November 3, 1871.

41. *Ibid.,* March 3, 1872.

42. Letter, Leiter to J. N. Field, December 28, 1871.

43. Advertising circular, Field, Leiter & Co., Wholesale, March 1, 1872.

44. *Mercer,* I (June 1891), 17; and accounting ledgers, 1873-1906, Comptroller's safe, Marshall Field & Co. General Offices.

45. *Report of the Industrial Commission on the Relations and Conditions of Capital and Labor,* VII (Washington: Government Printing Office, 1901), 45.

46. *Chicago Tribune,* March 3 and 25, 1872; and *Chicago Evening Journal,* April 2 and 4, 1872.

47. *Spring Catalogue,* Field, Leiter & Co., 1870, p. 4; and 1871, p. iv.

48. Agreement . . . stock, Field, Palmer & Leiter, January 4, 1865.

49. Accounting sheets, net sales, Retail, 1872-73, A. B. Jones folder, Marshall Field & Co. Archives; and accounting ledgers, 1873-1906, Comptroller's safe, Marshall Field & Co. General Offices.

50. *Chicago Tribune,* February 16, 1874; and McClintock, p. 199, quoting James O'Malley, Austin O'Malley, and Walter Haskell, carpet men who came to Field's in 1870 and 1872.

51. *Chicago Evening Journal,* May 29, 1872; and *Chicago Tribune,* September 29, 1872 and February 16, 1874.

52. Letters, Field, Leiter & Co. to Field, Leiter & Co., Manchester, England, June 16, 1875; Field, Leiter & Co. to Field, Leiter & Co., New York, June 8, 1875; and Marshall Field to Lorenzo G. Woodhouse, New York, September 27, 1876, Field Estate.

53. Accounting ledgers, 1873-1906, Comptroller's safe, Marshall Field & Co. General Offices.

54. Accounting sheets, profit and loss, retail and wholesale, 1872-91, and accounting sheets, recapitulation, retail departments, 1873, A. B. Jones folder, Marshall Field & Co. Archives.

55. *Chicago Tribune,* October 15, 1872.

56. Advertising circular, Field, Leiter and Company, November 7, 1876, Marshall Field & Co. Archives.

57. *Chicago Times,* April 5, 1872.

58. *Chicago Tribune,* October 13, 1868.

59. *Spring Catalogue,* Field, Leiter and Company, 1871, p. 80. The same goods were sold in the retail store (see again, contractual agreement, Alfred Ray with Field, Leiter & Co., January 4, 1873; Barbour (ed.), *Sketchbook of the Inter-State Exposition, Chicago, 1883;* contractual agreement, Dixon Bean with Field, Leiter & Co., January 1, 1877; and, for example, accounting ledgers, 1873-75, Comptroller's safe, Marshall Field & Co. General Offices).

60. "Price List, Notions Department," Field, Leiter & Co., Wholesale, 1877, pp. 112 and 114.

61. McClintock typescript, citing statement by Dowd. See also *Chicago Evening Journal,* April 17, 1872; *Spring Catalogue,* Field, Leiter & Co., Wholesale, 1870, pp. 46 and 48; *Ibid.,* 1871, pp. 48 and 50.

62. *Ibid.,* p. 60; *ibid.,* 1870, pp. 7, 46, 102 and 104; "Price List, Notions Department," Field, Leiter & Co., Wholesale, 1877, pp. 38, 56, 80, 86 and 120; and *Chicago Evening Journal,* April 17, 1872.

63. *Chicago Tribune,* June 30, 1872 and September 25, 1876; and *Chicago Times,* December 21, 1870 and September 25, 27, and 28, 1876.

64. See, for example, bill of sale, P. Palmer & Co., May 17, 1859; *Chicago Evening Journal,* November 8, 1861; and *Chicago Tribune,* September 10, 1861 and May 19, 1862.

65. See advertisements in *Chicago Tribune, Chicago Times,* and *Chicago Evening Journal* from December, 1871 through May, 1876. Also *Spring Catalogue,* Field, Leiter & Co., Wholesale, 1870 and 1871; and "Price List, Notions Department," Field, Leiter & Co., Wholesale, 1877.

66. *Chicago Tribune,* January 29, September 29, and November 1, 1872; *Spring Catalogues,* Field, Leiter & Co., Wholesale, 1870 and 1871; and "Price List, Notions Department," Field, Leiter & Co., Wholesale, 1877.

67. *Chicago Evening Journal,* April 3 and 4, 1872; and *Chicago Times,* April 5, 1872.

68. *Chicago Times,* April 5, 1872. See also *Chicago Tribune,* April 5, 1872; and letters, Field, Leiter & Co. to Field, Leiter & Co., Manchester, England, June 16, 1875; and Field, Leiter & Co. to Field, Leiter & Co., N. Y., June 8, 1875, Field Estate.

69. *Chicago Tribune,* March 3, 1872; and advertising circular, Field, Leiter & Co., Wholesale, March 1, 1872.

70. Nine months of 1872 and ten months of 1873 (*Inter-Ocean,* April

46-50

26, 1872; *Chicago Tribune,* September 29 and October 8 and 9, 1873; *Chicago Evening Journal,* October 3, 1873; and accounting sheets, net sales, retail, 1872-73, A. B. Jones folder).

71. *Chicago Tribune,* April 26, 1872; *Chicago Times,* April 26, 1872; *Inter-Ocean,* April 26, 1872; Advertising circulars, Field, Leiter & Co., Wholesale, March 1, 1872, and February 28, 1876.

72. *Chicago Times,* April 26, 1872.

73. *Chicago Commercial,* September 18, 1875, and Table XIV.

74. Advertising circular, Field, Leiter & Co., Wholesale, February 28, 1876. By 1876, the firm had in addition seven warehouses (Marshall Field Accounting Record Book, 1876, "Insurance Register").

75. Wholesale record, Marshall Field & Co., June 14, 1887, p. 162; and *Goodalls Daily Sun,* June 18, 1887.

76. *Chicago Tribune,* December 13, 18, and 21, 1871; June 29 and 30 and July 7, 1872; *Chicago Evening Post,* November 8 and 11, 1871; and *Chicago Evening Journal,* December 11, 1871. See also *Landowner,* April 1872, J. D. Stone Scrapbook, p. 15, Marshall Field & Co. Archives (Supplement).

77. *Chicago Tribune,* March 31, 1872; and *Chicago Times,* March 31, 1872.

78. *Ibid.,* March 31, 1872.

79. *Chicago Tribune,* April 24, 25, and 28, 1872; *Chicago Times,* January 9, 1873; and *Chicago Evening Journal,* May 7 and 18, 1872.

80. *Chicago Tribune,* April 28, 1872.

81. The last day was March 29, 1873 (*Chicago Times,* March 18, 25, and 28, 1873).

82. See Tables XIV & XV. Sales and profit figures of the two retail branches during the period they both existed are worthy of note:

	Sales		Profits	
	1872	1873	1872	1873
Retail No. 1	$1,789,000	$1,664,000	$31,300	$47,500*
Retail No. 2	965,000	999,000	19,900	73,200
Carpet & Upholstery Dept.	355,000	472,000	10,100*	7,000*
Total Retail	3,109,000	3,135,000	41,100	18,700

*LOSS

(accounting sheets, net sales, retail, 1872-1873, A. B. Jones folder; accounting sheets, profit and loss, wholesale and retail, 1872 *ibid.;* accounting sheets, recapitulation, retail departments, 1873, *ibid.*). Broken down, the profits listed were even less favorable than the above indicates. The firm in its accounting divided "total retail profits" as shown above into "net profit" and "retail department interest." The latter amount was interest (in 1872 and 1873 it was at the rate of 10%) which the firm charged each department for that portion of the total capital the department used to carry on its business. In 1873, for example "total" profits, as seen above and in Table XV, page 177, were $18,700. Actual "net profit" for that year, however, showed a loss of $16,900. The departmental interest of $35,-600 put the total amount in the black:

Retail department interest		$35,600
Retail net profit .... (loss)		16,900
Total retail profit		$18,700

Net profits broken down according to branches of retail for 1873:

Retail No. 1 .... (loss)		$60,800
Retail No. 2		69,100
Retail Carpet & Upholstery Dept. .... (loss)		25,200
Net retail profit (loss)		$16,900

("John G. Shedd Record Book, 1872-1906"; and accounting sheets, retail departments, 1873, A. B. Jones folder). The poor showing in 1873 was not, of course, due entirely to the West and South Side locations, but due partly to the fact that the last half of 1873 was the start of a period of business depression. It was during the latter portion of the year that all retail departments were moved to State and Washington. Retail No. 2 ceased to exist *(Chicago Tribune,* September 29 and October 3, 8, and 9, 1873) and was thus not much affected by the panic. Undoubtedly the unfavorable profit totals resulting from those months were credited entirely to "Retail No. 1" (then the only retail), thus accounting for its especially unfavorable showing.

83. *Landowner,* April 1872 (Supplement), Stone scrapbook, p. 15,

Marshall Field & Co. Archives; *Chicago Times,* March 19 and June 21, 25, and 26, and October 9 and 10, 1873.

84. *Chicago Evening Journal,* November 7, 1871; Letter, Leiter to J. N. Field, December 28, 1871.
85. *Chicago Tribune,* August 3, 1873.
86. Letter, Marshall Field to William P. Draper, Union Bank, London, July 7, 1875, Field Estate.
87. *Chicago Times,* November 15, 1877.
88. *Chicago Tribune,* August 3 and October 9, 1873.
89. *Chicago Tribune,* August 3 and October 9, 1873.
90. *Ibid.,* October 8, 1873, and November 15, 1877.
91. *Chicago Times,* November 15, 1877.
92. *Chicago Tribune,* August 3, 1873.
93. *Chicago Times,* November 15, 1877.
94. *Chicago Tribune,* October 9, 1873.
95. *Chicago Times,* October 13, 1868.

CHAPTER SIX

1. *Chicago Tribune,* October 11, 1873.
2. *Chicago Times,* October 18, 1873; *Scribner's Monthly,* X (1875), 533. See also, *Dry Goods Economist, Jubilee Number, 1846-1896,* p. 104.
3. *Dun, Barlow's . . . Ratings, 1873,* as quoted in letter, A. M. Sullivan, Dun & Bradstreet, Inc., to R. W. Twyman, February 12, 1948.
4. Advertising circular, Field, Leiter & Co., Wholesale, September 25, 1873, Marshall Field & Co. Archives.
5. *Chicago Tribune,* October 11, 1873; advertising circular, Field, Leiter & Co., Wholesale, September 25, 1873; and *Chicago Times,* October 18, 1873.
6. *Ibid.*
7. Compare Table XIV, p. 175, and U. S. Bureau of the Census, *Historical Statistics of the United States, 1789-1945* (Washington: Government Printing Office, 1949), Series L15-25, pp. 233-34.
8. Computed on basis of accounting ledgers, 1873-78, Comptroller's safe, Marshall Field & Co. General

Offices; and M. Field personal record book, real estate and salaries (per cent of profits—1869-1901).
9. See, for example, letter, Marshall Field to C. L. Mozrin, Iowa City, January 15, 1876, Field Estate.
10. *Chicago Times,* October 18, 1873. "Buying light" for Field, Leiter & Co. was not necessarily contradictory to the firm's other maxim of demanding discounts for buying in quantity. The firm's sales volume was so great by this time that in most items of merchandise buying lightly still meant making purchases heavy enough to earn large discounts.
11. See, for example, numerous "notices" in wholesale record, Marshall Field & Co.; letters, Field, Leiter & Co. to Mr. C. P. Panich, Manchester, November 10, 1875, Field Estate; and M. Field to J. G. Shedd, August 7, 1905, Marshall Field & Co. Archives.
12. For example, advertising circular, Field, Leiter & Co., Wholesale, February 28, 1876.

13. Statements, Porter Case and Joseph Yates, Marshall Field & Co. General Offices; and letter, E. C. DeWitt to Marshall Field & Co., November 6, 1896, Field Estate.

14. Wholesale record, Marshall Field & Co., August 24, 1905. See also *ibid.*, June 29, 1888, and February 28, 1905; and letter, Marshall Field to Hollister & Gorham, June 24, 1875, Field Estate.

15. Wholesale record, Marshall Field & Co., *circa* February, 1891, p. 81; and Red "Record," general and special house orders, Marshall Field & Co., March 10, 1881, p. 45, Marshall Field & Co. Archives.

16. For example, letter, W. F. Hypes, salesman, Wholesale, Marshall Field & Co., to F. D. Yaw, Cherokee, Iowa, December 3, 1896, H. H. Bettcher record book, Marshall Field & Co. Archives; and Cleveland, *System Magazine*, November 1906, p. 462.

17. Wholesale record, Marshall Field & Co., *circa* November 1875, p. 23; January 20, 1888, p. 70; July 29, 1901, p. 357; and February 5, 1903, p. 385; and letter, Van Brocklin, general salesman, Wholesale, Marshall Field & Co., to Capt. G. M. Bailey, Charge of Canteen, Fort Robinson, Nebraska, March 20, 1890, R. H. Bettcher record book, Marshall Field & Co. Archives.

18. Statement, George Young, one-time sales manager of Wholesale and later vice-president, Marshall Field & Co. General Offices.

19. *Ibid.; Chicago Evening Journal,* November 19, 1877; and see M. Field personal record book, real estate and salaries [1869-1901], which lists property acquired by Field's as a result of driving this type of creditor out of business.

20. U. S. Congress, House of Representatives, *Congressional Record,* 55th Cong., 2nd Sess., 1907 (Washington: Government Printing Office, 1907), p. 1898.

21. *Ibid.*

22. Higinbotham, *The Making of a Merchant*, pp. 202-3.

23. *Dun, Barlow's . . . Ratings,* 1873-78, as quoted in letter, A. M. Sullivan, Dun & Bradstreet, Inc., to R. W. Twyman, February 12, 1948.

24. *Scribner's Monthly,* X (1875), 533.

25. *Infra,* p. 85.

26. *Chicago Times,* September 23, 1876; and *Chicago Tribune,* August 29, 1876.

27. Field Estate letters, September 1876 to April 1877, *passim.*

28. Letter, W. J. Flood, Chicago branch of A. T. Stewart and Co. to Field, Leiter & Co., May 6, 1870, Marshall Field & Co. Archives.

29. Field Estate letters, September 1876 to April 1877, *passim.*

30. *Chicago Tribune,* August 29, 1876; wholesale circulars, A. T. Stewart & Co., March 28, 1877, and other dates, Chicago, Marshall Field & Co. Archives; and *Seven Days in Chicago* (Chicago: J. M. Wing & Co., 1877), p. 63.

31. *Seven Days in Chicago,* p. 63 and back cover; *Chicago Times,* September 23, 25, 26, and 27, 1876; and *Chicago Tribune,* August 29, 1876.

32. *Ibid.*

33. See, for example, *Chicago Times,* November 22, 1876.

34. Letter, Marshall Field to Field, Leiter & Co., N. Y., October 28, 1876, Field Estate.

35. *Chicago Tribune,* January 19, 1883.

36. M. Field personal record book, real estate and salaries [1869-1901]; salary record books, 1871-87; 1876-77; and 1876-78 [pages not numbered], Marshall Field & Co. Archives (hereafter cited as "salary record, 1876-78").

37. Letters, Field, Leiter & Co. to Field, Leiter & Co., N. Y., October 14, 1876; and Marshall Field to Lorenzo G. Woodhouse, September 29, 1876, Field Estate.

38. *Ibid.;* and letters, Marshall Field to Field, Leiter & Co., N. Y., September 23 and October 28, 1876, Field Estate.

39. Letter, Field, Leiter & Co., to Field, Leiter & Co., N. Y., October 14, 1876, Field Estate.

40. Letter, Marshall Field to Lorenzo G. Woodhouse, September 29, 1876, Field Estate.

41. Letter, Marshall Field to Field, Leiter & Co., N. Y., October 18, 1876, Field Estate.
42. Letters, Marshall Field to Lorenzo G. Woodhouse, September 29, 1876, and February 16, 1877, Field Estate; and letter, Marshall Field to Field, Leiter & Co., N. Y., October 4, 1876, Field Estate.
43. *Ibid.;* letter, Field, Leiter & Co. to Field, Leiter & Co., N. Y., Otcober 14, 1876, Field Estate; wholesale circulars, A. T. Stewart & Co., March 28 and November 10, 1877, Chicago, Marshall Field & Co. Archives; and letter, Marshall Field to Lorenzo G. Woodhouse, February 16, 1877, Field Estate.
44. *Ibid.;* letters, Marshall Field to Field, Leiter & Co., N. Y., October 4 and 18, 1876, and March 3, 1877; and Field, Leiter & Co. to Field, Leiter & Co., N. Y., October 14, 1876, Field Estate.
45. Letters, Marshall Field to Lorenzo G. Woodhouse, April 6, 1877; Marshall Field to Field, Leiter & Co., March 30, 1877; and Field, Leiter & Co. to Field, Leiter & Co., N. Y., November 16, 1876, Field Estate.
46. *Ibid.*, and letters, Field, Leiter & Co. to Field, Leiter & Co., N. Y., October 21 and November 16, 1876, Field Estate.
47. Letter to Field, Leiter & Co., N. Y., October 14, 1876, Field Estate.
48. Letter to Field, Leiter & Co., N. Y., October 18, 1876, Field Estate.
49. Letter to Field, Leiter & Co., N. Y., October 28, 1876, Field Estate. See also letter, Field, Leiter & Co. to Field, Leiter & Co., N. Y., October 14, 1876, Field Estate.
50. Letter to Field, Leiter & Co., N. Y., December 2, 1876, Field Estate.
51. Field Estate. See also, letter, Marshall Field to Field, Leiter & Co., N. Y., March 30, 1877, Field Estate.
52. Field Estate letters, April, 1877, *et seq.*
53. Stewart died April 10, 1876 *(Dictionary of American Biography,* XVIII, 4).
54. *Chicago Tribune,* April 15, 16, 17, 1882. See also Gibbons, *John Wanamaker,* II, 2-3. By 1880, A. T. Stewart & Company had declined to such an extent that Marshall Field served notice that he no longer cared to have his store referred to as the "A. T. Stewart of Chicago" *(Chicago Tribune,* June 24, 1880).
55. *The Modern Encyclopedia,* p. 266.
56. For example, see letters, Marshall Field to Field, Leiter & Co., New York, July 1, 1875, December 2, 1876, and March 30, 1877, Field Estate.
57. Gibbons, *Wanamaker,* I, 237-38.
58. See Table XIV, p. 175.
59. Wright, *Chicago,* p. 148.
60. *Hurst, Garlock & Co.'s Western Reports,* 1871, p. 521.
61. *Ibid.*
62. Andreas, *History of Chicago,* II, 694; and *Chicago's First Half-Century, 1833-1883* (Chicago: The Inter-Ocean Pub. Co., 1884), p. 89.
63. See Table XIV, p. 175.
64. Letter, J. Chalmers O'Brien, Assistant to the President, Carson Pirie Scott & Co., to R. W. Twyman, September 16, 1949.
65. Wright, *Chicago,* p. 148.
66. *Hurst, Garlock & Co.'s Western Reports,* 1871, p. 522.
67. Letter, J. Chalmers O'Brien, Assistant to the President, Carson Pirie Scott & Co., to R. W. Twyman, September 16, 1949.
68. Statement, Porter Case, former general sales manager of Wholesale, February 1946.
69. *Chicago Times,* November 15, 1877.
70. *Ibid.;* and *Chicago Tribune,* November 15, 1877.
71. *Ibid.;* and *Chicago Evening Journal,* November 15, 1877.
72. *Chicago Times,* November 15, 1877.
73. *Ibid.,* and *Chicago Tribune,* November 15, 1877.
74. *Ibid.; Chicago Times,* November 15, 1877; and *Chicago Evening Journal,* November 15, 1877.
75. Letter, Marshall Field to C. A. Spring, general-manager, McCormick Reaper Co., November 15, 1877, Marshall Field & Co. Archives.
76. *Chicago Evening Journal,* November 16, 1877.
77. *Ibid.,* November 19; and *Chicago Tribune,* November 18 and 19, 1877.
78. Accounting ledgers, "Statement of Business—1878," Marshall Field &

Co. General Offices; and *Chicago Evening Journal,* November 19, 1877.

79. *Chicago Tribune,* November 25, 27, and 28, 1877.

80. *Ibid.,* November 28.

81. *Ibid.,* December 2, 1877; postcard circular, Field, Leiter & Co., November 28, 1877, Marshall Field & Co. Archives; and *Chicago Evening Journal,* November 27 and December 1, 1877.

82. *Chicago Tribune,* December 10, 1877.

83. Accounting ledgers, "Statements of Business — 1878," Comptroller's safe, Marshall Field & Co. General Offices; *Chicago Evening Journal,* December 10, 1877; and *Chicago Tribune,* December 10 and 14, 1877, and January 5 and 12, 1878.

84. *Ibid.,* February 27, and March 2, 4, 5, 6, 7, and 8, 1878; and *Chicago Evening Journal,* February 27 and March 9, 1878.

85. Letter, Singer Manufacturing Co., to Marshall Field, December 19, 1890, Field Estate; and *Chicago Tribune,* January 27, 1881.

86. *Ibid.;* and *Chicago Times,* January 27, 1881.

87. Record book, "Rents, June 1, 1900," Marshall Field & Co. Archives; complete inventory, Estate of Marshall Field, Deceased; accounting sheets, "Retail Departments' Expenses," 1879-86, A. B. Jones folder, Marshall Field & Co. Archives; and accounting ledgers, 1898-1904, Comptroller's safe, Marshall Field & Co. General Offices.

88. *Chicago Tribune,* April 25, 26, and 28, 1879.

89. The City Council felt, in the second place, that if the building were to be rented at all, the Council should get the rent and not the Exposition Building Company (*Chicago Evening Journal,* November 27, 1877).

90. Accounting ledgers, 1876, 1878.

Comptroller's safe, Marshall Field & Co. General Offices.

91. *Ibid.,* 1878.

92. See Table XV, p. 177.

93. R. M. Fair personal record book of rents and property, "compiled June 1, 1901."

94. *Chicago Daily News,* April 26, 1879; *Chicago Times,* April 26 and 28, 1879; *Chicago Evening Journal,* April 26, 1879; and *Daily Telegraph,* April 26, 1879.

95. *Ibid.,* April 28; and *Chicago Tribune,* April 29, 1879.

96. *Ibid.*

97. See Plate V.

98. *Mercer,* I (June 1891), 15; Barbour (ed.), *Sketchbook of the Inter-State Exposition, Chicago, 1883.*

99. *Ibid.*

100. Barbour (ed.), *Sketchbook of the Inter-State Exposition, Chicago, 1883;* and *Chicago Tribune,* April 29, 1879.

101. *Mercer,* I (June 1891), 15-16.

102. Barbour (ed.), *Sketchbook of the Inter-State Exposition, Chicago, 1883.*

103. *Ibid.*

104. *Ibid.;* and accounting sheets, "Retail Departments' Expenses," 1879-86, A. B. Jones folder. The wholesale building obtained its first engines and lights in the first month of 1883 (*ibid.;* and wholesale record, Marshall Field & Co., January 31, 1883), but most of its early lights were arc lights rather than the Edison type (accounting ledgers, "Statement of Business—1868," Comptroller's safe, Marshall Field & Co. General Offices).

105. The last use made of gas was by Wholesale, for night lights (wholesale record, Marshall Field & Co., May 5, 1899, p. 297; June 25, p. 370; and July 25, p. 375, 1902; and "Views of the Retail Store of Marshall Field & Co., Chicago" [Chicago: Souvenir of National G. A. R. Encampment, 1900], [pages not numbered]).

CHAPTER SEVEN

1. See, for example, Gustavus Myers, *History of the Great American Fortunes* (New York: Random House, Inc., 1907), p. 195. Also see John Dennis, Jr., "Marshall Field," *Everybody's Magazine*, XIV (March 1906), 298; *Mercer*, I (June 1891), 18; and Stoddard, *Men of Business*, p. 293.
2. Letters, Marshall Field to Field, Leiter & Co., N. Y., August 12, 1875, Field Estate; to Marshall Field & Co., N. Y., March 13, 1882 and June 7, 1888, unidentified scrapbook; and to John G. Shedd, July 2, 1905, Marshall Field & Co. Archives; wholesale record, Marshall Field & Co., November 12, 1875, p. 21; April 18, 1877, p. 37; and January 6, 1888, p. 70; and "Store Rules, extracts from 'Book of Rules of Marshall Field and Company, Retail Store,'" *Chicago Dry Goods Reporter*, XXVII (October 9, 1897), 11.
3. M. Field personal record book, real estate and salaries [1869-1901].
4. *Chicago Tribune*, December 23, 1890.
5. 7 per cent.
6. 10/25.
7. M. Field personal record book, real estate and salaries [1867-1901]; and co-partnership, Field, Leiter, *et al.*, January 1, 1869.
8. For the years 1873 through 1875 Higinbotham obtained 3 per cent of the wholesale profits; from 1876 through 1878 he obtained 2½ per cent of the total (wholesale plus retail) net profits before the shares were divided among the regular partners (*ibid.*; and M. Field personal record book, real estate and salaries [1867-1901]). The capital at this time was also increased from $1,200,000 to $2,550,000 (Marshall Field personal memorandum, "Statement my affairs," January 1, 1874, Marshall Field & Co. Archives).
9. Two years before (1877) a general readjustment had been made among the junior partners. Leiter and Marshall Field had kept their ⅓ interests (that is, 4/12), but Woodhouse had been granted a 10 per cent interest, Willing an 8⅓ per cent interest, and Marshall Field's two brothers 7½ per cent each. When Henry Field dropped out of the firm in the latter part of 1878, Higinbotham was allowed to purchase his 7½ per cent interest (M. Field personal record book, real estate and salaries [1867-1901]).
10. *Chicago Times*, January 27, 1881; letter, R. M. Hitchcock to J. Simpson, May 10, 1922, Marshall Field & Co. Archives; and statement, Charles B. Nash, department head, china, Marshall Field & Co. General Offices.
11. *Chicago Tribune*, January 27, 1881.
12. McClintock typescript.
13. *Chicago Tribune*, January 27, 1881.
14. *Chicago Times*, January 27, 1881; McClintock typescript; and statement, Stanley Field, Marshall Field & Co. General Offices. Marshall Field personally denied the truth of this account of the split (*Chicago Tribune*, January 28, 1881).
15. *Ibid.*; and general house notice, Field, Leiter & Co., January 26, 1881, Marshall Field & Co. Archives.
16. *Chicago Tribune*, January 19, 1883. See also *ibid.*, January 27, 1881.
17. *Chicago Times* and *Chicago Tribune*, January 27, 1881.
18. *Chicago Tribune*, January 27, 1881.
19. F. A. Eastman, "The Man in the Street," unidentified newspaper clipping, "Fifty-Year Club" scrapbook; and *Chicago Tribune*, June 10, 1904.
20. *Ibid.*; and *Chicago Chronicle*, June 10, 1904.
21. M. Field personal record book, real estate and salaries [1869-1901]. Two years later Willing and Henry Field suddenly retired (*Chicago Tribune*, January 19, 1883, December 23, 1890, and September 30, 1903), permitting the notions superintendent, J. G. McWilliams (contractual agreement, John G. McWilliams with Field, Leiter & Co., January 1, 1879, Marshall Field & Co. Archives), to assume a minor

interest and resulting in a new arrangement which lasted until 1890. From 1883 to 1890 the percentage of interest retained by each partner was as follows:

M. Field 42.5/89
L. G. Woodhouse 20/89
H. N. Higinbotham 10/89
J. N. Field 10/89
J. G. McWilliams 6.5/89

M. Field personal record book, real estate and salaries [1867-1901]. The division of the first year's (1883) profits under this partnership was as follows:

M. Field .... $ 796,151.37
L. G. Woodhouse ...   374,659.47
H. N. Higinbotham..   187,329.73
J. N. Field 187,329.73
J. G. McWilliams 121,764.33
                      —————————
                      $1,667,234.63

("Balance Jany 5, 1885," accounting sheets, profits, A. B. Jones folder, Marshall Field & Co. Archives.)

22. See, for example, "Marshall Field & Company," *Fortune*, XIV (October 1936), p. 82; and Stoddard, *Men of Business*, pp. 291-92.

23. See, for example, Ernest Poole, *Giants Gone; Men Who Made Chicago* (New York: Whittlesey House, 1943), p. 122. Wayne Andrews, *Battle for Chicago* (New York: Harcourt, Brace & Co., 1946), p. 122.

24. M. Field personal record book, real estate and salaries [1869-1901]; *Chicago Tribune,* January 19, 1883; *Chicago Record,* January 9, 1895; and *Chicago Chronicle,* January 13, 1905.

25. Co-partnership, Field, Leiter, *et al.,* January 1, 1869.

26. Statement, John McKinlay, president, Marshall Field & Co. General Offices. See also, *Chicago Tribune,* January 19, 1883.

27. *Ibid.; Chicago Record,* February 7, 1900; *Chicago Times-Herald,* February 8 and December 27, 1900; *Chicago Chronicle,* January 13, 1905; general house notice, Marshall Field & Co., December 31, 1900, Marshall Field & Co. Archives; *Chicago Daily News,* May 14, 1904; and form letter, H. N. Higinbotham to the firm and its

patrons, December 31, 1900, Stone scrapbook, p. 82, Marshall Field & Co. Archives.

28. Harry Gordon Selfridge, "Selling Selfridge, Some Random Reflections of an American Merchant in London," *Saturday Evening Post,* July 27, 1935, pp. 19 and 51; *Chicago Record-Herald,* January 17, 1906; and *Chicago Evening Post,* January 16, 1906.

29. Marshall Field personal salary record book, 1869-72; salary record books, 1871-87, 1872-74, 1876-77, and 1876-78; salary record book, 1884-85, Marshall Field & Co. Archives [hereafter cited as "salary record, 1883-85"]; M. Field personal record book, real estate and salaries [1867-1901]; and accounting sheets, sales of general salesmen, wholesale, 1871-72, A. B. Jones folder, Marshall Field & Co. Archives.

30. *Chicago Tribune,* September 15, 1927; and Ditchett, *Marshall Field and Company,* p. 151.

31. Interoffice communication, Chapin A. Day, treasurer, to J. E. Holden, merchandise manager, July 23, 1900, Marshall Field & Co. Archives; John G. Shedd address to "fifty-year" men in *Fifty Years of Service,* December 18, 1922; Marshall Field personal salary record book, 1869-72; salary record books, 1871-87, 1872-74, 1876-77, 1876-78, and 1883-85; and M. Field personal record book, real estate and salaries [1869-1901].

32. Letter, February 3, 1876, Field Estate.

33. Letter, Marshall Field to Field, Leiter & Co., N. Y., December 22, 1876, Field Estate.

34. Wholesale record, Marshall Field & Co., May 18, 1876, p. 31; memoranda, H. G. Selfridge and W. P. Warren to section managers and assistants, August 9, 1901 to March 10, 1904, in "Business Ideas," p. 3, Marshall Field & Co. Archives; "Marshall Field & Co., Retail," *Chicago Dry Goods Reporter,* XXXII (October 11, 1902), 29-30; and *Chicago Tribune,* May 12, 1902.

35. Cleveland, *System Magazine,* May 1907, pp. 45-47; and Henry P. Wil-

liams, "Evolution of the Moral Idea in Business," *Interior,* December 18, 1902, Reprint [pages not numbered].

36. *Chicago Tribune,* May 12, 1902; and memoranda, H. G. Selfridge and W. P. Warren to department heads, August 8, 1901, in "Business Ideas," p. 1, Marshall Field & Co. Archives.

37. Wholesale record, Marshall Field & Co., *passim: Chicago Times,* October 13, 1868; and statements, George Young, vice-president, John McKinlay, president, and Porter Case, sales manager, Wholesale, Marshall Field & Co. General Offices.

38. Contractual agreements, Dixon Bean, January 1, 1876 and 1877, and November 15, 1880; and Alfred Ray, January 24, 1873, and January 23, 1880, with Field, Leiter & Co.; J. G. Shedd with Marshall Field & Co., July 1, 1887, Marshall Field & Co. Archives; M. Field personal record book, real estate and salaries [1869-1901]; record book, "Rents, June 1, 1901"; accounting sheets, recapitulation of profit and loss accounts, "Share Profits above guaranteed salaries," 1885-88, A. B. Jones folder, Marshall Field & Co. Archives; accounting ledgers, 1890-1906, Comptroller's safe, Marshall Field & Co. General Offices; "New State Street Firm," *Chicago Dry Goods Reporter,* XXXIV (May 21, 1904), 37, citing R. M. Fair on management; *Mercer,* I [June 1891], 19; and wholesale record, Marshall Field & Co., August 7, 1896, p. 213; September 12, 1898, p. 273; and July 28, 1904, p. 406.

39. Barbour (ed.), *Sketchbook of the Inter-State Exposition, Chicago, 1883;* statements, John McKinlay, Philip James, Helen Duggan, and Charles C. Bunker, Marshall Field & Co. General Offices; "Notice to Section Managers, Assistants, and others," January 9, 1905, in John McKinlay, *Old Advertising Policy* [scrapbook], Marshall Field & Co. Archives; and M. Field personal record book, real estate and salaries [1867-1901].

40. Previous to 1874 these three were all one department. In that year, however, they were divided into two — upholstery, and rugs and carpets. In 1886, they became three separate departments (accounting sheets, net sales, retail, 1872-73, A. B. Jones folder; and accounting ledgers, 1873-1906, Comptroller's safe, Marshall Field & Co. General Offices).

41. In some instances, the same man who headed one of these retail departments also headed the corresponding wholesale department (M. Field personal record book, real estate and salaries, 1869-1901; salary record, 1871-87; and contractual agreement, Dixon Bean with Field, Leiter & Co., January 1, 1876 and 1877; and November 15, 1880).

42. Barbour (ed.), *Sketchbook of the Inter-State Exposition, Chicago, 1883;* "A Monument to Enterprise," *Dry Goods Retailer and Jobber,* October 1893, p. 17; *Mercer,* I (June 1891), 16; *Dry Goods Reporter,* XXXII (October 11, 1902), 19; *Chicago's First Half Century, 1833-1883,* p. 87; and memoranda, H. G. Selfridge and W. P. Warren to department heads, August 8, 1901, in "Business Ideas," p. 1, Marshall Field & Co. Archives.

43. Contractual agreements, J. G. Shedd with Marshall Field & Co., July 1, 1886 and 1887; and Alfred Ray with Field, Leiter & Co., January 23, 1880; and interdepartmental communication [to department heads], September 1, 1883, unidentified scrapbook, Marshall Field & Co. Archives.

44. General house notice from manager to heads of sections, August 3, 1904; Dennis, *Everybody's Magazine,* March 1906, p. 298; and accounting ledgers, 1902-06, Comptroller's safe, Marshall Field & Co. General Offices.

45. M. Field personal record book, real estate and salaries, [1869-1901].

46. Mimeographed copy of "Notes on Subjects Referred to at the Meeting [of section managers] of July 2d, 1902"; and Barbour (ed.),

Sketchbook of the Inter-State Exposition, Chicago, 1883.

47. *Ibid.;* contractual agreement, Dixon Bean with Field, Leiter & Co., January 1, 1877; accounting ledgers, 1873-1906, Comptroller's safe, Marshall Field & Co. General Offices; and *Chicago's First Half Century, 1833-1883,* p. 87.

48. Before 1887 the general managers were called "superintendents" *(ibid.;* and salary record, 1871-87).

49. *Mercer,* I (June 1891), 18-19; and statements, John McKinlay, president, and Charles C. Bunker, president, Frederick & Nelson, Seattle.

50. See, for example, wholesale record, Marshall Field & Co., *passim.*

51. Interoffice communication, W. B. Weaver to Paul H. Howard, July 2, 1946, *re* interview with Edgar Moreland, cashboy in 1883, Marshall Field & Co. Archives; statements, Henry J. Stadelman to S. McClintock, Marshall Field & Co. Archives; and Stanley Field, Philip James, Thomas H. Eddy, George Young, H. P. Shedd, and J. W. Hughes, operating department, Marshall Field & Co. General Offices; and personal interview, Mr. Henderson.

52. Statement, Helen Duggan, buyer, women's wear, Marshall Field & Co. General Offices.

53. House notice, J. B. Fair to section managers [1902], unidentified scrapbook; Red "Record," general and special house orders, Marshall Field & Co., p. 33, Marshall Field & Co. Archives; *Chicago Dry Goods Reporter,* XXVII (October 9, 1897), 31; and *ibid.* (August 21, 1897), 38.

54. House notice, J. B. Fair to section managers [1902] (unidentified scrapbook), Marshall Field & Co. Archives; notices issued from office of Retail Manager to heads of sections, June 7 and 28, 1904, Marshall Field & Co. Archives; and *Chicago's First Half Century, 1833-1883,* p. 87.

55. Wholesale record, Marshall Field & Co., *passim;* and Red "Record," general and special house orders, Marshall Field & Co., *passim,* Marshall Field & Co. Archives.

56. Marshall Field accounting record book, 1876, Marshall Field & Co. Archives.

57. See, for example, salary record, 1871-87.

58. Letters, Field, Leiter & Co. to R. Moir & Co., Oquawka, Illinois, April 19, 1872; and H. L. Pinney, Field, Leiter & Co., general salesman, to Robt. Moir & Co., Oquawka, Illinois, January 3 and 24, 1875, Warshaw Collection of Business Americana; salary record, 1871-87, "General salesmen"; and wholesale record, Marshall Field & Co. [February, app.], 1891, p. 81, and December 9, 1897, p. 251.

59. *Ibid.* [1873, app.], pp. 3 and 11; [January 1876, app.], p. 25; December 10, 1888, p. 122; and February 11, 1903, pp. 387-88; letter, M. Field to L. G. Woodhouse, August 11, 1875, Field Estate; and Red "Record" general and special house orders, Marshall Field & Co., pp. 13, 15, 37, and 38.

60. Invoice, Field, Leiter & Co., October 7, 1871; letters, H. L. Finney, general salesman, Field, Leiter & Co., January 3 and 24, 1873, to Robt. Moir & Co., Oquawka, Illinois, Warshaw Collection of Business Americana; and W. F. Hypes to A. B. Edee, Pawnee City, Nebraska, March 9; and to A. H. Sanford, Seattle, Washington, June 18, 1900, R. H. Bettcher record book, pp. 66 and 69, respectively; and wholesale record, Marshall Field & Co., November 17, 1884, p. 63; and [March, app.], 1891, p. 81; and Cleveland, *System Magazine,* April 1907, pp. 387-88; and statement, George Young, Marshall Field & Co. General Offices.

61. See, for example, Marshall Field personal salary record book, 1869-72; salary record, 1871-87; M. Field personal record book, real estate and salaries [1867-1901]; and personal interview, John Rau.

62. *Chicago Tribune,* May 12, 1902.

63. See, for example, "Day Book," Marshall Field & Co., 1889-96, pp. 191 and 226, Marshall Field & Co. Archives.

64. Marshall Field personal salary record book, 1869-72; salary records,

1871-87, 1872-74, 1876-77, 1876-78; M. Field personal record book, real estate and salaries, 1869-1901; salary record, "Marshall Field, Jany 1st, 1901"; and *Chicago Daily News*, June 11, 1904.

65. Barbour (ed.), *Sketchbook of the Inter-State Exposition, 1883;* and Marshall Field personal memorandum, "Number of Employees, Jany 1882," Marshall Field & Co. Archives.

66. M. Field personal record book, real estate and salaries, 1869-1901; and salary record, "Marshall Field, Jany 1st, 1901."

67. Statement, Ellen Jane Bredin and Charles Nash, Marshall Field & Co. General Offices.

68. Marshall Field personal salary record book, 1869-72; salary records, 1871-87, 1872-74, 1876-77, 1876-78, 1883-85; M. Field personal record book, real estate and salaries, 1869-1901; salary record, "Marshall Field, Jany 1st, 1901," Marshall Field & Co. Archives [pages not numbered]; and "C.A.D. Fund Papers in *re* Will of Marshall Field," Marshall Field & Co. Archives.

69. "Fifty-Year Club" scrapbook, Marshall Field & Co. Archives; *Chicago Herald-Examiner*, February 5, 1930; *Chicago Evening American* and *Chicago Daily News*, October 22, 1924.

70. Statement, J. J. Reilly, Marshall Field & Co. General Offices.

71. "Notes from Retail Advertising," 1900-[1921]), p. 30, Marshall Field & Co. Archives, Typescript; *Mercer*, I (June 1891), 20; and Dennis, *Everybody's Magazine*, XIV (March 1906), 299.

72. Marshall Field personal salary record book, 1869-1872; salary records, 1871-87, 1872-74, 1876-77, 1876-78, 1883-85; M. Field personal record book, real estate and salaries, 1869-1901; and salary record, "Marshall Field, Jany 1st, 1901."

73. Dennis, *Everybody's Magazine*, XIV (March 1906), 298-99; and statements, John McKinlay, J. E. Hughes, Helen Duggan, and John Rau, Marshall Field & Co. General Offices. In wholesale, persons re-

ceiving over $12.00 per week in 1887 constituted only from one-third to one-half of the total employees (salary record, 1871-77).

74. John T. Bramhall, "In Memoriam: John Graves Shedd" (pamphlet), Marshall Field & Co. Archives.

75. *Chicago Dry Goods Reporter*, XXVII (July 24, 1897), 35; *ibid.* (October 9, 1897), 35; *Chicago Evening Journal*, April 2, 1872; and salary records, 1872-74, 1871-87, 1876-78, 1876-77, 1883-85.

76. Letter, "Elements of Success," M. Field to the Rev. N. D. Hillis, D.D., February 15, 1896.

77. Memorandum, H. G. Selfridge and W. P. Warren, to section managers and assistants, August 9, 1901-March 10, 1904, in "Business Ideas," p. 3. See also wholesale record, Marshall Field & Co., February 26, 1903, p. 391; notices issued from office of Retail Manager to section managers and employees, October 27, 1904 and November 16, 1905, Marshall Field & Co. Archives; and accounting sheets, "Retail Departments' Expenses," 1882-83, A. B. Jones folder, Marshall Field & Co. Archives.

78. Marshall Field personal memorandum, "Number of Employees Jany 1882." After 1900, the proportion was much smaller ("Marshall Field & Co.'s Opening," *Apparel Gazette*, XXVI [October 7, 1902], 46).

79. Interoffice communication, W. B. Weaver to Paul H. Howard, July 2, 1946, *re* interview with Edgar Moreland, cash boy in 1883; and interview, J. G. Hall with Mr. Luehman, courtesy History of Chicago Project.

80. Memorandum, J. G. Shedd to McClintock, June 19, 1926, Marshall Field & Co. Archives; statement, Fred Morgan, division head, Bullock's, Los Angeles; and interviews, J. G. Hall with Luehman and Berleman, courtesy History of Chicago Project.

81. Red "Record," general and special house orders, Marshall Field & Co., p. 12; and *Marshall Field & Company* [1903] (Chicago: Marshall Field & Co., [1903]), Marshall Field & Co. Archives.

82. By 1879 an electrical contrivance flashed the boy's numbers on a central board. An "enunciator" watched the signals and sent the boys scurrying to the counters where they were needed (*Chicago Tribune,* April 29, 1879; *Chicago Daily Telegraph,* April 28, 1879; and statements, Fred Morgan and Michael Carey).

83. *Ibid.; Chicago Dry Goods Reporter,* XXVII (October 9, 1897), 13; interviews, J. G. Hall with Fred Bonk, Mr. Luehman, and Mr. Berleman, courtesy History of Chicago Project; letter, Frank Langosch, Inspection Division to S. V. Sutton, Marshall Field & Co., internal correspondence, April 25, 1942, Marshall Field & Co.; and see again *Chicago Daily Telegraph,* April 28, 1879; and *Chicago Tribune,* April 29, 1879.

84. A pneumatic cash carrier system was installed for the first time in the new 1902 building (*Chicago Dry Goods Reporter,* XXXII [October 11, 1902], 35). The last cash boys were finally dispensed with completely in September 1904 (company record on repair . . . and statistics [1902-43]).

85. Statements, George Young, Ellen Jane Bredin, Charles C. Bunker, Marshall Field General Offices; Henry J. Stadelman to S. McClintock, Marshall Field & Co. Archives; salary record, 1876-78; Marshall Field personal salary record book, 1869-72; Marshall Field & Co. personnel record card, Richard Peel, September 12, 1899, Marshall Field & Co. Archives.

86. Statement, J. J. Reilly, Marshall Field & Co. General Offices. See also, in this connection, delivery boy record book, 1860-1900, p. 55 (1876), and p. 85 (1879); and "carfare account" (1880-1900), p. 432.

87. Delivery boy record book, 1860-1900, pp. 79, 375, 383, and 403, Marshall Field & Co. Archives.

88. Earl R. Beckner, *A History of Labor Legislation in Illinois* (Chicago: University of Chicago Press, 1929), pp. 162-63.

89. Statements, G. Michael and Joseph Yates, department heads, Marshall Field & Co. General Offices.

90. *Ibid.;* Marshall Field personal salary record book, 1869-72; salary record, 1872-74.

91. *Ibid*

92. Statement, Charles Nash, department head, citing H. G. Selfridge, Marshall Field & Co. General Offices.

93. Salary record, 1871-87.

94. *Ibid.;* and Marshall Field personal salary record book, 1869-72.

95. Salary record, 1872-74.

96. *Ibid.;* Marshall Field personal salary record book, 1869-72; salary records, 1871-77, 1876-77, and 1883-85.

97. Marshall Field personal salary record book, 1869-72; salary records, 1871-87, 1872-74, 1876-77, 1876-78, 1883-85; M. Field personal record book, real estate and salaries, 1869-1901; and salary record, "Marshall Field, Jany 1st, 1901."

98. Letter, [Ida?] M. Cray, Chicago, to Henry D. Lloyd, March 29, 1888, Henry D. Lloyd *Papers,* MS. Wisconsin State Library (courtesy *History of Chicago* project).

99. Marshall Field personal salary record book, 1869-72.

100. Salary record, 1872-74.

101. *Ibid.*

102. Marshall Field personal salary record book, 1869-72; salary records, 1871-87, 1872, 1872-74, 1876-77, 1876-78, 1883-85; M. Field personal record book, real estate and salaries, 1869-1901; and salary record, "Marshall Field, Jany 1st, 1901," *passim.*

103. Salary records, 1876-77, 1876-78, 1883-85; M. Field personal record book, real estate and salaries, 1869-1901; salary record, "Marshall Field, Jany 1st, 1901"; and "Marshall Field Record Book," January 1, 1902, Marshall Field & Co. Archives.

104. Accounting ledgers, 1880-1906, Comptroller's safe, Marshall Field & Co. General Offices; accounting sheets, recapitulation of profit and loss accounts, "Share Profits above guaranteed salaries," 1885-88, A. B. Jones folder; contractual agree-

ments, Alfred Ray, January 24, 1873, and John G. McWilliams, January 1, 1879, with Field, Leiter & Co.; M. Field personal record book, real estate and salaries, 1869-1901; and salary records, 1883-95, and 1871-87.

105. *Ibid.;* salary records, 1876-78; and "Marshall Field, Jany 1st, 1901."

106. Contractual agreement, Dixon Bean with Field, Leiter & Co., January 1, 1876.

107. Contractual agreement, Dixon Bean with Field, Leiter & Co., November 15, 1880.

108. M. Field personal record book, real estate and salaries, 1869-1901. See other examples in this same source.

109. Copy of contractual agreement for 1889 and 1890, Marshall Field with J. G. Shedd and H. G. Selfridge, November 13, 1889, Marshall Field & Co. Archives.

110. Accounting ledgers, 1898-1906, Comptroller's safe, Marshall Field & Co. General Offices.

111. *Ibid.*, 1885-1906; and statement, J. W. Hughes, Marshall Field & Co. Archives.

112. Accounting ledgers, 1898-1904, Comptroller's safe, Marshall Field & Co. General Offices; Marshall Field personal salary record book, 1869-72; salary record, 1871-87; and salary record, "Marshall Field, Jany 1st, 1901."

113. Red "Record," general and special house orders, Marshall Field & Co., pp. 12 and 14.

114. *Dry Goods Reporter*, XXXII (October 11, 1902), 76; and wholesale record, Marshall Field & Co., June 21, 1900, p. 327.

115. *Ibid.*, 1873, p. 5; and June 21, 1900, p. 327; mimeographed copy of "Notes on Subjects Referred to at the Meeting [of section managers] of July 2d, 1902," Marshall Field & Co. Archives; and Red "Record," general and special house orders, Marshall Field & Co., pp. 12 and 14; and September 4, 1873, p. 19.

116. *Daily Democratic Press*, May 24, 1856.

117. Wholesale record, Marshall Field & Co., 1873, p. 9. See also Red "Record," general and special house orders, Marshall Field & Co., p. 12.

118. Wholesale record, Marshall Field & Co., 1873, p. 9; and August 28, 1873, p. 14; and Red "Record," general and special house orders, Marshall Field & Co., August 28, 1873, p. 18.

119. *Ibid.* [n.d.], p. 12.

120. "The Department Store," *Department Store Journal*, II (August 1897), 369.

121. Interview, T. Dreiser with M. Field, quoted in *Success*, December 8, 1898, pp. 7-8.

122. Wholesale record, Marshall Field & Co., 1881, p. 141; October 10, p. 143 and p. 146. For a few years after 1881, apparently the Retail remained open to a later hour during certain seasons (*Chicago Tribune*, January 3, 1883).

123. "State Street Openings," *Chicago Dry Goods Reporter*, XXXVII (October 5, 1907), 57; "Greater Efficiency the Aim; What Marshall Field & Co. Do to Interest Employees in Store and Promote Efficiency," *ibid.*, XL (January 8, 1910), 71; H. Hull, "Impressions of a Great Store," *Marshall Field & Company* (Chicago, 1907), Marshall Field & Co. Archives; *Chicago Tribune*, March 11, 1901; and April 14, 1902; and wholesale record, Marshall Field & Co., February 23, 1904, p. 403.

124. *Ibid.*, March 6, 1901, p. 345. See also *ibid.*, July 2, 1902, p. 372; and February 23, 1904, p. 403.

125. *Ibid.* [app.] 1881, p. 141; August 17 and October 19, 1881, p. 143; February 24 and March 8, 1882, p. 144; May 5 and August 15, 1882, p. 145; October 16, 1882, p. 146; and February 22 and March 8, 1883, p. 147.

126. Employee record book, "Day Book," 1889-96, p. 298, Marshall Field & Co. Archives; and statement, Fred Morgan, Marshall Field & Co. General Offices.

127. *Dry Goods Reporter*, XL (January 8, 1910), 71; and *Marshall Field & Company* [1903], Marshall Field & Co. Archives.

128. *Women's Wear*, October 22, 1926, J. G. Shedd scrapbook of clippings, Marshall Field & Co. Archives; and

statement, John McKinlay, Marshall Field & Co. General Offices.

129. Letter, Fred E. French of John V. Farwell & Co. to A. B. Jones, June 6, 1887, Field Estate; *Chicago Tribune,* June 24, 1887; and June 26 and 28, 1894; advertising circular, Marshall Field & Co., Retail, 1899, scrapbook of advertising circulars, p. 112, Marshall Field & Co. Archives; *Chicago Times,* July 7, 1893; *Marshall Field & Company* [1903], Marshall Field & Co. Archives; and wholesale record, Marshall Field & Co., April 16, 1890, p. 178. After 1904, in Wholesale alone, the one o'clock Saturday closing hour was made a year-around provision *(ibid.,* February 23, 1904, p. 403).

130. Underlining mine. *Dry Goods Reporter,* XXXII (October 11, 1902), 29.

131. Marshall Field personal salary record book, 1869-72.

132. Wholesale record, Marshall Field & Co., July 3, 1888, p. 72; and delivery boy record book, 1860-1900, Marshall Field & Co. Archives.

133. *Chicago Dry Goods Reporter,* XXVII (October 9, 1897), 13.

134. "Vacation Time," *American Artisan,* XXXVIII (August 19, 1899), 34.

135. Wholesale record, Marshall Field & Co., May 2, p. 145, and November 29, p. 146, 1882; May 29, 1883, p. 148; May 28, 1884, p. 151; May 27, 1885, p. 153; June 29, 1886, p. 158; April 16, 1890, p. 178; May 12, 1898, p. 265; and July 2, 1902, p. 372; letter, Marshall Field & Co. to Marshall Field & Co., N. Y., November 26, 1888, Marshall Field & Co. Archives; and *Chicago Daily News,* May 27, 1904.

136. Wholesale record, Marshall Field & Co., October 17, 1892, p. 195; July 19, 1897, p. 248; October 14, 1898, p. 280; and September 16, 1901, p. 360; *Chicago Evening Post,* October 6, 1893; *Chicago Herald,* September 26, 1881; and general house notice to department heads, November 3, 1873, A. B. Jones folder, Marshall Field & Co. Archives.

137. Letter [A. B.] Jones to Marshall Field & Co., N. Y., November 3, 1888, unidentified scrapbook, Marshall Field & Co. Archives; and wholesale record, Marshall Field & Co., November 2, 1882, p. 169; November 5, 1883, p. 58; March 8, 1886, p. 66; November 1, 1886, p. 159; April 1, p. 161, and November 6, 1887, p. 164; March 30, 1888, p. 166; November 4, p. 174, and December 11, 1889, p. 176; and March 14, 1898, p. 263.

138. *Ibid.,* November 4, 1882, p. 146; and March 31, 1883, p. 147; and *Chicago Tribune,* November 3, 1884.

139. Wholesale record, Marshall Field & Co., December 11, 1889, p. 176.

140. *Ibid.,* March 3, 1881, p. 51; and June 21, 1883, p. 57; Red "Record" general and special house orders, Marshall Field & Co., March 7, 1881, p. 42, and "Day Book," Marshall Field & Co., 1889-96, pp. 292-96, Marshall Field & Co. Archives.

141. Delivery boy record book, 1860-1900, p. 85; wholesale record, Marshall Field & Co., March 3, 1881, p. 51; and January 8, 1884, p. 149; Amos W. Wright, "Marshall Field I," *Harper's Weekly,* XXXV (March 21, 1891), 211; and salary record book, "J. G. Shedd, Dept. Heads, etc., Jan. 1, 1901, to July 1, 1904," Marshall Field & Co. Archives.

142. Statements, Dr. J. L. Munson, Joseph Yates, and Charles C. Bunker, Marshall Field & Co. General Offices; and Field Estate Letters, *passim.*

143. *Marshall Field & Company* [1903], Marshall Field & Co. Archives; and Dennis, *Everybody's Magazine,* March 1906, p. 298.

144. Statement, Stanley Field, Marshall Field & Co. Archives; and interview, J. G. Hall with Luehman, courtesy History of Chicago Project.

145. *Chicago Herald,* December 28, 1881.

146. Barbour (ed.), *Sketchbook of the Inter-State Exposition, Chicago, 1883.*

147. Dennis, *Everybody's Magazine,* March 1906; *Chicago Tribune,* Oc-

tober 1, 1901; *Chicago Dry Goods Reporter*, XXXII (October 11, 1902), 34; wholesale record, May 16, 1903, p. 397; and *Chicago Evening Journal*, September 26, 1903.

148. See cash boys' picnic ribbon, July 21, 1883, attached to interoffice communication, W. B. Weaver to Paul H. Howard, July 2, 1946; and baseball championship pennant, 1904, Marshall Field & Co. Archives.

149. *Chicago Dry Goods Reporter*, XXXII (October 11, 1902), 38.

150. *Northwestern Christian Advocate*, November 12, 1902, p. 18; and *Chicago Evening Journal*, September 26, 1903.

151. Statement, F. O. Stevens, rug department, Marshall Field & Company General Offices.

152. Delivery boy record book, 1860-1900, see for example, pp. 69, 77, 87, 99, 321, 327, 391, 397, 401, Marshall Field & Co. Archives; notice issued from office of Retail Manager to employees, January 27, 1905; *"Don'ts" for Employees* (Chicago: Marshall Field & Co., 1904), *passim;* and *Chicago Dry Goods Reporter*, XXVII (October 9, 1897), 13.

153. Higinbotham, *The Making of a Merchant*, pp. 122-23.

154. Warren, "A Synopsis of the Meeting of Section Managers, November 13, 1902 . . ." (unidentified scrapbook); wholesale record, August 27, 1873, p. 13; Red "Record," general and special house orders, Marshall Field & Co., August 26, 1873; and *Chicago Dry Goods Reporter*, XXVII (October 9, 1897), 11.

155. Mimeographed copy of "Notes on Subjects Referred to at the Meeting of Section Managers of July 2d, 1902"; and *Mirror* (St. Louis), April 16, 1903.

156. Warren, "A Synopsis of the Meeting of Section Managers, November 13, 1902 . . ." (unidentified scrapbook).

157. Personal interview, Dr. J. L. Munson.

158. "Business Policy," *Chicago Dry Goods Reporter*, XXVII (October 9, 1897), 10, 11, and 15; "Topics Referred to at the Meeting of Section Managers of November 4th, 1902" (unidentified scrapbook), Marshall Field & Co. Archives; memoranda of meeting, section managers and assistants with H. G. Selfridge and W. P. Warren, October 18, 1901, in "Business Ideas," p. 2, Marshall Field & Co. Archives; and notice issued from office of Retail Manager to employees, November 22, 1904, Marshall Field & Co. Archives.

159. Statement, Charles C. Bunker, Marshall Field & Co. General Offices.

160. *Chicago Dry Goods Reporter*, XXVII (October 9, 1897), 11; Delivery boy record book, 1860-1900, pp. 245, 297, 375, and 427; wholesale record, Marshall Field & Co., (app. 1873), 7-8; November 28, 1898, p. 285; July 25, 1891, p. 191; December 3, (app. 1874), p. 17; November 4, 1882, p. 146; *"Don'ts"* for *Employees*, pp. 3, 11, 12, 13; and J. William Schulze, *The American Office, Its Organization, Management and Records* (2nd ed.), quoting the Marshall Field & Co. Book of Rules.

161. *Ibid.*, pp. 371-72; "Subjects Referred to at the Meeting [of Section Managers] of October 7, 1902," unidentified scrapbook, Marshall Field & Co. Archives; and notice issued from office of Retail Manager to employees, September 30, 1904, Marshall Field & Co. Archives.

162. *Chicago Dry Goods Reporter*, XXVI (October 9, 1897), 15.

163. *The Dry Goods Economist*, LXIV (November 20, 1909), 45; and Schulze, *The American Office*, pp. 371-72, quoting Marshall Field & Co. "Book of Rules."

164. Notice issued from office of Retail Manager to employees, January 27, 1905; and M. Field's Real Estate Record and Dept. Head Salary Record Book," Marshall Field & Co. Archives.

165. Unidentified newspaper clipping, Stone scrapbook, p. 80, Marshall Field & Co. Archives.

166. Wholesale record, Marshall Field & Co., January 15, 1872, p. 12; and Red "Record," general and special house orders, Marshall Field & Co., January 15, 1873, p. 16.

167. *Ibid.*, p. 40; "Don'ts for Employees," p. 13; and *Chicago Dry Goods Reporter*, XXVII (October 9, 1897), 11.

168. Wholesale record, August 19, 1904, p. 408. See also Red "Record," general and special house orders, Marshall Field & Co., March 1, 1881, p. 40.

169. Wholesale record, February 18, 1882, p. 133; and statement, Fred Morgan, Marshall Field & Co., General Offices.

170. *"Don'ts for Employees," passim.*

171. Wholesale record, Marshall Field & Co., February 16, 1903, pp. 388-89; *"Don'ts for Employees,"* pp. 6, 13; *Chicago Dry Goods Reporter,* XXVII (October 9, 1897), pp. 11, 13; J. William Schulze, *The American Office,* p. 375, quoting Marshall Field & Co. Book of Rules. Also compare advertisements in *Chicago Tribune* of December 16, 1868 and January 3, 1878 with those in *Inter-Ocean* of December 9, 1891 and November 25, 1904; and in *Daily Drovers Journal* of September 13, 1882.

172. Statement, Ellen Jane Bredin, Marshall Field & Co. General Offices.

173. "Marshall, [*sic*] Field & Co., First-Class Establishment," *Buyer and Seller,* I (October 12, 1895); *Chicago Dry Goods Reporter,* XXVII (October 9, 1897), 11 and 15; and XXXII (October 11, 1902), 25; *Mirror* (St. Louis), April 16, 1903; and *Chicago Evening Journal,* September 26, 1903.

174. MacLean, *American Journal of Sociology,* IV (May 1899), 724-25.

175. Interference on the part of Marshall Field and Company was insignificant, however, compared to some firms of that day. See, for example, descriptions of the Bon Marche, Louvre, and Printemps, all of Paris, in "Department Stores Abroad," *Department Store Journal,* I (September 15, 1896), 47-48; and "The Paris Department Stores," *ibid.* (October 15, 1896), pp. 115-16.

176. For comparison, see Hower, *History of Macy's,* pp. 200-208.

177. Wholesale record, Marshall Field & Co., November 28, 1898, p. 285; *Mercer,* I (June 1891), 20; statement, Charles C. Bunker, Marshall Field & Co. General Offices; and *Dry Goods Reporter,* XXXII (October 11, 1902), 20. See also *Buyer and Seller,* Vol. I (October 12, 1895), [n.p.].

178. Statements, Dr. J. L. Munson and C. F. Pritzlaff, Marshall Field & Co. General Offices; and interview, J. G. Hall with Luehman, courtesy History of Chicago Project.

179. Statement, Marshall Field & Co. General Offices.

180. *Ibid.*

181. Williams, December 18. See also James Simpson, "Our Organization," Marshall Field & Co. Archives (mimeographed); *Northwestern Christian Advocate,* November 12, 1902, p. 18.

CHAPTER EIGHT

1. *Chicago Times,* January 27, 1881; and *Chicago Tribune,* January 27, 28, 1881.

2. *Ibid.,* January 27, 1881.

3. Cook, *Bygone Days in Chicago; Recollections,* p. 190.

4. *Chicago Times,* January 27, 1881.

5. Letter, L. Leiter to M. Field, March 13, 1867, Marshall Field & Co. Archives. See also "M. Field's Real Estate and Dept. Head Salary Record Book," Marshall Field & Co. Archives.

6. *Ibid.;* and Marshall Field personal salary record book, 1869-72.

7. M. Field personal record book, real estate and salaries, 1869-1901; record book, "Rents, Oct. 30, 1906," [n.p.], Marshall Field & Co. Archives; record book, "Rents, June 1, 1901," Marshall Field & Co. Archives; and Hoyt, *Land Values in Chicago, 1830-1933,* pp. 89-90.

8. Letter, M. Field to W. N. Draper, London, July 7, 1875, Field Estate.

9. *Chicago Times* and *Chicago Tribune*, January 27, 1881.
10. Statement of services rendered, Lyman and Jackson, attorneys at law to Marshall Field, Marshall Field & Co. Archives; Complete Inventory, Estate of Marshall Field, Deceased, Marshall Field & Co. Archives.
11. T. W. Goodspeed, *University of Chicago Magazine*, VIII (1902), 42-43; and *Chicago Record Herald*, June 9, 1906.
12. Inheritance Tax Appraisement, Estate of Marshall Field, Marshall Field & Co. Archives.
13. *Economist*, January 26, 1907; and *Chicago Tribune*, January 17, 1906.
14. Inheritance Tax Appraisement, Estate of Marshall Field, Marshall Field & Co. Archives.
15. Record book, "Rents, June 1, 1901," Marshall Field & Co. Archives.
16. *Infra*, pp 154 ff.
17. Inheritance Tax Appraisement, Estate of Marshall Field, Marshall Field & Co. Archives.
18. Record book, "Rents, Oct. 30, 1906." Marshall Field & Co. Archives.
19. *Chicago Times* and *Chicago Tribune*, January 27, 1881.
20. *Ibid.*, June 10, 1904.
21. *Chicago Tribune*, June 14, 1898, and June 10, 1904.
22. Complete Inventory, Estate of Marshall Field, Deceased, Marshall Field & Co. Archives.
23. M. Field personal record book, real estate and salaries, 1869-1901; and letter, Marshall Field to Henry Foreman, Chicago, March 23, 1877, Field Estate.
24. Original unedited MS for article by James Simpson, "Simplifying Buying for the Merchant," to be published in *Nation's Business*, July 1929, Marshall Field & Co. Archives [Simpson was Marshall Field's personal secretary at the time]; statements, Robert Mandel of Mandel Bros., and witness to agreement between Marshall Field and Leon Mandel; F. W. Boyden [in charge of Field's real estate]; and Homer J. Buckley [advertising], Marshall Field & Co. General Offices; and Daniel F. Kelly, "Cut-Throat Competition Is Destruction," *Illinois Journal of Commerce*, November 1927, p. 18.
25. Simpson, *Nation's Business*, July 1929, pp. 41-42.
26. Marshall Field personal salary record book, 1869-72.
27. Marshall Field personal memorandum, "Statement my affairs," January 1, 1874, Marshall Field & Co. Archives.
28. *Chicago Tribune*, January 25, 1906.
29. Statement, Richard H. Peel, confidential bookkeeper for Mr. Field, Marshall Field & Co. General Offices.
30. Inheritance Tax Appraisement, Estate of Marshall Field, Marshall Field & Co. Archives.
31. T. W. Goodspeed, *University of Chicago Magazine*, VIII, 1922, 47-48; and letter, Marshall Field to C. H. McCormick, Chicago, July 23, 1880, courtesy McCormick Historical Association. See also *Economist*, January 26, 1907; and *Chicago Record-Herald*, January 17, 1906.
32. *Chicago Herald*, June 17 and 19, 1887; and Marshall Field personal salary record book, 1869-72.
33. Inheritance Tax Appraisement, Estate of Marshall Field, Marshall Field & Co. Archives; and Marshall Field personal letters, Field Estate, *passim*.
34. *Chicago Tribune*, August 18, 1887. See also *ibid.*, August 6, 1893.
35. Allan Nevins, *John D. Rockefeller; The Heroic Age of American Enterprise* (New York: Charles Scribner's Sons, 1940), II, 423.
36. Inheritance Tax Appraisement, Estate of Marshall Field, Marshall Field & Co. Archives; *Chicago Record-Herald*, December 1, 1901; and Illinois, *Reports to the General Assembly*, 1890, "Report of the Auditor of Public Accounts," p. 322.
37. *Ibid.*, p. 334; W. H. Harper and C. N. Ravell, *Fifty Years of Banking in Chicago*, 1857-1907 (Chicago: Merchants' Loan and Trust Co. [1908]), p. 67; statement, John W. Hughes, Marshall Field & Co. General Offices; and Marshall Field personal letters, Field Estate, *passim*.

38. *Chicago Record-Herald,* December 20, 1905; F. Cyril James, *The Growth of Chicago Banks, 1816-1938* (New York: Harper, 1938), I, 558-89, and II, 673-74; *Chicago Evening Post,* January 16, 1906; "Marshall Field," *Outlook,* LXXXII (January 27, 1906), 152-53; and R. G. Thomas, "Bank Failures in Chicago Before 1925," *Journal of the Illinois Historical Society, XXVIII* (October 1935), 196-97.

39. Marshall Field personal memorandum, "Statement my affairs," January 1, 1874, Marshall Field & Co. Archives; and Marshall Field personal salary record book, 1869-72.

40. Letter, Charles T. Yerkes to Marshall Field, December 10, 1887, Field Estate.

41. *Chicago Record,* May 18 and 19, 1900; letters, Charles T. Yerkes, North Chicago Street Railroad Co., to Marshall Field, December 1 and 10, 1887, Field Estate; "History and Statistics of Chicago Street Railway Corporations," *Economist* (Chicago: Economist Pub. Co., 1896), pp. 33, 35, 42, and 47-48. Supplement.

42. *Chicago Record-Herald,* January 11 and 12, August 17, and October 18 and 23, 1905.

43. Carter H. Harrison, *Stormy Years,* (Indianapolis: The Bobbs-Merrill Co., 1935), pp. 136-38; and Tomay F. Deuther, *First Issue of Civic Questions Pertaining Entirely to Local Transportation in the City of Chicago,* Report of Northwest Side Commercial Association (Chicago, 1924), p. 61.

44. *Ibid.,* pp. 56-57, 77.

45. *Ibid.,* p. 61.

46. *Chicago Record-Herald,* December 1, 1901; *New York Herald,* September 1, 1901; Inheritance Tax Appraisement, Estate of Marshall Field, Marshall Field & Co. Archives; *Poor's Railroad Manual,* 1905 (New York: Poor's Pub. Co., 1905), pp. 321 and 1507; and *ibid.,* 1900, p. 223.

47. Cleveland, *System Magazine,* December 1906, p. 582; statement, H. P. Shedd, Marshall Field & Co. General Offices; Edward Hunger-

ford, *The Story of the Baltimore & Ohio Railroad, 1827-1924* (New York: Putnam, 1928), II, 216; and *Chicago Record-Herald,* December 1, 1901.

48. *Ibid.; New York Herald,* September 1, 1901; *Chicago Evening Post,* January 16, 1906; and Inheritance Tax Appraisement, Estate of Marshall Field, Marshall Field & Co. Archives.

49. *Chicago Evening Post,* January 16, 1906; and C. L. Drain record book, 1900-07, Marshall Field & Co. Archives.

50. Statements, Stanley Field, H. P. Shedd, and J. W. Hughes, Marshall Field & Co. General Offices.

51. Table XIV, p. 175.

52. *Chicago Evening Post,* October 27, 1926; and *Chicago Evening American,* October 28, 1926.

53. Selfridge, however, did not die a rich man. *Chicago Record-Herald,* November 25, 1906; Selfridge, *Saturday Evening Post,* August 10, 1935, p. 69; *Chicago Sun,* May 9, 1947; *New York Times,* May 9, 1947.

54. Marshall Field personal salary record book, 1872, Marshall Field & Co. Archives.

55. Shedd was born July 20, 1850 *(Chicago Evening Post,* January 16, 1906; letter, Henry C. Metcalf, Town Clerk, Alstead, New Hampshire, to R. W. Twyman [August 5, 1949]).

56. John G. Shedd, "Roads to Success," *Economist,* repr., September 2, 1922 [n.p.], Marshall Field & Co. Archives.

57. Accounting sheets, sales of general salesmen, Wholesale, 1871-72, A. B. Jones folder.

58. Salary record book, 1872-74.

59. M. Field personal record book, real estate and salaries, 1869-1901.

60. Marshall Field personal salary record book, 1872, Marshall Field & Co. Archives.

61. Ditchett, *Marshall Field and Company,* p. 42, quoting Mr. Shedd.

62. Accounting sheets, sales of general salesmen, Wholesale, 1871-72, A. B. Jones folder.

63. Salary record book, 1872-74.

64. Salary record book, 1876-78.

NOTES

87-92

65. *Chicago Herald and Examiner,* October 23, 1926; statements, George Young, H. P. Shedd, and J. J. Reilly, Marshall Field & Co. General Offices; and *Chicago Tribune,* October 24, 1926.
66. *Ibid.,* January 19, 1883.
67. Accounting sheets, profit and loss, wholesale and retail, 1872-91, A. B. Jones folder; M. Field personal record book, real estate and salaries, 1869-1901; and salary record, 1883-85.
68. Tables XIV, p. 175; and XV, p. 177.
69. Accounting sheets, profit and loss, wholesale and retail, 1872-91, A. B. Jones folder.
70. Salary record book, 1883-85.
71. *Ibid.;* and wholesale record, Marshall Field & Co., February 2, 1883, p. 121.
72. Salary record book, 1871-87, and 1883-85.
73. Accounting sheets, profit and loss, wholesale and retail, 1872-91, A. B. Jones folder.
74. Contractual agreement, J. G. Shedd with Marshall Field & Co., July 1, 1886 and 1887; and M. Field personal record book, real estate and salaries, 1869-1901.
75. Accounting sheets, profit and loss, wholesale and retail, 1872-91, A. B. Jones folder; "John G. Shedd Record Book, 1872-1902"; and "J. G. Shedd" record book, 1902-06, Marshall Field & Co. Archives.
76. Accounting sheets, recapitulation of profit and loss accounts, "Share Profits above guaranteed salaries," 1885-88, A. B. Jones folder.
77. Copy of contractual agreement for 1889 and 1890, Marshall Field with J. G. Shedd and H. G. Selfridge, November 13, 1888.
78. Accounting ledgers, 1891-92, Comptroller's safe, Marshall Field & Co. General Offices.
79. John G. Shedd address to "fifty-year" men in *Fifty Years of Service,* December 18, 1922, Marshall Field & Co. Archives; *Chicago Herald and Examiner,* October 23, 1926; and *Chicago Tribune,* October 24, 1926.
80. Statements, John McKinlay, H. P. Shedd, R. H. Bettcher, and George Young, Marshall Field & Co. General Offices.
81. Statement, Charles C. Bunker, Marshall Field & Co. General Offices.
82. Statements, Hilton Thorpe, H. P. Shedd, George Young, and J. J. Reilly, Marshall Field & Co. General Offices; and Herma Clark, "John Graves Shedd," citing Mr. Yates (Chicago: Marshall Field & Co. Archives, 1946). Typescript.
83. Statements, R. H. Bettcher, J. W. Hughes, George Young, Hilton Thorpe, and R. H. Peel, Marshall Field & Co. General Offices.
84. Letter, M. Field to L. G. Woodhouse, August 11, 1875, Field Estate.
85. McClintock typescript, quoting Shedd.
86. Marshall Field accounting record book, 1876 (directions for keeping department records); wholesale record, Marshall Field & Co., March 10, and September 14, 1903, pp. 393 and 400, respectively; and Cleveland, *System Magazine,* February 1907, pp. 131-32.
87. Interdepartmental communication, "Addressed to heads of all Depts. [*sic*] *at* Chicago," Marshall Field & Co., February 19, 1883, unidentified scrapbook, Marshall Field & Co. Archives.
88. Wholesale record, Marshall Field & Co., March 9, 1891, p. 79.
89. *Ibid.,* August 19, 1886, p. 67.
90. Cleveland, *System Magazine,* March 1907, p. 230.
91. M. Field personal record book, real estate and salaries, 1869-1901.
92. Robert Fair was general manager of Wholesale; but his authority seems to have been nominal compared to that of Shedd (wholesale record, Marshall Field & Co., January 1, 1897, p. 215; December 18, 1900, p. 340; and February 19, and April 30, 1903, pp. 389-90 and 396, respectively; "Confirmed by the Trades: Improved Dry Goods Trade," *Chicago Dry Goods Reporter,* XXVII [August 7, 1897], 21; "Large Volume of Business," *ibid.,* XXVIII [March 12, 1898], 35).
93. *Chicago Tribune,* October 23, 1926; and *Chicago Daily News,* October 22, 1926.

207

94. Copy of contractual agreement for 1889 and 1890, Marshall Field with J. G. Shedd and H. G. Selfridge, November 13, 1888.
95. For example, letter, Field, Leiter & Co., to E. L. Jaffray & Co., April 20, 1876, Field Estate; and advertising circular, Field, Leiter & Co., wholesale, spring, 1876, Marshall Field & Co. Archives. Field's showed a certain inconsistency by sending through the mail sample selections of goods to choose from to anyone who requested them *(Spring Catalogue,* Field, Leiter & Co., Wholesale, 1870, p. 48; and *Chicago Tribune,* May 1, 1871). This, of course, had been done even when the firm was owned by Potter Palmer *(ibid.,* November 9, 1861; and *Chicago Evening Journal,* November 8, 1861).
96. *Chicago Tribune,* July 14, 1871; and letters, Field, Leiter & Co., to George C. Richardson & Co., and to Wright, Bliss & Fabyan, March 29, 1876, Field Estate.
97. Advertising circulars, Field, Leiter & Co., Wholesale, August 20, 1877, Autumn; and May 2, 1878, Marshall Field & Co. Archives.
98. For example, advertising circulars, Field, Leiter & Co., Wholesale, November 15, 1875, November 7, 1876, Autumn 1877, and May 2, 1878, Marshall Field & Co. Archives; postcard circulars, Field, Leiter & Co., Wholesale, November 28, 1877, and February 8 and March 16, 1878, Marshall Field & Co. Archives; letters, Marshall Field to Field, Leiter & Co., N. Y., October 4, 1876, and Field, Leiter & Co., to Field, Leiter & Co., N. Y., October 14, 1876, Field Estate.
99. Letter, Field, Leiter & Co., to E. L. Jaffray & Co., April 20, 1876, Field Estate.
100. *Chicago Commercial,* September 18, 1875; letters, W. F. Hypes, Marshall Field & Co. to J. J. O'Brien & Co., San Francisco, October 17, 1895; and to Conley & McTague, Deer Lodge, Montana, January 22, 1897, Bettcher record book, pp. 32 and 43, Marshall Field & Co. Archives; wholesale record, Marshall Field & Co., December 9, 1897, p. 251; and February 24, 1900, p. 320;

and letter, Marshall Field to Field, Leiter & Co., November 18, 1876, Field Estate.
101. McClintock typescript, quoting interview of McClintock with Mr. Walter Haskell, carpet salesman and department head in Wholesale.
102. Accounting ledgers, 1873-1906, Comptroller's safe, Marshall Field & Co. General Offices; wholesale record, Marshall Field & Co., November 17, 1884, p. 63; February 21, 1901, pp. 343-44; April 18, 1901, pp. 349-50; and March 29, 1905, p. 415; *Chicago Dry Goods Reporter,* XXVII (May 8, 1897), 4, adv.; and Red "Record" general and special house orders, Marshall Field & Co., February 28, 1881, pp. 38-39.
103. There had always been some by general salesmen, largely for purposes of "good will."
104. Statements, George Young and R. H. Bettcher, road salesmen, Marshall Field & Co. General Offices; and wholesale record, Marshall Field & Co., December 18, 1882, p. 107; and January 17, 1889, p. 184.
105. McClintock typescript, quoting interview of McClintock with William Zentell of the notions department.
106. Salary records, 1871-87, and 1883-85.
107. Statement, George Young, Marshall Field & Co. General Offices.
108. Statement, R. H. Bettcher, Marshall Field & Co. General Offices.
109. *Ibid.;* and wholesale record, *passim.*
110. Statements, R. H. Bettcher and George Young, Marshall Field & Co. General Offices. See also wholesale record, Marshall Field & Co., January 17, 1889, p. 184; and letter, Marshall Field & Co. to Chas. F. Wilt, Chicago, September 14, 1897, Bettcher Record Book, p. 63, reverse, Marshall Field & Co. Archives.
111. Letter, Marshall Field to Col. C. G. Sawtelle, Q. M. General, Philadelphia, May 29, 1893, Bettcher record book, p. 22, Marshall Field & Co. Archives; and "The Field Columbian Museum," *Interior,* XXVI (March 14, 1895), 352.

112. Wholesale record, Marshall Field & Co., [March] 1891, p. 81; February 21, and August 24, 1905, pp. 412 and 422, respectively; Advertising circular, Field, Leiter & Co., Wholesale, February 28, 1876; letters, Haskell, Field, Leiter & Co. general salesman, to Robt. Moir & Co., Oquawka, Illinois, June 5, 1878; and Barron, Field, Leiter & Co., general salesman, to Robt. Moir & Co., Oquawka, Illinois, June 19, 1878, Warshaw Collection of Business Americans; letters, W. F. Hypes, Marshall Field & Co. to A. H. Sanford, Seattle, June 18, 1900, and to Messrs. Pierr & Co., Moline, Ill., December 19, 1900, Bettcher record book, pp. 66 and 72; and letter, Wm. L. Hipsley, Table Grove, Ill., to W. F. Hypes, December 20, 1922, Marshall Field & Co. Archives.

113. *Chicago Times-Herald,* December 27, 1900; and *Chicago Chronicle,* June 10, 1904.

114. U. S. Bureau of the Census, *Abstract of the Twelfth Census of the United States; 1900, Population* (3rd ed.; Washington: Government Printing Office, 1904), pp. 32, 33 and 35.

115. Wholesale record, Marshall Field & Co., December 9, 1897, p. 251; and February 24, 1900, p. 320; letter, Geo. H. Partridge, Wyman, Partridge & Co., Minneapolis, to Marshall Field, May 28, 1896, Field Estate; M. Field personal record book, real estate and salaries, 1867-1901; and catalogue, "Marshall Field & Co. Notions," Wholesale, 1893, pp. 1-113, Marshall Field & Co. Archives.

116. Letter, S. G. Gould, Marshall Field & Co. road salesman, Salem, Oregon, to Marshall Field, May 15, 1890, Field Estate; and statements, George Young, John McKinlay, and Porter Case, Marshall Field & Co. General Offices. See also *Inter-Ocean,* January 28, 1890; and Bancroft, *Fifty Years of Service,* December 18, 1922. Field continued to take over the property of any firm that did not pay its debts (M. Field personal record book, real estate and salaries, 1867-1901).

117. Statements, Stanley Field, T. H. Eddy, John McKinlay, R. H. Peel, Porter Case, and George Young, Marshall Field & Co. General Offices. At the time of his death, Marshall Field had $4,301,382.06 in cash deposited in eight different banks and had $8,486,607.23 loaned out to Marshall Field and Company in addition to his share of the capital (Inheritance Tax Appraisement, Estate of Marshall Field, Marshall Field & Co. Archives).

118. *Goodalls Daily Sun,* June 18, 1887; and *Chicago Herald,* June 18 and 19, 1887.

119. *Chicago Tribune,* January 9, and May 29, 1881; *Chicago Times,* January 27, 1881; Inheritance Tax Appraisement, Estate of Marshall Field, Marshall Field & Co. Archives; and record books, "Rents, Oct. 30, 1906"; and "Rents, June 1, 1901," Marshall Field & Co. Archives.

120. M. G. Van Rennselaer, *Henry Hobson Richardson and His Works* (Boston: Houghton Mifflin Co., 1888), p. 36; and Louis R. Sullivan, *Kindergarten Chats on Architecture, Education and Democracy* (1st ed.; Scarab Fraternity Press, 1934), facing p. 16.

121. See pictures in an unidentified clipping, Marshall Field & Co. Archives; and Advertising circular, Marshall Field & Co., Wholesale, 1887, Marshall Field & Co. Archives. See also *Marshall Field & Company* [1903], Marshall Field & Co. Archives. Land and building together were valued at $2,332,000 when Field died (Inheritance Tax Appraisement, Estate of Marshall Field, Marshall Field & Co. Archives).

122. *Chicago Tribune,* June 18, 1887; *Goodalls Daily Sun,* June 18, 1887; and Wholesale record, Marshall Field & Co., June 14, 1887, p. 162.

123. Unidentified clipping, Marshall Field & Co. Archives.

124. Memorandum of departments, number, location, and goods, Wholesale, July 1887, Marshall Field & Co. Archives. See also catalogues, "1890-91 Wholesale Notions and Fancy Goods Catalogue," *passim;* "Marshall Field & Co. No-

tions," Wholesale, 1893, *passim;* Jewelry, Marshall Field & Co., Wholesale, 1893 and 1898, *passim;* and "Dry Goods, Carpets and Upholstery," Marshall Field & Co., 1900, *passim* [no page numbers], Marshall Field & Co. Archives.

125. For example, see *Chicago's First Half Century, 1833-1883*, p. 91.

126. General house notice to "General Salesmen," July 16, 1883, Marshall Field & Co. Archives; letters, Field, Leiter & Co. to Geo. C. Richardson & Co.; and to Wright, Bliss & Fabyan, New York, March 29, 1876; and to Field, Leiter & Co., New York, October 21, 1876, Field Estate; and Catalogue, "Price List, Notions Department," Field, Leiter & Co., Wholesale, 1877, p. 5.

127. Advertising circular, Field, Leiter & Co., Wholesale, August 20, 1877; and *Spring Catalogue,* Field, Leiter & Co., Wholesale, 1870, pp. 15, 21, 40, and 46. See also *Chicago Dry Goods Reporter and Wholesale Price List,* July 1894, p. 6.

128. *Spring Catalogue,* Field, Leiter & Co., Wholesale, 1870, p. 31. See also p. 74.

129. *Ibid.,* pp. 15 and 31; *Chicago Tribune,* April 10, 1873; Marshall Field personal salary record book, 1869-72; and Advertising circular, Field, Leiter & Co., Wholesale, November 5, 1872, Marshall Field & Co. Archives. Also see *Spring Catalogue,* Field, Leiter & Co., Wholesale, 1871, for other items.

130. Advertising circular, Field, Leiter & Co., Wholesale, August 20, 1877; Marshall Field & Co. Archives.

131. *Goodalls Daily Evening Sun,* March 19, 1887.

132. *Illustrated Catalogue of Holiday Goods, Druggists' Sundries, Stationery, Etc.,* Marshall Field & Co., 1890-91, Marshall Field & Co. Archives, pp. 199 and 395.

133. *Ibid.,* 1893, pp. 236, 243.

134. For other examples, see advertisement, *Scribner's Magazine Advertizer,* November 1895, p. 87; and "Records of the Houses: Marshall Field and Company," *Chicago Dry Goods Reporter,* XXIX (January 7, 1899), 95.

135. Letter, W. G. Northrup, North Star Woolen Mill Co., Minneapolis, to Marshall Field, July 25, 1893, Field Estate. Later factories aided in this fashion were some manufacturing fine china. Statement by Charles Nash, head of china department, Dec. 13, 1946.

136. Eastern Union Telegraph Co., cable messages, Marshall Field, Paris, to Levi Leiter, Chicago, March 2, 3, and 4, 1880, Marshall Field & Co. Archives.

137. Copy of contractual agreement, Field, Leiter & Co., Chicago and New York, with Fortin Fils & Deschamps, gloves manufacturer of Paris, France, May 15, 1880, Marshall Field & Co. Archives.

138. *Chicago Tribune,* January 17, 1865; and March 14 and September 19, 1874; and *Spring Catalogue,* Field, Leiter & Co., Wholesale, 1870, p. 46.

139. Copy of contractual agreement, Field, Leiter & Co., with Fortin Fils & Deschamps, May 15, 1880.

140. Accounting ledgers, 1873-1906, Comptroller's safe, Marshall Field & Co. General Offices; and "State Street Glove Talks," *Chicago Dry Goods Reporter,* XXVII (August 7, 1897), 19.

141. *Chicago Times,* November 13, 1876; and *Chicago Tribune,* March 14, 1874, January 13, 1879, June 21, 1880, and April 27, 1881; and C. Cody Collins, *Love of a Glove: the romance, legends and fashion history of gloves and how they are made* (New York: Fairchild Pub. Co., 1945), p. 119.

142. *Ibid.,* pp. 77 and 86; "Glove Manufacture," *Encyclopaedia Britannica,* Vol. X (1948); and letter, Marshall Field & Co. to Miss Claire Shulman, October 31, 1925, Marshall Field & Co. Archives. See also *Chicago Tribune,* September 14, 1900.

143. For example, *ibid.,* December 12, 1887, November 14, 1892, September 25 and 26, 1893, March 16 and 30, 1896; *Chicago Record,* September 25, 1899; *Chicago Record-Herald,* September 25, 1905; advertising circular, Marshall Field & Co., Wholesale, Autumn, August 1881, Stone scrapbook, p. 75; and post-

card circular, Marshall Field & Co., Retail, 1904, Marshall Field & Co. Archives.

144. Wholesale record, Marshall Field & Co., December 23, 1881; and letters, Marshall Field & Co. to Marshall Field & Co., New York, March 29 and April 23, 1883, Marshall Field & Co. Archives.

145. Contractual agreement, Field, Leiter & Co., with Fortin Fils & Deschamps, July 1, 1883, Marshall Field & Co. Archives; and letter, G. Deschamps & Co. [formerly Fortin Fils & Deschamps] to Marshall Field & Co., January 1907, Marshall chives).

146. Accounting ledgers, 1881-1906, Comptroller's safe, Marshall Field & Co. General Offices. Marshall Field & Company in 1890 made a similar arrangement with Messrs. E. and S. Jay of Alsace-Lorraine for another quality of glove (translation of contractual agreement, Marshall Field & Co., with E. & S. Jay, Grenoble, Alsace-Lorraine, January 21, 1890, effective July 1, 1890, Marshall Field & Co. Archives).

147. Letter, Field, Leiter & Co. to R. Moir & Co., Oquawka, Illinois, April 19, 1872, Warshaw Collection of Business Americana, New York.

148. Accounting ledgers, 1873-79 Comptroller's safe, Marshall Field & Co. General Offices; and record book, foreign buying, "Foreign Purchases," 1892-1900, pp. 13-14, Marshall Field & Co. Archives.

149. *Chicago Evening Post*, January 16, 1906.

150. Record book, foreign buying, 1892-1902; and record book, foreign codes and gold import and export rates, 1906, Marshall Field & Co. Archives.

151. Letters, Marshall Field to Field, Leiter & Co., New York, August 12, 1875, and August 4, 1876, Field Estate; and wholesale record, Marshall Field & Co., April 18, 1877, p. 37; August 5, 1890, p. 76; April 19, 1901, p. 350; and September 1, 1905, p. 432. Because of the magnitude of their orders, Marshall Field & Co. exacted rebates from both shippers and manufacturers as a

regular policy (M. Field personal record book, real estate and salaries, 1867-1901).

152. Letter, Marshall Field & Co. to Hon. Burton McMillin, House of Representatives, Washington, D. C., July 27, 1894, Marshall Field & Co. Archives; "The New Tariff Bill," *Chicago Dry Goods Reporter*, XXVII (May 15, 1897), 17; and "Want Prompt Actions," *ibid.*, June 5, 1897, p. 11.

153. Letter of instruction, M. Field to J. N. Field, May, 1871, Marshall Field & Co. Archives.

154. Letter, John G. Shedd to Victor F. Lawson, July 3, 1905, Victor F. Lawson *Papers*, Newberry Library, Chicago; and statements, Stanley Field, son of Joseph N. Field, partner and head of Manchester Office; and Hilton Thorpe, secretary and successor to Joseph N. Field in Manchester office, Marshall Field & Co. General Offices. By the time of Field's death, offices had been established in Plauen and Annaberg, Germany, and Yokohama, Japan *(Chicago Evening Post,* January 16, 1906).

155. Marshall Field personal memorandum, "Number of Employees Jany 1882," Marshall Field & Co. Archives; and statement, Hilton Thorpe, Marshall Field & Co. General Offices.

156. Letter, Marshall Field to L. G. Woodhouse, New York, June 10, 1875, Field Estate.

157. *Chicago Evening Journal,* September 26, 1903; "Book Gifts" [1900], unidentified scrapbook, Marshall Field & Co. Archives [pages not numbered]; *Chicago Tribune,* March 24, 1902; *Inter-Ocean,* March 10, 1902; and advertising circular, "From Over the Sea," Marshall Field & Co., November 4, 1901, scrapbook of advertising circulars, p. 85, Marshall Field & Co. Archives.

158. *Chicago Dry Goods Reporter and Wholesale Price List,* July 7, 1894, p. 6; and "Oriental Rugs and Carpets," *Carpet Trade and Review,* p. 17 [n.d.], in the William E. Clarke [head, home furnishings] personal scrapbook on Oriental

rugs, carpets, etc. [1874-1930], Marshall Field & Co. Archives [no page numbers].

159. Statement, Charles C. Bunker, Marshall Field & Co. General Offices. See also advertising circulars, Field, Leiter & Co., Retail, Spring; and Wholesale, August 20, 1877, Marshall Field & Co. Archives; unidentified clipping, December 15, 1902, p. 97, in the William E. Clarke personal scrapbook on Oriental rugs, carpets, etc. 1874-1930, Marshall Field & Co. Archives; *Chicago Tribune*, March 18, 1901; *Report of the Industrial Commission of 1901*, VII, 458, Courtesy History of Chicago Project; and *Chicago Record-Herald*, October 3, 1905.

160. *Supra*, pp. 44 ff.

161. Unidentified clipping, February 8, 1891, p. 52 in the William E. Clarke personal scrapbook on Oriental rugs, carpets, etc [1874-1930].

162. Letters, Field, Leiter & Co. to Field, Leiter & Co., New York, June 8, 1875; and to Field, Leiter & Co., Manchester, June 16, 1875, Field Estate.

163. Clipping, *Interior Furnishing*, [1889], p. 32 in the William E. Clarke personal scrapbook on Oriental rugs, carpets, etc. [1874-1930]. See also *Dry Goods Economist, Jubilee Number, 1846-1896*, p. 104.

164. Unidentified clipping, February 8, 1891, p. 52 in the William E. Clarke personal scrapbook on Oriental rugs, carpets, etc. [1874-1930].

165. Accounting sheets, profit and loss, wholesale and retail, 1872-91, A. B. Jones folder; accounting ledgers, 1878-79, Comptroller's safe, Marshall Field & Co. General Offices; "John G. Shedd Record Book, 1872-1902"; and "J. G. Shedd" record book. 1902-6.

166. Accounting ledgers, 1889-98, Comptroller's safe, Marshall Field & Co. General Offices; unidentified clipping, October 27, 1891, p. 67, in the William E. Clarke personal scrapbook on Oriental rugs, carpets, etc., 1874-1930; and *ibid.*, unidentified clipping, "Rugs from the Orient" (November 21, 1889), p. 2.

167. *Ibid.*; and unidentified clippings, December 15, 1902, p. 97; and October 27, 1891, p. 67; and Hull, *Marshall Field & Company*, 1907, p. 31. See also advertising circular, Field, Leiter & Co., Retail, Spring 1877.

168. Advertising circular, Marshall Field & Co., May 2, 1903, unidentified scrapbook, p. 61, Marshall Field & Co. Archives; *Chicago Tribune*, December 18, 1901, March 10 and 24, 1902; and *Chicago Evening Journal*, September 26, 1903. Rugs, exclusively for Marshall Field's, were also woven in Asia Minor (*Chicago Record*, October 11, 1897).

169. Advertising circular, Field, Leiter & Co., September 16, 1867. See also *Chicago Evening Journal*, April 27, 1872.

170. In 1877, for instance, the cloak-making "factory" alone employed two hundred. In the other manufacturing departments there were another one hundred (*Chicago Tribune*, November 15, 1877). By 1882, there were a total of over four hundred in all the workrooms (Marshall Field personal memorandum, "Number of Employees Jany 1882").

171. Record book, directions to retail clerks, 1876, Marshall Field & Co. Archives [no page numbers]; and Marshall Field accounting record book, 1876.

172. Advertising circular, Field, Leiter & Co., Wholesale, Spring 1876.

173. *Chicago Tribune*, September 29, 1872. See also *ibid.*, July 27, 1874.

174. Catalogue, "Dry Goods, Carpets and Upholstery," Marshall Field & Co., 1900.

175. Memorandum, "The Manufacturing Division, Marshall Field & Company Factories and Products," February 16, 1903, Marshall Field & Co. Archives; and Notice issued from office of Retail Manager to employees, September 25, 1905, Marshall Field & Co. Archives.

176. Postcard circular, 1903, Marshall Field & Co. Archives; and memorandum, "The Manufacturing Division, Marshall Field & Company Factories and Products," February

NOTES

101-105

16, 1903. There were 35 different factories located in the retail buildings by 1902 *(Inter-Ocean,* September 30, 1902).

177. Figures include departmental interest ("John G. Shedd Record Book, 1871-1902"; and "J. G. Shedd" record book, 1902-6).

178. Gibbons, *Wanamaker,* II, 206, quoting John Wanamaker's *Diary,* Chicago, September 21, 1903.

179. *Chicago Tribune,* June 8, 1903; *Chicago Evening Journal,* September 26, 1903; and advertising circular, "Our Fur Factory," Marshall Field & Co., August 28, 1901, scrapbook of advertising circulars, p. 82, Marshall Field & Co. Archives.

180. *Supra,* p. 43.

181. Advertising circular, Field, Leiter & Co., Wholesale, November 7, 1876. See also *Chicago Times,* December 6 and 16, 1876; and advertising circular, Field, Leiter & Co., Wholesale, August 20, 1877.

182. "John G. Shedd Record Book, 1872-1902"; and accounting sheets, wholesale departmental gross sales, 1886-89, A. B. Jones folder.

183. *Ibid.,* 1886; and letter, Marshall Field & Co. to Marshall Field & Co., N. Y., February 24, 1886, Marshall Field & Co. Archives.

184. Accounting sheets, wholesale departmental gross sales, 1886-89, A. B. Jones folder; "John G. Shedd Record Book, 1872-1902"; and pamphlet, "Fur Fashions," Marshall Field & Co., 1900-1, Marshall Field & Co. Archives [no page numbers].

185. *Ibid.;* and advertising circular, Marshall Field & Co., Manufacturers, 1900, Marshall Field & Co. Archives. See also "Fur Headquarters

of the West," *Chicago Dry Goods Reporter,* XXVII (December 11, 1897), 33, adv.

186. Advertising circular, Marshall Field & Co., Manufacturers, 1900.

187. Marshall Field & Co., fur storage record book, 1888-93, Marshall Field & Co. Archives; and *Chicago Tribune,* July 9, 1888.

188. *Ibid.,* July 3, 1903; and *Chicago Dry Goods Reporter,* XXVII (December 11, 1897), 33; *ibid.,* XXXII (October 11, 1902), 21, 31; "John G. Shedd Record Book, 1872-1902"; and "J. G. Shedd" record book, 1902-6.

189. *Ibid.;* and "John G. Shedd Record Book, 1872-1902."

190. *Spring Catalogue,* Field, Leiter & Co., Wholesale, 1871, p. vi.

191. Catalogue, "Price List, Notion Department," Field, Leiter & Co., Wholesale, 1877, see back cover.

192. Advertising circular, Field, Leiter & Co., Wholesale, February 28, 1876.

193. *Illustrated Catalogue of Holiday Goods, Druggists' Sundries, Stationery, Etc.,* Marshall Field & Co., 1890-91, pp. 344, 392, and 400.

194. *Ibid.,* 1895-96, pp. 204, 242, and 285.

195. *Illustrated Catalogue of Jewelry Department,* Marshall Field & Co., 1898, Marshall Field & Co. Archives, pp. 28 and 329.

196. Wholesale record, Marshall Field & Co., February 15, 1897, p. 224; and February 27, 1905, p. 414.

197. Tables XIV, p. 175; and XV, p. 177.

198. "Simpson Pays Tribute to J. G. Shedd," *American,* October 22, 1926; and *Chicago Daily News,* October 22, 1926.

CHAPTER NINE

1. *Chicago Dry Goods Reporter,* XXIV (May 21, 1904), 37; *Chicago Tribune,* May 15, 1904; *Yearbook of the Union Club* (Chicago: Union Club, pub., 1931), p. 23; letter, S. L. Tompkins to H. G. Selfridge, June 7, 1902, Marshall Field & Co.

Archives; and statements, Homer J. Buckley, Philip James, John McKinlay, and Joseph Yates, Marshall Field & Co. General Offices.

2. *Ibid.,* J. W. Hughes, Charles Nash, and Joseph Yates.

3. *Chicago Daily News,* May 14, 1904; and *Chicago Dry Goods Reporter,* XXIV (May 21, 1904), 37; and letter, S. M. Pedrick, relative of Selfridge, Ripon, Wisconsin, to R. W. Twyman, July 13, 1949.

4. *Chicago Dry Goods Reporter,* XXIV (May 21, 1904), 37; *Chicago Tribune,* May 15, 1904; and McClintock typescript, quoting John Devlin, p. 382.

5. Marshall Field personal salary record book, 1869-72.

6. Salary record book, 1883-85.

7. Salary record book, 1871-87.

8. Copy of contractual agreement for 1889 and 1890, Marshall Field with J. G. Shedd and H. G. Selfridge, November 13, 1888.

9. Statements, Joseph Yates, W. H. Miller, Michael Carey, C. C. Bunker, Ellen Jane Bredin, John McKinlay, T. H. Eddy, Charles Nash, and J. W. Hughes.

10. *Ibid.,* John McKinlay, Joseph Yates, J. W. Hughes, Homer Buckley, and Robert Mandel; *Chicago Dry Goods Reporter,* XXIV (May 21, 1904), 37; "Topics Referred to at the Meeting of section managers of November 4th, 1902," unidentified scrapbook, Marshall Field & Co. Archives; accounting sheets, "Retail Departments' Expenses," 1883-84, A. B. Jones folder; and *Chicago Tribune,* May 15, 1904.

11. Selfridge, *Saturday Evening Post,* September 7, 1935, p. 90. See also Neil M. Clark, "How to Get All That's Coming to You," *American Magazine,* CIX (May 1930), 45.

12. Statement, Homer J. Buckley. See also statements, Philip James, J. J. Reilly, and Joseph Yates, Marshall Field & Co. General Offices; and letter, William B. Clarke, Santa Monica, California, to Mr. Elmore, Chicago, September 1, 1946, Marshall Field & Co. Archives.

13. Statements, Joseph Yates, John McKinlay, F. W. Boyden, and Philip James, Marshall Field & Co. General Offices.

14. Picture postcard, Marshall Field & Co. [1907], Marshall Field & Co. Archives; "Notes on Subjects Referred to at the Meeting [of section managers] of August 21, 1902," unidentified scrapbook, Marshall Field & Co. Archives; advertising circular, Marshall Field & Co., Retail, 1902-3, unidentified scrapbook, Marshall Field & Co. Archives; "Observations," *Chicago Dry Goods Reporter,* XXVII (April 10, 1897), 10; "Hosiery and Underwear for Spring," *ibid.,* XXVIII (February 5, 1898), 15; "Spring Productions in Capes, Jackets, Suits and Shirts," *ibid.* (February 19, 1898), 23; and *Chicago Tribune,* September 26, 1890, November 6, 1899, March 18, 1901, and October 20, 1902.

15. *Ibid.,* September 17, 1900, October 6, 1902, and May 23, 1904; and catalogue, *Automobile Apparel and Accessories,* Marshall Field & Co., Retail, Fall and Winter, 1904-5, Marshall Field & Co. Archives n.p.

16. "State Street Ideas," *Chicago Dry Goods Reporter,* XXVII (February 13, 1897), 13 and 15; "Observations," *ibid.* (August 21), 10; advertising circular, Marshall Field & Co., January 25, 1901, scrapbook of advertising circulars, p. 78, Marshall Field & Co. Archives; *Chicago Record,* October 23, 1899; *Chicago Tribune,* February 2, 1888, April 6, 1896, October 16, 1899, June 2, July 8 and 13, 1903; and February 15, 1904; and Accounting Ledgers, 1906, Comptroller's safe, Marshall Field & Co. General Offices.

17. *Chicago Tribune,* May 23, 1904; *Inter-Ocean,* January 4, 1903; *Chicago Evening Post,* March 7 and 9, and January 31, 1903, and November 4, 1905; and Scrapbook of advertising circulars, Marshall Field & Co., *passim,* Marshall Field & Co. Archives.

18. *Goodalls Daily Sun,* March 19, 1887.

19. Accounting ledgers, 1873-1906, Comptroller's safe, Marshall Field & Co. General Offices. Most of these new departments are discussed in subsequent pages.

20. *Chicago Dry Goods Reporter,* XXXII (October 11, 1902), 34.

21. Accounting ledgers, 1873-1906, Comptroller's safe, Marshall Field & Co. General Offices; and *Chicago Tribune,* March 8, 1896.

22. *Dry Goods Retailer and Jobber,* October 1893, p. 17; and *Chicago Dry Goods Reporter,* XXXII (October 11, 1902) , 23.

23. Accounting ledgers, 1883-1906, Comptroller's safe, Marshall Field & Co. General Offices; and Barbour (ed.) , *Sketchbook of the Inter-State Exposition, Chicago, 1883.*

24. Selfridge, *Saturday Evening Post,* July 27, 1935, p. 19. Wanamaker also seriously considered doing the same thing (Gibbons, *Wanamaker,* II, 47) .

25. Selfridge, *Saturday Evening Post,* July 27, 1936, p. 51.

26. Copy of contractual agreement for 1889 and 1890, Marshall Field with J. G. Shedd and H. G. Selfridge, November 13, 1888.

27. M. Field personal record book, real estate and salaries, 1869-1901.

28. Selfridge, *Saturday Evening Post,* July 27, 1935, p. 19.

29. M. Field personal record book, real estate and salaries, 1869-1901.

30. Selfridge, *Saturday Evening Post,* July 27, 1935, pp. 19 and 51.

31. M. Field personal record book, real estate and salaries, 1869-1901.

32. The Fair, founded in 1875 by E. J. Lehman, is sometimes called the first American department store (Charles A. Bates, *The Art and Literature of Business* [New York: Bates Pub. Co., (1902)], II 308; Forrest Crissey, *Since Forty Years Ago: An account of the origin and growth of Chicago and its First Department Store* [Chicago: Privately Printed (The Fair) . 1915], [no page numbers]; John J. Flinn, *Chicago, the Marvelous City of the West; A History, an Encyclopedia and a Guide* [Chicago: Flinn & Sheppard, 1890], p. 517; and Hower, *History of Macy's,* pp. 144-45) .

33. Letter, William H. Wanamaker, Wanamaker & Brown, Oak Hall, Philadelphia, to Marshall Field, February 27, 1888, Field Estate; and "Popularity of General Stores," *Chicago Dry Goods Reporter,* XXIX (April 1, 1899) , 11-12.

34. Accounting ledgers, 1873-1906, Comptroller's safe, Marshall Field & Co. General Offices.

35. *Chicago Tribune,* March 12, 1900.

36. Col. McClurg owned a bookstore, A. C. McClurg & Company, at Wabash and Madison (see, for example, *ibid.,* December 21, 1889, and May 14, 1904) .

37. Statement, Homer J. Buckley, Marshall Field & Co. General Offices. See also *Buyer and Seller,* I (October 12, 1895) , [n.p.]; *Chicago Dry Goods Reporter,* XXXII (October 11, 1902) , 23; and Dennis, *Everybody's Magazine,* XIV (March 1906) , 297.

38. Stead, *If Christ Came to Chicago,* pp. 63-64.

39. See *Furniture Worker,* XXVIII (March 10, 1897) , 26; and *American Artisan,* XXXVI (September 3, 1898) , 29.

40. *Chicago Tribune;* and *Chicago Daily News,* March 29, 1889.

41. See, for example, *ibid.,* April 3, 1896; *Chicago Tribune,* July 10 and November 14, 1890, August 9 and 15, September 30, and November 4, 1893, June 16, 1894, April 11, 1896, August 24, 1898, and June 14, 1902; *Chicago Times,* October 24, 1891; *Chicago Evening Post,* October 9 and 23, 1891; and advertising circulars, Marshall Field & Company, Retail, July 30, 1899, scrapbook of advertising circulars, Marshall Field & Co. Archives.

42. Accounting ledgers, 1889-1906, Comptroller's safe, Marshall Field & Co. General Offices.

43. *Chicago Tribune,* September 21, 1889.

44. *Ibid.,* April 12, 1890.

45. *Ibid.,* January 6, 1900.

46. XXXII (October 11) , 33.

47. *Chicago Daily News,* June 11, 1904.

48. Accounting ledgers, 1896-1904, Comptroller's safe, Marshall Field & Co. General Offices; and *Chicago Tribune,* March 30, 1896.

49. *Ibid.,* September 29, 1872; *Daily National Hotel Reporter,* May 13, 1891; and advertising circular, Marshall Field & Co., 1898, scrapbook of home furnishings, 1893-1902, Marshall Field & Co. Archives.

50. Marshall Field accounting record book, 1876; and *Chicago's First Half Century, 1833-1883,* adv.

51. Statement, Ellen Jane Bredin, Marshall Field & Co. General Offices; interview, J. G. Hall with Mr. Luehman and Mr. W. H. Miller, head, antique furniture, courtesy History of Chicago Project; *Mercer,* I (June 1891), 16; and general house notice, Marshall Field & Co., 1893, Marshall Field & Co. Archives.

52. *Chicago Tribune,* March 30 and and April 11, 1896.

53. *Chicago Tribune,* January 5, 1900; *Chicago Daily News,* April 13, 1904, and April 11, 1905; and statement, W. H. Miller, head, antique furniture, Marshall Field & Co. General Offices.

54. *Ibid.*

55. *Mercer,* I (June 1891), 27; "Mr. Clarke's Department," *Upholsterer,* April 15, 1903, p. 97, in the William E. Clarke personal scrapbook on Oriental rugs, carpets, etc. [1874-1930]; and unidentified clipping, "Reproduction Furniture," September 15, 1902, p. 93 in *ibid.*

56. *Chicago Tribune,* September 24, 1900; and see March 1, 1898, October 31, 1900; and May 2, 1904; *Chicago Daily News,* October 11, 1904, and April 11, 1905; *Chicago Record,* September 25 and October 23, 1899; *Chicago Evening Journal,* September 26 and October 24, 1903; unidentified clippings, "Reproduction Furniture," September 15, 1902, p. 93; and October 15, 1902, p. 95, in the William E. Clarke personal scrapbook on Oriental rugs, carpets, etc. [1874-1930]; "Drumming" letter, Marshall Field & Co., July 31, 1899, scrapbook of home furnishings, 1893-1902, Marshall Field & Co. Archives; Williams, *Interior,* December 18, 1902 [n.p.]; *House Beautiful,* December 1903, adv.; and October 1902, p. xvii, adv.; Edmund Buckley, University of Chicago, "The Artistic Aspects of America's Greatest Store," *Fine Arts Journal,* XIX [April 1908], 212-13; and statement, W. H. Miller, Marshall Field & Co. General Offices.

57. *Chicago Tribune,* March 10 and 24, and October 6, 1902.

58. Accounting ledgers, 1898-1904,

Comptroller's safe, Marshall Field & Co. General Offices.

59. *Chicago Press and Tribune,* September 30, 1858; letter, L. Leiter to M. Field, March 13, 1867, Marshall Field & Co. Archives; *Chicago Times,* October 13, 1868; and *Chicago Tribune,* October 13, 1868, and November 15, 1877.

60. *Chicago Daily Telegraph,* May 1, 1879; and *Chicago Daily News,* May 2, 1879.

61. *Inter-Ocean,* January 26, 1880.

62. Barbour (ed.), *Sketchbook of the Inter-State Exposition, Chicago, 1883;* and see *Chicago Tribune,* January 5, 1884.

63. For example, see *ibid., Chicago Times, Inter-Ocean, Chicago Evening Journal,* May 1880 to January 1885, *passim.*

64. Accounting ledgers, 1879, Comptroller's safe, Marshall Field & Co. General Offices; and *Chicago Tribune,* November 8, 1868.

65. See, for example, *ibid.,* December 26, 1884.

66. *Ibid.,* May 10, 1888, and February 1, 1892; *Chicago Daily News,* April 12, 1890; and "Hints to Retailers and State Street Observations; Basement Salesrooms," *Chicago Dry Goods Reporter,* XXVIII (April 9, 1898), 43.

67. *Ibid.,* XXXII (October 11, 1902), 34; and *Dry Goods Retailer and Jobber,* October 1893, p. 17.

68. *Chicago Tribune,* March 23, 1885. See also *Chicago Evening Journal,* March 21, 1885.

69. See, for example, *ibid.,* April 10, 13, and 16, 1865; *Chicago Herald,* June 13, 1887; *Chicago Tribune,* April 13, 20, and 24, September 15, 19, and 29, October 6, November 9, 10, and 11, 1885, May 6, 1886, October 26, 1887, January 10, April 4, and May 10, 1888, April 17, 1889, April 7, 10, 14, and 15, 1890, February 1, 1892, and October 19, 1896; *Chicago Daily News,* April 12, 14, and 21, 1890; and "Drumming" letter, Marshall Field & Co. to basement trade, forms #B, #D, and #F, November 5, 1904, unidentified scrapbook, Marshall Field & Co. Archives.

70. See again *Chicago Daily Telegraph,* May 1, 1879; *Chicago Daily News,* May 2, 1879; *Chicago Evening Journal,* April 10, 13, and 14, and February 10, 1885; and *Chicago Tribune,* March 23, 1885.
71. Flinn, *Chicago, the Marvelous City,* p. 518.
72. *Chicago Herald,* June 13, 1887.
73. Sometimes the words used were "trustworthy" or "dependable" (*Chicago Tribune,* October 26, 1887, January 10, and April 4, 1888, April 17, 1889, April 10, 14, 15, and 17, 1890, February 1, and December 12, 1892, and September 19, 1893; *Chicago Times,* September 19, 1893; *Chicago Evening Post,* October 23, 1893; *Chicago Daily News,* April 12, 1890, and April 3, 1902; *Chicago Dry Goods Reporter,* XXXII [October 11, 1902], 19-21; and memoranda of meeting, section managers and assistants, with H. G. Selfridge and W. P. Warren, October 18, 1901, in "Business Ideas," p. 2, Marshall Field & Co. Archives).
74. *Chicago Daily News,* April 21, 1890; and *Chicago Tribune,* January 10, 1888, April 17, 1889, April 10, 1890, February 1, 1892, September 19, 1893, and January 2, 1902.
75. *Ibid.,* April 4, 1888, and September 19, 1893; *Economist,* March 22, 1892; and *Chicago Times,* September 19, 1893.
76. *Chicago Tribune,* April 10, 1890.
77. *Inter-Ocean,* January 26, 1880; *Chicago Daily News,* April 12, 1890, and April 3, 1902; and *Chicago Tribune,* June 29, 1886, January 10, April 4, and May 10, 1888, April 10, 1890, February 1, and December 12, 1892, September 19 and 25, October 30, November 4, 1893, and December 26, 1901.
78. *Chicago Daily News,* April 3.
79. *Infra,* pp. 156 ff.
80. *Chicago Dry Goods Reporter,* XXXII (October 11, 1902), 17. This was reputedly more than 135,-000 square feet (*ibid.,* and pp. 19-21. See also *Chicago Evening Journal,* September 26, 1903; and *Chicago Daily News,* January 17, 1901).
81. C. L. Drain record book, 1900-1907, Marshall Field & Co. Archives.
82. See Table XIV, p. 175.
83. See Table XV, p. 177.
84. Letter, Marshall Field & Co. to Victor W. [*sic*] Lawson [app. 1903], Victor F. Lawson *Papers,* courtesy Newberry Library; "State Street Trade," *Chicago Dry Goods Reporter,* XXVII (May 1, 1897), 15; and "Want Loop Bridges," *ibid.* (December 4, 1897), p. 13. Note Field advertising, for example, *Chicago Tribune,* December 30, 1901, March 12, 1902.
85. "Drumming" letter, Marshall Field & Co. to better residence districts, forms #C and #G, November 5, 1904, unidentified scrapbook, Marshall Field & Co. Archives; *Chicago Dry Goods Reporter,* XXVII (May 1, 1897), 15; *ibid.* (December 4, 1897), 13; "State Street Ideas," *ibid.,* XXVIII (January 29, 1898), 15; "Shows Increase; Marshall Field and Company," *ibid.,* XXIX (February 4, 1899), 15.
86. Statements, John McKinlay and Charles C. Bunker, Marshall Field & Co. Corporate Offices; and accounting ledgers, 1873-1906, Comptroller's safe, Marshall Field & Co. General Offices.
87. Wholesale record, Marshall Field & Co., March 31, 1894, p. 203.
88. *Ibid.,* January 1882, p. 133. See also *ibid.,* January 24, 1882, p. 52; March 14, 1888, p. 71; and March 31, 1894, p. 203; and general house notices [to department heads], January 24, 1882, and September 1, 1883, unidentified scrapbook, Marshall Field & Co. Archives.
89. November 4, unidentified scrapbook, Marshall Field & Co. Archives. See also wholesale record, Marshall Field & Co., March 10, 1903, pp. 393-94; notice issued from office of Retail Manager to employees, April 14, 1905, Marshall Field & Co. Archives; and *Chicago Tribune,* October 30, 1877.
90. *Ibid.,* March 18, 1901; Marshall Field accounting record book, 1876; advertising circular, Retail, Marshall Field & Co. [after 1893], Marshall Field & Co. Archives.
91. *Chicago Tribune,* October 27, 1902; and "Book Gifts" [1900], unidentified scrapbook, Marshall Field & Co. Archives [no page numbers].

92. *Goodalls Daily Sun,* March 19, 1887.

93. *Chicago Tribune,* April 17, 1888, and April 4, 1896.

94. *Ibid.,* March 18, 1901; *Inter-Ocean,* January 20, 1890; "Book Gifts" [1900], unidentified scrapbook, Marshall Field & Co. Archives; and accounting ledgers, 1875-1906, Comptroller's safe, Marshall Field & Co. General Offices.

95. *Ibid.*

96. *Ibid.,* 1873-1906; and Marshall Field accounting record book, 1876.

97 House notice, J. B. Fair to section managers [1902], unidentified scrapbook, Marshall Field & Co. Archives; and notice issued from office of Retail Manager to heads of sections, August 3, 1904, Marshall Field & Co. Archives.

98. Tables XIV, p. 175; and XV, p. 177.

99. Hower, *History of Macy's,* pp. 129, 133, 185-89, and 260-62.

100. Wholesale record, Marshall Field & Co., July 28, 1904, p. 406. Also see *ibid.,* August 7, 1905, p. 421.

101. *Supra,* pp. 50 ff.

102. For example, letter, Marshall Field to J. G. Shedd, Aug. 7, 1905, Marshall Field & Co. Archives.

103. For example, *Business Ideas,* p. 1.

104. Statement, George Young, Marshall Field & Co. General Offices; and typescript, "The Meaning of Field Leadership," pp. 1-2, Marshall Field & Co. Archives.

105. Wholesale record, Marshall Field & Co., *passim.*

106. Statements, John McKinlay, J. W. Hughes, and Stanley Field, Marshall Field & Co. General Offices.

107. Accounting ledgers, 1878-1906, Comptroller's safe, Marshall Field & Co. General Offices.

108. *Ibid.*

109. *Furniture Worker,* XXVIII (March 10, 1897), 26; "Ante-Lucem's Weekly Budget," *American Artisan,* XXXVII (April 8, 1899), 17-18; *ibid.,* XXXVI (September 3, 1898), 29; *ibid.* (December 24, 1898), 19; *ibid.* (July 9, 1898), 20; Hoyt, *Land Values in Chicago,* 1830-1933,

p. 158; and William T. Stead, *Chicago Today; or The Labour War in America* (London: Review of Reviews, 1894), p. 113. See also *Chicago Dry Goods Reporter,* XXIX (April 1, 1899), 11-12.

110. *Ibid.,* Hoyt, *Land Values in Chicago, 1830-1933,* p. 158; *Chicago Tribune,* August 11, 1893; and "English View of Department Stores," *Chicago Dry Goods Reporter,* XXVIII (February 12, 1898), 31. See also *Buyer and Seller,* I (October 12, 1895), [n.p.].

111. U. S. Congress, House, *Cong. Record,* 55th Con., 2nd Sess., 1907, p. 1910; and Hoyt, *Land Values in Chicago,* 1830-1933, p. 158.

112. *American Artisan,* XXXVI (July 30, 1898), 26; "Country Merchants Talk," *Chicago Dry Goods Reporter,* XXVII (April 1897), 17; and *ibid.,* XXVIII (February 12, 1898), 51.

113. *Ibid.,* XXVII (October 11, 1902), 23; *Chicago Tribune,* March 12, 1900; and *Chicago Record,* March 12, 1900.

114. Gibbons, *Wanamaker,* II, 46. See also "The Proposed Dry Goods Trust," *Chicago Dry Goods Reporter,* XXIX (September 2, 1899), 41.

115. Letter, E. Y. Eaton, T. Eaton Co., Ltd., Importers, Toronto, to Marshall Field, November 13, 1895, Field Estate; *American Artisan,* XXXVI (August 6, 1898), 27; and *ibid.,* XXXVII (February 18, 1899), 16; and *ibid.* (April 8, 1899), 17. See also *Chicago Dry Goods Reporter,* XXVIII (February 12, 1898), 51.

116. *American Artisan,* XXXVI (July 30, 1898), 26; *ibid.* (September 3, 1898), 29; *Furniture Worker,* XXVII (May 10, 1897), 26; "Observations," *Chicago Dry Goods Reporter,* XXVIII (October 8, 1898), 13; *ibid.,* XXVII (April 1897), 13, 15, and 17; "Ebb of Department Store Fight," *ibid.* (April 17, 1897), 9-10; "Department Store Agitation," *ibid.* (April 24, 1897), 27; and *ibid.,* XXVIII (February 12, 1898), 51.

117. *Ibid.* (July 9, 1898), 17; and *ibid.* (October 8, 1898), 13.

118. *American Artisan,* XXXVI (September 3, 1898), 29; and Gibbons, *Wanamaker,* I, 167n. See also Stead, *If Christ Came to Chicago,* pp. 63-64.

119. *American Artisan,* XXXVII (February 18, 1899), 16.

120. Table XIV, p. 175; letter, J. Chalmers O'Brien, Assistant to the President, Carson Pirie Scott & Co., to R. W. Twyman, September 16, 1949; and letter, The Fair to R. W. Twyman, August 15, 1949.

CHAPTER TEN

1. *Chicago Dry Goods Reporter,* XXVIII (February 12, 1898), 51.
2. Personal interview, Miss J. Rudy (62 years old), assistant in Patent and Newspaper Research, Chicago Public Library, September 2, 1948.
3. *Chicago Tribune,* October 16, 1899.
4. *Ibid.,* November 6, 1899.
5. *Ibid.,* November 14, 1892.
6. *Buyer and Seller,* I (October 12, 1895), [no page numbers].
7. *Chicago Dry Goods Reporter,* XXVII (May 1, 1897), 15; *ibid.* (December 4), 13; and statements, C. F. Pritzlaff, greeter, and Ellen Jane Bredin, Marshall Field & Co. General Offices.
8. *Chicago Times,* August 3, 1893.
9. *Chicago Tribune,* October 1, 1902; and *Chicago Dry Goods Reporter,* XXXII (October 11, 1902), 23.
10. *Ibid.,* and pp. 21 and 31-33.
11. *Chicago Dry Goods Reporter,* XXXII [October 11, 1902], 31-32.
12. *Ibid.,* pp. 21 and 23.
13. *Chicago Record,* April 20, 1896; and *Chicago Tribune,* March 11, 1882, October 19, 1887, December 24, 1900, and March 11, 1901.
14. *Chicago Tribune,* January 28, 1881.
15. *Chicago Times,* October 13, 1868.
16. "Drumming letters," Marshall Field & Co., to better residence districts, forms #C and #G; and to business, professional, and club men, form #H, November 5, 1904, unidentified scrapbook, Marshall Field & Co. Archives; *Chicago Tribune,* June 12, 1902; and *Chicago Dry Goods Reporter,* XXVII (May 1, 1897), 15.
17. *Ibid.,* XXXII (October 11, 1902), 23; "Drumming letters," Marshall Field & Co., to basement trade, suburbanites, and general class of men, forms #A, #B, #D, #E,

and #F, November 5, 1904, unidentified scrapbook, Marshall Field & Co. Archives; and *Chicago Daily News,* April 13, 1904.

18. *Chicago Tribune,* October 6, 1902. See also *ibid.,* December 30, 1901, March 25 and November 4, 1901, October 6, 1902, and June 22, 1903.

19. *Chicago Dry Goods Reporter,* XXXII (October 11, 1902), 23.

20. Notice issued from office of Retail Manager to employees, September 28, 1904, Marshall Field & Co. Archives.

21. *Chicago Times,* October 13, 1868.

22. *Ibid.,* October 6, 1902; *Chicago Record-Herald,* October 3, 1905; *Inter-Ocean,* September 30, 1902; and *Chicago Dry Goods Reporter,* XXXVII (October 5, 1907), 63.

23. *Economist,* Special News Bulletin, March 22, 1892.

24. Williams, *Interior,* December 18, 1902.

25. Statement, Dr. J. L. Munson, Marshall Field & Co. General Offices.

26. Salary record book, 1876-78, and 1872-74.

27. Statement, C. F. Pritzlaff, greeter, Marshall Field & Co. General Offices.

28. Statements, Charles C. Bunker, Michael Carey, and C. F. Pritzlaff, Marshall Field & Co. General Offices.

29. *Chicago Dry Goods Reporter,* XXXII (October 11, 1902), 38; *Inter-Ocean,* September 30, 1902; *Chicago Evening Journal,* September 26, 1903; and *Chicago Tribune,* December 30, 1901, and October 1, 1902. The first big corner clock outside the building was hung at the corner of State and Washington Streets in 1897, (*ibid.,* November 26, 1897). The clock at State

and Randolph was placed there in 1907 (Guy Norse Armstrong, "A Globe Trotter in Chicago," *Chicago*, V [January 1908], 59).

30. *Chicago Tribune*, April 11, 1896.
31. Statement, Charles C. Bunker, Marshall Field & Co. General Offices.
32. Interview with Mr. Luehman. From the files of Pierce, *History of Chicago*, University of Chicago; salary record book, 1876-77; pamphlet, Marshall Field & Co., Souvenir of the Republican and Democratic Conventions of 1884, p. 4; *Chicago Daily News*, August 5, 1893; *Chicago Tribune*, August 11, 1893, and October 1, 1902; and advertising circular, Marshall Field & Co., December 20, 1899, scrapbook of advertising circulars, p. 73, Marshall Field & Co. Archives. The Fair had a check room on the first floor in 1885 (*Chicago Tribune*, January 1, 1885).
33. *Supra*, p. 60.
34. Barbour (ed.), *Sketchbook of the Inter-State Exposition, Chicago, 1883*.
35. *Chicago Evening Journal*, August 8, 1893; *Chicago Times*, August 8, 1893; and *Chicago Daily News*, August 5, 1893.
36. *Ibid.;* and *Chicago Tribune*, August 11, 1893.
37. *Ibid.*, October 1, 1902; *Inter-Ocean*, September 30, 1902; *Chicago Evening Journal*, September 26, 1903; *Chicago Record-Herald*, September 30, 1902; *Marshall Field & Company* [1903], Marshall Field & Co. Archives; *Mirror*, St. Louis, April 16, 1903, Marshall Field & Co. Archives; and *Chicago Dry Goods Reporter*, XXXII (October 11, 1902), 38.
38. *Ibid.;* and Williams, *Interior*, December 18, 1902.
39. *Chicago Dry Goods Reporter*, XXXII (October 11, 1902), 38.
40. *Ibid.;* and Marshall Field & Company [1903], Marshall Field & Co. Archives.
41. *Inter-Ocean*, September 30, 1902; and *Chicago Dry Goods Reporter*, XXXII (October 11, 1902), 38.
42. Hull, *Marshall Field & Company*, 1907, p. 44, Marshall Field & Co. Archives.

43. *Ibid.*, p. 46; *Inter-Ocean*, September 30, 1902; and *Marshall Field & Company* [1903], Marshall Field & Co. Archives.
44. Hull, *Marshall Field & Company*, 1907, pp. 45 and 47, Marshall Field & Co. Archives.
45. *Chicago Tribune*, October 1, 1902; *Inter-Ocean*, September 30, 1902; and Williams *Interior*, December 18, 1902.
46. *Chicago Dry Goods Reporter*, XXXII (October 11, 1902), 38.
47. Higinbotham, *The Making of a Merchant*, pp. 118-20; and *Inter-Ocean*, September 30, 1902.
48. *Fashions of the Hour: 1852-1927* (Chicago: Marshall Field & Co., 1927), p. 38; *Marshall Field and Company and You*, 1941, p. 30.
49. Hower, *History of Macy's*, p. 160.
50. Gibbons, *Wanamaker*, I, 220.
51. *Chicago Tribune*, January 1, 1885. Mandel's first opened its tearooms in 1898 (*ibid.*, June 20).
52. *Chicago Tribune, Chicago Times, Inter-Ocean,* and *Chicago Evening Journal*, 1890, *passim*, make no mention of the opening either in their news columns or advertisements.
53. Statement, Mrs. Anna Nelson tearooms and restaurants, Marshall Field & Co. General Offices; *Fortieth Anniversary of the Tea Rooms: 1890-1930* (Chicago: Marshall Field & Co.), souvenir announcement, Marshall Field & Co. Archives; "Views of the Retail Store of Marshall Field & Co., Chicago," 1900; and accounting ledgers, 1891-96, Comptroller's safe, Marshall Field & Co. General Offices; and see 1948-49 menus.
54. *Mercer*, I (June 1891), 17-18.
55. Accounting ledgers, 1891-96, Comptroller's safe, Marshall Field & Co. General Offices.
56. *Mercer*, I (June 1891), 17-18. See also notice issued from office of Retail Manager, "Rules for Ushers in the Tea and Grill Rooms," *circa* September 1, 1904.
57. *Chicago Daily News*, August 5, 1893; *Chicago Times*, August 8, 1893; and *Chicago Evening Journal*, August 8, 1893.

58. "Views of the Retail Store, Marshall Field & Company, Chicago," 1900.

59. *Chicago Evening Journal,* September 26, 1903; and *Chicago Tribune,* October 1, 1902.

60. *Marshall Field and Company and You,* 1941, p. 30.

61. Williams, *Interior,* December 16, 1902; *Chicago Dry Goods Reporter,* XXXII (October 11, 1902), 38; *Chicago Evening Journal,* September 26, 1903; and *Inter-Ocean,* September 30, 1902.

62. *Inter-Ocean,* September 30, 1902.

63. *Chicago Evening Journal,* September 26, 1903.

64. *Chicago Dry Goods Reporter,* XXXII (October 11, 1902), 38.

65. Dennis, *Everybody's Magazine,* XIV (March 1906), 297.

66. Hull, *Marshall Field and Company,* 1907, Marshall Field & Co. Archives; *Chicago Dry Goods Reporter,* XXXVII (October 5, 1907), 67; *Chicago Tribune,* September 27, 1907; and Buckley, *Fine Arts Journal,* XIX (April 1908), 207-11. The *Chicago Evening American* of October 28, 1907, gives the seating capacity as 3,500.

67. *Chicago Times,* November 8, 1871; and letter, Marshall Field to Hollister & Gorham, June 24, 1875, Field Estate.

68. Dennis, *Everybody's Magazine,* XIV (March 1906), 297.

69. Williams, *Interior,* December 18, 1902.

70. "Subjects Referred to at the Meeting[s] [of section managers] of September 16 [and October 7], 1902," unidentified scrapbook, Marshall Field & Co. Archives; wholesale record, Marshall Field & Co., June 29, 1888, p. 111; February 12, p. 412; and August 24, 1905, p. 422; notices issued from office of Retail Manager to employees, May 2 and June 5 and 14, 1905, Marshall Field & Co. Archives; *"Don'ts" for Employees, passim;* and *Chicago Dry Goods Reporter,* XXVII (October 9, 1897), 11.

71. "Hints to Retailers and State Street Observations," *Chicago Dry Goods Reporter,* XXVIII (October 29, 1898), 53; mimeographed copy of "Notes on Subjects Referred to at the Meeting [of section managers] of July 2d, 1902," Marshall Field & Co. Archives; and poster advertisement, Marshall Field & Co., 1903, Marshall Field & Co. Archives.

72. *Chicago Evening Journal,* September 26, 1903.

73. *Chicago Dry Goods Reporter,* XXVII (October 9, 1897), 11. See also *Mirror* (St. Louis), April 16, 1904, Marshall Field & Co. Archives; and Schulze, *The American Office,* Marshall Field & Co. Book of Rules, p. 378.

74. *"Don'ts" for Employees,* p. 5.

75. *Supra,* p. 4.

76. *Chicago Dry Goods Reporter,* XXXII (October 11, 1902), 23 and 25.

77. *"Don'ts" for Employees,* p. 7.

78. See, for example, wholesale record, Marshall Field & Co., January 10, 1883, p. 88; and December 20, 1900, p. 338; and Higinbotham, *The Making of a Merchant,* p. 130. It should be noted, certainly, that recent experts point out that the customer is not always to blame. Returned goods are a measure of poor selling as well as spoiled customers. (Lew Hahn, *Stores, Merchants and Customers* [New York: Fairchild Publications, 1952], p. 203; and H. D. Comer, *Merchandise Returns in Department Stores* [Ohio State University Press, 1928], I, 42).

79. See, for example, "Why Customers Make Returns," *Journal of Retailing* (March 21, 1938), Vol. X, No. 12, p. 9, as cited by O. Preston Robinson and Norris B. Brisco, *Store Organization and Operation* (New York: Prentice-Hall, Inc., 1949), p. 467.

80. Accounting ledgers, 1877-1906, Comptroller's safe, Marshall Field & Co. General Offices.

81. *Chicago Dry Goods Reporter,* XXII [October 11, 1902], 2; letters, Mrs. H. deRoode to Marshall Field, September 22, 1890, Field Estate; and Marshall Field & Co. to Mrs. Frederick Loeb, September 3, 1903, unidentified scrapbook, Marshall Field & Co. Archives; and invoice,

Field, Leiter & Co., November 1, 1878, A. B. Jones folder, Marshall Field & Co. Archives.

82. *Chicago Dry Goods Reporter,* XXXII (October 11, 1902) , 27.

83. Record book, directions to retail clerks, 1876, Marshall Field & Co. Archives [no page numbers]; and letter, Mrs. H. de Roode to Marshall Field, September 22, 1890, Field Estate.

84. "Instructions to Drivers," Marshall Field & Co. [*circa* 1906], p. 2, Marshall Field & Co. Archives.

85. This refers to merchandise actually purchased. There is evidence that Field's sold some goods "on approval" at least during the seventies (Marshall Field accounting record book, 1876), but this was not done to any great extent and is not included in the statistics on "returns."

86. "Instructions to Drivers," Marshall Field & Co. Archives, p. 2.

87. Accounting ledgers, 1877-1906, Comptroller's safe, Marshall Field & Co. General Offices.

88. Hower, *History of Macy's,* p. 261.

89. Controllers' Congress, National Retail Dry Goods Association, *Merchandising and Operating Results of Department and Specialty Stores —1947* (New York: National Retail Dry Goods Association, 1948) , n.p., as cited by Robinson and Brisco, *Store Organization and Operation,* p. 466.

90. *Supra,* p. 19.

91. October 13, 1868.

92. *Ibid.*

93. "Price List, Notion Department" [catalogue], Field, Leiter & Co., Wholesale, 1877, p. 134; letter, H. L. Pinney, Field, Leiter & Co. general salesman, to Robt. Moir & Co., Oquawka, Illinois, January 3, 1873, Warshaw Collection of Business Americana, New York; and wholesale record, Marshall Field & Co., November 17, 1877, p. 69.

94. Advertisng circular, Field, Leiter & Co., November 15, 1872, Marshall Field & Co. Archives.

95. *Chicago Commercial,* September, 18, 1875.

96. Pacific Avenue was later renamed "LaSalle." *Chicago Times,* January 27, 1881; and *Chicago Tribune,* January 27, 1881.

97. Statements, John Rau, J. J. Reilly, in charge of delivery, and Joseph Yates, Marshall Field & Co. General Offices; Marshall Field personal salary record book, 1869-72; letter, Marshall Field to J. H. Kelley, November 13, 1875, Field Estate; delivery boy record book, 1860-1900, p. 315; and "Instructions to Drivers," Marshall Field & Co., *circa,* 1906, p. 5, Marshall Field & Co. Archives. In 1885 the firm owned 163 horses; in 1895, 344; and in 1904, 244. Each horse was kept an average of eight years (inventory record books, "Horses and Wagons," Marshall Field & Co., January 1, 1883 to January 1, 1893, pp. 1-1100; January 1, 1893 to January 1, 1902, pp. 1-108; and January 1, 1899 to July 1, 1907, pp. 1-119, Marshall Field & Co. Archives) .

98. *Chicago Daily Sun,* October 31, 1893; and inventory record book, "Horses and Wagons," Marshall Field & Co., January 1, 1883 to January 1, 1893, pp. 101-22.

99. Wholesale record, Marshall Field & Co., August 8, 1897, p. 232.

100. Accounting ledgers, 1873 and 1906, Comptroller's safe, Marshall Field & Co. General Offices.

101. Statement, C. F. Pritzlaff, Marshall Field & Co. General Offices; salary record book, 1876-77; and accounting sheets, "Retail Departments' Expenses," 1881-83, A. B. Jones folder, Marshall Field & Co. Archives.

102. Business statements, 1873-1906, Comptroller's safe, Marshall Field & Co. General Offices.

103. Delivery boy record book, 1860-1900, pp. 54-55.

104. Salary record book, 1872-74; and accounting sheets, "Retail Departments' Expenses," 1881-83, A. B. Jones folder, Marshall Field & Co. Archives.

105. The firm supplied the carfare (delivery boy record book, 1860-1900, p. 54, *et. seq.;* and see especially p. 432; statement, J. J. Reilly, in charge of delivery, Marshall Field & Co. General Offices; record book, "Shipping Room Expenses," Mar-

shall Field & Co., 1885, pp. 250-351, Marshall Field & Co. Archives; and accounting sheets, "Retail Departments' Expenses," 1881-83, A. B. Jones folder, Marshall Field & Co. Archives).

106. Accounting ledgers, 1873-79, Comptroller's safe, Marshall Field & Co. General Offices.

107. Accounting sheets, "Retail Departments' Expenses," 1879-86, A. B. Jones folder, Marshall Field & Co. Archives.

108. Salary records, 1871-87, and 1883-85.

109. Barbour (ed.), *Sketchbook of the Inter-State Exposition, Chicago, 1883.* See also record book, directions to retail clerks, 1876, Marshall Field & Co. Archives; and record book, "Shipping Room Expenses," Marshall Field & Co., 1875, p. 147, Marshall Field & Co. Archives.

110. Statement, J. J. Reilly, Marshall Field & Co. General Offices.

111. Delivery boy record book, 1860-1900, p. 63; notices issued from office of Retail Manager to employees, September 3, 1904 and November 18, 1905, Marshall Field & Co. Archives; and "A Model Delivery System," *Chicago Dry Goods Reporter,* XXXIV (March 19, 1904), 11.

112. *Ibid.;* and "Drumming" letters Marshall Field & Co. to basement trade and suburbanites, forms #E and #F, November 5, 1904, unidentified scrapbook, Marshall Field & Co. Archives.

113. "Views of the Retail Store of Marshall Field & Co., Chicago," 1900.

114. Memorandum, delivery file, 1902, Marshall Field & Co. Archives; picture postcard, advertisement, Marshall Field & Co. [1907], Marshall Field & Co. Archives; and *Chicago Dry Goods Reporter,* XXXII (October 11, 1902), 2. See also 1903, Marshall Field & Co. Archives; and inventory record books, "Horses and Wagons," Marshall Field & Co., January 1, 1893 to January 1, 1902, pp. 1-108 and 122-42; and January 1, 1895 to July 1, 1907, pp. 1-119, Marshall Field & Co. Archives.

115. Accounting ledgers, 1902, Comptroller's safe, Marshall Field & Co. General Offices; *American Artisan,* XXXVI (September 3, 1898), 29.

116. Delivery boy record book, 1860-1900, p. 423; notice issued from office of Retail Manager to employees, August 12, 1905; and *Chicago Dry Goods Reporter,* XXXIV (March 19, 1904), 11.

117. *Ibid.;* and XXXII (October 11, 1902), 17; and *Marshall Field & Company* [1903], Marshall Field & Co. Archives.

118. *Chicago Dry Goods Reporter,* XXXIV (March 19, 1904), 11.

119. *Chicago Tribune,* January 17, 1906; Marshall Field & Company [1903], Marshall Field & Co. Archives; Hull, *Marshall Field & Company,* 1907, Marshall Field & Co. Archives; and *Chicago Dry Goods Reporter,* XXXVII (October 5, 1907), 67.

120. Accounting ledgers, 1906, Comptroller's safe, Marshall Field & Co. General Offices.

121. *History of Macy's.* See especially pp. 133, 258, and 394. Professor Hower lists "packing" and "delivery" as separate expense items. These should be added together for purposes of comparison with the Field figures which include packing as part of delivery expenses. This makes the years 1902-6 difficult to compare since Hower provides no packing expenses for those years. It would appear, however, that were a percentage added for packing, similar to earlier years, that Macy's delivery-expense ratios for 1902-6 would be close to Field's. Unfortunately, for *all* years the two stores are only roughly comparable since Hower includes in his percentages "possibly some salaries" while Field's figures definitely include all wages and salaries directly attributable to delivery. The figures for Field's do not include any prepaid freight.

122. The figures for 1902-6.

123. *Chicago Dry Goods Reporter,* XXVII (October 9, 1897), 13; *Chicago Tribune,* July 27, 1903; and notice issued from office of Retail Manager to employees, December

10, 1904, Marshall Field & Co. Archives.

124. *Chicago Dry Goods Reporter,* XXVII (October 9, 1897), 13; and notices issued from office of Retail Manager to floormen, July 16, 1904, and August 10, 1905.

125. Letter, S. W. French to Marshall Field, November 3, 1894, Field Estate.

126. Letter, Mrs. H. de Roode to Marshall Field, September 22, 1890, Field Estate.

127. Letter, S. E. Hurlbut to Marshall Field, December 13, 1892, Field Estate.

128. Letter, Emily E. Bond to Marshall Field, March 15, 1891, Field Estate; *Chicago Dry Goods Reporter,* XXXII (October 11, 1902), 17; and see again *Northwestern Christian Advocate,* November 12, 1902, p. 19; and *Chicago Times,* August 8, 1893.

129. Mimeographed copy of "Notes on Subjects Referred to at the Meeting [of section managers] of July 2d, 1902," Marshall Field & Co. Archives.

CHAPTER ELEVEN

1. See, for example, *Chicago Tribune,* July 11 and 12, August 23, 24, and 30, September 4, 6, 7, 14, and 20, 1865; and *Chicago Times,* November 30, and December 15 and 18, 1865.

2. See, for example, *Chicago Tribune,* July 13, August 25 and 28, and September 4, 7, 18, and 19, 1865.

3. *Ibid.,* 1865-67, *passim;* and *Chicago Tribune,* 1865-67, *passim.* J. V. Farwell & Co., for example, ran a small advertisement in the *Chicago Republican* in 1861 without change from April 12 to June 28.

4. See, for example, *Chicago Tribune,* April 7, 1865.

5. *Ibid.,* January 17 and 20.

6. *Ibid.,* January 31 and February 1, 2, 3, and 4.

7. *Ibid.,* March 25 and 29.

8. *Ibid.,* May 27 and 29, 1865.

9. *Ibid.,* November 11, 14, 16, and 28, 1865; and *Chicago Times,* November 1, 15, and 28, 1885.

10. *Chicago Tribune,* December 20, 1865. See also *ibid.,* 14 and 18.

11. *Ibid.,* April 17 and May 18, 1866; and *Chicago Times,* May 4 and 8, and September 4, 1866.

12. *Chicago Tribune,* December 29, 1867.

13. See as early as *ibid.,* August 25, 1864.

14. See, however, *ibid.,* December 6 and 16, 1868; and *Chicago Times,* April 12 and December 6, 1868.

15. *Chicago Tribune,* September 17, 1867. See also *ibid.,* April 6 and October 8, 1867; and *Chicago Times,* December 29, 1867.

16. *Chicago Tribune,* December 16, 1868.

17. *Chicago Times,* May 1, 1870. See also similar type of advertisement, *ibid.,* May 8.

18. *Ibid.,* May 1. See also advertisement of Hamlin, Hale & Co. with 3-column picture, unusual for that time (*Chicago Tribune,* April 26, 1871).

19. *Ibid.,* April 28, May 12, and June 2, 1872, May 1 and June 8, 1874; and *Chicago Times,* April 24 and December 18, 1870.

20. Note, for instance, *Chicago Tribune,* January 13, 15, 20, 22, 23, 29, 30, and 31, March 25 and 27, April 1 and 2, 1872, and June 19, 20, 22, 23, 25, and 26, 1874; and *Chicago Evening Journal,* March 18 and April 3 and 4, 1872.

21. *Ibid.,* December 6, 1877; *Chicago Times,* September 23, 1876; and *Chicago Tribune,* December 18, 1871, October 20, 1872, August 7, 1874, November 5, 1875, November 14 and December 14 and 18, 1877, and January 3, 4, 5, 12, and 16, and March 1, 1878.

22. See especially *ibid.,* March 21 and November 16, 1878.

23. See, for example, *ibid.,* May 22, June 19, and December 27, 1871, January 23 and December 16, 1872,

September 25, 1876, December 18, 1877, and March 12, 1878; *Chicago Times,* December 16, 18, and 21, 1870, and September 25, 27, and 28, 1876; and *Chicago Evening Journal,* December 18, 1877, and February 26, 1878.

24. Wendt, *Holiday,* May 1947, pp. 42-43; Andrews, *Battle . . . Chicago,* p. 30; T. W. Goodspeed, *University of Chicago Magazine,* VIII (1922), 29; and Ditchett, *Marshall Field and Company,* pp. 23 and 76.

25. Letter, John G. Shedd to R. Lowrie, editor, *Elgin [Illinois] Daily News,* December 1, Marshall Field & Co. Archives.

26. See, for example, *Chicago Tribune,* December 29, 1867, December 6, 1868, and April 28, May 12, June 2 and 9, and November 3, 1872; and *Chicago Times,* April 12, November 8 and 22, 1868.

27. Copy of agreement, Retail Dry Goods Merchants of Chicago, April 5, 1876, Marshall Field & Co. Archives. The following firms signed the agreement: Field, Leiter & Co., Chas. Gossage & Co., W. S. Simpson & Co., Carson, Pirie, Scott & Co., Norwell & Simpson, Mandel Bros., and C. W. & E. Pardridge & Co.

28. *Chicago Tribune,* November 12 and 25, and December 2, 1877. Field's also ran a Sunday ad on September 25, 1881, to announce the closing of their store on the following Monday in respect to the martyred President James Garfield *(ibid.).*

29. Chicago newspapers from 1877 through 1906 do not reveal any further Sunday advertising of a strictly commercial nature.

30. See, for example, Mandel's Sunday ads in *Inter-Ocean,* January 4, 1885; and *Chicago Tribune,* November 18, 1883, October 6, 1884, February 15 and September 20, 1885, December 22, 1889, and June 10, 1894. Chas. Gossage & Co.'s ads, *ibid.,* March 1, 1885; Carson's ads, *ibid.,* November 18, 1883, October 6, 1884, March 1, 1885, January 9, 1887, December 29, 1901, and February 2, 1902; Pardridge & Co.'s ads, *ibid.,* October 7, 1877, Septem-

ber 26, 1880, February 10, 1884, and April 12 and 21, 1885.

31. Higinbotham, *The Making of a Merchant,* pp. 123-27.

32. Notice issued from office of Retail Manager to employees, September 26, 1905, Marshall Field & Co. Archives. See also *ibid.,* June 20, 1904.

33. See, for example, *Chicago Tribune,* May 11, June 8 and 22, July 27, and August 31, 1874, May 5, 1879, September 27 and October 25, 1880, and November 19, 1883.

34. *Ibid.,* October 20, 21, and 28, and November 3, 1871, March 3, 1872, and June 18, 1887; and *Chicago Herald* and *Goodalls Daily Sun,* June 18, 1887.

35. For rare instances of Wholesale advertising, see *Official Annual Labor Gazette,* p. 12, and *Daily Drovers Journal,* September 13, 1882.

36. *Spring Catalogue[s],* Field, Leiter & Co., Wholesale, 1870 and 1871, Marshall Field & Co. Archives.

37. See, for example, letter, Marshall Field & Co. to Capt. C. M. Bailey, Ft. Robinson, Nebraska, March 20, 1890, Bettcher record book, p. 1, Marshall Field & Co. Archives.

38. This type of literature was not a new device as of the seventies (see, for example, advertising circular, Field, Palmer & Leiter, December 3, 1866; and form letter to wholesale customers, Field, Palmer & Leiter, August 10, 1865, Marshall Field & Co. Archives), but many more were distributed during each year of this decade than in the sixties. (Advertising circulars, Field, Leiter & Co., Wholesale, March 1, Marshall Field & Co. Archives, August 10, November 5, and December 14, 1872, and November 10, 1873, Stone scrapbook, pp. 41, 47, 51, and 57, respectively; November 15, 1875, February 28, and spring, 1876, and autumn and August 20, 1877, Marshall Field & Co. Archives; and postcard circular, November 28, 1877, Marshall Field & Co. Archives.)

39. Advertising circulars, Field, Leiter & Co., Wholesale, spring, and November 7, 1876, August 20 and autumn, 1877, May 2, 1878, Marshall

Field & Co. Archives; and February 19, and August 1881, Stone scrapbook, pp. 73 and 57, respectively, Marshall Field & Co. Archives.

40. Postcard circulars, Field, Leiter & Co., wholesale, November 9, 1877, and February 8 and March 16, 1878; and postcard circulars, Marshall Field & Co., Wholesale, August 23, 1892, and January 16, 1894, Marshall Field & Co. Archives.

41. "Price List, Notions Department" [catalogue], Field, Leiter & Co., Wholesale, 1877, Marshall Field & Co. Archives.

42. *Illustrated Catalogue of Holiday Goods, Druggists' Sundries, Stationery, etc.,* Marshall Field & Co., 1890-91; *Marshall Field & Co. Notions & Fancy Goods Wholesale Catalogue, 1890-91; Marshall Field & Co. Notions* [catalogue], Wholesale, 1893; catalogues, jewelry, Marshall Field & Co., Wholesale, 1893 and 1898, Marshall Field & Co. Archives; and letter, Marshall Field & Co. to Captain C. E. Bailey, Ft. Robinson, Nebraska, March 20, 1890, Bettcher record book, p. 1, Marshall Field & Co. Archives.

43. Prices, however, were "subject to change without notice." ("Illustrated Catalogue of Jewelry Department," Marshall Field & Co. Archives; *Illustrated Catalogue of Holiday Goods, Druggists' Sundries, Stationery, etc.,* Marshall Field & Co., 1890-91; *Marshall Field & Co. Notions & Fancy Goods Wholesale Catalogue,* 1890-91; *Marshall Field & Co. Notions* [catalogue], Wholesale, 1893; and catalogue, jewelry, Marshall Field & Co., Wholesale, 1898.)

44. Wholesale record, Marshall Field & Co., October 2, 1902, pp. 378-80.

45. *Chicago Herald,* October 31, and November 5 and 9, 1881; and *Chicago Tribune,* March 11 and October 5, 1882; and December 1, 1884.

46. See, for example, *ibid.,* September 5, 7, 12, 21, and 29, 1881, and November 17 and 24, and December 8, 1884.

47. *Ibid.,* September 20 and October 25, 1880, September 27 and 28,

1881, January 1 and November 19, 1883, and December 26, 1884.

48. *Ibid.,* November 19, 1883, November 2, 9, and 16, and December 7, 1884, and December 3, 1885; and Crissey, *Since Forty Years Ago.* The first true full-page mercantile advertisement was supposed to have been purchased by John Wanamaker of Philadelphia in 1879 (Paul H. Nystrom, *Economics of Retailing—Retail Institutions and Trends* [3rd ed.]; New York: Ronald Press Co., 1932, p. 95). As early as August 25, 1864, however, a *Chicago Tribune* advertiser of Hemhold's Fluid Extract told of his product and its comprehensive abilities as a curative agent in the first column of one page and then repeated the same advertisement in the remaining eight columns to occupy the full page. This is the earliest-known full page advertisement in existing records of Chicago papers (letter, Charles T. Smutny, Librarian, *Chicago Tribune,* to R. W. Twyman, August 17, 1949).

49. *Chicago Tribune,* September 11, 1881.

50. *Ibid.,* October 5, 1882.

51. Accounting ledgers, 1873 and 1874, Comptroller's safe, Marshall Field & Co. General Offices.

52. Accounting sheets, "Expense Record," 1872-73, A. B. Jones folder, Marshall Field & Co. Archives.

53. Table XIV, p. 175.

54. Accounting ledgers, 1880-1906, Comptroller's safe, Marshall Field & Co. General Offices.

55. See *Chicago Evening Journal* and *Chicago Tribune,* 1885-90, *passim.*

56. *Ibid.,* October 6, and December 14, 1885, January 17 and 24, 1887, May 10 and 12, 1888, March 30, and September 21, 1889, February 1 and 11, 1892, and August 18, and November 6, 1893; *Goodalls Daily Sun,* July 13, 1887; *Evening News,* October 28, 1891; *Inter-Ocean,* December 9, 1891; and *Chicago Times,* October 24, 1891.

57. *Ibid.; Chicago Tribune,* September 24, October 5, November 4 and 5, and December 16, 1885, December 1, 1887, April 2, May 10, and January 9, 1888, March 30, 1889,

January 9 and 13, 1890, October 19, 1891, and May 21, and June 11, 1894; *Chicago Evening Post,* October 23, 1891; and *Inter-Ocean,* January 20, 1890, and December 9, 1891.

58. *Ibid.,* October 30, 1893; *Chicago Tribune,* February 1, 1892, October 30, 1893, March 8 and 30, April 6 and 20, and November 9, 1896, June 13, and July 18, 1898, December 4, 1899, September 10 and 24, 1900, September 2, 9, 16, 28, and 30, 1901, January 2, 1902, June 8 and 22, 1903, April 4, 11, and 25, and May 16, 1904; *Chicago Record-Herald,* March 17, 1902; *Chicago Daily News,* May 12, 1904; *Chicago Record,* December 3, 1894, October 4 and 11, 1897, and January 16, 1899; *Chicago Times-Herald,* January 16, 1899; and *Chicago Evening Post,* January 2, 1903.

59. Statements, Homer J. Buckley and J. W. Hughes, Marshall Field & Co. General Offices. In order to make his ads stand out still further, Selfridge later obtained from the *Chicago Daily News* almost exclusive use for Field's advertisements of a particular kind of type (letter, Harry G. Selfridge to Victor F. Lawson, January 3, 1903, Victor F. Lawson *Papers,* courtesy Newberry Library, Chicago).

60. *Chicago Tribune,* February 1, 1892.

61. See R. G. Walters, J. W. Wingate, and E. J. Rowse, *Retail Merchandising* (Cincinnati: South-Western Pub. Co. [*c.* 1943]), p. 246.

62. See, for example, *Chicago Tribune,* February 1, 1892, September 19, 1893, October 30, 1899, March 12 and December 24, 1900, September 2, 9, 16, 28, and 30, and December 30, 1901, April 7, May 5, June 8 and 22, 1903, and April 11 and 25, 1904; *Chicago Evening Journal,* September 26, 1903; *Chicago Record,* December 18, 1893, April 20, 1896, and January 16, 1899; *Chicago Daily News,* February 13 and April 3, 1902; *Chicago Times,* September 19, 1893; *Inter-Ocean,* April 3, 1905; and *Chicago Evening Post,* October 19, 1891.

63. Letter, Charles T. Smutny, Librar-

ian, *Chicago Tribune,* to R. W. Twyman, August 17, 1949; and see *Chicago Times* and *Chicago Tribune,* 1865-90, *passim.*

64. See *ibid.,* 1887-93. Note especially, advertisements of Siegel and Co., and The Fair in *ibid.* of December 10, 1893; and John T. Shayne, The Bee-Hive, and The Fair in *ibid.* of December 3, 1893.

65. See *ibid.,* January 4 and 5, 1883, January 3, 1884, January 1 and 3, 1887, May 10 and 12, 1888, and August 5, 1893.

66. Early examples may be seen in *ibid.,* April 4, May 2, June 6 and 13, and July 18, 1898; *Chicago Times-Herald,* February 28, 1898, and January 16, 1899; and *Chicago Record,* September 20 and October 4, 11, and 18, 1897, September 12, 1898, and January 16, 1899.

67. "Bargain Friday," *Buyer and Seller,* I (October 12, 1895), [n.p.]; and *American Artisan,* XXXVI (September 3, 1898), 29.

68. Memoranda, H. G. Selfridge and W. P. Warren to heads of departments, etc., in "Business Ideas," p. 2. See also notice issued from office of Retail Manager to employees, September 28, 1904, Marshall Field & Co. Archives.

69. Green, *Associated Advertising,* III (December 1921), 5; *Chicago Tribune,* April 19, 1871, February 2, 1892, May 25 and June 1, 1894, March 16, 1896, March 25, 1898, February 23, 1901, and April 4, 1904; *Inter-Ocean,* January 20, 1890; and *Chicago Record,* September 2, 1897.

70. *Ibid.,* April 20, 1896. See also *Chicago Tribune,* April 20, 1896, June 8, 1898, October 30, 1899, and March 25, 1901.

71. Schulze, *The American Office,* pp. 218-82, quoting Marshall Field & Co. Book of Rules. See also notice issued from office of Retail Manager to employees, September 28, 1904; "Notes on Subjects Referred to at the Meeting of section managers of August 21, 1902," unidentified scrapbook, Marshall Field & Co. Archives; and Green, *Associated Advertising,* XII (December 1921), 5.

72. Underlining mine *(Chicago Tribune,* March 10, 1902).

73. *Ibid.,* July 6, 1886, and November 26, 1892; *Inter-Ocean,* January 20, 1890; *Chicago Record,* April 20, 1896; *Chicago Evening Journal,* October 10, 1892; and advertising circular, Marshall Field & Co., retail [January], 1903, Marshall Field & Co. Archives.

74. See, for example, *Chicago Times-Herald,* January 16, 1899; and *Chicago Evening Post,* January 2, 1903.

75. *Chicago Tribune,* April 18, 1904; and *Chicago Daily News,* April 11, 1905.

76. See, for example, *Chicago Tribune,* October 27, 1890, February 8, 1892, September 25 and 26, 1893; *Chicago Daily News,* January 23, 1899, May 31, 1904, April 11, 1905, and January 2, 1906; *Chicago Record,* October 4, 1897, and January 16, 1899; advertising circulars, Marshall Field & Co., Retail, January 1898, and January 3, 1905; postcard circular, Marshall Field & Co., Retail, 1904; and "Drumming" letter, Marshall Field & Co. to Mrs. Chas. Graves, Winnetka, Illinois, April 1, 1899, Marshall Field & Co. Archives.

77. *Chicago Tribune,* January 4 and 5, 1883.

78. *Ibid.,* January 3 and 4, 1884.

79. See, for example, *ibid.,* January 1 and 3, 1887, January 2, 1888, January 1 and 2, 1890, January 1, 1896, and January 2, 1902.

80. *Ibid.,* January 17, 1887.

81. *Ibid.,* April 18, 1904.

82. *Chicago Evening Post,* January 2, 1903.

83. Advertising circular, Marshall Field & Co., March 27 to April 1, 1905, unidentified scrapbook, p. 38; notices issued from office of Retail Manager to employees, September 28 and 30, October 3 and 8, and November 15, 1904, March 20, 1905, and March 21, 1906; confidential notices issued from office of Retail Manager to section heads, September 13, 17, 23, 24, and 26, 1904, and March 14, 1904, Marshall Field & Co. Archives; *Chicago Record-Herald,* March 17, 1902; *Chicago Evening Post,* March 21 and

26, 1903; *Inter-Ocean,* January 4, 1903; and *Chicago Daily News,* March 13, 1900. The seasonal openings, however, date from the seventies *(Chicago Tribune,* September 21, 1871, April 26, 1872, September 21, 1874, September 25, 1876, April 5, 1879, September 25, 27, and 29, 1880, September 30 and October 1, 1885, and October 8 and 9, 1901; *Chicago Times,* September 25, 1876; *Chicago Record,* September 29, 1897; and *Chicago Herald,* September 28 and 29, 1881).

84. *Chicago Record-Herald,* October 3, 1905; and *Chicago Daily News,* October 3, 1905.

85. *Chicago Record-Herald,* October 3, 1905.

86. Letter, Marshall Field & Co. to Managers, St. James Orphanage, Chicago, October 5, 1903, unidentified scrapbook, Marshall Field & Co. Archives; and "Children's Day at Field's," *Chicago Dry Goods Reporter,* XXXIII (October 17, 1903), 72.

87. *Chicago Record-Herald,* October 3, 1905.

88. *Chicago Dry Goods Reporter,* XXXVII (October 5, 1907), p. 61; *Chicago Record-Herald,* October 3, 1905; *Chicago Evening Journal,* September 26, 1903; and *Inter-Ocean,* October 3, 1904.

89. Accounting ledgers, 1904, Comptroller's safe, Marshall Field & Co. General Offices.

90. *Chicago Daily News,* June 11 and 13, 1904.

91. Notice issued from office of Retail Manager to employees, November 7, 1904, Marshall Field & Co. Archives.

92. Accounting ledgers, 1904 and 1905, Comptroller's safe, Marshall Field & Co. General Offices.

93. "Notice to Section Managers, Assistants and Others," January 9, 1905, in John McKinlay, *Old Advertising Policy* (scrapbook), Marshall Field & Co. Archives. See also notice issued from office of Retail Manager to employees, November 7, 1904; and "Notice to Basement Section Managers," June 10, 1904, Marshall Field & Co. Archives.

94. The 1906 figure was $234,900 (accounting ledgers, 1906, Comptroller's safe, Marshall Field & Co. General Offices).

95. Letter, Adair, advertising department, *Chicago Daily News*, to Victor F. Lawson, September 7, 1905, Victor F. Lawson *Papers*, courtesy Newberry Library, Chicago.

96. Notice issued from office of Retail Manager to employees, February 16, 1905, Marshall Field & Co. Archives.

97. *Chicago Daily News*, November 29, 1895; letter, J. R. Brady & Associates, Sales Research Analysts, to R. W. Twyman, September 16, 1949; and *Chicago Tribune*, March 24, 1902.

98. *Chicago Daily News* balance sheet, March 1904, Marshall Field & Co. advertising totals in the *Daily News*, *Record-Herald*, and *Tribune*, Victor F. Lawson, *Papers*, courtesy Newberry Library, Chicago.

99. Interoffice communication, [March 1904], Rogers to Lawson, Victor F. Lawson *Papers*, courtesy Newberry Library, Chicago.

100. Letter, Charles T. Smutny, Librarian, *Chicago Tribune*, to R. W. Twyman, August 17, 1949. See also letter, J. R. Brady & Associates, Sales Research Analysts, to R .W. Twyman, September 16, 1949.

101. See, for example, advertising circulars, Field, Leiter & Co., Retail, [1876]; September 16, 1867; Spring 1877; and Marshall Field & Co., and Spring 1881, Marshall Field & Co. Archives.

102. Foreign lithographed cards, Field, Leiter & Co., *passim*, Marshall Field & Co. Archives.

103. Marshall Field & Co. Archives.

104. See, for example, advertising circulars, Marshall Field & Co., [January] 1903; January 1898; January 3, 1899; March 1, 1901; March 1, 1902; advertising enclosure cards, Marshall Field & Co., Retail, September 16, 1901-3, Marshall Field & Co. Archives; "Catalogue of an Exhibition of the Works of John La Farge," December 1 to 20, 1902, advertising scrapbook, 1902-6, Marshall Field & So. Archives; "Drum-

ming" letter, Marshall Field & Co. to Mrs. Chas. Graves, Winnetka, Illinois, April 1, 1899, Marshall Field & Co. Archives; notice issued from office of Retail Manager to Section Managers, Assistants, and Others, April 4, 1905, Marshall Field & Co. Archives; advertising poster, Waldo P. Warren, "Ideas— A Souvenir Thought from the Art Exhibit of the Advertising Bureau of Marshall Field & Co., Chicago, September, 1901," Marshall Field & Co. Archives; and catalogue, *Automobile Apparel and Accessories*, Marshall Field & Co., Retail, Fall and Winter, 1904-5, Marshall Field & Co. Archives.

105. Accounting ledgers, 1890-1906, Comptroller's safe, Marshall Field & Co. General Offices.

106. See "Views of Portions of the Retail Store of Marshall Field & Co., Chicago," [1893], Marshall Field & Co. Archives. See also *Chicago Times*, August 5, 1893.

107. "Views of the Retail Store of Marshall Field & Co., Chicago," 1900.

108. Accounting ledgers, 1899, Comptroller's safe, Marshall Field & Co. General Offices.

109. Actual expenses were: 1901, $20,100; 1902, $58,500 (*ibid.*, 1901-2).

110. See, for example, form letters, Marshall Field & Co. to Mrs. James Cummings, July 13, 1903; and to Mr. John C. Graves, May 4, 1903; and form letter, Marshall Field & Co. to Agnes M. O'Donohue, March 22, 1904 (6000 of similar type mailed to Chicago schoolteachers), advertising scrapbook, 1902-6, Marshall Field & Co. Archives.

111. Expenses for circulars, pamphlets, etc., for the remainder of the period:

    1903 ....$36,000
    1904 40,000
    1905 20,400
    1906 22,800

    (Accounting ledgers, 1903-6, Comptroller's safe, Marshall Field & Co. General Offices.)

112. Hower, *History of Macy's*, pp. 133, 180, 258, and 394.

113. *Marshall Field and Company and You*, 1941, p. 29; and *Marshall*

Field and Company and You, 1943, p. 31.
114. *Chicago Tribune*, October 13, 1868.
115. Accounting sheets, "Retail Departments' Expenses," 1883, A. B. Jones folder, Marshall Field & Co. Archives.
116. *Ibid.*, 1884.
117. McClintock typescript, citing M. P. Ford; and see Plate V.
118. *The Dry Goods Retailer and Jobber*, October 1893, p. 17.
119. August 8, 1893.
120. Earl A. Dash, "Fraser Was the Greatest Displayman of Them All," *Women's Wear Daily*, July 8, 1947.
121. *Ibid.*
122. Letter, John G. Shedd to R. Lowrie, editor, *Elgin Daily News*, Illinois, December 1, 1919, Marshall Field & Co. Archives; and *Northwestern Christian Advocate*, November 12, 1902, p. 19.
123. Dash, *Women's Wear Daily*, July 8, 1947.

124. *Chicago Dry Goods Reporter*, XXVII (April 10, 1897), 10.
125. Picture postcard, Marshall Field & Co., 1906, Marshall Field & Co. Archives. In this connection see *Chicago Tribune*, July 28, 1902.
126. *Chicago Evening Journal*, September 26, 1903.
127. *Chicago Tribune*, September 30 and October 1, 1902; "Scroll Designing," *Chicago Dry Goods Reporter*, XXXVII (November 16, 1907), 25; "Formal Opening of a Great Store," *Drygoodsman and General Merchant*, October 12, 1907, pp. 15-21; *Chicago Examiner*, September 29, 1907; *Chicago Daily News*, October 3, 1905, and September 30, 1907; *Chicago Record-Herald*, October 3, 1905; Hull, *Marshall Field and Company*, 1907; and letter, Bryan L. Smith, Northern Trust Co., Chicago, to R. G. Shedd, September 30, 1907, Marshall Field & Co. Archives.

CHAPTER TWELVE

1. *Chicago Tribune*, April 7, 1902.
2. Statements, Joseph Yates, John W. Hughes, Thomas H. Eddy, and F. W. Boyden, Marshall Field & Co. General Offices.
3. R. M. Fair personal record book of rents and property, "compiled June 1, 1901," Marshall Field & Co. Archives; and complete inventory, Estate of Marshall Field, Deceased, Marshall Field & Co. Archives.
4. *Ibid.; Chicago Tribune*, August 11, 1893, and January 17, 1906; *Chicago Record-Herald*, January 3, 1906; and M. Field personal record book, real estate and salaries, 1867-1901.
5. Complete inventory, Estate of Marshall Field, Deceased, Marshall Field & Co. Archives; and R. M. Fair personal record book of rents and property "compiled June 1, 1901."
6. *Ibid.;* and *Economist*, Special News Bulletin, March 22, 1892.
7. The total cost of the building was $1,008,000. The firm paid $208,000 of the total *(ibid.;* and R. M. Fair

personal record book of rents and property, "compiled June 1, 1901").
8. *The Marshall Field & Company Building* (Chicago: J. L. Bridgford & Co. [1892]; *Economist*, May 6, 1893; *Chicago Daily News*, August 5 and 8, 1893; and *Chicago Times*, August 3 and 5, 1893.
9. *Ibid.*, August 8, 1893; and *Chicago Evening Journal*, August 8, 1893.
10. *Ibid.; The Marshall Field & Company Building* [1892].
11. *Economist*, Special News Bulletin, March 22, 1892; and *Chicago Evening Journal*, August 8, 1893.
12. *Economist*, April 29, 1893, and *ibid.*, March 22, 1892; and *Chicago Evening Journal*, August 8, 1893.
13. *Ibid.; The Marshall Field & Company Building* [1892]; *Chicago Daily News*, August 8, 1893; *Economist*, Special News Bulletin, March 22, 1892; and *ibid.*, April 29, 1893.
14. *Ibid.;* and *Chicago Tribune*, October 1, 1902.
15. *Chicago Daily News*, August 8, 1893; *Chicago Evening Journal*,

August 8, 1893; and *Chicago Times*, August 8, 1893.

16. *Ibid.*, August 3 and 5, 1893.

17. *Chicago Evening Journal*, August 4 and 7, 1893; *Chicago Tribune*, August 11, 1893; and *Chicago Times*, August 8, 1893.

18. Statement, John W. Hughes, Marshall Field & Co. General Offices.

19. *Chicago Evening Journal;* and *Chicago Daily News*, August 8, 1893; and R. M. Fair personal record book of rents and property, "compiled June 1, 1901."

20. *Chicago Daily News* and *Chicago Times*, August 8, 1893; *Chicago Tribune*, August 11, 1893; and *Dry Goods Retailer and Jobber*, October, 1893, p. 15.

21. Fred A. Shannon, *America's Economic Growth* (N. Y.: Macmillan Co., 1940), pp. 406-7; and Davis Rich Dewey, *Financial History of the United States* (12th ed.; New York: Longmans, 1934), pp. 445-47.

22. Table XIV, p. 175.

23. George E. Plumbe (ed.), *The Chicago Daily News Almanac and Political Register for 1896* (Chicago: Chicago Daily News Co., 1896), pp. 370-71.

24. Table XIV, p. 175.

25. "The Tide Has Turned," *Department Store Journal*, II (July 1897), 295.

26. "Views of the Retail Store," 1900; and record book, "Rents, June 1, 1901," Marshall Field & Co. Archives.

27. *Chicago Daily News*, July 20, 1891.

28. Company record on repair . . . building accounts, 1902-43.

29. *Proceedings of the City Council of City of Chicago for the Municipal Year 1900-1901* (Chicago: John F. Higgins, 1901), June 29, 1900, p. 794.

30. Complete inventory, Estate of Marshall Field, Deceased, Marshall Field & Co. Archives.

31. *Chicago Record-Herald*, January 3, 1906; and *Chicago Tribune*, January 17, 1906.

32. *Chicago Dry Goods Reporter*, XXXII (October 11, 1902), 31.

33. *Ibid.*, pp. 31 and 35; and advertising circular, Marshall Field & Co.,

May 15, 1905, Marshall Field & Co. Archives.

34. "Traffic Check, Marshall Field and Company's Loop Store, Saturday, December 16, 1944." Submitted by Ross Federal Research Corporation, Chicago, Illinois, December 21, 1944. Marshall Field & Co. General Offices.

35. *Chicago Dry Goods Reporter*, XXXII (October 11, 1902), 17, 31, 33, and 35; *Mirror*, St. Louis, April 16, 1903, Marshall Field & Co. Archives; and Williams, *Interior*, December 18, 1902.

36. *Chicago Tribune*, October 1, 1902.

37. *Ibid.*, June 10, 1901.

38. *Ibid.*, February 3, 1902.

39. *Ibid.*, April 14, 1902. See also *ibid.*, February 13, April 17, May 19, and September 15, 1902; and *Chicago Daily News*, April 3, 1902. See also *Inter-Ocean*, May 5, 1902.

40. Engraved invitation, Stone scrapbook, p. 91, Marshall Field & Co. Archives; *Chicago Tribune* and *Inter-Ocean*, September 29 and 30, 1902.

41. *Ibid.*

42. *Chicago Tribune*, October 1, 1902.

43. Record book, "Rents, June 1, 1901," Marshall Field & Co. Archives.

44. Table XV, p. 177.

45. Complete inventory, Estate of Marshall Field, Deceased, Marshall Field & Co. Archives; record book, "Rents, June 1, 1901," Marshall Field & Co. Archives; and *Economist*, Special News Bulletin, March 22, 1892.

46. *Ibid.*

47. Complete inventory, Estate of Marshall Field, Deceased, Marshall Field & Co. Archives.

48. Notice issued from office of Retail Manager, January 6, 1905, Marshall Field & Co. Archives; *Chicago Record-Herald*, January 23, 1906; and *Chicago Tribune*, January 17, 1906.

49. Letter, M. Field to J. G. Shedd, August 7, 1905, Marshall Field & Co. Archives.

50. Record book, "Rents, June 1, 1901," Marshall Field & Co. Archives. See addenda of December 31, 1905.

51. *Chicago Evening Post,* January 3, 1906.

52. Letter, M. Field to J. G. Shedd, July 4, 1905, Marshall Field & Co. Archives.

53. *Ibid.* Marshall Field had little use for Edward F. Dunne, the newly elected reformist mayor, who wanted Chicago to take over the street railways *(Chicago Tribune,* October 23, 1905).

54. Letter, M. Field to J. G. Shedd, August 7, 1905, Marshall Field & Co. Archives.

55. Letter, M. Field to J. G. Shedd, July 4, 1905, Marshall Field & Co. Archives.

56. Cablegram, Marshall Field, Burgenstock, to [J. G. Shedd], August 6, 1905, Marshall Field & Co. Archives.

57. *Chicago Record-Herald,* January 3, 1906; and *Chicago Evening Post,* January 3, 1908.

58. *Daily Trade Record,* N. Y., January 6, 1906, Marshall Field & Co. Archives; and *Chicago Record-Herald,* January 3, 1906.

59. *Inter-Ocean,* September 30 and October 4, 1907; *Chicago Tribune,* September 27 and 30 and October 3, 1907; and *Chicago Daily News,* September 28, 1907.

60. *Daily Trade Record,* N. Y., January 6, 1906, Marshall Field & Co. Archives.

61. *Chicago Tribune,* September 30, 1907. For details on the opening, see the *Chicago Dry Goods Reporter,* XXXVII (October 5, 1907), pp. 57-67.

62. *Chicago Tribune,* December 10, 1906, and September 27, 1907.

63. *Ibid.,* December 10, 1906; and Buckley, *Fine Arts Journal,* XIX (April 1908), 199-206.

64. *Chicago Evening American,* October 28, 1907; and Hull, *Marshall Field & Company,* 1907.

65. Inheritance Tax Appraisement, Estate of Marshall Field, Marshall Field & Co. Archives.

66. *Supra,* p. 000.

67. R. M. Fair personal record book of rents and property, "compiled June 1, 1901."

68. The total rent figure rose from $385,245 in 1901 to $668,304 in 1906. (Accounting ledgers, 1901-6, Comptroller's safe, Marshall Field & Co. General Offices.)

69. Falling prices cause the dollar volume of sales to drop even though the number of individual sales transactions remains the same.

70. The greatest differences appeared in the depression years of the nineties. While Macy's expense ratio between 1892 and 1894 rose less than 1 per cent, Field's ratio, already slightly higher, shot up more than 5 per cent because of plunging sales. The gap, however, was gradually closed over the years.

71. Unfortunately accurate figures on the cost of labor to the firm are impossible to obtain from Field's early accounting records. Comparison of numbers of employees with Macy's is likewise difficult because of the lack of accurate figures for either store. For available figures on numbers of Field employees, see page 69. For Macy's, see Hower, *History of Macy's,* especially pp. 192 and 305.

72. The Wabash building was completely occupied and the first floor of the new South State building was put into use in December 1906 *(Chicago Tribune,* December 10).

73. *Ibid.,* January 17, 1906.

74. Statements, John McKinlay, Philip James, J. W. Hughes, and Charles Nash, Marshall Field & Co. General Offices.

75. Selfridge, *Saturday Evening Post,* July 27, 1935, pp. 18, 19, and 51.

76. Higinbotham retired on December 31, 1900 (general house notice, Marshall Field & Co., December 31, 1900, Stone scrapbook, p. 82, Marshall Field & Co. Archives).

77. *Chicago Record,* February 23, 1901.

78. *Chicago Tribune,* February 23, 1901.

79. *Chicago Record-Herald,* November 28, 1905; and personal interview, Marshall Field III.

80. *Commercial and Financial Chronicle,* I (April 26, 1890), 572-73, and *Chicago Tribune,* February 23, 1901.

81. *Chicago Evening Post* and *Chicago News Record,* February 23, 1901;

and M. Field personal record book, real estate and salaries, 1869-1901.

82. *Ibid.* R. M. Fair retired in 1905 *(Chicago Chronicle,* January 13; and *Chicago Evening Journal,* January 12, 1905).

83. *Chicago Tribune,* October 23, 1926; and *Chicago Daily News,* October 22, 1926.

84. *Ibid.,* May 14, 1904; *Chicago Record-Herald,* May 15, 1904; and *Inter-Ocean,* May 15, 1904.

85. *Chicago Dry Goods Reporter,* XXIV (May 21, 1904), 37; and *Chicago Daily News,* May 14, 1904.

86. Selfridge, *Saturday Evening Post,* p. 51; and M. Field personal record book, real estate and salaries, 1869-1901.

87. *Inter-Ocean,* May 15 and June 13, 1904; *Chicago Tribune* and *Chicago Daily News,* June 13, 1904.

88. *Ibid.,* August 12, 1904; and *Chicago Chronicle* and *Chicago Record-Herald,* August 12, 1904.

89. Selfridge, *Saturday Evening Post,* p. 51.

90. Statement, J. W. Hughes, Marshall Field & Co. General Offices.

91. *Chicago Daily News,* August 12, 1904; and statements, George Young and John McKinlay, Marshall Field & Co. General Offices.

92. Selfridge had paid Schlesinger and Mayer $5,000,000; but soon afterwards he sold the building and leasehold to Otto Young for $1,-485,000, cutting the cost of the business for himself to $3,515,000. This is the amount that Carson's paid, plus the $250,000 bonus *(Chicago Tribune,* June 19 and August 12, 1904; *Chicago Daily News,* August 12, 1904; and Selfridge, *Saturday Evening Post,* p. 51).

93. *Times* (London), May 9, 1947, Marshall Field & Co. Archives; George Seal, "The Passing of the Founder of This Business," *Key of the House; Staff Magazine of the House of Selfridge,* May-June 1947, pp. 15-16; and H. J. Clarke, Director of Selfridge's Ltd., "Most Powerful Personality I Met," *ibid.,* p. 10, reprinted from *Drapers' Record,* Marshall Field & Co. Archives.

94. *New York Times,* May 9, 1947.

95. *Supra,* Chapter VII.

96. Letter, Marshall Field to Victor F. Lawson, December 22, 1903, Victor F. Lawson *Papers,* courtesy Newberry Library, Chicago.

97. William T. Hutchinson, *Cyrus Hall McCormick, Harvest, 1856-1884* (New York: D. Appleton-Century Co., 1935), II, 617. See also letters, D. R. Goudie, editor and publisher of *Best of Everything,* to Marshall Field, February 26, May 11, and December 6 and 13, 1887, Field Estate.

98. Letter, Charley E. Koch, Headquarters, First Infantry, Illinois National Guard, Chicago, to Marshall Field, February 13, 1891, Field Estate; and *Chicago Tribune,* February 11, 1894.

99. Letters, Marshall Field to Victor F. Lawson, December 22, 1903, Victor F. Lawson *Papers,* courtesy Newberry Library, Chicago; Frank J. Loesch, Attorney, to Arthur B. Jones, secretary to Mr. Field, June 5, 1890, Field Estate; and John S. Cooper, Attorney, to Marshall Field, February 26, 1891, Field Estate.

100. Clippings, *Journal,* October 9, 1925; and *Decorative Furnisher,* September 1, 1927, "Fifty-Year Club" scrapbook, Marshall Field & Co. Archives. For Marshall Field's part in punishing the alleged instigators of the Haymarket Riot, see Caro Lloyd, *Henry Demarest Lloyd,* 1847-1903 (New York: G. P. Putnam's Sons, 1912), I, 90.

101. Letter, May 27, 1903, Victor F. Lawson *Papers,* courtesy Newberry Library, Chicago.

102. Letter, Marshall Field to Victor F. Lawson, May 31, 1905, *ibid.* See attached.

103. Beckner, *A History of Labor Legislation in Illinois,* p. 91. See also *Chicago Tribune,* June 3, 4, and 5, 1902.

104. Wholesale record, Marshall Field & Co., June 3, 1902, pp. 369-70.

105. Beckner, *A History of Labor Legislation in Illinois,* p. 91. See also letter, John G. Driscoll, Sec'y, Coal Owners' Association of Chicago and Furniture Movers and Expressmen's Association of Chicago, to

H. G. Selfridge, June 7, 1902, Marshall Field & Co. Archives.

106. McGuire Agency Reports to James Simpson, July 26, 29, and August 26, 1902, Marshall Field & Co. Archives. The story, that Marshall Field would not tolerate union men as employees (Dennis, *Everybody's Magazine*, XIV [March 1906], 299) is not true; for he did have some union people in the firm (Beckner, *A History of Labor Legislation in Illinois*, p. 91). Exactly how many or even in which department they worked, however, there are no records to indicate.

107. *Ibid.*, p. 94.

108. John Cummings, "The Chicago Teamsters' Strike—A Study in Industrial Democracy," *Journal of Political Economy*, XIII (September 1905), 540; *Chicago Tribune*, July 21, 1905; and *Chicago Record-Herald*, July 20, 1905. Marshall Field & Company drivers did not go out until April 27 (*ibid.*, April 27; *Inter-Ocean*, April 27, 1905; and general house notice, Marshall Field & Company, April 27, 1905, Marshall Field & Co. Archives).

109. Howard H. Myers, "The Policing of Labor Disputes in Chicago; A Case Study" (Ph.D. dissertation, Dept. of Economics, University of Chicago, 1929), p. 557.

110. Myers, "The Policing of Labor Disputes in Chicago," p. 561.

111. Accounting ledgers, 1905, Comptroller's safe, Marshall Field & Co. General Offices.

112. Myers, "The Policing of Labor Disputes," pp. 570-74.

113. Letter, Marshall Field to Victor F. Lawson, May 11, 1905, Victor F. Lawson *Papers,* courtesy Newberry Library, Chicago.

114. Letters, Marshall Field to J. G. Shedd, July 2 and 4, New York, and August 7, 1905, Switzerland, Marshall Field & Co. Archives.

115. Letter, Marshall Field to J. G. Shedd, July 4, 1905, New York, Marshall Field & Co. Archives.

116. Letter, Marshall Field to J. G. Shedd, August 7, 1905, Switzerland, Marshall Field & Co. Archives; and *Chicago Tribune*, July 21, 1905.

117. *London Mail*, September 6, 1905; *Inter-Ocean*, September 5 and 6, 1905; and *Chicago Daily News,* September 5, 1905.

118. October 23, 1905.

119. *Ibid.*, November 28, 1905; and *Chicago Record-Herald*, November 28 and 29, 1905.

120. *Chicago Tribune*, October 23, 1905; and *Chicago Record-Herald*, October 23, 1905.

121. *Ibid.*, January 17, 1906; and *Chicago Evening Post* and *Chicago Daily Journal*, January 16 and 17, 1906.

122. *Economist*, January 30, 1906; "Three Men of Chicago," *Review of Reviews*, XXXIII (February 1906), 144; *Chicago Examiner*, January 17, 1906; *Chicago Record-Herald*, January 18, 1906; *Chicago Evening Post*, January 16, 1906; letter file #21, "Letters and Messages on Death of Marshall Field I," Marshall Field and Company Archives; and *Chicago Tribune*, January 17, 1906, and January 22, 1909.

123. *Ibid.*, January 16, 1906.

124. Copy of Will, Marshall Field & Co. Archives.

125. The exact value of the inheritance is difficult to state. Estimates ran all the way from $100,000,000 to $174,000,000 (*Chicago Tribune*, January 17, 1906). The courts placed the value at only $79,262,-659 (*Chicago Record-Herald*, April 22, 1910; and Inheritance Tax Appraisement, Estate of Marshall Field, Marshall Field & Co. Archives). In any event, before the boys received their complete inheritance, its value was certain to increase greatly; for the fortune by itself brought a continuous income.

126. Copy of Will, Marshall Field & Co. Archives.

127. *Ibid.*

128. See, for example, Albert M. Kales, "Reforms in the Law of Future Interests Needed in Illinois," *Illinois Law Review*, I (December 1906), Part I, 317-18; Dennis, *Everybody's Magazine,* XIV (March 1906), 301; and *Economist.* December 22, 1906. See also J. M. Patterson, "Marshall Field's Will," *Collier's*, June 2, 1906.

129. Illinois, *Revised Statutes*, 1945 (State Bar Association Edition; Chicago: Burdette Smith Company, 1945), Chap. 30, Section 153, p. 822.

130. Contemporary literature makes this claim and all available evidence seems to bear it out. For Field's place in retailing, see *Chicago Tribune*, October 30, 1899, and August 11, 1893; *Inter-Ocean*, September 30, 1902; *Chicago Dry Goods Reporter*, XXXII (October 11, 1902), 17; and Nystrom, *Economics of Retailing*, p. 140. For wholesaling, see Hull, *Marshall Field & Company*, p. 51; and *Chicago Evening Journal*, September 26, 1903. Also compare sales figures in Table XIV of the Appendix with those in the H. B. Claflin Co. "Report for the season ending December 31st, 1898," Marshall Field & Co. General Offices; and in Hower, *History of Macy's*, p. 348. The sales totals of Field's largest retail and wholesale competitors in Chicago did not even approach those of Marshall Field and Company (letters, The Fair Store Chicago, to R. W. Twyman, August 15, 1949; and J. Chalmers O'Brien, Assistant to the President, Carson Pirie Scott & Co., to R. W. Twyman, September 16, 1949).

131. Table XIV, p. 175.
132. *Ibid.*
133. Mr. Barger's ten-year estimates were built up from commodity output by projecting backwards ratios for finished to unfinished goods, proportion passing through wholesale channels, freight charges, and retail and wholesale margins; also included were commodity composition of sales of different types of stores, the starting point being nearly always 1929 Census material. For the reason that his results are admittedly only preliminary estimates, he has requested that they not be published for the present.

For purposes of making the above comparisons, Mr. Barger's estimates on retail sales for "dry goods" and "department stores" were added together. The same procedure was followed for his estimates on "wholesale sales to department stores" and "sales to dry goods stores."

134. *Chicago Tribune*, January 1, 1895, and December 31, 1904.
135. This does not mean to imply that Field's did not grow at a rate more rapid than many other *individual* dry-goods firms. They did, of course. The point is, however, that Chicago as a business center was apparently expanding more rapidly than Field's was as an individual company.

136. The "capital employed" (capital invested plus loans) throughout the history of the firm was always much greater than the "capital invested." For example, in 1906 the capital invested was only $6,000,-000, whereas the capital employed was $15,190,100 (accounting ledgers, "Capital Employed," 1878-1906, Comptroller's safe, Marshall Field & Co. General Offices).

137. See Table XVI, p. 178.
138. "Business Review," *Ten Eventful Years* (c. 1947), I, 480.
139. Computed from wholesale and retail sales figures for the years 1886 and 1906 in Table XIV, p. 175.
140. Table XIV, p. 175.
141. Computed from accounting ledgers, 1886, 1896, and 1906, Comptroller's safe, Marshall Field & Co. General Offices.

142. Apparently as early as 1877, Field's Wholesale experienced some concern over this fact. In the Notions' Catalogue for 1877 it was announced that ". . . by placing extensive orders none but the *largest* manufacturers can compete with us. *We guarantee* to undersell *any* manufacturer that finds it necessary to go to the Retail Trade." (Marshall Field & Co. Archives.)

143. Statement, Stanley Field, Marshall Field & Co. General Offices.
144. *Chicago Tribune*, September 23, 1925.
145. *Ibid.*, November 26, 1935.
146. Letter, J. Chalmers O'Brien, Assistant to the President, Carson Pirie Scott & Co., to R. W. Twyman, September 16, 1949.

Bibliography

Published Material

BOOKS

Andreas, A. T. *History of Chicago from the Earliest Period to the Present Time*. Vols. II and III. Chicago: A. T. Andreas, 1884-85.

Andrews, Wayne. *Battle for Chicago*. New York: Harcourt, Brace & Co., 1946.

Angle, Paul M. (ed.). *The Great Chicago Fire: Described in Seven Letters by Men and Women Who Experienced Its Horrors*. Chicago: The Chicago Historical Society, 1946.

Barbour, George M. (ed.). *Sketchbook of the Inter-State Exposition, Chicago, September 5 to October 20, 1883*. Chicago: Lakeside Press, 1883.

Bates, Charles A. *The Art and Literature of Business*. Vol. II. New York: Bates Pub. Co. (1902).

Beckner, Earl R. *A History of Labor Legislation in Illinois*. Chicago: The University of Chicago Press, 1929. Chapters VI and XI.

Burnley, James. *Millionaires and Kings of Enterprise*. Philadelphia: J. B. Lippincott Co., 1901.

Chicago's First Half Century, 1833-1883. The Inter-Ocean Pub. Co., 1884.

Collins, C. Cody. *Love of a Glove: The Romance, Legends and Fashion History of Gloves and How They Are Made*. New York: Fairchild Pub. Co., 1945.

Comer, H. D. *Merchandise Returns in Department Stores*. Vol. I. Columbus: Ohio State University Press, 1928.

Cook, Frederick F. *Bygone Days in Chicago: Recollections of the "Garden City" of the Sixties*. Chicago: A. C. McClurg & Co., 1910.

Crissey, Forest. *Since Forty Years Ago: An Account of the Origin and Growth of Chicago and Its First Department Store*. Chicago: Privately printed [The Fair], 1915.

Dewey, Davis Rich. *Financial History of the United States*. 12th ed. New York: Longmans, 1934.

Ditchett, S. H. *Marshall Field and Company, the Life Story of a Great Concern*. 1st ed. New York: Dry Goods Economist, 1922.

Farwell, John V., Jr. (ed.). *Some Recollections of John V. Farwell: A Brief Description of His Early Life and Business Reminiscences*. Chicago: R. R. Donnelley & Sons, 1911.

Ferry, Mrs. Abby Farwell. *Reminiscences of John V. Farwell by His Elder Daughter*. 2 vols. Chicago: Ralph Fletcher Seymour, 1928.

Flinn, John F. *Chicago, The Marvelous City of the West: A History, an Encyclopedia and a Guide*. Chicago: Flinn & Sheppard, 1890.

Gibbons, Herbert A. *John Wanamaker*. 2 vols. New York: Harper, 1926.

Hahn, Lew. *Stores, Merchants and Customers*. New York: Fairchild Publications, 1952.

Harper, W. H., and Ravell, C. H. *Fifty Years of Banking in Chicago: 1857-1907*. Chicago: Merchants' Loan and Trust Co., [1908].

Harrison, Carter H. *Stormy Years: The Autobiography of Carter H. Harri-*

236

son, Five Times Mayor of Chicago. Indianapolis: Bobbs-Merrill Co., 1935.

Hayes, Dorsha B. *Chicago, Crossroads of American Enterprise: A Cities of America Biography.* New York: Julian Messner, Inc., 1944. Chapter IV.

Higinbotham, Harlow N. *The Making of a Merchant.* Chicago: Curtis publishing Co., 1902.

Hower, Ralph M. *History of Macy's of New York, 1858-1919.* Cambridge, Mass.: Harvard University Press, 1943. Chapters I, VI, and XI.

Hoyt, Homer, *One Hundred Years of Land Values in Chicago: 1830-1933.* Chicago: University of Chicago Press, 1933.

Hungerford, Edward. *The Story of the Baltimore & Ohio Railroad, 1827-1927.* Vol. II. New York: Putnam, 1928.

Hutchinson, William T. *Cyrus Hall McCormick, Harvest, 1856-1884.* Vol. II. New York: D. Appleton-Century Co., 1935.

James F. Cyril. *The Growth of Chicago Banks, 1816-1938.* 2 vols. New York: Harper, 1938.

Johnson, Allen (ed.). *The Dictionary of American Biography.* New York: Charles Scribner's Sons, 1928-.

Lloyd, Caro. *Henry Demarest Lloyd, 1847-1903.* Vol. I. New York: G. P. Putnam's Sons, 1912.

McIlvaine, Mabel. *Chicago: Her History and Her Adornment.* Chicago: C. D. Peacock, Inc., 1926.

MacLeish, Andrew. *Life of Andrew MacLeish, 1838-1928.* Chicago: Privately Printed, 1929.

Monroe, Harriet (ed.). *Harlow Niles Higinbotham: A Memoir with Brief Autobiography.* Chicago: Privately Printed, 1920.

Moses, J., and Kirkland, J. *History of Chicago, Illinois.* Vol. I. Chicago: Munsell & Co., 1895.

Myers, Gustavus. *History of the Great American Fortunes.* New York: Random House, Inc., 1907.

Nevins, Allan. *John D. Rockefeller, The Heroic Age of American Enterprise.* 2 vols. New York: Charles Scribner's Sons, 1940. Chapter VII.

Nystrom, Paul H. *Economics of Retailing—Retail Institutions and Trends.* 3rd ed. New York: Ronald Press Co., 1932.

Pierce, Bessie Louise. *A History of Chicago: From Town to City, 1848-1871.* Vol. II. New York: Alfred A. Knopf, 1940.

Plumbe, George E. (ed.). *The Daily News Almanac and Political Register for 1896.* Chicago: Chicago Daily News Co., 1896.

Poole, Ernest. *Giants Gone: Men Who Made Chicago.* New York: Whittlesey House, 1943.

Poor's Railroad Manual. New York: Poor's Pub. Co., 1901 and 1905.

Robinson, O. Preston, and Brisco, Norris B. *Store Organization and Operation.* New York: Prentice-Hall, Inc., 1949.

Schulze, J. William. *The American Office, Its Organization, Management and Records.* 2nd ed. New York: Ronald Press Co., 1914.

Seven Days in Chicago. Chicago: J. M. Wing & Co., Publishers, 1877.

Shannon, Fred A. *America's Economic Growth.* New York: Macmillan Co., 1940.

Stead, William T. *Chicago Today: or, The Labour War in America.* London: Review of Reviews, 1894.

——— ———. *If Christ Came to Chicago!* London: Review of Reviews, 1894.

Stoddard, William O. *Men of Business.* New York: C. Scribner's Sons, 1895.

Sullivan, Louis H. *Kindergarten Chats on Architecture, Education and*

Democracy. 1st ed. Washington, D. C.: Scarab Fraternity Press, 1934.

Upton, G. P., and Sheahan, J. W. *The Great Conflagration: Chicago, Its Past, Present and Future.* Chicago: Union Pub. Co., 1871.

Van Rensselaer, M. G. *Henry Hobson Richardson and His Works.* Boston: Houghton Mifflin Co., 1888.

Walters, R. G., Wingate, J. W., and Rowse, E. J. *Retail Merchandising.* Cincinnati: South-Western Pub. Co., [c. 1943].

Wood, David W. *Chicago and Its Distinguished Citizens: or the Progress of Forty Years.* Chicago: Milton George & Co., 1881.

Wright, John S. *Chicago: Past, Present, Future.* Chicago: Western News Co., 1868.

Yearbook of the Union Club. Chicago: Union Club, Publishers, 1931.

ARTICLES

American Artisan, XXXVI (July 9, 1898), 20; (July 30, 1898), 26; (August 6, 1898), 27; (September 3, 1898), 29; and (December 24, 1898), 19.

American Artisan, XXXVII (February 18, 1899), 16.

"Ante Lucem's Weekly Budget," *American Artisan,* XXXVII (April 8, 1899), 17-18.

Armstrong, Guy N. "A Globe Trotter in Chicago," *Chicago,* V (January 1908), 59. Courtesy History of Chicago Project.

"Bargain Friday," *Buyer and Seller,* I (October 12, 1895), [n.p.]

Buckley, Edmund. "The Artistic Aspects of America's Greatest Store," *Fine Arts Journal,* XIX (April 1908), 195-213.

"Business Policy," *Chicago Dry Goods Reporter,* XXVII (October 9, 1897), 9-11.

"Chicago," *Scribner's Monthly,* X (September 1875), 529-51.

Chicago Dry Goods Reporter and Wholesale Price List, July 7, 1894, pp. 6 and 7.

Chicago Dry Goods Reporter, XXVII (May 8, 1897), 4, adv.; and (July 24, 1897), 35.

Chicago Dry Goods Reporter, XXVII (August 21, 1897), 38.

Chicago Dry Goods Reporter, XXVIII (February 12, 1898), 4, adv.; and (July 9, 1898), 17.

"Children's Day at Field's," *Chicago Dry Goods Reporter,* XXXIII (October 17, 1903), 72.

Clark, Neil M. "How To Get All That's Coming To You," *American Magazine,* CIX (May 1930), 44-45 and 184-86.

Cleveland, Harold I. "Fifty-five Years in Business, The Life of Marshall Field," *System Magazine,* May 1906-April 1907

Commercial and Financial Chronicle, I (April 26, 1890), 572-73.

"Confirmed by the Trade: Improved Dry Goods Trade," *Chicago Dry Goods Reporter,* XXVII (August 7, 1897), 21.

"Country Merchants Talk," *Chicago Dry Goods Reporter,* XXVII (April 1897), 13, 15, and 17.

Cummings, John. "The Chicago Teamsters' Strike—A Study in Industrial Democracy," *Journal of Political Economy,* XIII (September 1905), 536-73.

Dash, Earl A. "Fraser Was the Greatest Displayman of Them All," *Women's Wear Daily,* July 8, 1947, [n.p.].

Dennis, John, Jr. "Marshall Field," *Everybody's Magazine,* XIV (March 1906), 290-97.

"Department Store Agitation," *Chicago Dry Goods Reporter,* XXVII (April 24, 1897), 27.

"Department Store, The," *Department Store Journal,* II (August 1897), 368-69.

"Department Stores Abroad," *Department Store Journal,* I (September 15, 1896), 47-48.

"Distribution of Textiles in the Early Part of the Last Half Century, The," *Dry Goods Economist, Jubilee Number, 1846-1896,* 1896, pp. 102-4.

Dreiser, Theodore. "Life Stories of Successful Men: Marshall Field," *Success,* December 8, 1898.

"Ebb of Department Store Fight," *Chicago Dry Goods Reporter,* XXVII (April 17, 1897), 9-10.

"Edward Nevers," *Dry Goods Economist,* August 28, 1920, p. 52.

Encyclopaedia Britannica. 14th ed. Vol. X. Article, "Glove Manufacture."

"English View of Department Stores," *Chicago Dry Goods Reporter,* XXVIII (February 12, 1898), 51.

"Formal Opening of a Great Store," *Drygoodsman and General Merchant,* October 12, 1907, pp. 15-21.

"Field Columbian Museum, The," *Interior,* XXVI (March 14, 1895), 350-57.

"Fur Headquarters of the West," *Chicago Dry Goods Reporter,* XXVII (December 11, 1897), 33, adv.

Furniture Worker, XXVIII (March 10, 1897), 26; and (May 10, 1897), 26.

Goodspeed, Thomas W. "Marshall Field," *University of Chicago Magazine,* VIII (January 1922).

"Greater Efficiency the Aim: What Marshall Field and Company Do to Interest Employees in Store and Promote Efficiency," *Chicago Dry Goods Reporter,* XL (January 8, 1910), 71.

Green, William P. "Marshall Field Store Reflects Business Building Policies," *Associated Advertising,* XII (December 1921), 5-32.

"Mr. Higinbotham's Views of the Cash and Credit Systems," *Chicago Dry Goods Reporter,* XXVII (February 20, 1897), 11.

"Hints to Retailers and State Street Observations," *Chicago Dry Goods Reporter,* XXVIII (October 29, 1898), 53.

"Hints to Retailers and State Street Observations: Basement Salesrooms," *Chicago Dry Goods Reporter,* XXVIII (April 9, 1898), 43.

"History and Statistics of Chicago Street Railway Corporations," *Economist,* 1896, pp. 33, 35, 42, and 47-48. Supplement.

"Hosiery and Underwear for Spring," *Chicago Dry Goods Reporter,* XXVIII (February 5, 1898), 11, 13, and 15.

Kales, Albert M. "Reforms in the Law of Future Interests Needed in Illinois," *Illinois Law Review,* I (December 1906), Part I, 317-18.

Kelly, Daniel F. "Cut-Throat Competition Is Destruction," *Illinois Journal of Commerce,* November 1927, p. 18.

"Large Volume of Business," *Chicago Dry Goods Reporter,* XXVIII (March 12, 1898), 35.

MacLean, Annie M. "Two Weeks in Department Stores," *American Journal of Sociology,* IV (May 1899), 721-41.

"Marshall Field," *Outlook,* LXXXII (January 27, 1906), 152-53.

"Marshall Field & Co.," *Fortune,* XIV (October 1936), 78-87.

"Marshall Field & Co.'s [sic], Chicago," *Mercer,* I (June 1891), 13-20.

"Marshall, [sic] Field & Co., First-Class Establishment," *Buyer and Seller,* I (October 12, 1895), [n.p.].

"Marshall Field & Co., Retail," *Chicago Dry Goods Reporter,* XXXII (October 11, 1902), 17-38.

"Marshall Field & Co.'s Opening," *Apparel Gazette,* XXVI (October 7, 1902), 45-47.

"Model Delivery System, A," *Chicago Dry Goods Reporter,* XXXIV (March 19, 1904), 11.

Modern Encyclopedia. 8th ed. Article, "Horace Brigham Claflin."

"Modern Institution, A," *Northwestern Christian Advocate,* November 12, 1902, pp. 18-19.

"Monument to Enterprise, A," *Dry Goods Retailer and Jobber,* October 1893, pp. 15-17.

"New State Street Firm," *Chicago Dry Goods Reporter,* XXXIV (May 21, 1904), 37.

"The New Tariff Bill," *Chicago Dry Goods Reporter,* XXVII (May 15, 1897), 15 and 17.

"Observations," *Chicago Dry Goods Reporter,* XXVII (April 10, 1897), 10.

"Observations," *Chicago Dry Goods Reporter,* XXVII (August 21, 1897), 10.

"Observations," *Chicago Dry Goods Reporter,* XXVIII (October 8, 1898), 13.

Patterson, J. M. "Marshall Field's Will," *Collier's,* June 2, 1906, pp. 24-26.

"Paris Department Stores, The," *Department Store Journal,* I (October 15, 1896), 115-16.

"Popularity of General Stores," *Chicago Dry Goods Reporter,* XXIX (April 1, 1899), 11-12.

"Proposed Dry Goods Trust, The," *Chicago Dry Goods Reporter,* XXIX (September 2, 1899), 41.

"Records of the Houses: Marshall Field and Company," *Chicago Dry Goods Reporter,* XXIX (January 7, 1899), 95.

"Saleswomen's Appearance," *Dry Goods Economist,* LXIV (November 20, 1909), 45.

Scribner's Magazine Advertiser, November 1895, p. 87, adv.

"Scroll Designing," *Chicago Dry Goods Reporter,* XXXVII (November 16, 1907), 23-25.

Seal, George. "The Passing of the Founder of This Business," *Key of the House: Staff Magazine of the House of Selfridge,* May-June 1947, pp. 15-16.

Selfridge, Harry Gordon. "Selling Selfridge, Some Random Reflections of an American Merchant in London," *Saturday Evening Post,* July 27, August 10, August 24, and September 7, 1935.

"Shows Increase: Marshall Field and Company," *Chicago Dry Goods Reporter,* XXIX (February 4, 1899), 15.

Simpson, James. "Simplifying Buying for the Merchant," *Nation's Business,* July 1929, pp. 41-42.

"Simpson Pays Tribute to J. G. Shedd," *American Magazine,* October 22, 1926.

"Spring Productions in Capes, Jackets, Suits and Shirts," *Chicago Dry Goods Reporter,* XXVIII (February 19, 1898), 17 and 23.

"State Street Ideas," *Chicago Dry Goods Reporter,* XXVII (February 13, 1897), 13 and 15.

"State Street Ideas," *Chicago Dry Goods Reporter,* XXVIII (January 29, 1898), 15 and 17.

"State Street Glove Talks," *Chicago Dry Goods Reporter,* XXVII (August 7, 1897), 19.

"State Street Openings," *Chicago Dry Goods Reporter,* XXXVII (October 5, 1907), 57-67.

"State Street Trade," *Chicago Dry Goods Reporter,* XXVII (May 1, 1897), 15.

"Store Rules, Extracts from Book of Rules of Marshall Field and Company's

BIBLIOGRAPHY

Retail Store," *Chicago Dry Goods Reporter,* XXVII (October 9, 1897), 10, 11, 13, and 15.

Ten Eventful Years. Vol. I. Article, "Business Review."

Thomas, R. G. "Bank Failures in Chicago Before 1925," *Journal of the Illinois Historical Society,* XXVIII (October 1935), 188-203.

"Three Men of Chicago," *Review of Reviews,* XXXIII (February 1906), 143-44.

"Tide Has Turned, The," *Department Store Journal,* II (July 1897), 295.

"Vacation Time," *American Artisan,* XXXVIII (August 19, 1899), 34.

"Want Loop Bridges," *Chicago Dry Goods Reporter,* XXVII (December 4, 1897), 13.

"Want Prompt Action," *Chicago Dry Goods Reporter,* XXVII (May 15, 1897), 11 and 13.

Wendt, Lloyd. "Marshall Field's," *Holiday,* May 1947, pp. 40-43 and 128-29.

Williams, Henry P. "Evolution of the Moral Idea in Business," *Interior,* December 18, 1902. Reprint. n.p.

Wright, Amos W. "Marshall Field I," *Harper's Weekly,* XXXV (March 21, 1891), 210-11.

PUBLIC DOCUMENTS AND REPORTS

Circuit Court, Cook County, Illinois. *The Joint and Several Answers of Francis B. Cooley, John V. Farwell and Marshall Field, Defendants to the Bill of Complaint of Elisha S. Wadsworth.* [1863] Chicago Historical Society.

Deuther, Tomay F. *First Issue of Civic Questions Pertaining Entirely to Local Transportation in the City of Chicago.* Report of Northwest Side Commercial Association. Chicago: Northwest Side Commercial Association, 1924.

Hurst, Garlock & Co. *Hurst, Garlock & Co. Western Reports.* Chicago: Hurst, Garlock & Co., March 1, 1871.

Illinois. *Revised Statutes, 1945.* State Bar Association Ed. Chicago: Burdette Smith Co., 1945.

Proceedings of the City Council of the City of Chicago for the Municipal Year 1900-1901. Chicago: John F. Higgins, 1901.

Report of the Industrial Commission on the Relations and Conditions of Capital and Labor. Vol. VII. Washington: Government Printing Office, 1901.

U. S. Bureau of the Census. *Abstract of the Twelfth Census of United States: 1900 Population.* 3rd ed. Washington: Government Printing Office, 1904.

U. S. Bureau of the Census. *Historical Statistics of the United States, 1789-1945.* Washington: Government Printing Office, 1949.

U. S. Congress, House of Representatives. *Congressional Record.* 55th Cong. 2nd Sess. Washington: Government Printing Office, 1907.

NEWSPAPERS (Titles often varied slightly in different years.)

Chicago Chronicle, 1895-1907.
Chicago Commercial, 1875.
Chicago Daily Democrat, 1852-61.
Chicago Daily Democratic Press, 1852-58.
Chicago Daily News, 1875-1907, and 1926.
Chicago Daily Press and Tribune, 1858-60.

Chicago Daily Sun, 1893.
Chicago Daily Telegraph, 1878-81.
Chicago Evening American, 1900-1907.
Chicago Evening Post, 1890-1907.
Chicago Evening Journal, 1852-1907.
Chicago Herald, 1881, 1887.
Chicago Herald-American, 1906-7.
Chicago Herald-Examiner, 1926.
Chicago Record, 1893-1901.
Chicago Record-Herald, 1901-7.
Chicago Republican, 1861-72.
Chicago Sun, 1949.
Chicago Times, 1857-95.
Chicago Times-Herald, 1895-1901.
Chicago Tribune, 1860-1907.
Daily Drovers Journal, 1882.
Daily National Hotel Reporter, 1891.
Daily Trade Record (New York), 1906.
Economist, 1892-93.
Goodalls Daily Sun, 1887.
Inter-Ocean, 1872-1907.
London Mail, 1905.
Mirror (St. Louis), 1903, 1904.
New York Herald, 1901.
New York Times, 1947.

Pamphlets and Unpublished Material

Bramhall, John T. "In Memoriam: John Graves Shedd." Chicago: Marshall Field & Co. Archives.

Clark, Walter Scott. "Presentation Address: R. M. Hitchcock Banquet." Chicago: Marshall Field & Co. Archives, 1915.

" 'Don'ts' for Employees." Chicago: Marshall Field & Co., 1904.

"Fashions of the Hours: 1852-1927." Chicago: Marshall Field & Co. Archives, 1927.

"Fifty Years of Service." Chicago: Marshall Field & Co. Archives, 1922.

"Fur Fashions." Chicago: Marshall Field & Co. Archives, 1900-1901.

"Marshall Field & Company." Chicago: Marshall Field & Co. Archives, 1903.

"Marshall Field & Company, Retail." Chicago: Marshall Field & Co. Archives, 1905.

"Marshall Field & Company." Chicago: Marshall Field & Co. Archives, 1907.

"Marshall Field & Company and You." Chicago: Marshall Field & Co. Archives, 1941.

"Marshall Field & Company and You." Chicago: Marshall Field & Co. Archives, 1943.

"Marshall Field & Company Building, The." Chicago: J. L. Bridgford & Co., 1892. Marshall Field & Co. Archives.

Myers, Howard H. "The Policing of Labor Disputes in Chicago; Case Study." Ph.D. dissertation, Dept. of Economics, University of Chicago, 1929.

"Views of Portions of the Retail Store of Marshall Field & Co., Chicago." Chicago: Marshall Field & Co., [1893].

Bibliography

"Will of Marshall Field." Chicago: Marshall Field & Co. Archives.
"Views of the Retail Store of Marshall Field & Co., Chicago." Chicago: Marshall Field & Co. Archives, 1900.

Miscellaneous

Marshall Field & Company Papers. General Offices, Chicago.
  Comptroller's safe:
    Accounting ledgers (Yearly Business Statements) 1873-1908. General Offices.
  Marshall Field & Co. Archives:
    Miscellaneous Accounting Sheets. Varied dates, 1871-91. Profit & loss, wholesale and retail, net sales, retail, expenses, etc.
    Merchandising catalogues.
      Wholesale: 1870, 1871, 1877, 1887, 1893, 1898 and 1900. Retail: 1890 and 1904.
    Advertising circulars, folders and postcards. Varied dates: Wholesale, 1864-1906; Retail, 1867-1905.
    Contracts. Marshall Field & Co. with other firms. Marshall Field & Co. with individual salaried employees.
    Employee Statements. Personal interviews and those of Lloyd Lewis, historian and newspaper reporter, and others. Those not identified otherwise are by Mr. Lewis.
    House Notices. Topics of General Interest to or instructions to employees. Issued by department heads or executives. Varied dates, 1881-1905.
    Invoices, early Field partnerships and competitors. Varied dates, 1859-78.
    Letters. Assorted business, customer, and personal. Varied dates, 1863-1949.
    Record books. For example, Departmental financial records, employer attendance records, foreign codes and trips, rents and properties, instructions to wholesale, wholesale credit ratings, etc. Varied dates, 1860-1906.
    Scrapbooks. Newspaper and journal clippings. Sundry memorabilia. Compiled by divers firm employees.
    Salary record books. M. Field's personal records of employee wages and salaries and others. 1871-1904.
    Typescripts. Employee reminiscences, historical sketches, term papers and doctoral dissertations on related subjects, biographical sketches, advertising manuscripts, etc.
    Miscellaneous. For example:
      Legal papers—deeds, leases, reports, bills, receipts.
      Cable messages, business cards, souvenirs.
      M. Field's personal memorandums
        Income tax (1874), Will, Inventory of Estate, Inheritance Tax, etc.
      Company memorandums—on delivery, departments, manufacturing divisions, etc.
Field Estate Letters. Office, Marshall Field III, Chicago.
Victor Lawson Letters. Newberry Library, Chicago.
McCormick Letters. McCormick Association Library, Chicago.
Warshaw Collection of Business Americana. Invoices. New York.

Index

Post Office, 123, 169
Prices, the firm's, 6, 7, 9, 16, 19, 26, 31, 32-33, 35, 36, 37, 44, 49, 122, 139, 161, 169, 235n
Prices, general market, 8, 13, 14, 20-21, 53, 97
Private branding, 97-104 passim., 116
Profits, 21, 30, 42, 50, 177; in carpets, 44; in furniture, 111; Palmer's, 8-9, 180n; retail, 25, 59, 115, 158, 177; tearoom's, 125; wholesale, 104-5 177
Profit-sharing, 62, 65, 74, 75, 195n. See also Partnerships
Promotions. See Employees
Pulman Sleeping Car Company, 88
Purchasing. See Buying

Quality goods. See Buying

Railroad strike of 1877, 165
Refunds. See Returned goods
Rent, 59-60, 65, 85, 159-60
Rest rooms (customer), 60, 124, 155, 169
Rest rooms (employee), 78-79
Retail: advertising, 136-43, 144-53; building program after 1893, 154-62; conclusions about, 168-73 passim; customer treatment, 121-35 passim; departments in, 65-66; early methods, 24-29; employees in, 61-83 passim; expansion of, 43-46, 107-14; expenses, 160-61; in Exposition Building, 57-58; under Field, Palmer and Leiter, 18-19, 20; fire (1877), 56-58; number employed, 68-69; opening of new building, 23-24 (1868), 60-61 (1879); under Palmer, 3-6, 9; relationship to Wholesale, 30, 115, 169; reopens in car barns, 40-41; return to State Street, 47-48 (1873); 58-59 (1879); rise in importance, 115-20, 173-75; under Selfridge, 105-20, passim; value of building (1907), 209n; on Wabash Avenue, 58
"Retail No. 1," 190n
"Retail No. 2," 46, 190n
Returned goods, 3-4, 7, 26, 30, 127-31, 161, 169, 179n, 221n
Rockefeller, John D., 86
Rock Island R.R., 87
Ross and Gossage, 136
Ross, Foster and Company, 136
Rugs and carpets: added to firm, 43-44; divided into separate sections, 66; exclusively designed, 101-2; separated from upholstery, 197n; stock-turn, 118, 119

St. Louis, 2
Salaries. See Wages and Salaries
Sales, 6, 111, 136, 142, 148

Sales clerks, 67, 72
Sales volume, 2, 6, 9, 19, 29, 49, 88, 104-5, 115, 155, 168, 170-71, 173-74, 175-76, 182n, 183n, 190n; basement, 114; carpets, 44; furniture, 111
Salesman, departmental, 51, 67
Salesman, general, 67, 68, 74, 94, 208n
Salesman, specialty, 94
Salesman, traveling, 92-95, 161, 172
Samples, 93, 208n
Schlesinger and Mayer, 84, 85, 120, 162-64, 233n
Sears, Roebuck and Company, 144
Section head. See Buyer
Section manager. See Buyer
Sections, arrangement of, 121
Selfridge, Harry G., 80; advertising policy, 146-47, 149, 151; becomes general manager, 88; building expansion, 154; expansion of departments, 107-8, 108-14; leaves firm, 162-64; personality and career, 105-6; Schlesinger and Mayer purchased, 233n; sells building to Otto Young, 233n; stock held in firm, 163; tearoom introduced, 125
Selfridge, Harry G., and Company, 163 (Chicago); 164 (London)
Sewing girls, 39, 69, 102
Shedd, John G., 70, 142, 164; becomes partner, 108; becomes vice-president, 163; "best merchant," 105; handles strike, 166; personality and career, 88-92; Saturday half-holiday, 76; stock held in firm, 163
Shoe department introduced, 107, 109-10
Shopper. See Customers
Showcases, 154, 157
Silence room (customer), 124
Simpson, James, 166
Singer Building. See Sites, building, 158, 159
Singer Sewing Machine Company, 48, 58, 59
Sites: building, 154-60; Annex (1893), 124, 151, 152, 154-55, 230n; car barns (1871), 38, 40, 42; Exposition Building (1877), 57, 58, 142; Madison and Market building, Wholesale (1872), 42; Middle Wabash building (1904-5), 158, 159, 232n; Middle State building (1902), 156-58; Palmer adds building (1863), 9; Palmer moves next door (1857), 4; Palmer's new location (1858), 5; Singer Building (1873), 48; Singer Building (1879), 59, 155, 158, 159; South State building (1907), 158-59; Wabash Avenue building (1878-79), 58; Wholesale building (1887), 96
Smyth, John M., and Company, 111

248

INDEX